A HISTORY OF THE BRITISH ISLES

Also by Jeremy Black

British Foreign Policy in the Age of Walpole

The British and the Grand Tour

Natural and Necessary Enemies: Anglo-French Relations in the Eighteenth Century

The English Press in the Eighteenth Century

The Collapse of the Anglo-French Alliance, 1727–31

Eighteenth-Century Europe, 1700–89

Robert Walpole and the Nature of Politics in Early Eighteenth-Century Britain

The Rise of the European Powers, 1679–1793

A System of Ambition? British Foreign Policy, 1660–1800

A Military Revolution? Military Change and European Society, 1550–1800

Culloden and the '45

War for America: The Fight for Independence, 1775–1783

Pitt the Elder

The British Abroad: The Grand Tour in the Eighteenth Century

History of England

The Politics of Britain, 1688–1800

European Warfare, 1660–1815

Convergence or Divergence? Britain and the Continent

British Foreign Policy in an Age of Revolutions, 1783–93

The Cambridge Illustrated Atlas of Warfare: Renaissance and Revolution

Illustrated History of Eighteenth-Century Britain

A History of the British Isles

Jeremy Black

St. Martin's Press
New York

A HISTORY OF THE BRITISH ISLES
Copyright © 1996 by Jeremy Black
All rights reserved. No part of this book may be used or reproduced
in any manner whatsoever without written permission except in the
case of brief quotations embodied in critical articles or reviews.
For information, address:

St. Martin's Press, Scholarly and Reference Division,
175 Fifth Avenue, New York, N.Y. 10010

First published in the United States of America in 1996

Printed in Hong Kong

ISBN 0–312–16063–1

Library of Congress Cataloging-in-Publication Data
Black, Jeremy.
A history of the British Isles / Jeremy Black.
p.   cm.
Includes bibliographical references (p.) and index.
ISBN 0–312–16063–1 (cloth)
1. Great Britain—History.   2. Ireland—History.   I. Title.
DA30.B6   1996
941—dc20   95–43055
                                                   CIP

To Timothy

Contents

Contents

List of Maps

List of Plates

Preface

In some respects this has been the most interesting and most difficult book that I have attempted. Most interesting because I have had to read so widely, most difficult because of the discipline of writing in accordance with particular guidelines and to a tight word-limit. What has been discarded in endless redrafting could have made several books, which shows not only the richness and variety of the history of the British Isles, but also the different ways in which it could be approached. Any history inevitably invites suggestions about different approaches, contrasting arguments, divergent conclusions. The history of the British Isles is the history of the English, Irish, Scots and Welsh. Britain itself has a shorter history as a united state and it is important to place due weight on separate and diverse national traditions. Particular emphasis has been placed on the history of Wales, too often subsumed into accounts of English history but an area of great interest because it was the 'Celtic' area most exposed to English pressure and rule. At the risk of anachronism, terms such as England, Wales, Scotland, Ireland, France and East Anglia are used throughout so that modern readers can better understand the areas they refer to. Britain is generally used to denote England, Wales and Scotland. It is sometimes termed Great Britain. The British Isles is the term used for Britain and Ireland. Ireland refers to the geographical area currently divided between the Republic of Ireland, and Northern Ireland which is a part of the United Kingdom, the state otherwise comprised of Britain.

This book is dedicated to my son Timothy, but while writing my thoughts have often turned to those who taught me English history, to David Griffiths at Haberdashers', and to Tim Blanning, Martin Brett, Marjorie Chibnall, John Morrill, Jonathan Riley-Smith and John Walter at Cambridge. Many thanks to Paul Hammond, Michael Jones and Kenneth Morgan for letting me quote from their work. I am most grateful to Ian Archer, Stuart Ball, Chris Bartlett, Sarah Black, John Blair, John Bourne, George Boyce, Richard Brown, Duncan Bythell, Tony Carr, P.J. Casey, Rees Davies, John Davis, John Derry, Grayson Ditchfield, Sean Duffy,

Alan Ford, Robin Frame, William Gibson, Ralph Griffiths, Steve Gunn, David Gwynn, Robert Harris, Paul Harvey, Alan Heesom, Philip Jenkins, Gareth Elwyn Jones, J. Gwynfor Jones, John R. Kenyon, Keith Laybourne, David Loades, Alex Murdoch, Jon Parry, Murray Pittock, John Plowright, Bernard Porter, Michael Prestwich, Nigel Ramsay, David Rollason, Nigel Saul, Geoffrey Searle, Peter Shilston, Henry Summerson, Christopher Williams and John Young, for commenting on sections of earlier drafts. I am most grateful for the secretarial assistance of Wendy Duery.

JEREMY BLACK

Introduction

That the past, our past, can be seen in so many different lights adds to its fascination. There is not only the question of what to discuss, but the problem of how best to do so. If it is difficult enough for us to establish the course of history, it is even harder to assess causes. This is particularly a problem with a book of this scale. There is a powerful tendency, when writing a history that stretches over more than two millennia but relatively few pages, to shape the past into patterns and to stress the beneficial nature of the changes that have occurred. This Whiggish approach to British history was particularly dominant in the nineteenth and early twentieth centuries; it emphasised a Protestant identity for the nation, respect for property, the rule of law and parliamentary sovereignty as a means to secure liberty and order, and a nationalistic self-confidence that combined a patriotic sense of national uniqueness with a xenophobic contempt for foreigners, especially Catholics. The positive contribution of Protestantism and liberty to prosperity and social development was stressed, but a very partial account of the latter was offered, concentrating on the growth of a strong middle class.

In modern academic circles Whig history is apparently dead, displaced by the scholarly developments of the last sixty years. At the popular level, however, traditional history and historical images are still popular, generally reflect Whiggish notions and often have little to do with academic developments. In addition, the academic works that sell best and are most accessible to the general reading public are generally those that are written in a traditional fashion. Biographies and narratives are at a premium. Narrative history is especially popular. This can be seen in child, adolescent, and adult reading patterns, and there is a parallel in literature, where continued popular preferences defy powerful academic literary fashions. The persistent popularity of the detective novel, with its stress on the role of the individuals and chance, and with a strong narrative structure, and, in most cases, its strong moral element, is especially noteworthy. The genre offers exciting, often exemplary, stories, which are precisely what are sought by most readers of history. In combination, narrative and the Whig approach offer a readily accessible means to produce a clear account of a highly complex subject: human history.

This book, however, seeks to avoid an emphasis on inevitability. It is important to appreciate that choices have always existed, that policy was not pre-ordained by the 'structures' of economic or other circumstances, that contingencies and the views of individuals were of consequence. It is necessary to grasp the uncertainties of the past, the roles of chance and perception; to restore a human perspective to an historical imagination too often dominated by impersonal forces. If this can lead to greater difficulties in posing and answering questions of the relationships between change and continuity, the short term and the long, it is appropriate to point out that history is not an unbroken mirror reflecting our views, but a fractured glass turning in the wind, with pieces missing or opaque and a general pattern that is difficult to distinguish and impossible to do so to general satisfaction.

The selection of central themes is therefore in large part a personal response to the multifaceted nature of the past. Two emerge clearly: first the political relations both between the constituent parts of Britain and between them and the rest of Europe; and secondly the impact of technology. The latter is particularly important and becoming more so. The impact of man on his environment has been far more insistent in the age of industrialisation and urbanisation than hitherto. People no longer have to live by the sweat of their brow; they are more likely to sit in an office, manipulating electronic machinery, whether manufacturing goods or working in the financial or service industries. They do not face starvation if they fall ill. They take longevity, perhaps even prosperity, for granted. People themselves have changed. Inoculations to prevent serious diseases are now universal. Mechanical and chemical contraception has led to the replacement of earlier patterns of sexual activity and procreation. Technical and medical advances have led to the ability effectively to replace parts of the body, such as hips. Much work is currently under way on creating artificial knee joints, a far more complex task. People look different: they are taller than in the past; teeth have been filled or crowned or replaced by dentures; the water is fluoridated. Clothes are made from man-made or enhanced fibres; food is processed, coloured and preserved as a result of the combination of modern science and mass-production techniques.

These changes are emphasised in the chapter on the twentieth century, but they are, of course, more general, as have been shifts towards a more immediate 'mass culture'. Widespread literacy in the nineteenth century, followed by the spread of new media in the twentieth, led to a dynamic, constantly renewed relationship between the producers and consumers of information and images. This was subversive of earlier means of disseminating and inculcating ideas. A vastly expanded press, and new media such as the television, did not necessarily lead to the spread of radical ideas – they could equally serve to reiterate conservative views – but, by regularly providing information and stimuli, they played a major role in a democratisation or equalisation of society that has been a predominant theme over the last century and a half. In the nineteenth century the newspaper became an accepted means for the pursuance of disputes, possibly contributing to a more peaceful and public means of conducting political, social, economic and religious disagreements. Democratisation was not the same as democracy, publicity did not entail the public nature of all politics, but in the twentieth century the information presented to the public has become more extensive and its impact more insistent. Whereas Edward VIII's relationship with Mrs Simpson (later the Duchess of Windsor) in the 1930s was known only to a restricted circle, the same has not been true of the activities of his grand-nephew, Prince Charles. Politicians today press avidly for equal exposure on television, but there are also worries about privacy.

This book itself is a testimony to changing circumstances. Technology is all-pervasive: the use of a word processor permitted frequent redrafting. There is also the clear sense that it is necessary to produce a work that is accessible to a wide audience. Consumer choice is crucial, and censorship, or the need to follow a 'party line', is a not a factor. Indeed, it is the freedom with which this book has been written that is the most encouraging feature of this work. In Britain it is possible to write a book of this type without the problems and fears that an author would experience in much of the world. There is no room for triumphalism: the position may not last. The situation in Northern Ireland scarcely offers encouragement about the use of the past. Nevertheless, it is part of the strength of much of British society that it can look at itself and its past without complacency or the need to reiterate national myths. Would that that were true more widely.

JEREMY BLACK

ROMAN BRITAIN

• Places

1	London	6	York	11	Inchtuthil
2	Chester	7	Lincoln	13	Halkyn
3	St Albans	8	Wroxeter	14	Dolaucothi
4	Gloucester	9	Colchester	15	Stonehenge
5	Caerleon	10	Exeter	16	Avebury

Areas

A	Suffolk	E	Wales	I	Shropshire
B	Kent	F	Anglesey	J	Hereford
C	Cumbria	G	Glamorgan	K	East Anglia
D	Yorkshire	H	Clwyd		

□ Legionary fortresses
not all occupied at once

++++++ Antonine Wall

+++++ Hadrian's wall

⟶ Caesar's invasion route in 55 and 54 BC

--► Claudius's invasion route in 43 AD

▩ Over 200 m

▬ Over 500 m

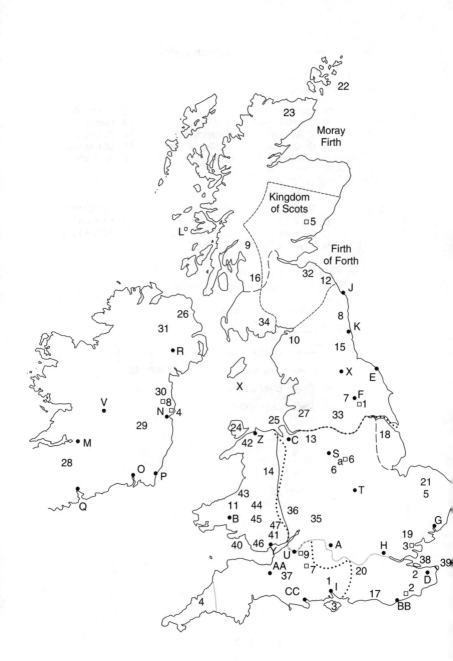

Moray
Firth

Kingdom
of Scots
□ 5

Firth
of Forth

22

23

L °

9

16

34

32

12

10

8

J

K

15

X

E

26

31

R

30
□ 8
N □ 4

X

7 ● F
□ 1

29

V

M

O

P

Q

28

24
42 Z

25

C 13

27

33

18

S
a □ 6
6

21
5

T

43

14

11
● B

44

45

36

35

47
41

G

40

46

U □ 9
□ 7

A

19
3 □

H

38
2
D

39

AA
37

CC

1
I

3

20

17

BB

2 □

4

ANGLO-SAXON BRITAIN

- Places

A Dorchester-on-Thames	H London	P Wexford	Y Caerleon
B Carmarthen	I Southampton	Q Cork	Z Degannwy
C Chester	J Lindisfarne	R Armagh	AA Athelney
D Canterbury	K Jarrow	S Derby	BB Pevensey
E Whitby	L Iona	T Leicester	CC South Cadbury
F York	M Limerick	U Bath	
G Ipswich	N Dublin	V Clonmacois	
	O Waterford	X Catterick	

Areas

1 Hampshire	13 Cheshire	25 Wirral	37 Wessex
2 Kent	14 Powys	26 Antrim	38 Sheppey
3 Isle of Wight	15 Northumbria	27 Lancashire	39 Thanet
4 Cornwall	16 Strathclyde	28 Munster	40 Gower
5 East Anglia	17 Sussex	29 Leinster	41 Gwent
6 Mercia	18 Lindsey	30 Meath	42 Gwynedd
7 Deira	19 Essex	31 Ulster	43 Ceredigion
8 Bernicia	20 Surrey	32 Lothian	44 Builth
9 Argyll	21 Norfolk	33 Elmet	45 Brycheiniog
10 Cumbria	22 Orkney	34 Rheged	46 Glywysing
11 Dyfed	23 Caithness	35 Hwicce	47 Ergyng
12 Gododdin	24 Anglesey	36 Magonsaetan	

- Battles

1 Stamford Bridge	6 Repton
2 Hastings	7 Edington
3 Maldon	8 Tara
4 Clontarf	9 Wroughton
5 Nechtansmere	

······ Boundary of Mercia in 800   — — Boundary of Northumbria in 650

—— Boundary of Wessex in 830   ----- Kingdom of Scots in 1018

—— Offa's Dyke

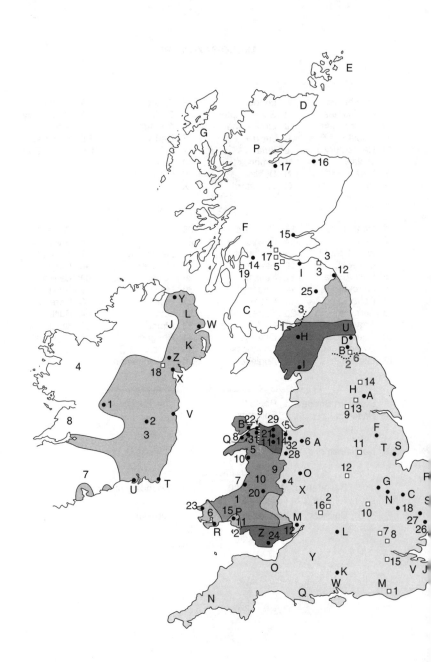

MEDIEVAL BRITISH ISLES

- Places

A	York	P	Camarthen	6	Chester	21	St Asaph
B	Durham	Q	Bangor	7	Aberystwyth	22	Beaumaris
C	Ely	R	Tenby	8	Caernarfon	23	St Davids
D	Newcastle	S	Boston	9	Conwy	24	Llandaff
E	Norwich	T	Wexford	10	Harlech	25	Roxburgh
F	Lincoln	U	Waterford	11	Denbigh	26	Hadleigh
G	Stamford	V	Dublin	12	Berwick	27	Long Melford
H	Carlisle	W	Carrickfergus	13	Edinburgh	28	Holt
I	Kendal	X	Dundalk	14	Glasgow	29	Rhuddlan
J	Canterbury	Y	Coleraine	15	Perth	30	Lavenham
K	Winchester	Z	Newry	16	Elgin	31	Degannwy
L	Dorchester-	1	Athlone	17	Inverness	32	Hawarden
	on-Thames	2	Kildare	18	Cambridge		
M	Tintern	3	Dover	19	Great		
N	Peterborough	4	Montgomery		Yarmouth		
O	Shrewsbury	5	Flint	20	Builth		

Regions

A	Cheshire	L	Antrim	W	Hampshire	8	Thomond
B	Anglesey	M	Sussex	X	Herefordshire	9	Powys
C	Galloway	N	Cornwall	Y	Wiltshire	10	Deheubarth
D	Caithness	O	Somerset	Z	Glamorgan	11	Kidwelly
E	Orkney	P	Ross	1	Ceredigion	12	Gwent
F	Argyll	Q	Dorset	2	Gower	13	Moray
G	Western Isles	R	Norfolk	3	Leinster	14	Clwyd
H	Yorkshire	S	Suffolk	4	Connacht	15	Dyfed
I	Lothian	T	Lincolnshire	5	Gwynedd		
J	Ulster	U	Northumbria	6	Pembrokeshire		
K	Down	V	Kent	7	Desmond		

□ Battles   Rivers ⋯⋯

1	Lewes	8	Barnet	15	Sevenoaks	1	Solway Firth
2	Evesham	9	Wakefield	16	Tewkesbury		(bay)
3	Dunbar	10	Northampton	17	Bannockburn	2	Tees
4	Stirling	11	Stoke	18	Faughart	3	Liddel
5	Falkirk	12	Bosworth	19	Largs	4	Conway
6	Neville's Cross	13	Towton				
7	St Albans	14	Boroughbridge				

▢ Areas under effective control of
the English crown and its subjects
at the death of William I, 1087.

▨ Additions to this area by 1100

▢ Additions to this area by 1189

▨ Additions to this area by 1290

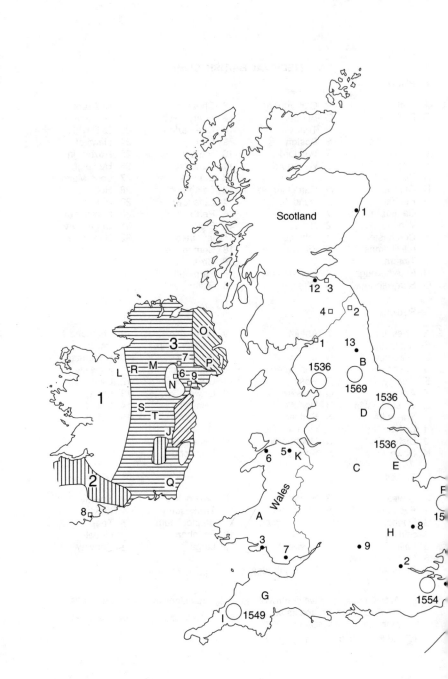

THE SIXTEENTH CENTURY

● Places

1	Aberdeen	6	Bangor	11	Calais
2	London	7	Llandaff	12	Edinburgh
3	Swansea	8	Cambridge	13	Durham
4	Canterbury	9	Oxford		
5	St Asaph	10	Norwich		

Counties

A	Cardiganshire	H	Bedfordshire	O	Antrim
B	Durham	I	Cornwall	P	Down
C	Derbyshire	J	Kildare	Q	Wexford
D	Yorkshire	K	Flintshire	R	Leitrim
E	Lincolnshire	L	Sligo	S	Longford
F	Norfolk	M	Fermanagh	T	Westmeath
G	Devon	N	Monaghan		

□ Battles

1	Solway Moss	6	Clontibret
2	Flodden	7	Yellow Ford
3	Pinkie	8	Kinsale
4	Ancrum Moor	9	Moyry Pass
5	Dussindale		

Regions (larger than counties)

1 Connacht
2 Munster
3 Ulster

○ Centres of Rebellion in England

▨ The Pale c. 1550

▥ Plantations established before 1603

▨ Scottish settlements

▤ Plantations established 1603-49

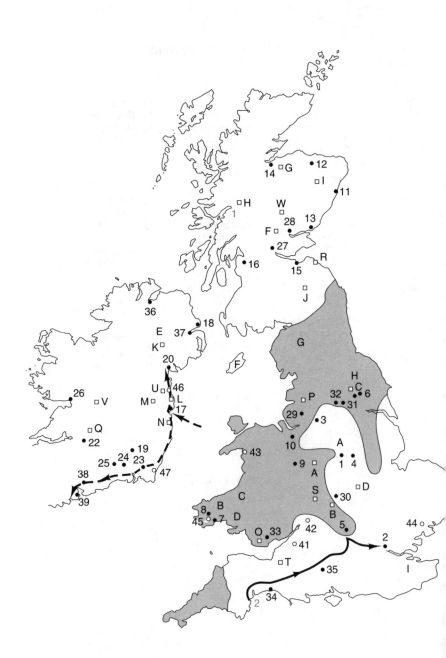

THE CIVIL WARS 1638 –1691

• Towns

1 Derby	11 Aberdeen	22 Limerick	32 Bradford
2 London	12 Elgin	23 Ross	33 Llandaff
3 Manchester	13 Dundee	24 Carrick	34 Lyme Regis
4 Nottingham	14 Inverness	25 Clonmel	35 Salisbury
5 Oxford	15 Edinburgh	26 Galway	36 Derry
6 York	16 Glasgow	27 Stirling	37 Belfast
7 Tenby	17 Dublin	28 Perth	38 Cork
8 Haverfordwest	18 Carrickfergus	29 Wigan	39 Kinsale
9 Shrewsbury	19 Kilkenny	30 Warwick	
10 Chester	20 Dundalk	31 Leeds	

▫ Battles

A Hopton Heath 1643	J Philiphaugh 1645	R Dunbar 1650
B Edgehill 1642	K Benburb 1646	S Worcester 1651
C Marston Moor 1644	L Julianstown 1641	T Sedgemoor 1685
D Naseby 1645	M Dungan Hill 1647	U Boyne 1690
F Tippermuir 1644	N Baggot-rath 1649	V Aughrim 1691
G Auldearn 1645	O St Fagan's 1648	W Killiecrankie 1689
H Inverlochy 1645	P Preston 1648	
I Alford 1645	Q Scarrifhollis 1650	

○ Besieged Towns   Areas

41 Bristol 1643	A Derbyshire	H Yorkshire
42 Gloucester 1643	B Pembrokeshire	I Kent
43 Harlech 1647	C Cardiganshire	
44 Colchester 1648	D Carmarthenshire	Places
45 Pembroke 1648	E Ulster	
46 Drogheda 1649	F Isle of Man	1 Glencoe
47 Wexford 1649	G Cumberland	2 Torbay

▨   Areas of Royalist support in England and Wales 1 May 1643

Campaigns

⟶ William of Orange's route in 1688

– – ➤ Cromwell's route in 1649

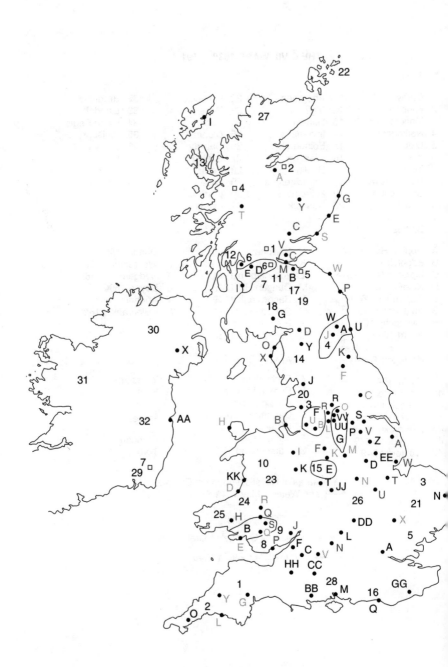

BRITAIN OF INDUSTRIALIZATION & REFORM 1750 – 1900

• Places

A	London	O	Truro	I	Troon	F	Darlington
AA	Dublin	P	Doncaster	J	Tintern	G	Exeter
B	Edinburgh	Q	Brighton	K	Stockton	H	Holyhead
BB	Wimborne	R	Bradford	L	Plymouth	I	Crewe
C	Bath	S	Scunthorpe	M	Forth Bridge	J	Gateshead
CC	Wilton	T	Birmingham	N	Swindon	K	Burton-on-Trent
D	Grantham	U	Sunderland	O	Workington	L	Huddersfield
DD	Wolverton	UU	Dewsbury	P	Bambrugh	M	Nottingham
E	Glasgow	V	Dunfermline	Q	Merthyr Tydfil	N	Leicester
EE	Sleaford	VV	Batley	R	Halifax	O	Leeds
F	Bristol	W	Newcastle	S	Ebbw Vale	P	Cardiff
G	Dumfries	X	Carrickfergus	T	Spalding	Q	Rhondda
GG	Battle	Y	Penrith	U	Stamford	R	Brecon
HH	Bruton	Z	Lincoln	V	Gainsborough	S	Dundee
I	Stornoway	A	Louth	W	Boston	T	Fort William
J	Lancaster	B	Liverpool	X	Whitehaven	U	Bolton
JJ	Stoneleigh	C	Perth	Y	Braemar	V	Devizes
K	Shrewsbury	D	Carlisle	A	Inverness	W	Berwick
KK	Aberdovey	E	Montrose	B	Manchester	X	Cambridge
L	Oxford	F	Derby	C	York	Y	Launceston
M	Southampton	G	Aberdeen	D	Aberystwyth		
N	Norwich	H	Carmarthen	E	Swansea		

Regions

1	Devon	12	Renfrew	23	Montgomeryshire
2	Cornwall	13	Skye	24	Cardiganshire
3	Norfolk	14	Lake District	25	Pembrokeshire
4	Durham	15	Black Country	26	Northamptonshire
5	Essex	16	Sussex	27	Sutherland
6	Strathclyde	17	Selkirk	28	Hampshire
7	Lanarkshire	18	Dumfries	29	Wexford
8	Glamorgan	19	Roxburghshire	30	Ulster
9	Monmouthshire	20	Lancashire	31	Connacht
10	Merioneth	21	East Anglia	32	Leinster
11	Midlothian	22	Orkney Islands		

□ Battles

1 Sheriffmuir 1715
2 Culloden 1746
3 Preston 1716
4 Glenshiel 1719
5 Prestonpans 1745
6 Falkirk 1746
7 Vinegar Hill 1798

Major Coalfields

(A) North-East   (D) Strathclyde
(B) South Wales   (E) Midlands
(C) Fife   (G) Nottinghamshire/Yorkshire

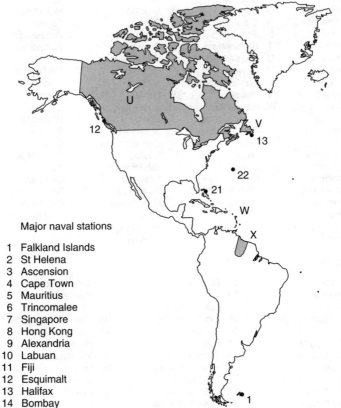

Major naval stations

1 Falkland Islands
2 St Helena
3 Ascension
4 Cape Town
5 Mauritius
6 Trincomalee
7 Singapore
8 Hong Kong
9 Alexandria
10 Labuan
11 Fiji
12 Esquimalt
13 Halifax
14 Bombay
15 Calcutta
16 Lagos
17 Gibraltar
18 Malta
19 Aden
20 Sydney
21 Bahamas
22 Bermuda
23 Adelaide
24 Seychelles

THE BRITISH EMPIRE IN 1914

A Australia	I India	Q Nigeria
B New Zealand	J Cyprus	R Gold Coast
C Tasmania	K Sudan	S Sierra Leone
D Malaya	L Egypt	T Gambia
E New Guinea	M Uganda	U Canada
F Kenya	N S. Africa	V Newfoundland
G Ceylon	O N. Rhodesia	W British West Indies
H Burma	P S. Rhodesia	X British Guiana

1

Pre-Roman and
Roman Britain

The long and complex history of the British Isles reflects the interaction of man and a very varied natural environment. The British Isles are both part of Europe and yet separated from it by the sea. They have a very varied topography, climate and natural vegetation. We should be careful about projecting the modern environment on to the past: climate and economic factors, even the coastline and water levels, were different. Yet in simple terms the bulk of the west and north of Britain are higher and wetter, their soils poorer and their agriculture pastoral rather than arable: centred on animals not crops. Much of Ireland is like west and north Britain, although there is less high land. Yet there are many exceptions to this description of the British Isles as a result of a complex geological history and of great climatic variations. Thus the north and west contain fertile lowlands such as the central lowlands of Scotland, the vale of York in Yorkshire and the vale of Eden in Cumbria while the south and east contain areas of poor fertility, such as the sandy wastes of the Breckland in Suffolk or the hilly greensand of the Weald in Kent. Despite this, the essential contrast in England is between the colder, hillier north and the warmer, lower south, the wetter west and the drier east. Upland areas such as the Pennines, the backbone of northern England, have not served as centres of political power. For most of English and Scottish history wealth and influence have been disproportionately present in the south and east.

Wales clearly shows the consequences of terrain and climate. It is largely mountainous: 60 per cent of the surface area is above the

200-metre line. Until nineteenth-century bridge-building and tunnelling, such terrain acted as an effective brake on communications: the natural links in Wales run east–west, not north–south, and this has had historical and political implications over the centuries. In addition, mountainous terrain is difficult to cultivate. Exposed to prevalent westerly winds that are forced to rise to cross its mountains, Wales, like Ireland, west Scotland and north-west and south-west England, receives a heavy rainfall. This plays a major role in washing the soil from its uplands. Thus, much of Wales, like much of upland Britain, has relatively poor, often acidic, soil and is unsuitable for continuous or intensive cultivation. This encourages a dependence on the rearing of animals, a form of agriculture that cannot support the higher population levels of arable regions. As in much of the north of England, the more fertile areas of Wales are separated by the poor terrain. There is a limited amount of good land on Anglesey and the northern coast, particularly the vale of Clwyd, and far more in the vale of Glamorgan to the south of the main massif, and in other parts of southern Wales. However, there is a clear shift from there, or from the good farmland of Shropshire and Hereford in the neighbouring region of England, to the mountains of central Wales. Although the rich coastal regions of Wales are small, their wealth and power became so great as to quite dominate the whole society of Wales, and in many ways to make up for the poverty of the inland regions. The same was true of northern England.

For most of their history, the map of power in the British Isles was one that was heavily influenced by the geography of agriculture and agrarian systems. This was particularly true of the pre-Roman period. Coins, proto-towns and 'states' with monarchical patterns of government existed in southern England, but not in the north or in Wales. In the latter two, relatively low population levels and a poorly developed agricultural base ensured that there was only a small surplus of wealth for taxation and thus only a limited ability to support political and governmental activity. Most of late-Iron-Age Wales, for example, has left no trace of pottery.

In contrast, southern England was linked in this period to nearby areas of the Continent: to northern Gaul (France) and the Low Countries. The nature of these links is contentious, as, more generally, are the ethnic origins of the inhabitants of the British Isles. Early Hominoids and Neanderthals were both present. Human settlement in the British Isles increased as the climate improved with the retreat of the last Ice Age. Britain was still joined to the Continent by a wide land-bridge between the east coast of England and the Low Countries, but this was broken by the rising sea level in about 6500 BC. Hunter-gatherers turned to agriculture from about 4500 BC and villages developed in fertile regions. The plough was adopted in southern England in about 3500 BC. The sophistication of Neolithic society is indicated by the numerous tombs or megaliths that survive and by the religious monuments such as Avebury and Stonehenge in southern England that would have each required at least hundreds of thousands of man-hours to construct. Stone alignments and circles were created in England, Ireland, Scotland and Wales: there are remains of about 1,000. Dating from about 3200–1500 BC, they became progressively more complex, suggesting a tendency towards ritual and maybe political centralisation. The religious practices of the people are obscure, although astronomical knowledge clearly played a major role. The midsummer sun rises along the axis of Stonehenge. Animals played a major role in the economy, culture and religion. Animal motifs were incorporated in art and animals had religious symbolism, being linked with particular deities.

Trade developed as the flint necessary for agricultural tools and axes was mined and traded. By the third millennium BC copper metallurgy had spread into southern Britain. This was followed by bronze, a copper-tin alloy that was harder and therefore better for tools and weapons. Britain was a source of copper, gold and tin. The Bronze Age was followed by iron-working which reached Britain by the end of the eighth century BC. The ethnic history of the first millennium BC is complex, but it is apparent that from a heartland in France, Germany and the Alpine lands, Celts spread into Britain. The population rose and agriculture improved. Britain was far from stagnant on the eve of the Roman conquest.

ROMAN CONQUEST

Having conquered Gaul (France), the Roman military leader Julius Caesar claimed that it was necessary to stop British support for the Celts still resisting there; there may indeed have been British assistance for the Veneti of Brittany. Caesar was also probably motivated by a desire for glory and plunder, and by the need to employ his troops. In 55 and 54 BC he launched expeditions against southern England, but met unexpectedly strong resistance and storms. As a result, Caesar was happy to return to Gaul.

Under his successors trade links developed with Britain, but there was no military action until AD 43 when the Emperor Claudius invaded, both in order to gain a necessary military reputation and because Rome's protégés in southern Britain had lost control. The Romans rapidly conquered lowland England, although there was considerable resistance, led initially by the Catuvellani and, in particular, their leader Caratacus, to give them the Roman spelling of their names – inevitably, since almost all our knowledge of this period comes from Roman written sources. In pursuit of him the Romans invaded Wales.

In AD 60 the Governor Suetonius Paulinus was campaigning in north Wales against the Druids, anti-Roman priests and their supporters, when a major rising was staged by the Iceni tribe of East Anglia under their female leader Boudicca (Boadicea is a later corruption of the name). They were enraged by callous Roman rule and by their treatment of the royal family, including the flogging of Boudicca and the rape of her daughters. The major Roman settlements were destroyed, but Paulinus crushed the Iceni in battle and they were then brutally 'pacified'. Boudicca died, probably by suicide.

In the seventies the Romans pressed forward again. The Brigantes of northern England were subjugated in 71–4, Wales following. By 78 all of England and Wales was under Roman control, and this remained the case until links with Rome collapsed in 409. However, the British Isles were not conquered in their entirety, and the continued presence of a frontier zone ensured that Britain absorbed a relatively high percentage of Roman military expenditure, and had a comparatively large number of troops. As a result, Britain played an important role during struggles for control in the empire. Highland Scotland was never conquered by the Romans: the terrain was far more difficult for an invading power than lowland Britain and it was well defended. Agricola, governor 77–83, invaded Scotland, winning a notable victory at Mons Graupius, but only the Scottish lowlands were conquered. Although Agricola considered its conquest, Ireland was not attacked by the Romans. The Roman conquest thus, even as it united southern Britain for the first time in its history, also demonstrated a central feature of British history: a lack of uniformity that in part reflected a variety of local socio-environmental systems stemming from the physical variety of the country.

The frontier zone was most clearly marked by Hadrian's Wall, built by the Emperor Hadrian from about 122 along the Tyne-Solway line, across the narrowest part of the island, to protect England from invasion from the north and a means to control the upland zone by preventing free movement. To the south, the generally peaceful nature of Roman society encouraged a process of romanisation. Roman citizenship was restricted neither to Romans nor to Italians. Non-Romans could rise to the heights of power. Similarly, Roman conquest did not mean expropriation of all power. Roman Britain acquired an urban system linked by roads, as well as romanised farms or villas. Towns such as Londinium (London), Deva (Chester) and Eboracum (York) were centres of authority, consumption and Roman culture, including, eventually, Christianity. Some towns emerged alongside Roman fortresses, but others developed as a result of initiatives by the native elites keen to adopt Roman culture and material life. Links with the Continent increased and fostered economic development. Britain was valuable as a source of mineral exports, especially silver, lead, gold and iron. Thus, Britain made a major contribution to the economics and finances of the empire. Mining was of particular importance in Wales. Although there was pre-Roman mining, there was a tremendous expansion under the Romans, of gold at Dolaucothi, lead at Halkyn and copper in Anglesey.

THE END OF ROMAN BRITAIN

Like other parts of the Roman empire, Britain suffered increasing attack from 'barbarians', from the third century onwards. Picts attacked from Scotland, Scots from Ireland and Angles, Jutes and Saxons from northern Germany and Denmark. Such assaults played a major role in the decline of trade and urban stagnation that affected Britain in the fourth century. At Verulamium (St Albans), for example, urban decay led to the use of the theatre as a rubbish dump. The ability of the empire to resist these attacks was progressively eroded, and links with Rome were further weakened by Roman usurpers based in Britain, such as Magnus Maximus in 383–8 and Constantine III in 407–9. As more serious challenges to Roman power were mounted across the Rhine and the Danube, troops were also withdrawn from Britain. In 409 the Romano-Britons expelled the officials of Constantine III and were left to their own devices to resist barbarian attack. This was the end of the Roman empire in Britain, although not of Roman Britain. Nevertheless, the subsequent break-up of Roman Britain into a number of kingdoms suggests that its internal unity should not be exaggerated.

2

Saxons, Vikings and Celts, AD 400–1066

THE ANGLO-SAXON INVASIONS

The fifth century is an especially obscure period. It is far from clear how far continuity or discontinuity should be stressed between Roman and post-Roman Britain. In particular, it is unclear how far there were large-scale movements of people or invasions by smaller warrior groups. The invaders attacked eastern and southern England. The Jutes established themselves in Kent, the Isle of Wight and parts of Hampshire, the Saxons elsewhere in southern England, the Angles further north. Barbarian progress was, however, resisted, for longer and more successfully than in France, Spain or Italy, although resistance was gravely handicapped by internal divisions. Resistance may have been greater because there was more at stake for the Romano-British elite: the assimilation with invaders that characterised France, for example, was absent. In about 500 the Romano-Britons possibly won a major battle under Artorius (Arthur) at Mons Badonicus, and it is possible that a large hall at the hillfort at South Cadbury was the feasting hall of a warrior of the period, the basis of the legend of Arthur's Camelot.

England, nevertheless, was gradually conquered, and much of Roman Britain was destroyed or fell into decay. However, romanised town and villa life and Christianity did not cease abruptly. Continuity at many of the major towns has now been established by archaeological work which is throwing light on a period for which the written sources are very limited. In conquered areas many Romano-Britons survived as slaves and peasants: the landscape continued to be managed. The high levels of population that had characterised Roman Britain appear to have persisted until the mid-sixth century outbreak of the bubonic plague that devastated much of the ancient world.

Yet the languages and culture of Roman Britain were largely lost in England, and, as trade declined, England became a subsistence economy and a violent society with few ceramics or coins in the archaeological record. The invaders were all pagans: Christianity withered. Under the Romans, the religion had not been widespread in Britain, although Christianity was part of the Roman legacy, at least at the upper levels of society. In the sixth century the Angles and Saxons advanced considerably; the Jutes made scant impact. The most important Saxon kingdom, Wessex, that of the West Saxons, based around Dorchester-on-Thames and in Hampshire, advanced west, although it was not to conquer Cornwall until 838. The Angles established kingdoms in East Anglia, the Midlands (Mercia), Yorkshire (Deira) and north of the Tees (Bernicia). The latter two joined to become Northumbria, which conquered the Romano-British kingdoms of Elmet and Rheged so as to dominate the north of England.

SCOTLAND AND IRELAND

The situation in Scotland is far more obscure. The Picts, who occupied the lands north of the Firth of Forth, left scant remains, and their political and social organisation is unclear, as is the process in which the kingdom of Alba was formed by the Picts and the Scots. The kingdom was poor, had no coinage and its trading links were few. On the other hand, the kings of the Picts could wield considerable power. Brude mac Bile was able to devastate the Orkneys in 682 and, after his victory at Dunnichen Moss (Nechtansmere) in 685, to drive the Northumbrians back to the Forth. In addition, the views of the kings appear to have been decisive in the spread of Christianity at the start of the eighth century, while Pictland also produced art of a high order. The Picts, however, absorbed by the Scots, left few traces. Their own Celtic language probably did not outlast the tenth century, its loss a crucial part of the process by which the Picts were extinguished culturally. The Scots were Irish-speakers who settled in Argyll from perhaps as early as the fourth century, displacing the Picts.

The position in Ireland is also obscure; as in Scotland there was no question of post-Roman continuity. It is clear that Christianity spread in Ireland in the fifth century. It may have reached southern Ireland from parts of western Britain the previous century. St Patrick came from Britain, possibly Cumbria, in the fifth century and there were Christian settlements before his arrival. Ireland also had cultural links with Spain and western France. Ireland was thus affected by Christianity, but not, directly, by Roman cultural influence. Its culture was a complex mix of influences: pagan and Christian, oral and literate, native and imported.

WALES

Fifth-century Wales is also obscure. Town life continued in the Roman settlement in Caerleon and, possibly, Carmarthen, and Roman estate units may have continued to function in south-east Wales. Rome continued to cast a shadow over Wales, both politically and culturally, but the Roman system collapsed. Wales ceased to be part of a major empire and instead became an assortment of political units focusing on the largely tribal leadership of locally powerful warlords. Trade links by sea remained important in post-Roman Wales, and the same routes served both for the expansion of Christianity there, and for settlement from Ireland. Missionary activity from Gaul began in the fifth century. Illtud, from Brittany, established a school and monastery probably at Llaniltud Fawr in Glamorgan and these became a centre for missionary activity. St David was active in Dyfed.

If reliable information on the history of Wales for the rest of the first millennium AD is sparse, a product of its relative lack of political and cultural development compared to much of England, a number of themes nevertheless emerge. Christianity was clearly a major and growing force. There is evidence of ecclesiastical sites from all over Wales – monasteries, churches and hermitages – and it is clear that the church played an important role in cultural matters. Nevertheless, although Latin was used for liturgical (religious) purposes and for post-Roman gravestones and other inscriptions, the Celtic language of the pre-Roman and Roman periods survived as an active vernacular and began its development into Welsh. It was at this stage that the Celtic language rapidly evolved into Breton (in Brittany), Cornish, Welsh and Strathclyde/Cumbrian. Little survives in Wales in terms of the visual arts of the period, but Wales had a 'Celtic culture' in common with other areas of Britain not conquered by the Anglo-Saxons. An older culture, or at least language, had survived both Rome and the Anglo-Saxon invaders.

Nevertheless no one, not the people who lived in what is now Wales, not the Angles, nor the Saxons, nor the Romans, had any consciousness of Wales or for that matter of England as such until the sixth century or later. Surviving Welsh poetry is claimed to begin in the sixth century with Taliesin and Aneirin. Taliesin composed a series of poems in praise of Urien of Rheged and his son Owain. Rheged was in the Carlisle area. Aneirin wrote one long poem, *The Gododdin*, about how his lord, Mynyddog Mwynfawr of Gododdin, the region between the Forth and the Tyne, sent a warband to recover the strategically important town of Cattraeth (Catterick) in what is now Yorkshire. That is to say, these men composed in Welsh for Welsh warriors and their courts, but they were living in what is now the English Lake District or southern Scotland. Wales, although it is a geographical expression, is culturally far more problematic, being as much as anything a survivor from an older civilisation which the Anglo-Saxons mainly supplanted. The struggle with the invaders lasted a long time; ultimately, the building of Offa's Dyke in the late eighth century by King Offa of Mercia was to mark the definition of a border and of Wales and England. Nowhere else in the British Isles was a frontier quite so crucial. The advance of the Anglo-Saxons and later the Normans was to help condition Welsh history. Indeed Wales was given its identity by the conquerors in terms of otherness: the Saxons used *Walas* or *Wealas* to describe the Britons and it meant both serfs and foreigners.

As the Anglo-Saxons advanced westwards, the links between the surviving Romano-British communities were severed: Cumbria/Strathclyde, Wales and Cornwall could not unite to any purpose. The struggle for control of northern England helped to define the future political shape of Britain. In 616 Ethelfrith of Northumbria conquered Cheshire, killing the king of Powys in a battle at Chester, and separated Wales from Cumbria. A pagan, Ethelfrith slaughtered many of the monks of Bangor Is-coed, who had prayed for his defeat and possibly fought against him. His successor, Edwin, continued Northumbrian pressure on the Welsh, defeating Cadwallon of Gwynedd in 629. Cadwallon, a Christian, then formed an alliance with the pagan Penda of Mercia, and in 633 invaded Northumbria, defeating and killing Edwin at Heathfield in 633. Cadwallon was, however, in turn defeated and killed by Edwin's nephew Oswald the following year, and the Welsh lost their links with the Cumbrians. Links with the Celts of the south-west had been lost as a result of the battle of Dyrham (577). Wales became the most important area of surviving Romano-British civilisation.

THE SPREAD OF CHRISTIANITY

The replacement of the religious pluralism of Roman and post-Roman Britain by Christianity was to align the British Isles culturally far more closely with the Continent. A mission from Pope Gregory the Great, under Augustine, came in 597 to Canterbury, the capital of Kent, and had some success in the south-east, but it was the Irish Church that was the base for the conversion of much of England. Christian missionaries came to Scotland from Ireland with the Scots. Although the Irish Church had a system of bishoprics, the numerous monasteries, such as Armagh and Clonmacnois, were more important. They were centres of devotional, missionary and cultural activity, including writing. The church of Iona, off the west coast of modern Scotland, was founded by Columba, an Irish monk, in 563, and the Picts were converted by the early eighth century. A mission from Iona, under Aidan, founded Lindisfarne in Northumbria in 635. From there Mercia was converted. The Irish Church also had a major cultural influence in Anglo-Saxon England. There was tension over the authority of the papacy, but, as a result of the support of King Oswy of Northumbria at the Synod (Church meeting) of Whitby in 664, Roman customs prevailed, the authority of Iona over the Northumbrian Church was broken, and the path cleared for the organisation of the English Church by Theodore of Tarsus, who the pope appointed archbishop of Canterbury.

England, in turn, now became a major base for missionary activity, spreading Christianity in the Low Countries, Germany and, later, Scandinavia. Within the British Isles, pagan cults and practices were gradually destroyed or worn down by the Church, now sure of secular support. From the late seventh century, monastic churches were constructed at important centres, though most local parish churches were probably not founded until the tenth and eleventh centuries. Christianity meant a spread of education and literacy, and the beginnings of written law, not least to protect churchmen and their property; written instruments might serve to convey rights in land. Society was becoming at least partly institutionalised.

THE RISE OF LARGE KINGDOMS

The most important political development from the sixth and seventh centuries in England was the coalescence of the numerous small kingdoms into three major kingdoms, Northumbria, Mercia and Wessex. The process can be seen in cellular terms, with small units, probably based on successful warbands, amalgamating into larger units. Chance, especially the personalities of rulers and the results of warfare, helps to explain why some areas ceased to be independent kingdoms, while others flourished. The west Midland kingdoms of the Hwicce and the Magonsaetan were absorbed by Mercia, which from 654 and possibly the 630s also dominated East Anglia: the king was killed in battle by Penda in the 630s. The same process occurred in Wales: the less successful kingdoms, such as Gower, Gwent, Ergyng, Ceredigion, Builth, Brycheiniog and Powys, were taken over. The most expansive in Wales were Gwynedd in the north-west, Dyfed in the south-west and Glywysing in the south-east. They were the kingdoms based on the largest amount of fertile lowland, but, in addition, they benefited from a degree of immunity from the English. In contrast, Powys in the north–east suffered considerably at the hands of the Mercians. Ireland was divided into about 100, mostly small kingdoms, each occupied by a tribe. Ties of dependence linked lesser kings to their more powerful counterparts, and by the eighth century certain kings had thus considerably extended their area of authority. The notion of the 'high king' developed in Ireland and, to some extent, elsewhere in the British Isles.

The relationship between kingdoms was very volatile. It was difficult to perpetuate any hegemony. In England Aethelbert of

Kent was able to act as an overking in the 590s, but for most of the following century this position belonged to Oswald (634–41), Oswy (641–70) and Egfrith (670–85) of Northumbria. They ruled between the Humber and the Forth in eastern Britain and the Mersey and the Ayr on the west, and were at times treated as overlords by the rulers of Mercia, Wessex, Strathclyde and the Pict and Scottish territories. Northumbrian power was contested by Penda of Mercia (632–54).

Defeat at the hands of Mercia (678) and the Picts (685) brought Northumbrian hegemony to an end. It was replaced by that of Mercia, especially under Offa (757–96). He controlled such formerly independent kingdoms as Essex, Lindsey, East Anglia, Kent and Sussex. Wessex recognised Mercian protection in 786 and Offa's charters (formal documents) used the term 'King of the English' at least once. Offa is most famous for the earth dyke, a frontier line running from the Severn estuary to the Dee, that may well have been a defensive work. The building of it must have entailed considerable organisation, a testimony to the administrative capability of Mercian England. Offa's Dyke reflected the degree to which pressure from the English east shaped the extent of Wales, a process unmatched in this period for Scotland and Ireland. The dyke was not the end of Mercian expansion. In 822 Offa's successor, Cenwulf, invaded northern Wales, destroyed the fortress of Degannwy on the Conway, and annexed Powys. Dyfed was also attacked in Cenwulf's reign.

Durable and effective control of much of Britain was, however, beyond the capability of any one of the kingdoms. Wessex rejected Mercian protection in 802; Mercia was weakened in the 820s by conflict in Wales and dynastic feuds; and in 825, after defeating the Mercians at Wroughton, Egbert of Wessex conquered Kent, Essex, Surrey and Sussex. Mercia followed in 829 but was soon independent again. Thus, there was little sign of political unification. There were faint indications of a sense of national identity: the canons of the Synod of Hertford (672) were issued for and applied to the whole English Church, and Bede, a Northumbrian monk, wrote his *Ecclesiastical History of the English People* in 731. However, these had no political echoes. In 829 Northumbria had also acknowledged Egbert's overlordship, but there was scant sense that Wessex would emerge as the centre of an English state.

SOCIETY

The nature of the sources ensure that any account of society in the British Isles in the half-millennium after the ending of political links with Rome is necessarily tentative. Archaeological research can only reveal so much, particularly for the life of the bulk of the population, and written sources are very limited. Nevertheless new archaeological methodologies offer many insights. For example work on fossilised human stool has indicated the unhealthy nature of life in York in about 950.

The rationale and conduct of power were both violent. Feuds within and between royal families and between tribes ensured that society remained violent, the ethos of heroism revealed in the epic poem *Beowulf* being one of glory won through fighting. Society was also clearly unequal. Within each kingdom, below the ruling group, society was divided on both sides of the Irish Sea between free and unfree men; the latter worked the land. In modern society there is a clear distinction between the sovereign power (the state/government) and a citizenry enjoying equal rights and status; but premodern society was characterised by the pervasive impact of different privileges and, within the elite, of relationships joining ruler and ruled which were deliberately personal, rather than distant and impersonal; the ethos of the warband. Status was measured by *wergild*: the different sums payable in disparate social groups as compensation for killing a man. Unfree men included both slaves and serfs, but the status of the two groups was different.

Society was not only hierarchical, but also male-dominated, deferential and patriarchal, while respect for age and authority, religious and secular, legal and law-enforcing, was crucial. The roles of the environment and the human eco-system were only slightly affected by technology. Patterns of life and death reflected the dominant role of the seasons. Physical strength and stature were of considerable importance, and wisdom was attached to age. There was no cult of youth or value attached to novelty: both are essentially developments of the last 350 years, and more particularly the last 75. Instead, society was reverential of and referential to the past. Inegalitarian social practices and institutions were taken for granted, and were also central to 'politics', an activity restricted to the social elite. Kinship groups were of considerable importance and had defined legal roles in inheritance and in taking vengeance for hurts to kin members. Kin links were central to the practice of blood feuds. As farming systems became more settled, local manorial lordship developed. Hereditary tenure of land became more important and there was a closer definition of the status, rights and duties of *thegns* (nobles).

The basic distinction was between the sexes. Women were subordinated to men and expected to defer to them, and wives were represented by their husbands in court. Gender roles were embodied in religious models such as the Virgin Mary and the saints. Women nevertheless played a vital role in the economy. Households were economic units to which women contributed greatly; not least by making clothes and processing food. Women were not without rights. In the later Anglo-Saxon period there is evidence of their inheriting, holding and bequeathing lands, while married women could control separate property. Aside from the 'enclave' world of the nunnery, individual women could gain prominence, most obviously as members of royal families, as with Aethelflaed, who ruled English Mercia in 911–18, or Emma, successively influential wife of Aethelred the Unready and Cnut. The Pictish royal succession was matrilineal. Furthermore, whatever the superior status and rights of men, relationships within marriage reflected both strength of personality and affection, a pattern that was also true of parent–child relations. And yet personality and affection operated within a context of differential power and authority. A society of inherited status ensured that many women were treated like chattels or political counters. The centrality of military activity and ethos left scant independent role for women. Furthermore, female behaviour was classified and stereotyped by reference to religion. Alongside positive images of the woman as bride, wife and mother, there was a strong negative tradition of the woman as whore or harlot.

Inheritance was important to social and political relationships, because of the nature of the economic system. Land, and labour on it, were central, and its ownership was markedly inegalitarian. The British Isles were predominantly rural, in location, economy, politics and ethos; more so than during the Roman period. A small number of major ports – Ipswich, London, Southampton and York – developed spectacularly in the eighth century, and by the tenth century a more extensive urban network was in place, with numerous *burhs* (fortified towns) founded by Alfred and his successors.

Southampton, planned by King Ine of Wessex (688–726), is estimated to have covered 111 acres and was a major centre of trade
and minting. Yet, although domestic and foreign trade became
more important, agriculture remained dominant. Wool was the
major export and towns depended on a rural surplus of food.

Agriculture suffered from limited knowledge and technology in,
for example, power sources and transmission, and selective breeding of crops and animals. There was a serious shortage of fertiliser,
and fields therefore had to be left fallow (uncultivated) to restore
their fertility. Livestock were smaller than their Roman predecessors and far smaller than their modern descendants; and meat and
milk yields were much lower. Most labour was manual, repetitive,
often arduous and usually monotonous. Communications were
relatively primitive, both for goods and for people. Long-distance
bulk transport was only economic by water, but rivers were affected by freezing and drought, while sea travel was at the mercy of
wind, waves and tides. Horses were used for power and as pack
animals for transport, as well as for military service and pleasure.
Despite these limitations, settlement spread during the period. In
Norfolk, for example, the seventh and eighth centuries saw a
fleshing out of the earlier settlement pattern. It was to be a relatively prosperous society that attracted the attention of the Vikings.

VIKING ATTACKS

Much of Europe suffered a second wave of 'barbarian' attacks in
the eighth, ninth and tenth centuries: Magyars from the east, Arabs
from the south and Vikings from Scandinavia. The Vikings, tra-
ders, colonisers and fighters, spread east to Russia, and west to
Iceland, Greenland and the coast of North America. The main
burden of Viking attack was on the British Isles, northern France
and the Low Countries in the ninth century, with a fresh wave of
attacks on Britain between 980 and 1075. The Vikings, possibly
with limited land available for colonisation in Scandinavia, were
motivated by opportunities for raiding and settlement in more
prosperous and fertile lands, such as much of the British Isles,
which were vulnerable to the amphibious operations that the Scan-
dinavians could mount so well. Viking longboats, with their sails,
stepped masts, true keels, and steering rudders, were effective

ocean-going ships able to take to the Atlantic; but also able, thanks to their shallow draught, to be rowed in coastal waters and up rivers, even if there was only three feet of water.

England had been free from attack from the Continent for two centuries, but in 789 Danish ships were first recorded in English waters and in 793–4 the pagan Danes brutally sacked the monasteries of Lindisfarne and Jarrow, the cultural and religious centres of Northumbria. Viking pressure increased in the 830s and 840s and the coastal regions of the British Isles were all affected. The Norwegians (Norse) overran and settled the Orkneys, the Shetlands, the far north of Scotland, and much of its west coast, as well as coastal regions of Ireland. In the Northern Isles and northeast Caithness the settlement was so extensive that the local language became a Norse dialect until replaced by Scots in the sixteenth to eighteenth centuries. The monks of Iona were dispersed by the Norwegians in about 800, although monastic activity continued there.

The Norwegians made a major impact on Ireland. They were first recorded in 795 when they sacked Lambay Island. The wealthy Irish monasteries attracted attack, and the numerous rivers and lakes facilitated Viking movement. From the 840s their military presence became stronger with larger forces that overwintered in Ireland and developed permanent coastal bases. The first, Dublin, established in 841, was followed by Limerick, Wexford, Waterford and Cork. From such bases the Norwegians dominated the Irish Sea and its trade and intervened in Wales and on the west coast of England. Viking pressure on Ireland increased from the early tenth century. The Norwegians from the 850s began pressing on the north Welsh coast, especially Anglesey, and plundered the royal seat of the major Welsh kingdom of Gwynedd in 968. In the first two decades of the tenth century the Norwegians colonised the coastline of north-west England, invading the Wirral from Dublin in 902. The place-names of Scandinavian settlements, with their typical endings of -by and -thorp, are quite extensive in Cumbria and coastal Lancashire. Other Scandinavian place-names occur in parts of Ireland, such as east Antrim.

Danish pressure also increased on southern and eastern England. From the mid-ninth century the Vikings came not to plunder, but to conquer and stay. Danish invaders took up winter quarters in south-eastern England: in Thanet in 850 and Sheppey in 854. The

Danish 'Great Army' abandoned operations in northern France and overran East Anglia (865) and Yorkshire (866–7): York was stormed in 866. Wessex, attacked in 871, owed its survival in large part to the determination and skill of King Alfred (871–99), although the struggle was a desperate one and Alfred was nearly crushed in 871 and 878.

Wessex's resistance led the Danes to turn on Mercia, which was conquered in 874: King Burgred was defeated at Repton and fled to Rome. In 878 the Danes launched a sudden attack on Alfred, leading him to flee to the Somerset marshes at Athelney. He successfully reorganised his forces and defeated the Danes at Edington (878). The victory was followed by a treaty leaving the Danes with what became known as the Danelaw: England east and north of a line from Chester to London. The Danish advance had been stopped.

There was considerable Scandinavian settlement in the Danelaw. This is indicated by place-names, the names of individuals noted in documents and material remains; although there is no agreement on the proportion of the population of the Danelaw that was Scandinavian. As earlier with the Anglo-Saxon invasions, some interpretations stress major immigration, others a transfer of political control. The concentration of Scandinavian place-names in particular parts of the Danelaw suggests extensive but patchy immigration.

THE GROWTH OF WESSEX

Having stopped the Danes, Alfred went onto the offensive, capturing London in 886, and sought to strengthen Wessex. He built a fleet, created a more effective system of military recruitment and constructed a system of *burhs* (fortified towns). These policies helped Alfred to defeat further Danish attacks in 892–6. At the same time resistance to the Norwegians increased in Ireland. They were increasingly confined to their bases and were driven from Dublin in 902 although they regained control there in 914.

Alfred's policies were continued by his successors. Conflict with the Vikings played a crucial role in the development of the English state, just as the Viking invasions of Scotland played a part in the growing power of the kingdom of the Scots. The earlier destruction of the other Anglo-Saxon ruling houses allowed Alfred and his successors to be portrayed as 'English', rather than merely 'West Saxon', kings. The process of advance under Alfred's heirs could be, was and has been presented as one of reconquest, the driving back of the Danes and the Norwegians, but it was also one of conquest, in which the rulers of Wessex brought modern England under their authority.

A succession of able rulers was crucial. Edward the Elder (899–924) and his sister Aethelflaed, Lady of the Mercians (911–18), Athelstan (924–39), and Edmund (936–46) conquered East Anglia, and Danish Mercia and Northumbria, and English (western) Mercia was absorbed by Wessex in 918, the end of what had been a major independent power. Aethelflaed took Derby, obtained control of Leicester and received the submission of York, exploits which the (West Saxon) *Anglo-Saxon Chronicle* appropriated to her brother, King Edward. The defeated Danes were allowed to keep their lands and the Danelaw retained distinctive features, including its own legal system. The Danes, however, converted to Christianity.

The conquest of the north was a more protracted affair than that of the Midlands and the Viking kingdom of York received important support from the Vikings in Dublin in resisting the advance of Wessex. The West Saxon rulers also laid claim to the overlordship of all Britain. In 920 the rulers of Scotland, York, English Northumbria (the area north of the Tees that had resisted the Vikings), and the Strathclyde Britons are said, by West Saxon sources, to have accepted Edward's lordship. His successor Athelstan captured York (927), invaded Scotland (934), defeated a united force of Scots, Strathclyde Britons and Norwegians from Ireland at Brunanburh (937) and formed alliances with leading continental rulers. Athelstan saw himself as a king or overking or even emperor of Britain and this came out in his charters.

After Athelstan's death, however, Olaf II Guthfrithson, king of Dublin, gained York and the north Midlands with the support of the local population. York did not finally accept West Saxon control until 954 when Eric Bloodaxe, its last Norwegian king, was killed in an ambush. This left the West Saxon dynasty dominant in England. Eadred (946–55) could be described as the first king of the English. In 973 Edgar (959–75) was able to stage an elaborate coronation at Bath in which he was the first ruler to be *crowned* as king of the English; the title itself had been used by Offa and Athelstan.

The expanding West Saxon state also developed internally. A county or shire system was consolidated and extended. The shires were in turn divided into hundreds or *wapentakes* which were responsible for maintaining law and order. Their public courts were a link between rulers and free men; a system of officials – *ealdormen*, sheriffs, port-reeves and hundredmen – linked the ruler and the localities. Service to the king led to gains of land and status: what had been the personal loyalties of the warband were increasingly given territorial form, regularity and aristocratic status and continuity.

There was also a system of assessment for taxation and military service. The coinage was improved and under Edgar it was re-minted on average every six years, a major administrative achievement that would not have been possible a century earlier. The state of the coinage indicated the development both of a cash economy and of an administrative system in which taxation and expenditure played major roles.

The development of a sophisticated and spatially defined governmental system was matched by a revival of the Church, which had been greatly disrupted by Viking invasion and settlement. New monasteries were founded and monastic life was revived. This process began with the initiatives of Alfred, but continued under his successors to culminate in a period of impressive activity in the late tenth century. The Church lent ideological support to the monarchy and also provided the context for cultural activity, including manuscript illumination (illustrations) and stone carving.

IRELAND

Resistance to Viking invasion also served to bring a measure of political consolidation in the Celtic lands: the history of the British Isles became very much a matter of the survival of the fittest or at least most fortunate. Máel Sechnaill I (d. 862) was the first ruler to wield authority over most of Ireland. At the battle of Tara (980), Máel Sechnaill II, high king of Ireland, defeated the Dublin forces and seriously weakened the Vikings. Brian Boru (*c*.926–1014), the son of a minor Irish king, defeated the Norse of Limerick at the battle of Sulcoit in about 968, gained control of Munster, captured Dublin in 1000, deposed Máel Sechnaill II, and was recognised as high king in 1002. His defeat of his Irish rival Máel Mórda, king of Leinster, and of the latter's Viking allies from Dublin, Orkney and Scandinavia, at Clontarf (1014) decisively weakened the Vikings in Ireland, although Brian was killed in the battle. Brian was replaced by Máel Sechnaill II, but after his death no high king ruled without significant opposition. The crucial political level became that of the sub- or provincial kingdoms: Connacht, Leinster, Meath, Munster and Ulster. Each, especially the last, was in turn divided into independent lordships based essentially on tribal domains. Powerful sub-kings such as Turloch O'Brien of Munster (d. 1086) and his son Muircertach (1086–1119), and Turloch O'Connor of Connacht (1119–56) and his son Rory (1166–83), won and maintained the high kingship in bitter struggles.

SCOTLAND

In Scotland Kenneth I MacAlpin (d. 858), the king of the Scottish kingdom of Dál Riáta, conquered the Picts, whose throne he claimed by matrilinear succession, and united them with the Scots, becoming king of Scotia. However, a separate Scottish invasion led to the conquest of the northern Pictish kingdom centred on the Moray Firth and this Scottish kingdom resisted control from the other until the early twelfth century. Kenneth MacAlpin's descendants were more interested in expanding south, overrunning Strathclyde early in the tenth century and Lothian later that century. There was no obvious geographical boundary between Scotland and England, and no ethnic unity to either. What eventually became Scotland was ethnically, geographically, economically and culturally diverse, and included Scots, Picts, the Britons of Strathclyde and the Angles of Lothian. Until the mid-twelfth century it was unclear whether much of what is now northern England, and especially Cumbria and Northumbria, would be part of England or of Scotland.

WALES

Wales was the least affected of the four 'countries' by the Vikings, although the most affected by pressure from within the British

Isles. Important as English pressure was, however, it would be wrong to juxtapose overly coherent realities of Welshness and Englishness, to argue that the English set the terms for Welsh political development, and to neglect the role of internecine, particularly dynastic, struggles. The failure of the kingdoms of Ceredigion and Gwrtheyrnion in central Wales to survive was due in part to the greater strength of Gwynedd and Dyfed. Gwynedd was the basis of the power of Rhodri Mawr (d. 878), but he also ruled much of central Wales. Rhodri fought the Vikings and the Mercians, and was killed when the latter invaded in 878.

Welsh inheritance customs – the division of property among sons – may have made it difficult to translate territorial gains into more cohesive statehood, although kingship was, at least in theory, indivisible. What probably happened in the case of such rulers as Rhodri Mawr was that they might accumulate several kingships and on their deaths individual kingships would be inherited by different sons. Rhodri's grandson, Hywel Dda, Howel the Good (d. 950), initially succeeded only to Ceredigion, although he eventually came to rule over most of Wales. Hywel was a major figure, the first Welsh king who certainly issued his own coinage, and in about 928 he went on pilgrimage to Rome. By later tradition Hywel is also held to have been the codifier of Welsh law (though this may be a twelfth-century appeal to history). The laws attributed to him were the basis of an ordered kindred society, until 1284 in some respects and until 1536 in others.

Hywel's death was followed by internecine conflict in which the English state, with its growing pretensions to overlordship in Britain, came to intervene with increasing frequency. The South Welsh in 886 made some kind of submission to Alfred, to whom they turned for help against the Vikings, and this may have lasted into the early tenth century. Welsh rulers attended Athelstan's court and were regarded by him as subordinates. Under Edward the Confessor (1042—66), the royal titles of king of the English and of the British were used indifferently and, although Ireland was completely independent, Wales and Scotland were in part dependent.

The political geography of Wales may be compared with that of England; kingship was inherent in the individual kingdoms and there was no kingship of Wales. But, whereas in England unity was created by the Viking destruction of all kingships bar one (Wessex), this did not happen in Wales, and a similar process of consolidation in the face of foreign attack was delayed until the Anglo-Normans conquered much of Wales.

The Welsh rulers of the period spent much of their time in fighting. The rise of Gwynedd under Llywelyn ap Seisyll (d. c.1023) and his son Gruffudd ap Llywelyn (d. 1063) formed the most important development in the pre-Norman period. Both Llywelyn and Gruffudd had to fight to gain control of Gwynedd and both campaigned in south Wales, most of which was conquered between 1039 and 1055. The length of the process reflected the difficulty of obtaining a decisive 'political' settlement, short of slaying rivals as Gruffudd did twice.

Territorial consolidation was also complicated by foreign intervention: the Dublin Norse assisted Gruffudd's opponents. Welsh rulers, including Gruffudd, were willing to seek such support. Gruffudd, however, had serious clashes with the English, particularly with Harold Godwinson of Wessex. In 1063 Harold, campaigning by land and sea, harried Wales until Gruffudd was killed by some of his men and his head delivered to Harold, who also took his wife. Gruffudd's half-brothers were allowed to inherit Gwynedd and Powys on condition that they swore allegiance.

It is unclear whether Gwynedd could have developed as Wessex did in the tenth and eleventh centuries, serving as the basis for a Welsh state. Unlike England, there is little sign of governmental sophistication in Wales, though that is also true of Scotland in this period. The 'conquest' of one part of Wales, Scotland or Ireland by the ruler of another amounted to a personal submission and the giving of hostages rather than the loss of administrative control and consolidation. What is clear is that the power of the rulers of Gwynedd, Scotia and the high kings of Ireland rested on military success. After the Norman conquest of England the military pressure on these rulers was to increase appreciably.

A CENTURY OF INVASION

In the eleventh century the largest British state, the English kingdom created by the rulers of Wessex, was overthrown twice by foreign invasion. In each case England became the subject part of a polity (political organisation) based on the Continent. The second conquest, that by the Normans, was followed by a social recasting of England; but not the first.

The first invasion arose from the revival of Danish vitality; although now the Danes came not as independent warbands but as the forces of another well-developed kingdom. Danish raids on coastal regions of England resumed in 980 and were followed by major attacks from 991, the year in which the Danes defeated the Essex militia at Maldon. English resistance was organised by Edgar's younger son, Aethelred 'the Unready' (978–1016), who came to the throne after his supporters murdered his elder brother. Like King John, Aethelred, who ruled for nearly forty years, has been underrated. He made major efforts to organise an effective response to the Danes, but, like John, and later Charles I, he lacked the ability to command or elicit trust, both vital facets of kingship in an aristocratic society.

Aethelred may have faced Danish armies that at times were larger than those that had attacked Alfred's Wessex. He attempted to buy the Danes off with Danegeld (protection money). At least £240,000 was paid, testimony to the wealth and organisation of the English state, although the figures given in the *Anglo-Saxon Chronicle* may be exagerated and anyway the policy was unsuccessful in the long term. Although resistance continued for many years, King Swein of Denmark led major attacks in 1003—6 and 1013. The last led Aethelred to flee to Normandy, and after Swein died in 1014 his son, Cnut, continued the struggle. By the Peace of Alney (1016), England was divided between Cnut and Aethelred's eldest son, the vigorous Edmund Ironside, and when Edmund soon died Cnut became king of all England (1016—35).

After Cnut inherited Denmark from his elder brother in 1019, England became part of a multiple kingdom. He executed or exiled his opponents, introduced a number of Danes into the aristocracy and divided the kingdom into a small number of earldoms. Yet Cnut sought to rule not as a conqueror, but as a lord of both Danes and non-Danes. He was the king of a number of kingdoms, not a monarch seeking to enlarge one kingdom. Cnut took over an effective governmental system, did what an English monarch was supposed to do as head of state and, unlike the Norman William the Conqueror, did not have to face rebellions. In 1018, he reiterated the legislation of his predecessors. Cnut did not purge the Church, was the benefactor of a number of prominent English monasteries and was not culturally alienated from the Anglo-Saxon world. He made London his military and governmental centre in England.

Cnut's empire fell apart after his death. His son Harthacnut, who succeeded to Denmark and had a claim to England, was challenged for the latter by his half-brother, Harold Harefoot. Powerful support from the earls of Mercia and Wessex led Harold to gain control of the entire kingdom in 1037. Harthacnut replaced him when Harold died in 1040, only himself to die without children in 1042.

Although the Norwegians continued to be important around the Irish Sea and in northern and western Scotland, the Viking age was over in England. There were to be later attacks – Harald Hardrada of Norway invaded in 1066, the Danes in 1069–70 and 1075 – but they were unsuccessful. England was no longer to look to Scandinavia, but, instead, was soon to be immersed in the politics of France.

Under Edward 'the Confessor' (1042—66), Aethelred's surviving son, the house of Wessex was restored. His reign shared in the demographic growth and agrarian expansion of the tenth and eleventh centuries, but was dominated by the question of the succession. The childless Edward favoured the ducal house of Normandy, the family of his mother Emma which had sheltered him for many years. Norman influence was resisted by Edward's father-in-law, Earl Godwin of Wessex. In 1051–2 Godwin rebelled and was exiled, only to return and oblige Edward to reinstate him and expel his Norman friends. After Godwin died in 1052 his eldest son, Harold, succeeded him and dominated England for the rest of Edward's reign.

After Edward died on 5 January 1066, Harold was elected or recognised as king by the Witan, the great council of the kingdom. Harold stated that Edward had granted him the kingdom on his deathbed; but Duke William of Normandy claimed that Edward had promised him the succession when he visited England in 1051 and that Harold had acknowledged this claim in 1064.

Fearing Norman invasion, Harold concentrated his forces on the south coast, but William was delayed by contrary winds and Harold therefore marched north to confront a Norwegian invasion under Harald Hardrada that was supported by Harold's exiled brother, Tostig. The invaders defeated the local forces and seized

York, only to be surprised and crushed by Harold in their camp at Stamford Bridge (25 September). Harald and Tostig were both killed.

Three days later, William landed at Pevensey on the south coast. Harold rushed south to attack William before the Normans established themselves. The English army, however, was weakened by casualties at Stamford Bridge and fatigue, and was outnumbered by about 7,000 to 5,000. Harold chose a strong defensive position on the slopes of a hill, thus offering protection against the Norman cavalry. The battle was hard-fought, its outcome far from certain, but the shieldwall of the English *housecarls* was disrupted by advances designed to exploit real or feigned retreats by the Normans and at last the English position was broken, Harold falling with an arrow in his eye, at least in legend; although he may have been hacked down by horsemen.

William then moved rapidly to exploit his victory, advancing on London where the demoralised defenders lacked determined leadership: many of the natural leaders had died at Hastings. On Christmas Day William was acclaimed king in Westminster Abbey. The most powerful of the British states had fallen with unprecedented speed. England was now to be exposed to the full force of new political, social and cultural impulses, and, largely through English, or, as they became, Anglo-Norman intermediaries, these impulses were to affect or influence the subsequent history of the rest of the British Isles.

3

The Middle Ages

INTRODUCTION

The two dates that are most commonly associated with the Middle Ages in the British Isles are 1066 and 1485. William the Conqueror's victory at Hastings in 1066 brought the Normans to the throne of England. Richard III's defeat by Henry Tudor at the battle of Bosworth in 1485 is popularly seen to mark the close of the Middle Ages. There are dangers in endowing either of these dates, particularly 1485, with too much significance, but both are in a way appropriate. They both relate to England and they each centre on changes in ruling dynasties. Although there are no reliable figures – the first national census was not until 1801 – medieval England contained more people and was wealthier than Ireland, Scotland or Wales. It was also the most united of the constituent parts of the British Isles and the one that featured most in European politics. The politics of England centred on the ruler, on his views and entourage. The character of his reign depended on the personality of the monarch and this was of great importance for the stability of the country, for the personal relationship between the monarch and the great nobles (aristocrats) was crucial to political order. It is therefore possible to write a history of medieval England that centres on the rulers and is merely an account of their reigns in chronological order. Such an approach captures much of the reality of the high politics of the period, but it would also omit much that was of consequence to the development of medieval England. Two crucial aspects that would be omitted are social history and the regional dimension. Both must therefore be addressed in addition to the high political history of the period. In order to capture the variety of developments, particular attention will be devoted to two areas: prosperous East Anglia in lowland eastern England, particularly the counties of Norfolk, Suffolk and Lincolnshire, and Wales, a part of Celtic Britain under pressure from England and Anglo-Norman practices. Examples will not be restricted to these two areas, but stress on them will serve to highlight the diversity of Britain and the danger of concentrating on any one train of change.

Information on England at the outset is provided by the Domesday Book (1086), a land survey ordered by William the Conqueror so that he could ascertain his own resources and those of his tenants. Its contents provide a guide to the extent to which English landowners had been replaced by Normans. Both as a result of the 1066 campaign and as a consequence of the suppression of subsequent rebellions, there had been a social revolution at the level of the elite. This had had far less effect at the level of the bulk of the population. Their life continued to be dominated by the pressures of agricultural life and the rhythms of a harsh demographic regime. Domesday revealed the extent to which the detailed nature of local environments influenced settlement patterns and economic activities. Thus, the silts and peat fens in the south-east of Lincolnshire were little settled: the marshland attracted few bar salt makers. In Norfolk, the fertile, well-drained river valleys were far more heavily populated than the high, dry interfluves; and readily worked lighter soils were easier to plough than poorly drained heavy soils.

Under the Normans the crucial economic unit was the manor, the possession of a lord consisting of a demesne (home farm) directly under the lord and the rest of the estate from which the lord was entitled to day labour, rent and the profits of justice. Food-rents and labour services had existed under the Anglo-Saxons. The Normans brought heavier tenurial burdens as a consequence of their social system of feudalism under which manors were granted to vassals in return for military service. Peasants became subject to closer control and some free men had their status and rights lessened by the new lords. The Norman conquest thus changed more than simply the world of high politics.

NORMANISATION

Unlike the Danish seizure of the throne by Cnut, that by William was followed by a social revolution. William, who claimed to be the rightful successor of Edward the Confessor, may not have intended this, for Englishmen who submitted at the beginning of his reign were allowed to keep their lands and William appointed two in succession as Earl of Northumbria, but the scale of the resistance to the spread and consolidation of Norman rule led to the adoption of a harsher attitude. In 1068, for example, both Edgar, Edward the Confessor's grand-nephew who had submitted to William in late 1066, and Earl Gospatric of Northumbria, rebelled, leading William to establish garrisons at York and Durham. The latter was, however, massacred in 1069, the revolt spread, and William responded with severity. The brutalisation of the population in the 'harrying of the north' in the winter of 1069–70, was followed by a Normanisation of both Church and land, the latter largely to the benefit of those who had helped most in the conquest. Clerical appointments (and thus the control over Church lands) were denied to the English and the majority of English landlords were dispossessed. Most of the new rulers of the localities were Normans, though others from northern France also benefited. Alongside a ruling dynasty that linked England and Normandy, a united aristocracy had been created, while the foundation of 'daughter' houses of Norman monasteries created new links in the Church as did the appointment of foreign clerics such as the Italian Archbishops of Canterbury, Lanfranc 1070–89 and Anselm 1093–1109. The pope had supported the Norman invasion. Latin replaced English in official documents in the 1070s: William was not simply acting as the Confessor's heir.

These changes reflected the strength of the resistance to William: like the Anglo-Saxon resistance to the Danes in the late ninth- and early eleventh-centuries, it was considerable, and there was an additional factor in the shape of supportive foreign intervention from Denmark and Scotland. Risings in Herefordshire, Kent, the north, and the south-west (1067–8), were followed by a major crisis in 1069 involving risings in the north, the West Country, the west Midlands and Danish and Scottish invasions. Under Hereward the Wake, the Isle of Ely resisted. Lack of coordination among the rebellions and the failure of sustained Scandinavian assistance were crucial to the consolidation of the new regime, but the length of time that that took means that it is inappropriate to think of the Norman conquest as being completed in 1066. Norman authority north of the Tees did not become a reality until 1072 when William led an army north, forced Malcolm III of Scotland to do homage for Lothian, installed Waltheof, a member of the native ruling house whom he had married to a niece, as Earl of Northumbria, and built a castle at Durham. In 1075, a rebellion by disaffected Normans was combined with English and Danish action, but they were unsuccessful. Waltheof, one of the rebels, was executed, and the new bishop of Durham, a Lorrainer, was made Earl, but he was killed in a fresh rebellion in 1080, and William had again to send forces to restore order. A castle was erected at what was to become Newcastle, and effective Norman power thus reached the Tyne. A Norman was appointed Bishop of Durham. Northumberland was not normanised until the reign of Henry I.

The devastation and dislocation that these conflicts brought helped to ensure that the new order created by the Normans, a warrior people, had a military logic. This was demonstrated most clearly by the construction of numerous castles, as much signs of Norman power as the roads and forts of Roman Britain and the fortified towns of late-Saxon England. Early Norman castles were generally earth-and-timber constructions, for these could be built quickly, and were thus a flexible means of defence. Early Norman castles, such as Norwich, built by 1075, were 'motte and bailey' structures: wooden stockades atop earth mounds. As with the Romans, a process of consolidation led to more imposing and permanent structures. By 1125 Norwich's mound was crowned by a strong square stone keep. It is entirely appropriate that the most prominent surviving remains from Norman England are stone castles, such as the White Tower in London, and stone cathedrals, such as Durham. They were expressions of power and control, centres for government, political and religious. The first castles constructed in Lincolnshire were Lincoln and Stamford, both built for William in 1068 to control the major routes in the county.

Power is an appropriate theme: the expropriations of the early Norman period constituted and reflected a change that was more sweeping than anything subsequent in English history: the only comparison is with the destruction of Catholic power and expropriation of Catholic lands in late-seventeenth-century Ireland. Castles were royal or private. They were the centres of power, of royal government and of what has been termed the feudal system. Though the second is generally attributed to the Norman conquest, aspects of it existed in Anglo-Saxon England and might have become stronger even without the conquest. The essential characteristics of the system were the personal relationship, cemented in an act of homage, between lord and vassal. In this relationship the lord promised support and protection in return for service, principally military, and the granting of lands, or fiefs, to vassals, again in return for service, principally military. Norman lords held their estates by a military tenancy obliging them to provide a number of knights for service roughly proportionate to the size of the estate, an obligation that was usually discharged by enfeoffing the required number with lands of their own in return for service. However, the *familia regis*, the king's military household, was a permanent and professional military body that was therefore more important than the feudal host. The first three Norman monarchs were capable military leaders and this was important to the consolidation of their position.

THE POLITICS OF NORMAN ENGLAND

Initially designed to assist in the consolidation of Norman rule, castles rapidly lost the function of holding down the English, for the latter were turned into a conquered people remarkably quickly. Though there was considerable assimilation, there was no comparison with the Roman attempt to co-opt and romanise local elites: the Normans were too land-hungry, and they had a different ethos from that of the Romans. Castles, however, were swiftly required for another function: dealing with disputes within the Norman elite. In addition, the energy and strength of Norman England were expressed in a determination to push the frontiers back, and castles played a crucial role in this process.

Rivalry within the Norman elite reflected competition between nobles, disputes between them and monarchs and, most seriously, succession problems in the Norman dynasty. Impartibility (undivided inheritance) vied with the practice of all members of a family having a claim; and while male primogeniture (succession by the eldest male child) became the rule very quickly, it was resisted by other claimants. William I (1066–87) died as a result of injuries sustained when thrown by his horse in the French town of Mantes, which he had burnt as a result of a border conflict. William bequeathed Normandy to his oldest son Robert, who was in rebellion against him when William died, and England to the second, William II 'Rufus' (1087–1100). The latter tried to reunite the inheritance and, after some fighting, Robert pawned Normandy to William in 1096 in order to raise funds to go on the First Crusade. Politically and militarily successful, Rufus became unpopular with the Church because of his treatment of it, though he had a very high reputation in lay knightly circles. In 1092 he entered Cumbria with an army. The area had been disputed between the kings of the Scots and the Earls of Northumbria, but Malcolm III of Scotland had been acknowledged as overlord in 1058. Rufus created a town and built a castle at Carlisle, established a Norman ally at Kendal and made the Solway and the Liddel the northern border of the kingdom. He was also successful against Norman rebels and the French. By leaving bishoprics vacant, Rufus was able to enjoy their revenues, while a dispute with Archbishop Anselm of Canterbury over Rufus's lack of support for ecclesiastical reform and his hostility to papal authority led Anselm to leave the country in 1097. Rufus's death in the New Forest in 1100 was probably a hunting accident, though there have been claims that he was murdered.

Rufus was succeeded in England by his younger brother, Henry I (1100–35). Robert, who had taken part in the capture of Jerusalem (1099), returned to Normandy in 1100 and in 1101 invaded England, but Henry persuaded him to renounce his claim to the throne. Relations between the two brothers remained poor, however, and in 1105 Henry invaded Normandy. In 1106 he defeated Robert at Tinchebrai and conquered Normandy, imprisoning his brother until his death in 1134. The duchy, however, had a long land frontier and, in the kings of France and counts of Anjou, aggressive neighbours. Furthermore, the creation of the Anglo-Norman polity upset the political situation in northern France. Just as Cnut had concentrated on Scandinavia, so the often brutal Henry devoted most of his energies to consolidating his position in northern France, by war and diplomacy. Norman power was extended by bringing the neighbouring principalities of Maine and Brittany under control, and Louis VI of France was defeated at Brémule (1119). Henry was an effective military leader. It was important to keep England and Normandy together, because so many barons had lands on both sides of the Channel.

The costs of Henry's protracted conflicts were in large part met by England, the administration being conducted by the exchequer, which was able to provide a regular and methodical collection of royal revenues and control of expenditure. The precocious administrative development of England was in part a result of Henry I's concentration on Normandy. Means had to be found of ruling England efficiently in the absence of the king. In part it resulted from the application of new ideas and methods, notably the abacus, used as the basis of exchequer methods of calculation, though much of the governmental machinery of the Anglo-Saxon monarchy was continued. Old institutions were used for the benefit of new rulers with particular concepts of justice and government, and novel problems, especially those arising from the Norman link. Both royal and ecclesiastical government therefore changed appreciably. The expansion of royal judicial activity under Henry I and the appointment by the Crown of local and itinerant justices, were signs of a more sophisticated and settled administration. Thanks to an adroit mixture of ruthlessness, patronage and consultation with the magnates, and his effective administration, Henry kept England stable, though the *Anglo-Saxon Chronicle* presents a picture of an oppressively predatory government.

Stability was jeopardised by the succession. Henry I failed in the most crucial obligation of a monarch, that of leaving an uncontested succession. He was very fertile, siring over twenty illegitimate children, but his only legitimate son, William, died, wrecked during a Channel crossing in the *White Ship* in 1120, and, despite Henry's remarriage, there was to be no other son. Henry's hopes therefore rested on his daughter, Matilda, who in 1128 married Geoffrey Plantagenet, heir to Anjou. When Henry died in 1135, the throne, however, was seized by the initially popular Stephen of Blois (1135– 54), son of William I's daughter Adela. Matilda invaded in 1139 and captured her cousin Stephen at the battle of Lincoln (1141). Her haughty behaviour soon lost her London, however; she was defeated at Winchester by Stephen's wife, also Matilda, and had to exchange Stephen for her captured half-brother Robert of Gloucester (1141). Prominent nobles, such as John the Marshal in Wiltshire and Hampshire, used the civil war to consolidate their own positions and pursue their own interests. Local authority was seized by such nobles and much of Henry I's system of government collapsed. Stephen's reign acquired a reputation as a period of anarchy when in the words of the *Anglo-Saxon Chronicle* 'Christ and his saints slept'. David I of Scotland took over Cumbria and

Northumberland. In 1144 Geoffrey completed the conquest of Normandy and in 1152 his heir Henry invaded England. The nobility on both sides wanted peace and their lands on both sides of the Channel, and in 1153 they obtained the Treaty of Westminster. Stephen was to remain king, but agreed to adopt Henry as his heir. Stephen died within a year and Henry II (1154–89) came to the throne starting the Angevin dynasty.

Norman England thus ended, as it had begun, in war. Indeed, conflict had been the dominant theme of the period: the conquest of England, campaigns against Welsh and Scots, frequent hostilities with other rulers in France, and, most seriously, after the death of William the Conqueror, civil war within the Norman elite, most crucially the ruling dynasty. It was scarcely surprising that military obligation should have played such a prominent role in the social structure, that fealty, loyalty and protection should have been so crucial to political links, nor that so much should have been expended on constructing and maintaining castles. Not all castles had massive stone keeps: those have survived better than the initially far more numerous mottes and ringworks, which relied on earthworks; but they exemplify the resources, not least of money, skill and labour, taken from a relatively poor, low-productivity agrarian economy and devoted to war and military matters (while the cathedrals and churches of the period demonstrate that the same was true of expenditure on the Church). In 1138, for example, Stephen's influential brother, Henry of Blois, Bishop of Winchester, is reported to have begun six castles. In some respects this consistent expenditure had a more serious impact on the lives of the people of Norman England than the individual wars of the period. The most serious, the civil wars of Stephen's reign, were traditionally regarded as devastating, though more recently, as with the Wars of the Roses, historians have tended to reduce earlier assessments of their destructiveness. Nevertheless, it is worth considering the psychological costs of a lengthy civil war, and the impact of an abrupt change on people who had known over three decades of civil peace under Henry I. More significantly, the wars of the period placed greater weight on the already-strong military values of society. England was scarcely unique in this emphasis, but it was an essential feature of her society.

The other essential characteristics of society were determined by environment, technological level and socio-cultural inheritance.

The Judeao-Christian inheritance, clearly enunciated in the teachings and laws of the Church, decreed monogamy and forbade polygamy, marriage with close kin, incest, homosexuality, abortion, infanticide, adultery, pederasty and bestiality. Birth was stipulated as the purpose of matrimony, and condemned outside it. Divorce was very difficult. This moral 'agenda' was decreed and enforced with greater vigour after the disruption of the ninth- and early-eleventh-century Viking invasions, and even more so after the Norman conquest, though the effectiveness of this enforcement was probably limited until the bureaucratic developments of the twelfth century. The Norman conquest led to a reassertion of episcopal authority, a further expansion of the parochial (parish) system at the expense of the older minster system, monastic revival, and the creation of a new monastic structure firmly linked to developments in northern France. New institutional developments were related to the imposition of a 'foreign' emphasis, but they also reflected a widespread movement for Church reform that characterised the late eleventh century, and was supported by archbishops Lanfranc and Anselm of Canterbury (1070–1109). Lanfranc established the primacy of Canterbury over York and the authority of the archbishops over the bishops. The diocesan system was reorganised with some sees transferred to more major centres, for example from Dorchester-on-Thames to Lincoln, and new bishoprics were founded at Ely and Carlisle. New monastic orders spread, especially the Cistercians, who by 1154 had established about forty monasteries, including Rievaulx, Fountains and Rufford. The reform impulse led to attempts to enforce clerical celibacy and to end the clerical dynasties that had been important among the parochial clergy. Foreign prelates sought to discipline the mainly English lesser clergy. Lay ownership of churches declined. By 1200 the parish system as it was substantially to continue in rural England into the modern period had been created through a vast increase in the numbers of local churches. Most surviving medieval parish churches have an eleventh- or twelfth-century core. The Romanesque style of architecture also spread to England, bringing large churches characterised by thick walls, long, vaulted naves, and massive columns and arches, as for example at Durham, Ely and Peterborough. Romanesque architecture probably arrived in England in the 1050s, for Edward the Confessor used Norman architects for Westminster Abbey, but it became much more important after the conquest. Cultural links after 1066 were very much with France. The conquest brought in a French-speaking elite and it was not until the late fourteenth century that English became an acceptable language in upper-class circles.

THE NORMANS AND WALES

The Norman conquest of England was in time to have a major impact on Ireland, Scotland and Wales. The last was affected most immediately, though in the eleventh and twelfth centuries Wales did not follow England in being rapidly overrun by the Normans. Instead, its position was more like that of Scotland under the Romans: conquered only in part. William the Conqueror was not interested in the conquest of Wales; which, unlike Scotland, did not exist as a political unit anyway. He saw himself as the legitimate heir of the West Saxon dynasty and therefore as the inheritor of that dynasty's relationship with its Welsh and Scottish neighbours. What William and his successors probably sought in Wales was stability, and this may explain William's agreement with Rhys ap Tewdwr of Deheubarth. Such royal campaigns as there were in Wales were not aimed at conquest; there was always a specific and more limited objective.

Conquest in Wales was of individual kingdoms or political units by individual Norman adventurers: this was a land of opportunity for land-hungry younger sons, although some of the most significant early Normans, such as Roger de Montgomery and William fitz Osbern, were leading court magnates. In one case, that of Glamorgan, a whole overkingdom in all its political complexity was conquered. These Normans were operating outside the kingdom of England; they were not under the direct auspices of the king. However, they would not touch a ruler who had a formal agreement with the king; they tended to move in when there was a vacancy or a disputed succession. Initially the Normans advanced with great momentum, along the lowlands near the south and north coasts, and up the river valleys. The Welsh, however, benefited not only from their terrain, much of which offered little advantage to the feudal cavalry of the Normans, but also from the military skills and determination honed by conflict within their own ranks, conflict that continued throughout the period, and was particularly acute in the 1070s and 1080s.

The Normans sought to anchor their advance with castles and settlements, but the latter were restricted to lowland areas, especially in coastal south Wales. Nevertheless, Norman victories, such as the defeat and killing of Rhys ap Tewdwr (1093), were followed up by the seizure of territory by the land-hungry Norman baronage. The 'march' thus created was the result of Norman invasion and conquest, but it remained part of Wales, not a kind of no-man's-land between Wales and England. Marcher lordship has generally been seen essentially as Welsh political authority exercised by Anglo-Norman lords by right of conquest, Welsh royal rights in baronial hands. More recently, however, it has been presented as compact feudal lordships, with much in common with lordships in northern France (whose lords made war and peace and exercised 'high justice'), and with the 'castleries' of early Norman England. Marcher lordships came to look increasingly odd as the march stayed outside the orbit of the developing common law and centralised government in England.

The independence of the early marchers was affected by the strong court connections and major landholdings in England and Normandy of many of their leading figures. Events in the march were always closely connected with wider politics. Thus, the troubles in Wales at the beginning of Henry I's reign were a sub-plot to the high political struggle between Henry and his elder brother, Robert: Robert de Bellême, the Montgomery Earl of Shrewsbury, was a supporter of Robert's with estates ranging from mid-Wales to Maine, rather than simply a disobedient marcher baron. And although the marcher lordships were part of Wales rather than England, they came to be regarded as held of the Crown, which exercised rights of wardship, marriage and escheat: indeed in the twelfth and thirteenth centuries many lordships were retained for lengthy periods in the king's hands, or were pushed towards his supporters through marriage to heiresses.

The fighting was not all one-sided: the Welsh at times regained the initiative, in 1094, during the English civil war in Stephen's reign, and again in the mid-thirteenth century. In these periods much territory was regained. In 1094 much of Dyfed was won back and the Normans were pushed back from Ceredigion (Cardigan), which they had captured the previous year, and from west of the river Conway. William II failed to repair the situation in 1097. Rhys ap Tewdwr's son, Gruffudd (d. 1137), was able in the 1110s to inflict much damage on the Flemings newly settled in southern Wales by Henry I, and he also succeeded in capturing some castles. Yet, he made little impact during the reign of Henry I, a period of vigorous Anglo-Norman advance. Henry acquired the site of Carmarthen in 1109. He was aided by the willingness of Welsh kings to seek his support. Similarly, the Welsh were sometimes willing to ally with the Norman lords. Thus Cadwgan ap Bleddyn, who played a major role in the 1094 rising, became the man of Robert, Earl of Shrewsbury in 1100 and accepted that he held Ceredigion as a fief from him. Cadwgan's son Owain, who carried off the beautiful wife of Gerald of Windsor in 1110, was less accommodating, and Henry granted Ceredigion to Gilbert of Clare who conquered it in 1111, and consolidated his position by building a number of castles. In 1114 and 1121 Henry invaded north Wales, receiving the submission of its rulers.

In addition, the authority of the archbishopric of Canterbury was extended over the sees of St David's and Llandaff. Roman usage had spread in the Celtic Church prior to the Norman conquest, Bangor in 768 being the first to conform; but, as in England, the role of clerical dynasties remained important until after the conquest. It was then that a diocesan and parochial structure was introduced: Llandaff was established as a bishopric in 1107, St David's in 1115, Bangor in 1120 and St Asaph in 1143. As in England, the Cistercian monastic order brought new energy. Cistercian abbeys were founded both by Norman – Neath (*c.* 1129), Tintern (1131) and Margam (1147) – and by Welsh lords: Whitland (1143), Strata Florida (1164).

The situation left by Henry I – conquest in the south and hegemony in the north – was reversed in 1136 at the outset of Stephen's reign: the Anglo-Normans were defeated in Cardigan and Gower. Carmarthen fell to the Welsh in 1146, Tenby in 1153.

SCOTLAND

While neither Wales nor Ireland made significant moves towards political unification and governmental development in the century following the Norman conquest of England, the Scottish kingdom became more powerful. The authority of the kings over much of their kingdom, especially Galloway, the Highlands and the Isles, was limited, but the fertile central belt was under secure control. Although ethnically diverse, Scotland was given political direction by its capable rulers. As a consequence, the movement of Norman nobles, mostly from England, into Scotland in the twelfth century, families that were to play a major role in Scottish history, such as Barclay, Bruce, Hay, Menzies, Lindsay, Montgomery and Wallace, was not a matter of the piecemeal conquest of the more vulnerable lands, as initially in Wales and Ireland, but an immigration reflecting the sponsorship of the kings. It was related to the introduction of Norman administrative methods and French secular culture by David I (1124–53). David was educated at the court of his brother-in-law Henry I and held the Earldom of Huntingdon in England. As king, David introduced feudal tenures and organised the central government on the Anglo-Norman pattern, although the older-style Celtic social organisation also continued. Normanisation also affected the Scottish Church, leading to new monastic foundations and stronger continental links. David was a very generous benefactor; his extensive monastic foundations also extended royal influence. Yet normanisation was not accompanied by the massive expropriation and disruption that had affected England after 1066.

The Scottish kingdom of the twelfth and thirteenth centuries was strong. The Norman military machine of knights and castles, improved administrative mechanisms, especially the use of sheriffs, the skill of the rulers, and the economic expansion of the period, served as the basis for an extension of royal authority. English and Flemish immigrants played a major role in a growth of urban activity that was very important for economic development. Throughout Europe, these centuries were a period of substantial demographic and economic growth as recovery from the so-called Dark Ages gathered pace. This recovery fuelled the development of states and the pursuit of their wars, as well as the cultural expansion that focused on the Gothic style, the expansion of education and the growing density of Christian institutions. Within the British Isles these processes were most pronounced in England.

THE ENGLISH ECONOMY 1100–1350

Greater activity led to a nucleation of settlement in lowland England by the eleventh century. It was particularly important for the open-field system, in which large unhedged arable fields were divided into narrow strips cultivated by individual peasants under a system of communal supervision. Though sometimes seen as the standard form of medieval English agriculture, it was in fact typical of the Midlands and was largely absent from the upland areas of north and west, as well as from Kent. In these regions pasture was predominant, though there was also some arable farming.

The technological basis of medieval agricultural life was not unvarying. Windmills, for example, were introduced in the 1170s and spread particularly fast in east England in the 1180s. There was a switch from oxen to the faster and more adaptable, but costlier, horses for ploughing, though this change was not completed until the fifteenth century. Large-scale field cultivation of legumes, which enriched the soil and provided fodder, began in the early thirteenth century, vetches being first recorded in 1268. Natural fodder thus gave way to cultivated. Norfolk crop yields rose to levels that were not to be surpassed until the eighteenth century, in large part because the development of integrated mixed-farming systems offered the benefit of both arable and pastoral husbandry. An increase in the cultivated area and in agricultural productivity permitted a doubling of the English population between 1180 and 1330 to over five million, and a rise in the percentage involved in non-agricultural occupations. The twelfth and thirteenth centuries saw significant increases in town foundation, both planned and unplanned. In already existing towns growth within town defences led to denser occupation, while from the twelfth century suburbs developed outside the walls. Society became more complex, with broadened distribution of wealth, increases in monetary transactions, the volume of the currency, economic diversification and trade, both domestic and foreign. There was greater specialisation in occupations, increased social mobility and literacy, and the spread of industry into some rural areas. By the thirteenth century, for example, there were few places in Lincolnshire which were further than five miles from a market: seven markets in the county were mentioned in Domesday Book in 1086; fifty-five licensed from 1250 to 1299 alone. These markets linked the localities into wider commercial networks, transmitting goods, demands, information and innovation. Through rapidly growing ports, such as Boston in Lincolnshire, the leading wool exporter in the country, the localities were linked to European markets. By the early fourteenth century possibly a fifth of the population may have depended on trade and services. The value of coin circulating in England may have risen from about one shilling per head in 1180 to six in 1467.

Chattel slavery became extinct in the early twelfth century as a result of the ready availability of labour, Church pressure and the power of lords over their serfs (villeins): peasants who owed their lords often heavy labour services, as well as other obligations, such as use of the lord's mill alone. Given the limited scope for increasing the productivity of cultivated land, rising population entailed an expansion in the acreage of cultivated land, much woodland being cleared in, for example, the Lake District, but also soil deterioration, falling yields and pressure on the living standards of the agricultural labour force, especially if they had little if any land. Lowland England showed signs of overcrowding in the early fourteenth century, and this was possibly responsible for a rise in the age of marriage. Work on skeletal remains suggests a decline in living standards.

The increasing role of money in the economy throughout the British Isles, and thus in revenue and taxation, helped to ensure that socio-economic shifts had direct governmental and political consequences. The feudal system established by William I was based on land, but the burdens of vassals were very speedily commuted into cash. This reflected a number of factors including the subdivision of knights' fees, so that by the early twelfth century fractions of knights were owed as military service, fractions that were fulfilled by cash payments. In addition, some lords preferred to fulfil their military obligations by employing household knights and expecting their tenants to provide money, not military service. The initial relationship created by the allocation of land slackened with time and with the impact of hereditary property rights, and altered from that of lord and man to landlord and tenant and lord and client, a cause of growing tension that probably helped to increase litigation during the reign of Henry II. Aristocratic society was never static. By 1200 what has been termed bastard feudalism, and more commonly associated with the later medieval period, was already in evidence in magnate retinues: instead of all dependants being landed tenants, some were in receipt of robes and probably fees. Far from being static or changing only slowly and with reluctance, medieval society had a dynamic response to altering economic and political circumstances. By 1130 money rents were very common on royal manors and other large estates in England.

Over the following 150 years the amount and proportion of governmental revenues coming from taxation increased substantially. This was to help in a political transformation in which the essentially personal links between monarch and greater nobles, and the consequent politics of patronage and protection, of the eleventh century, both Anglo-Saxon and Norman, were joined by a more coherent sense of national political identity, in which issues related to taxation played a major role. Thus the men who represented 'the community of the realm', principally the greater nobles, were by the late thirteenth century also to express their views in Parliament, a new sphere of political pretension and activity, and one that reflected the stress on national financial demands and national grievances that were so important in the thirteenth century.

Economic and institutional changes were vital to this development, but so also was the crucial legacy of Norman England: war stemming from continuous confrontation with a neighbouring state. The Welsh and the Scots were only able to press on frontier areas. But after 1066 England was part of a state that spanned the Channel, one that found itself obliged to ward off the ambitions of other expanding states, most significantly the kingdom of France. The continuous military effort that this entailed was to be a central theme in the three centuries following the death of Stephen in 1154. Indeed, from the Roman conquest onwards, a united England was often to be politically associated with part of the Continent: as under the Romans (78–409), Cnut and his sons (1016–42), the medieval rulers (1066–1453) and the Hanoverians (1714–1837). The nature of this relationship was far from constant, but the resultant political strains were most apparent in the medieval period.

ANGEVIN KINGSHIP

Between 1154 and 1453 England was involved in the quest for territory and control, both in the British Isles and in France; although empire was not a term that contemporaries used, as to them the empire was the German empire. Henry II did not try to develop a single cohesive system; instead he expected to divide the large group of lordships he had accumulated among his sons. This quest was due largely to the ambitions of England's rulers, who saw themselves not simply as kings of England, but as rulers of or claimants to the wider inheritance of Henry II (1154–89), and, in time, to the French throne. Unlike his Norman predecessors, Henry's succession in England was not a signal for conspiracy and conflict: the war for succession had already been fought during Stephen's reign. Henry's most important step was his retrieval of Cumbria and Northumbria from Malcolm IV of Scotland, for the fluid Anglo-Scottish frontier reflected the respective strength of the powers and it had been pushed south during Stephen's reign, despite the English victory at the Battle of the Standard (1138). Until the mid-twelfth century it had been unclear whether what is now northern England would be part of England or of Scotland, but Henry II settled the matter in 1157.

The situation in France was less happy. In 1152 Henry had married Eleanor of Aquitaine, the imperious divorced wife of Louis VII, who brought control of the Duchy of Aquitaine (most of south-west France). Combined with the Norman and Angevin (Anjou) inheritances which he had gained in 1151, this made him the most powerful ruler in France, with more land and power than the king of France, his suzerain (feudal lord for his French territories), and in his first twelve years Henry used this power to resolve inheritance disputes in his favour, gaining control of Brittany and more of southern France. He received the homage of the Count of Toulouse and affirmed his hegemony over Auvergne. The enmity of the kings of France, however, ensured that when Henry's family divided over the inheritance (for like William the Conqueror, Henry II had several sons) and Henry was faced by a general rebellion in 1173–4, Louis VII was willing to intervene. Such foreign intervention was a problem in Henry II's continental empire, but not for him in the British Isles. There, it was Henry's power that was dynamic. The campaigns of 1157, 1163 and 1165 made little impact on Wales, but were a sign that the situation had changed since Stephen's reign.

INVASION OF IRELAND

Anglo-Norman colonisation was not confined within and near England's far-from-fixed borders. On 1–2 May 1169 a 600-strong force landed at Bannow Bay between Wexford and Waterford. With some Irish and Norse support, the Anglo-Normans seized Wexford and its neighbourhood: their skilful combination of cavalry and archers gave them a military advantage over the Irish. Further Anglo-Norman forces arrived in 1169 and 1170 including Richard of Clare, 'Strongbow', a prominent Anglo-Norman from Wales. In 1170 Strongbow seized Waterford and, in alliance with the king of Leinster, Dermot MacMurrough, Dublin. In 1171 Strongbow defeated the displaced Norse king of Dublin, Asgall, and the Irish high king, Rory O'Connor. Henry II arrived in late 1171 in order to establish his rights in accordance with the papal bull of 1155 from the only English pope, Adrian IV. The pope approved the invasion on the grounds of advancing ecclesiastical reform in Ireland, although the authenticity of the bull is open to question. Henry II imposed his authority on his barons, granting Strongbow Leinster, but taking control of Dublin, Waterford and Wexford himself. Henry also obtained the submission of many of the Irish kings and of the Irish Church, which also promised to adhere to English practices. The Treaty of Windsor of 1175 recognised Henry as lord of Ireland and O'Connor as only king of Connacht and as overlord of the as yet unconquered parts of the country. The kings of England only became kings of Ireland in the sixteenth century. In 1177 Henry granted Anglo-Normans Desmond and Thomond. In about 1185 the Anglo-Normans issued a coinage of silver pennies for Ireland.

Much of Ireland was rapidly captured, including much of Ulster from 1177. Anglo- Norman progress was marked by the construction of castles, such as Carrickfergus, Dundalk, Coleraine, Trim, Athlone and Kildare. Like Wales, and in contrast to Scotland and England, Ireland was far from unified, which provided opportunities for aristocratic and royal Anglo-Norman ambitions. A new order was established in Ireland, with a lordship, based on Dublin, under royal control and the introduction of English administrative practices. The extent to which this control was to be disrupted by Scottish invasion in 1315 was an indication of the value to earlier English rulers of Ireland of an absence of foreign intervention. It was far more important, practicable and profitable for the ruthless Philip Augustus, king of France 1180–1223, to undermine the Angevin empire in France than in the British Isles, though later French kings were to find the latter policy a way to weaken first the

English effort in France and finally English foreign policy more generally. Anglo-Norman control was extended in the thirteenth century, including a gradual expansion across the Shannon into Connacht. In *c*.1210 the Irish Justiciar, Bishop John de Grey, led a force to Athlone and built a stone bridge over the Shannon and a stone castle. This replaced earlier wooden works and provided the security that allowed the town to develop as a centre of English influence. From the 1280s, however, resistance mounted. Like Wales, Anglo-Norman Ireland was divided into the area where the king's writ ran effectively, by the fifteenth century called, in Ireland, the Pale, and regions under feudal lords, who held their own courts and ran their own administrations. The more fertile areas of Ireland, for example the plains of the east-centre, acquired a network of towns, while numerous nucleated villages developed.

HENRY II AND HIS SONS

Henry II is best remembered for his quarrel with Thomas à Becket, Archbishop of Canterbury, which led to Becket's murder in 1170. Like a later Chancellor, Sir Thomas More, who fell out with a powerful and demanding king, in his case Henry VIII, with fatal results, Becket was initially a friend of the monarch's, but after being made archibishop defended the rights of clerics to trial in Church courts. Also at stake was freedom of appeal and access to the Pope, at a time when the papal Curia (government), under a succession of lawyer popes, was becoming effectively the legal centre of Christendom and thus a prime source of papal authority and money. Freedom of appeal to Rome defined ecclesiastical jurisdictions and almost Church life as such. Becket had fled the country in 1164 when Henry turned the resources of royal judicial power against him. As with the rifts in his own family, Henry had to consider the views of a foreign power, in this case the papacy, and they helped to lead him towards compromise. Returning in 1170, Becket was unwilling, however, to abide by the spirit of compromise that was necessary both if his return was to be a success, and, more generally, for workable royal–papal and church–state relations. Henry's outraged explosion, 'Will no one rid me of this turbulent priest?', was taken at face value by four of his knights, who killed the archbishop in his cathedral. Becket was to be canonised, and his shrine at Canterbury to become a major centre of pilgrimage, but his death changed little: the balance of compromise had not shifted greatly, though restrictions on appeals to Rome were lifted and the basic immunity of criminous clerics from lay jurisdiction was confirmed.

No such upsets affected the processes of administrative development that were so important in Henry's reign, both in finance and in justice. The standardised common law gained in strength. Bar for some special privileges for the Danelaw, pre-conquest kings had issued laws for all their subjects and Henry II therefore built on well-laid foundations. English common law helped to consolidate England as a remarkably homogeneous state by European standards and in the thirteenth century played a role in fostering a sense of common Englishness.

The expansion of government activity required increasing numbers of professional administrators, a group that had first emerged clearly in the reign of Henry I. These *curiales* were mostly 'new men' who were resented by better-born nobles. The enforcement of justice and the collection of royal revenues improved and the processes of government became more effective and regular. This was shown by the introduction of regular record-keeping: the exchequer pipe rolls continually from early in Henry II's reign, the close and patent rolls of the chancery from just after 1200. The development of justice was a royal initiative, land actions were begun by royal writs, law and order enforced by royal justices itinerant. Procedure was regularised through the king's actions. The processes of government were less dependent on the personal intervention of the monarch than had been the case under the Normans, which was just as well as Henry II spent most of his reign on the Continent, although continuity was provided by the officer of justiciar.

On the other hand, the Crown became more dependent on financial windfalls as its landed income declined, while improvements in the administration of justice were balanced by a striking arbitrariness on the part of the Crown. Tenants-in-chief were very much at the king's will. The area designated as royal forest and its law were both extended as far as possible in order to make people pay for exemptions from them. Forest law was not affected by the forms and standards of the common law, but, instead by royal will. The greater coercive power of government made it a formidable instrument of tyranny. This was one reason for the popularity in some quarters of Becket, who had stood up to royal power, and for the immense resentment royal government aroused under King John. Bureaucratic principles of impartial government were slow to develop. In 1207–8 John wrote, 'it is no more than just that we should do better by those who are with us than by those who are against us'. The views and interests of the monarch were also crucial to government procedure. The medieval period was to witness changing patterns of royal administration, with the emphasis either on household government or on government through exchequer and chancery. Under John, Henry III and Edward I the household, initially the chamber and then the wardrobe, was very dominant; whereas under Edward III there was far greater exchequer control. Such variations remained the pattern during the Tudor period, and indeed medieval English monarchy prefigured Tudor government in many respects, including the scale of royal patronage and of office-holding under the Crown.

Three of Henry's five legitimate sons predeceased him, and he was succeeded by his third son, Richard I (1189–99). Richard had joined his brothers in 1173–4 in their French-supported rebellion against Henry II, and thereafter had acquired considerable military experience in suppressing rebellions in Aquitaine, the duchy of which he had inherited. As king he spent an even greater proportion of his reign abroad than Henry had done. A key participant in the Third Crusade, he captured Acre and defeated Saladin at the battle of Arsuf (1191), though he narrowly failed to reach Jerusalem. When he was imprisoned in Germany on his way back (1192–4), his absence was exploited by his younger brother John and, more seriously, by Philip Augustus. Richard was ransomed for 150,000 marks, a huge sum, and a considerable tribute to English wealth and government that the money was raised. Richard spent most of the rest of his reign in France recovering what had been lost during his absence, a process that led to his death in a siege.

Without legitimate children, Richard was succeeded by his brother John. John's position was weakened by the tactless handling of his French vassals, which was exacerbated by accurate rumours that he had been responsible for the death in 1203 of his nephew Arthur, Duke of Brittany, the son of his older brother Geoffrey, who had predeceased Henry II. The determination and military success of Philip Augustus led to John losing much of his father's vast continental possessions, including Normandy and Anjou, in 1203–4. Naturally avaricious and suspicious, adversity did not improve John. He was tough and nasty, lacked the skills of man-management, and could not soften the impact of intrusive and aggressive government. John's efforts to raise funds to help in the reconquest of lost lands, and his determined exploitation of the royal position aroused opposition, while a dispute over an election to the archbishopric of Canterbury led to a quarrel with a very determined adversary, Pope Innocent III. In 1208 Innocent laid England under an interdict, suspending all church services, and in 1209 excommunicated John.

MAGNA CARTA

John was able to buy his peace with Innocent by making England a fief of the papacy (1213), but his other enemies were harder to deal with. John's attempt to recover his continental inheritance ended in failure when his allies were defeated at Bouvines (1214). This helped to encourage John's domestic opponents to rise in rebellion, and in 1215 he was forced to accept the terms of what was to be later called Magna Carta in order to end what was for him an unsuccessful conflict. This charter of liberties was a condemnation of John's use of feudal, judicial and other governmental powers, for it defined and limited royal rights. Magna Carta was in effect an enormous list of everything that was wrong with government as John applied it. It covered practically everything, hence later calls for its confirmation. Baronial liberties were protected and freemen were provided with some guarantees against arbitrary royal actions. The Crown was not to be able to determine its rights alone. Constraining monarchs to accept limitations was always, however, a problematic course of action, for the effectiveness of such a settlement depended on royal willingness to change attitudes and policy or on the creation of a body able to force the monarch to do so. John's unwillingness to implement the agreement led his opponents to offer the throne to Philip Augustus's son, Louis. England drifted into a serious civil war and John died in 1216, shortly after the quicksands and tide of the Wash had claimed a valuable part of his baggage train.

John's son, Henry III (1216–72), was a more acceptable monarch: as a child of 9 he was no threat. Helped by victory in war,
especially the battle of Lincoln and Hubert de Burgh's naval
victory off Dover, both in 1217, Henry's supporters drove Louis
to abandon the struggle (Treaty of Lambeth, 1217). Henry did not
gain effective power until 1232, but neither during his minority nor
subsequently was it possible to defeat the French on the Continent
and regain the lands lost by John. The disastrous 1242 Poitevin
campaign damaged the king's reputation and finances, and in the
Treaty of Paris (1259) Henry finally accepted the losses that left
him only Gascony, part of Aquitaine with its principal centre at
Bordeaux.

During Henry's minority the idea of restricting a ruler through
written regulations and insisting that he seek the advice of the
nobility developed. 'Great Councils' were summoned to win baronial consent and thus cooperation; Magna Carta was frequently
reissued. Henry's unpopularity was due to his granting of favour to
French friends and advisors rather than only members of the
English elite; and to the fact that his government entailed as much
financial pressure as the king could exert, and that there was much
misrule and corruption by both royal and baronial officials. Like
his father, Henry proved unable to sustain acceptable relations with
his leading subjects, and by the Provisions of Oxford (1258) and of
Westminster (1259) they sought to take power out of his hands, to
enforce what they regarded as good kingship. War broke out in
1264 and that year many of the barons, under the king's brother-in-
law, the French-born Simon de Montfort, Earl of Leicester, defeated Henry at Lewes. His victory left de Montfort in control of
king and government, but Henry's son Edward escaped from
custody in 1265, raised an army and defeated de Montfort decisively at Evesham in 1265. The royal cause was helped because quite
a number of the barons had stayed loyal, while others had been
alienated by de Montfort. Royal authority was restored, though
Henry took pains to adopt a more careful attitude.

THE END OF WELSH INDEPENDENCE

The history of Wales from the 1150s to the 1280s sheds light on the
strengths and weaknesses of English rule, but it also throws valu-

able comparative light on the nature of political and governmental developments in the British Isles. The conquest of Wales was a central event in British history, reflecting and entrenching the superiority of the English state and bringing a longlasting Celtic community under the English crown.

Henry II sought to regain the authority his grandfather, Henry I, had had in Wales, but he had a formidable opponent in Gruffudd's son Rhys (d. 1197). Henry II's invasion in 1158 led to the submission of several Welsh princes, but Rhys, angered by the extension of Anglo-Norman territorial claims, especially by Roger of Clare in Cardigan, attacked with success. Henry II again marched into Wales, forcing Rhys to submit in 1163, but he started fighting again in 1164, while Henry's advance into north Wales in 1165 was unsuccessful. In 1165 Rhys took Cardigan castle, and in 1167, in co-operation with Gwynedd, he gained Rhuddlan.

Henry accepted Rhys's position in 1171, realising after the failure of his campaign in 1165 that a working relationship was the only answer. For the rest of Henry's reign, Rhys was in effect left as a powerful and independent sub-king, who in return for doing homage had effective control over his dominions, control that he strengthened by building his own castles. He endowed the new monastery at Strata Florida and patronised bards and harpists. As well as being king of Deheubarth, Rhys was 'Lord Rhys', Henry's justiciar for south Wales; he may be compared with the other great feudatories of Henry II's empire. Rhys dominated Wales and ensured stability. When Henry died, Rhys took the initiative against the Anglo-Normans, and the Welsh definitely had the advantage in the 1190s. In 1196 Carmarthen, which had so often defied the Welsh, was taken by Rhys.

This was the period in which Gerald of Wales (c.1145–1223), the Norman-Welsh Archdeacon of Brecon, was writing. Gerald was an educated cleric, only one quarter native Welsh, writing in the revived ethnographic tradition fashionable in the 'twelfth-century renaissance'. Gerald accompanied the Archbishop of Canterbury on his preaching tour of 1188 to gain support for the Third Crusade and described it in *The Journey Through Wales*; he also wrote a *Description of Wales*. Gerald is not a particularly reliable source, and, as in other such works of travel, there are numerous generalisations: 'the Welsh are the most particular in shaving the lower parts of the body . . . the Welsh sing their traditional songs, not in unison . . . but in parts, in many modes and modulations . . . Both sexes take great care of their teeth . . . for the Welsh generosity and hospitality are the greatest of all virtues.' Nevertheless, Gerald had a clear sense of Welshness: he was not writing of Gwynedd and Deheubarth as if their people were different. This reflected the idea of the Welsh as *cymry*, 'compatriots', or *cymru*, 'the country', a community united by a shared and mutually supporting culture, mythology, language, customs and laws. Despite their fissiparous politics, the Welsh saw themselves as one people occupying one country. However, the fragmentation of power and the practice of partible inheritance were fundamental weaknesses in a political structure confronted with a powerful external threat. Rhys's quarrelsome sons divided his kingdom.

Cymru was taken closest to political fulfilment by Llywelyn the Great (d. 1240) and his grandson, Llywelyn ap Gruffudd, 'the Last', (d. 1282) of Gwynedd. They united native Wales (*pura Wallia*). The thirteenth century is the period when Gwynedd finally emerged as the dominant power and the two Llywelyns sought to create a Welsh political unit and single political authority where none had existed before. It is not known who thought of this in the first place, but the new development was associated with the general growth of jurisdictional definition and written government in the thirteenth century, together with the growth in moveable wealth, which gave a sharper focus to princely claims everywhere. In Wales, traditions of 'national' history and identity, which had been invented and propagated by the native intelligentsia, were given more political reality by 'modernising' princes, who built castles, developed rights and resources, founded monasteries and granted borough charters, and were served by a small circle of administrators (including churchmen educated outside Wales); in order to resist English claims, the princes had to copy their methods. The object of the two Llywelyns was to extend overlordship over the other native rulers and at the same time to persuade the English Crown to accept the homage of the prince of Gwynedd for the whole of native Wales, the other rulers having done homage to the prince. What was needed to confirm this was a treaty with the Crown.

Llywelyn the Great first established himself by defeating close kindred (1194–1202). In 1208 he conquered Powys from its ruler Gwenwynwyn. King John turned a blind eye. Llywelyn followed this up by seizing Ceredigion (Cardigan), but in 1211 he fell out with John, who had restored Gwenwynwyn. Supported by Powys and the sons of Rhys, John campaigned in Gwynedd, driving Llywelyn back into Snowdonia. Llywelyn was forced to sue for peace and to cede the Four Cantrefs in north-east Wales (modern Clwyd), but in 1212 he rose again, this time supported by the other major Welsh princes. The English lost their new castles in Gwynedd, and John was handicapped by opposition to his policies in England. John was obliged in Magna Carta to promise to restore all lands illegally taken from Welshmen. Much of south Wales then rose with Llywelyn's assistance and he was able to raze Carmarthen castle to the ground. In 1216, at a sort of parliament at Aberdovey, Llywelyn dealt with competing territorial claims within *pura Wallia*. He did homage after the accession of Henry III, but he maintained his position against both English and Welsh rivals: in 1219 he devastated Pembrokeshire and in 1221 defeated Rhys Gryg of Deheubarth, who had joined the Earl of Pembroke. Llywelyn annexed Kidwelly and Gower. When English forces under the nominal command of the young Henry III advanced in 1223 Llywelyn made peace and renewed his homage, but hostilities frequently flared up anew, and in 1231 Llywelyn invaded Gwent, a region that had for long been under secure Anglo-Norman control.

Llywelyn died in 1240, still in control of native Wales, among the Cistercians of Aberconwy, whom he had actively supported. He had been a generous patron of the native bards (poets), who celebrated his talents. Nevertheless, he had failed to secure the treaty with the English Crown necessary to cement his position. The principality that he had built up depended entirely on his personality and had no institutional framework to sustain it, so it fell apart on his death. As in other monarchical states, stability was threatened by a disputed succession. Llywelyn sought to leave a clear succession by both designating Dafydd, his son by John's illegitimate daughter, Joan, and gathering all the princes of Wales together to swear fealty in 1238, but this was contested by Llywelyn's eldest son, Gruffudd, the child of an irregular union. Dafydd may have been the chosen successor because his mother was a Plantagenet; this could help to admit him to the contemporary European royal network. In 1239 Gruffudd was seized by Dafydd at a peace conference and imprisoned. Gruffudd, however, enjoyed considerable support, and in 1241 Henry III forced Dafydd to hand him over to his custody. In 1244 Gruffudd tried to escape from the Tower of London using a rope made from his linen, but he was too heavy and fell, breaking his neck. War then resumed between Dafydd and the English marcher lords. He invaded Herefordshire in 1244 and captured Mold the following year. Henry III advanced with a great army to Degannwy in Gwynedd, but Dafydd retired into Snowdonia and, being short of supplies, Henry had to retreat, although much damage was done by ruthless devastation. When Dafydd died childless in 1246, Gruffudd's eldest sons, Owain and Llywelyn, divided the inheritance, performing homage to Henry III in 1247 after the English seneschal of Carmarthen had overrun the southern dependencies of Gwynedd. In addition, all the lands east of the Conwy went to Henry.

Once again, the princes of Gwynedd now fought each other. Owain, supported by his younger brother Dafydd, attacked Llywelyn in 1254, who beat and imprisoned him in 1255, and set out to regain the dominions of his grandfather. This led to tension with the Welsh leaders in south Wales. Furthermore, in 1254 Henry granted his eldest son Edward the Earldom of Chester and the royal lands in Wales. This led to a new energy in the enforcement of the English crown's pretensions. In the south, Edward's agents sought to establish a shire system using English laws.

Llywelyn intervened, overrunning north-east Wales in 1256 and central Wales in 1256–7, and invading south Wales in 1257. Henry's counterattack in 1257 achieved nothing and Llywelyn continued to extend his power, taking Builth Castle in 1260. Enjoying greater support from the Welsh, Llywelyn backed Simon de Montfort and his baronial allies against Henry, and in 1263 the leading castle in north Wales, Degannwy, was surrendered by its blockaded garrison. In 1265 Henry, now held by de Montfort, was made to seal a convention granting Llywelyn and his heirs the title of Prince of Wales with the homage of all the Welsh magnates, as well as Hawarden and Montgomery. De Montfort was defeated at Evesham but by the Treaty of Montgomery (1267), as part of the postwar reconciliation, Henry felt it prudent to grant Llywelyn essentially the same terms that had been agreed in 1265. The concession of Llywelyn's newly claimed title of Prince of Wales indicated the extent to which the reimposition of royal power in England did not extend to Wales. This was the treaty with the English Crown that Llywelyn the Great had not achieved.

Between 1272 and 1277 there was a sequence of crises in Anglo-Welsh relations, although it is unlikely that either side wanted war. Llywelyn failed to do homage to Edward I and in 1274 his brother and heir, Dafydd, and the ruler of southern Powys plotted to assassinate him, fleeing to England when Llywelyn found out about the abortive plot. Where previous English monarchs had sought dominance, Edward I was a conqueror. In 1277 Edward invaded with massive force and the support of the other Welsh rulers and the Welsh exiles. While secondary forces advanced in central and south Wales, Edward attacked Gwynedd, using his navy to cut off Anglesey, Gwynedd's major source of food. Bottling up Llywelyn in Snowdonia, Edward kept him short of supplies until he accepted terms at the Treaty of Aberconwy (1277). Llywelyn was made to do homage to Edward and to surrender the lands east of the Conwy. His Welsh opponents were granted territories, and the homage of most of the Welsh leaders was transferred to the king: Welsh Wales was not to be united by Gwynedd. The principality was now restricted to Snowdonia and Anglesey.

The peace was followed by a degree of anglicisation of government and church that created problems. Archbishop Peckham of Canterbury told Llywelyn that Welsh customs were only to be observed if reasonable. In 1282 Dafydd rebelled. Whether or not Llywelyn joined the war at the outset is unclear, but he certainly became involved, attacking the other native Welsh rulers and seizing the castles of Flint, Rhuddlan and Hawarden: English rule in north-east Wales was unpopular. South Wales also rebelled. Edward repeated his strategy of 1277; Llywelyn, fearing winter starvation, broke out of Snowdonia, but was killed near Builth on 11 December. Dafydd, who was largely responsible for the rebellion, became a fugitive in Snowdonia. In 1283 he was captured and executed at Shrewsbury: hanged, his entrails torn out, beheaded and quartered.

The contrasting military fate of Wales and Scotland cannot be attributed to divisions among the Welsh or to the extent to which the English received Welsh support; the same was true of Scotland. The failures of earlier expeditions indicated that there was no inevitability in Welsh defeat, but the English undoubtedly were helped by the relatively compact nature of Gwynedd, by the proximity of bases, especially Chester and Shrewsbury, by their far superior resources in terms of men, money and supplies, by naval power and by the absence of foreign assistance for Llywelyn: there was no help from France or Scotland and the only intervention from Ireland was of troops sent to help the English.

POST-CONQUEST WALES

The conquest was secured by a new military order and followed by a political settlement. The English presence in Wales had for long been based on castles, and the campaigns of 1277 and 1282 were each followed by extensive construction. After 1277 there was work at Aberystwyth, Builth, Flint and Rhuddlan castles, but after 1282 there were new sites for fortification and a new strategic task because Gwynedd was now Crown property. Caernarfon, the intended centre of royal power, Conwy, Harlech and Beaumaris were all coastal castles that could be supplied by sea. The construction of these massive works, stone-built unlike the early earth and wood-castles, was a formidable undertaking, costing at least £93,000, an immense sum, and using thousands of workers. Lordship castles were also constructed at Chirk, Denbigh and Holt. Thirteenth century native Welsh rulers had previously built castles, such as Dolbadarn and Bere, but now castle-building was to be under English control.

The new political settlement ended Welsh independence, although the political and constitutional achievements of the rulers of Gwynedd served as a basis for rule by Edward I and his successors. The principality recognised in 1267 did survive – it retained its constitutional integrity from 1284, was granted to Edward I's eldest son in 1301 and was not annexed to England until 1536 – but it was no longer independent. Edward applied feudal law and saw himself as the heir to Llywelyn's forfeited estate, and the Crown thus obtained much of Wales, including all of Gwynedd. In effect the 'frontier' had been closed and it was therefore necessary and possible to create a new administrative and judicial structure for the Crown lands. The Statute of Wales (1284) added an extra tier of government to the principality, extending the English system of shire administration to Anglesey, Caernarfon, Flint and Merioneth, in addition to Cardigan and Carmarthen which had emerged as counties earlier in the thirteenth century. English criminal law was introduced although civil law remained largely Welsh. Caernarfon and Carmarthen became centres of royal administration, while the new castles of Aberystwyth, Beaumaris, Caernarfon, Conwy, Denbigh, Flint and Rhuddlan were associated with new or transformed towns that were created for settlement by English craftsmen and merchants and that were clearly seen as centres of English influence and culture – although by 1305 the richest burgess in Beaumaris was a Welshman. The principality of Wales was eventually allocated an essentially honorific, rather than independent, position for the heirs to the English throne, the future Edward II being created Prince of Wales in 1301.

The conquest of Gwynedd was a major achievement for Edward I, although the conscious imitation of the Theodosian landwall of Constantinople at Caernarfon was a disproportionate echo of imperial power. Although Cornwall was the first 'frontier' to be closed, it had never posed a military challenge comparable to Wales. Edward's conquest made larger defensive works in Cheshire relatively valueless and the castles there fell into ruin. The very failures of Edward's father and grandfather had encouraged him to act, as did the extent to which the Welsh problem was interwoven with English domestic politics: Llywelyn had indeed married a daughter of Simon de Montfort.

There was further resistance after 1283, including a revolt in 1287. This was not a major national rising; it was limited to Carmarthenshire and was led by one of the Welsh lords who had supported Edward in 1282 and who was disappointed with his reward. The heavy taxation levied in 1292–3 to pay the ransom of Edward's cousin, Charles of Salerno, led to discontent in England and a serious rebellion in Wales led by Madog, a member of a cadet branch of the Gwynedd dynasty. It was primarily a protest against government policy, including the levying of troops from Wales for service in France and the continuance of the exceptional financial demands of Llywelyn's last years, rather than against English control. The revolt broke out simultaneously in the north, the west and the south-east, which suggests concerted planning. The uncompleted castle at Caernarfon was badly damaged and the failure of the initial English response forced Edward to intervene. The Earl of Warwick defeated Madog in a night attack on his camp in 1295 and Edward received the submission of the Welsh. He also did something about Welsh grievances. In 1316 Llywelyn Bren rebelled in Glamorgan, but was suppressed by the overwhelming force of the marcher lords.

It is unclear how far the Welsh saw themselves as a conquered people. There was resentment at the domination of administration and Church by Englishmen and also at the commercial privileges granted to the inhabitants of the new towns. The political system worked to the benefit of those who had the necessary patrons at court, which was crucial in the administration of justice. The use of patronage annoyed the leaders of the native Welsh community, who regarded local offices as theirs by right. Llywelyn Bren was dismissed from his official position in Glamorgan by an English superior and when he complained was accused of sedition. Edward II's rejection of Llywelyn's attempt to justify himself led to the revolt.

Such an account can be seen as an indication of mistreatment, and yet it is also significant that Llywelyn, like many Welsh landholders, had held high office. Just as generations of Welsh princes, especially in Powys, had looked to the English for support, so others were able to accommodate themselves to the new regime. It was not followed by a wholesale expropriation of property comparable to that after the Norman conquest of England and although the Church was brought more into line with English practice there was again nothing to compare with the situation under William I. At the local level there was little change: the same families, the traditional leaders of the community, remained in charge.

Much of Wales was still under the control of the Anglo-Norman marcher families that had conquered it. Known collectively as the Welsh march, these lordships were not integrated into shires and were autonomous: their lords had effective administrative and legal control. Most marcher lordships gradually came, by marriage or inheritance, into the possession of magnate families. Prominent lordships included Glamorgan (which belonged to the Clare family), Maelienydd and Radnor (Mortimer), Brecon (Bohun), Abergavenny (Hastings), Ruthin (Grey) and Pembroke (Valence). Edward I thus made no attempt to create an integrated state: instead he dealt with the immediate problem of Gwynedd. Yet the great power of the marcher lords was a potential threat to the stability of the Crown, and Edward tried to assert his powers as sovereign over them too. So long as this contrast in government remained, royal authority was fragmented and there was no government agency that could lend bureaucratic shape to the notion of Wales. As in so much of the pre-modern British Isles, diversity was the keynote.

THE ANGLO-SCOTTISH STRUGGLE

In the thirteenth century the British Isles had two strong states, England and Scotland. They drew on similar administrative and military legacies. Each faced internal challenges, but in many respects the English monarchy was less successful in charting an internal political course without civil war and constitutional struggle. The Scottish kings spread their power out from the central lowlands. Thus, for example, William the Lion (1165–1214), the grandson of David I, both sought to increase his authority in Galloway and, in 1187, at the battle of the Muir of Mamgarvy, defeated a powerful dynastic rebellion in Moray. William was also able to defeat an invasion of Moray by Harald, Earl of Orkney, a product of the Viking diaspora, and to invade Caithness, which was part of Harald's earldom, and nominally subject to the king of the Scots. William's son, Alexander II (1214–49), extended royal control in Argyll and Caithness and repelled a Norse invasion in 1230. Alexander died while attempting to gain the Hebrides from Norway. His son Alexander III (1249–86) maintained the pressure to create a stronger and more centralised state. This was resisted by Hakon IV of Norway, but at the battle of Largs (1263) Hakon's amphibious force was checked and the more general failure of the entire Norwegian axis led to Scotland gaining the Western Isles by the Treaty of Perth (1266). The Viking political axis along the northern and western axis of Scotland had been gravely weakened.

The kings had encountered resistance in extending their authority over the ethnic hybrid that was Scotland. Galloway, for example, for long felt little affinity with the Scottish Crown: in the anti-foreign revolt of Uhtred and Gilbert of Galloway, in 1174, the Gallovodians slew the officials placed over them and attacked Anglo-Norman lords. Yet the monarchs were generally successful. For example, the position of the Scottish Crown in Caithness improved considerably in 1150–1266.

Furthermore, the formation of a distinctively Scottish Church contributed to a developing sense of national identity. In 1192 Pope Celestine II granted William the Lion a bull, *Cum Universi*, placing the nine Scottish bishoprics directly under the see of Rome and by implication denying the metropolitan claims of jurisdiction of the English archbishoprics of York and Canterbury. This brought to an end a long controversy. The papal bull halted what was essentially a matter of jurisdictional dispute and pride, but which could have developed eventually into a form of English ecclesiastical imperialism, and it thus strengthened the authority of the Scottish monarchy.

Under Alexander III, the power of the Canmore dynasty of Scottish rulers reached its zenith, but, as so often, dynastic chance was to bring weakness and strife. Alexander died in 1286, to be succeeded by a young grand-daughter, Margaret, the Maid of Norway. Edward I saw this as an opportunity to increase his family's power and in 1289 secured the Treaty of Salisbury by which the marriage of Margaret and the future Edward II was agreed. The rights and laws of Scotland were to be preserved, but, in essence, the union of the Crowns that was eventually to happen in 1603 seemed likely in 1289. Had it done so, it is interesting to consider how far the two countries could have remained united, and, if so, how far a process of convergence, political, administrative and cultural, would have occurred.

Margaret, however, died *en route* for Scotland in 1290, leaving a number of claimants to the throne. Edward I was asked to adjudicate and in 1291 had his overlordship over the Crown of Scotland recognised by the claimants, before eventually declaring John Balliol king. Balliol swore fealty and did homage to Edward. English hegemony in the British Isles seemed established. Edward's subsequent position, not least his encouragement of appeals by Scots to English courts, was, however, unacceptable to many Scots and, with tension rising due to Scottish links with Philip IV of France, who had seized Gascony in 1294, Edward invaded Scotland (1296). Berwick, the assault on which Edward led in person, fell, several thousand Scots being put to the sword. After a successful campaign, in which the Scots were defeated at Dunbar, Balliol surrendered the kingdom to Edward. Edward's triumph was shortlived, as in 1297 William Wallace rebelled and defeated the English at Stirling. He then revealed the danger of a hostile Scotland by ravaging Northumbria. Edward I was in Flanders, fighting the French and their allies: yet again continental commitments were weakening the position of the English Crown within Britain.

A truce with France enabled Edward I to march north in 1298. Attacking Wallace at Falkirk, he found the Scottish pikemen massed in tightly packed *schiltroms*, able to defy the English cavalry, but they were broken by Edward's archers. Further campaigns brought territorial gains, but Edward's forces were over-stretched and resistance was not crushed, though Wallace was captured and executed in 1305. The following year, Robert Bruce rebelled and had himself crowned king of Scots, and in 1307 Edward I died at Burgh-on-Sands on his way to campaign in Scotland. Edward II (1307–27) had inherited none of his father's military ability or ambition, and the less intense pace of English military pressure helped Bruce (Robert I), to consolidate his position in Scotland. In 1314 Edinburgh fell to Bruce and Stirling promised to surrender if not relieved. Poorly led by Edward, the English relieving force was defeated at Bannockburn by the Scottish army, pikemen on well-chosen ground routing cavalry. The English had very few archers at the battle and they were handled very badly. Edward fled and, after the surrender of Stirling, the English position was challenged in Ireland, which was invaded by Robert I's brother Edward Bruce in 1315, and in northern England. In 1318 Berwick fell and in 1319 the Scots ravaged Yorkshire. English counter-attacks were unsuccessful and in 1328, by the Treaty of Northampton, Scottish independence was recognised.

This was not the end of the Scottish wars of independence. The treaty was highly unpopular in England, even in the northern shires which had suffered most from Scottish attacks. It was always likely that the war would resume. In 1332 Edward Balliol claimed the throne and declared himself Edward III's liegeman. He was driven out by the adherents of Bruce's infant son, David II (1329–71), but the following year English archers under Edward III defeated the Scots at Halidon Hill and captured Berwick; and in 1334 Edward III restored Balliol and received Lothian from him. The weak Balliol was, however, driven out, and the English invaded Scotland again in 1335, 1336 and 1341, holding, for a while, much of the country, but Edward III had to divert most of his resources to war with France. David, urged on by his French allies, was able to invade England in 1346, though he was defeated at Neville's Cross, Durham, taken prisoner and held captive until 1357. Edward III invaded Scotland again in 1356, but peace was made in 1357.

England was far stronger than Scotland, and it is worth considering whether she could have conquered her but for the diversion of her strength to war with France, a conflict whose scale is suggested by the term 'The Hundred Years War'. Hostilities arose with Scotland in 1296 largely because of the quarrel from 1293 between Edward I and Philip IV of France, in which the Scots became involved. Had there not been that additional complication, Edward might have run Balliol on a looser rein, and the Scots might have acted more cautiously. Again in the 1330s Scotland mattered largely because, like the Low Countries, it was an area in which Edward III and Philip VI were competing. David II was an exile under Philip's protection in 1334–41. In addition, war with France did not preclude, as in 1346 and 1356, attacks on Scotland. The vulnerability of the centres of Scottish power and economy to English invasion is notable in any account of English attacks. In 1335 Edward III found no difficulty in occupying Glasgow and Perth, and in 1336 north-east Scotland; in 1356 Henry of Lancaster occupied Perth, Elgin and Inverness.

Had the English been able to maintain and support a permanent military presence in lowland Scotland, then the Scottish kingdom might have been so weakened and divided as to cease to be a powerful challenge. Divisions among the Scottish nobility, which greatly helped the English, might have been exploited to spread the power of the king of England, who would have been able to mount a more effective claim to the Crown of Scotland, either for himself or for a protégé. However, the episodic military commitment dictated by Scotland's secondary role in English military policy from the late 1330s, exacerbated the natural logistical problems of campaigning there and ensured that fixed positions were given insufficient support. This left the Scots with the military initiative, which was fatal to the English cause. When the English invaded, the Scots could avoid battle and concentrate on harrying the English force and denying them supplies, a policy that thwarted Edward's invasion of Lothian in 1356. In addition, it would have been staggeringly expensive to maintain a large number of English garrisons, and, as Scotland itself would not have been rich enough to be made to fund its own occupation, the cost would have fallen on England. Successful war in France, by contrast, was partially self-financing.

FAILURE IN IRELAND

Defeat for the English in Scotland was matched by failure in Ireland. Edward Bruce invaded Ireland in 1315 and it has been argued that Robert I wished it conquered as a prelude, with the hope of a Welsh alliance, to a pan-Celtic invasion of England. The Anglo-Irish were defeated by the Scots, who campaigned with great savagery, until Edward Bruce was crushed and killed at Faughart (1318), one of the more important battles of the Middle Ages. The scheme for a Scottish conquest of Ireland had been wrecked. Nevertheless, English lordship in Ireland had been gravely weakened, and, despite major expeditions from England in the 1360s, 1370s and 1390s, the situation continued to deteriorate. Athlone was burnt on several occasions in 1218–1315, its bridge broken down in an attack of c.1272 and after the burning of 1315 there was no further mention of the medieval town. The Dublin administration retained only nominal control by allowing the Anglo-Irish Dillons to act as hereditary constables of the castle and, even so, they were often driven out by the Gaelic O'Kellys of Ui Maine. The royal estates and castles at Roscommon and Rindrown were overrun in the 1350s. By the following century, direct English control was limited to the Pale, the area around Dublin, while the semi-autonomous Anglo-Irish lords and the independent Gaelic chieftains controlled most of the island. The Anglo-Irish Earldom of Ulster contracted markedly from 1333 in the face of the Gaelic resurgence. A branch of the Tyrone O'Neills overran the southern half of Antrim and the northern half of County Down and by 1460 the Ulster centre of Carrickfergus was paying them protection. The expedition by Richard II in 1399 was the last by an English king until William III invaded in 1689, although there were important English expeditions in the late-sixteenth and mid-seventeenth centuries. The fifteenth century was a lowpoint of English interest in Ireland.

THE CONTINUING DIVISION OF THE BRITISH ISLES

Political division was to be one of the most important political legacies of the Middle Ages. The British Isles were not united politically before the religious divisions stemming from the Reformation in the sixteenth century, and the subsequent strengthening of national consciousness made any such process far less easy. In hindsight it is possible to emphasise the difficulty of the task. The

English relied in Scotland not on colonisation but on collaboration, but it proved impossible to sustain the necessary level. The centre of English power was in the south of England, far distant from Scotland and Ireland. War in both countries posed formidable logistical difficulties for any invader. The Romans had not managed to conquer Scotland. Scotland had already developed an effective monarchy and acquired 'modern' military techniques.

And yet the extraordinary vitality of the Normans, who, through conquest, created kingdoms in southern Italy as well as England, and the fluidity of boundaries on the Continent, are reminders of the possibilities that existed. There were definite opportunities in the medieval period for enlarging, through marriage or conquest, the kingdom of England, and thus creating the basis of a British state, a British aristocratic elite and a British consciousness. The very fluidity of political circumstances and chance that characterised the international politics of the period, a situation exacerbated by the central role of the vagaries of dynastic chance, the births, marriages, skill and deaths of monarchs, would necessarily have challenged any such achievement. It is unclear that any British unity could have survived the conspiracies and civil conflict of the fifteenth century. The break-up of the Union of Kalmar, by which Sweden, Norway and Denmark had been jointly ruled (1397–1523), is instructive, but so also is the unification of Spain, at least at the dynastic level, a process in which war as well as marriage played a role.

If the division of the British Isles was one of the crucial political legacies of the medieval period, another was the loss, with the exception of Calais, of the continental territories of the kings of England. After the reigns of John and Henry III, relatively little remained of the legacy of Henry II, but Edward I was determined to protect Gascony from the consequences of French overlordship. His ability to do so was lessened by the domestic strains produced by his policies, especially his heavy financial demands. These affected the response to the extensive reform of law and administration that he carried through by a series of statutes in 1275–90. Edward's relations with the nobility were very tense in the 1290s, and the issues of taxation and grievances came to play a major role. The clergy and the merchants were also alienated. Unrest culminated in a political crisis in 1297 in which many nobles resisted demands for high war taxation. The situation was to deteriorate seriously in the following century.

FOURTEENTH-CENTURY CRISES IN ENGLAND

The fourteenth century was a period of political crisis. That was scarcely surprising. Most political systems with any degree of sophistication have periodical crises, and a period without crisis would require particular explanation. In the case of the fourteenth century, however, there was the additional socio-economic crisis caused by the end of the long period of demographic and economic expansion that had underpinned social development since the tenth century. Population growth had led to demand-led economic activity and an expansion of the social fabric: new towns and villages, roads and markets. This came to an end in the fourteenth century.

The most decisive episode in this crisis was the Black Death, an epidemic, probably of bubonic plague, which killed about a third of the English population between 1348 and 1351, seriously disrupted the economy and contributed to a loss of confidence. The Black Death originated in central Asia, reached Italy in 1347 and spread thence through trading links, reaching England and Ireland in 1348 and Scotland and Wales in 1349. Plague now became endemic until the seventeenth century (the last major episode in Scotland was in 1649 and in England in 1665) and held the population down until about 1500. Thereafter, it could still be savage in its effects. 30–33 per cent of the population of Norwich died as a result in 1587, 12 per cent of that in London in 1593, 40–50 per cent of that of Kendal in 1598, 12,000 in Edinburgh and its environs in 1644–9. Infected houses were marked with a sign and in effect quarantined, the only possible remedy for a society that lacked the scientific knowledge of transmission via rats and fleas.

Yet the Black Death was only the most spectacular instance of a more general crisis. Like the Great Famine of 1315–17 caused by harvest failure resulting from bad weather, the plague hit population levels that were anyway under pressure as a result of earlier expansion: population growth was not matched by a sufficient rise in food production and progressive under-nourishment probably weakened resistance to disease. Soil exhaustion, caused by over-cultivation and an absence of sufficient fertiliser, was another serious aspect of the crisis.

The Black Death had minimal direct political repercussions, but a cumulative socio-economic crisis exploded in the Peasants' Revolt of 1381. This was more wide-ranging and reflected a longer tradition of dissidence than is generally appreciated. Strains in rural society had arisen from increased agricultural production for market and the determination of landlords to benefit fully from this, not least by using their feudal powers. They also sought to prevent peasants exploiting the relative scarcity of labour arising from the Black Death by claiming higher wages. Resistance to landlords became common and frequently violent. The situation was exacerbated by failure in the Hundred Years War with France, which led to raids on the coast; the problems of the important East Anglian cloth industry; and a pervasive anti-clericalism which sapped respect for authority. One indicator of the social crisis was the evidence of rural depopulation presented by deserted and shrunken villages, especially in the Midlands and north-east of England and East Anglia.

A poll tax designed to fund the war with France pressed hard on the depressed rural economy, leading to high rates of evasion and to riots in 1379, and the process culminated in the Peasants' Revolt of 1381. This began in Essex and spread throughout southern England, being especially strong in Kent and East Anglia, but also leading to important disturbances in Sussex, Winchester, Somerset, Cornwall and Yorkshire. The destruction of manorial records reflected peasant hostility to baronial jurisdiction. The Chief Justice, Sir John Cavendish, who had enforced the attempt to fix low, pre-plague labour rates by the Statute of Labourers (1351), was killed in Suffolk. Led by Wat Tyler and a priest, John Ball, the rebels occupied London with the help of dissatisfied Londoners. The Tower of London was seized and prominent figures, including Simon of Sudbury, archbishop of Canterbury and Chancellor (head of the legal system), who was responsible for the poll tax, were murdered. This was a crisis at the centre of power.

The rebels did not, however, wish to create a new governmental system, but rather to pressurise the king, Richard II, into changes of policy. On 15 June Richard met the main body of the rebels under Tyler at Smithfield near London. During the meeting, William Walworth, Mayor of London, believing that Tyler was threatening Richard, lunged forward and killed him. Astutely Richard averted violence by promising to be the rebels' leader. The rebellion lost momentum with both the death of Tyler and Richard's grant of charters of freedom to the rebels. However, as soon as they had returned to their homes Richard revoked the charters and punished their leaders.

The Peasants' Revolt was the most serious challenge to the established order until the crisis of the 1640s. It indicates the lack of social and ideological quiescence on the part of the bulk of the population, a group whose lives and views are obscured by their illiteracy and the emphasis on the elite in the surviving records. The nature of popular alienation can, however, be grasped by the events of 1381. Thus in Norfolk the rebels took control of all the major towns, attacked, plundered or killed prominent figures, particularly landlords who were also JPs (justices of the peace), burned manor court rolls and attacked foreign (Flemish) settlers. The rebellion there, however, was crushed within a month by the warlike Bishop Despenser of Norwich, who brought leadership and determination to the gentry.

EDWARD II, 1307–27

The Peasants' Revolt would ultimately be the most serious social crisis of the medieval period, but there were even more serious political crises for the monarchs of fourteenth-century England. Edward II inherited serious problems, including war in Scotland, but he exacerbated them by his character and political incompetence. Edward's inability to deal with the Scots owed much to his quarrels with his leading barons, especially over Piers Gaveston, his arrogant Gascon favourite. Edward I, who regarded him as a sinister influence, had banished Gaveston, but he was recalled by Edward II, made Earl of Cornwall and given much wealth and influence. This led to a political crisis. In 1311 Edward was forced to accept ordinances restricting his power and in 1312 Gaveston was murdered by hostile nobles. The king's cousin, Thomas, Earl of Lancaster, a supporter of the ordinances, then controlled the government, until Edward was able to defeat him at Boroughbridge (1322) and have him executed. The ordinances were then repealed, but Edward remained unpopular, not least because of his new favourites, the Despensers, father and son. Their regime was very rapacious and ignored inheritance rights.

Edward II was not a martial ruler. Furthermore, he failed to conform to contemporary notions of kingship: he lacked dignity and had unroyal hobbies, such as boating and ditching. Edward's focusing of patronage on and via his favourites led to discontent which was exploited by his wife Isabella, daughter of Philip IV of France. With her lover, Roger Mortimer, she captured Edward in 1326. He was then deposed in favour of his son and disposed of in Berkeley Castle, probably by a red-hot poker inserted through his anus, a means of death that left few incriminating signs (1327). This first murder of a king since 978 (assuming that William II was shot accidentally), was to be followed by the murders of Richard II (1400), Henry VI (1471) and Edward V (1483), evidence both of the instability of the period and of the continued importance of the monarchy.

EDWARD III, 1327–77

Isabella and Mortimer controlled the first years of Edward III's reign, but in 1330 Edward and his friends seized Mortimer and had him hanged and his mother imprisoned. Edward restored royal authority and prestige after the chaos of his father's reign and was particularly successful in winning the support of the barons: he avoided favourites and brought many barons into his circle as knights of the Order of the Garter, which he established in 1348.

Edward's reign was dominated by the beginning of the Hundred Years War with France. The extinction of the male line of Philip IV, Edward's grandfather, led Edward to challenge Philip's nephew, Philip VI, by claiming the French throne in 1337. Initially the war went well. The French fleet was smashed at Sluys (1340), a battle dominated by the boarding of ships. France was invaded and, at Crécy (1346) and Poitiers (1356), longbowmen decimated the French cavalry. This led to the Treaty of Brétigny (1360), in which Edward promised to renounce his claim to the French throne, to Normandy and to Anjou, but was recognised as Duke of the whole of Aquitaine, as well as ruler of Calais, which had been gained in 1347. John II of France, who had been captured at Poitiers by Edward's eldest son, Edward, the 'Black Prince', promised to renounce his claim to sovereignty over Edward's continental dominions, but the treaty was never ratified.

Had the treaty held it would have been the high-water mark of the medieval English monarchy: they would have been the most powerful rulers in western Europe. However, the triumph proved illusory and the attempt to preserve it led to heavy political costs.

War resumed in 1369 because the French encouraged opposition to the Black Prince's governorship of Aquitaine. Edward III reasserted his claim to the French throne, but the war went badly for him both in Aquitaine and at sea. Poitou was lost in 1369–73. By the Truce of Bruges (1375), Edward retained little more than the coastal bases of Calais, Bordeaux and Bayonne.

Even the early decades of success had not prevented bitter criticism of the cost of conflict and the conduct of government, with a serious crisis in 1339–41 and renewed criticism of tax requests in the Parliaments of 1343, 1344, 1346, 1348 and 1352. In the second half of the long reign criticism mounted. The war was no longer successful and Edward lost his political grip. His costly and unpopular mistress, Alice Perrers, served as a focus for tension. The government was criticised for failing to protect the country from papal demands. Tax requests caused problems at the parliaments of 1372 and 1373, and in 1376 the so-called Good Parliament saw a major attack on the government. The Commons took the initiative, electing their first speaker to represent them, impeaching (prosecuting) two senior officials for corruption and rejecting tax demands.

DEVELOPMENT OF PARLIAMENT

From the early thirteenth century there was an increasing sense of the need for and importance of a political body that would serve, however episodically, as a national political focus. The concept of representation was outlined in the writs summoning representatives of the clergy, counties and boroughs to the 1295 Parliament. They were instructed to appear with authority to give advice and consent on behalf of the communities they represented; the nobles appeared on their own behalf. During the fourteenth century the institutional practices and pretensions of Parliament were established and elaborated. During the reign of Edward III the representatives of the counties and boroughs became a fixed part of Parliament and began to meet as a separate assembly, the origins of the House of Commons. In its early stages, Parliament was no different, to any great extent, from its continental counterparts, but the frequent need to raise taxation to pay for warfare led to Parliament becoming more important. War could not pay for itself, not least because the government relied on paid troops rather than a feudal host.

Parliament was a developing institution, the political consequences of which were far from clear. It could serve as a means
for eliciting and expressing support and funds for royal policies, as
in 1377 when the taxation refused the previous year by the Good
Parliament was granted. Yet the use of parliamentary demands to
influence the composition and intentions of government was another consequence, and the development of the corporate identity
and continuity of Parliament constrained monarchical freedom of
political manoeuvre. A statute (law passed by Parliament) of 1362
stated that Parliament must agree to all taxation of wool, England's
crucial export. The growing role of taxation, as opposed to landed
income, in royal revenues further increased Parliament's importance. It became an important focus for, and source of, political
activity.

RICHARD II, 1377–99

Because the Black Prince predeceased his father, Edward III was
succeeded by his grandson, the young Richard II, born in 1367.
Wilful and no warrior, Richard lacked personal prestige, and as he
grew older he found the lords who had dominated his minority
unwilling to surrender power. At the 1386 'Wonderful Parliament'
there was bitter criticism of Richard's favourites, especially Michael
de la Pole, a merchant's son, whom he had made chancellor and
Earl of Suffolk. Pole was impeached and a great council appointed
to oversee the royal household. Richard had the judges declare
Parliament's demands illegal (1387), but his leading supporter,
Robert de Vere, Earl of Oxford, was routed at Radcot Bridge. A
group of leading nobles then 'appealed' (accused) Richard's closest
supporters of treason and the 'Merciless Parliament' of 1388 agreed
their execution.

Although the appellants appointed pliable ministers, they were
dismissed by Richard in 1389. In the early 1390s he ruled in a less
provocative fashion, but tensions persisted. In 1394 one of the
appellants, the Earl of Arundel, turned up late for Queen Anne's
funeral, and the angry Richard struck him unconscious with an
usher's baton. In 1397 Richard turned on the appellants. A Parliament packed with supporters annulled the acts of the Merciless
Parliament. Arundel was beheaded for treason, Thomas, Duke of

Gloucester, one of Richard's uncles, was murdered. Richard followed this up by behaving in what was seen as a tyrannical fashion. People were intimidated into giving forced loans, and Richard used his army of Cheshire guards to terrorise his opponents.

Richard's policies led to a reaction. In 1399 he deprived his cousin, the exiled Henry Bolingbroke, a former appellant, of his inheritance, a step that dramatically underlined the insecurity of landed rights in the face of royal pretensions; and then led a second expedition to restore royal power in Ireland. While he was away, Bolingbroke invaded England. Richard's unpopularity and incompetence left him with scant support, and when he returned from Ireland he was outmanoeuvred, seized, forced to abdicate and imprisoned. The following year Richard was killed to prevent him from acting as a focus for opposition.

Richard's reign indicated the potential instability of the monarchical system. Each monarch reinterpreted the conventions of royal behaviour and readjusted the patronage system to reward his own supporters. This was difficult for magnates (great lords) who wished to be consulted, not least about the disposal of patronage. Economic difficulties and the role of money in social, economic, military and political relations ensured that this disposal was of ever greater importance. 'Bastard feudalism' was becoming more significant: a system in which lords rewarded and maintained their followers by annual payments of money, rather than land. This helped to make the political situation more volatile and made it easier for magnates who had access to wealth to maintain a substantial affinity (following), which could act on occasion as a small army. It also ensured that they had less of a cushion against the political consequences of financial difficulties. The removal of Richard II both reflected and facilitated a situation in which it was thus logical to try to coerce the monarch in order to ensure a favourable disposal of patronage.

WALES IN THE LATER MIDDLE AGES

Socio-economic problems were also significant in Wales. The Welsh had played an important role in support of the English Crown in the fourteenth century. Many bowmen and spearmen from all over Wales, especially from Gwent, served in the Hundred

Years War. Nevertheless, between 1369 and 1378 Owain ap Thomas ap Rhodri, or, as the French called him, Yvain de Galles, the great-nephew of Llwyelyn ap Gruffudd and the last heir of the Gwynedd dynasty, was active in French service. In 1369 and 1372 there were abortive expeditions to Wales and he was assassinated by an English agent at Mortagne-sur-Gironde in 1378. The rising of Owain Glyndŵr (Owen Glendower) in 1400–8 was an indication of the extent of disaffection and the survival of separatist feeling in Wales. Yet Glyndŵr's earlier career testified to the process of accommodation. An important landowner, as a young man he was a squire to the Earl of Arundel. In 1385 he took part in Richard II's Scottish campaign. Glyndŵr's revolt had probably been planned for a long time and may be seen as part of a whole series of revolts which occurred in Europe between about 1350 and 1450. It was in some ways a reaction to the successive crises of the fourteenth century, including the Black Death, but it was also a protest by the leaders of the native community at their neglect by the authorities.

Proclaiming himself Prince of Wales in 1400, Glyndŵr rose in north Wales, helped by dissatisfaction with the financial demands of English landowners. Henry IV led an army into Wales, but Glyndŵr avoided battle and in 1401 invaded central Wales, although he was unsuccessful at Caernarfon. Fresh victories against marcher forces and unsuccessful though destructive advances by royal armies were followed by negotiations with English opponents of Henry and unsuccessful attempts to win Scottish, Irish and French support. Carmarthen and most of south Wales were captured in 1403, Cardiff, Harlech and Aberystwyth in 1404. Glyndŵr sealed a treaty of alliance with the French who promised assistance, and sought to organise regular government, as well as an independent church and universities. A Welsh Parliament was summoned, while some of the English marchers bought peace from Welsh raids by truces. In 1405 Glyndŵr agreed the Tripartite Indenture with Edmund Mortimer and Henry Percy, Earl of Northumberland, by which they were to depose Henry IV and divide England. Glyndŵr's share included, besides Wales, England west of a line from the Mersey to the source of the Trent and then to the Severn just north of Worcester.

A French expeditionary force arrived in 1405 and Carmarthen fell for the second time, but the French then faltered in the face of

English naval power. In 1405 Glyndŵr, with French help, advanced as far as Worcester, but then withdrew. Although another of Henry IV's expeditions achieved very little, his vigorous son Prince Hal, later Henry V, began to inflict serious defeats. Harlech and Aberystwyth were recaptured in 1408 and the south entirely reconquered. Support for the rebellion ebbed and the English were increasingly successful.

Glyndŵr disappeared in 1415. He has recently served as a potent symbol of Welsh nationalism, and is certainly more appropriate than the princely house of Gwynedd, whose members, albeit through necessity, spent much of their energy fighting each other and other Welsh rulers. There was however a strong opposition to him among some native gentry too; they saw alliance with the English Crown as the best way to maintain their privileges. Glyndŵr was a warrior of his times, who used devastation without remorse. The cathedrals of St Asaph and Bangor were burnt down, as were Cardiff and Carmarthen, but Prince Hal also brought widespread destruction, and the English had often used this technique. The destruction of homes and farm implements and the seizure of farm animals were the equivalent for many, especially the weak, of sentences of death or at least severe hardship and malnutrition. Glyndŵr, heavily outnumbered, prudently avoided battle on many occasions and his military career was not conventionally heroic. More significantly, he was leading his followers towards a dead end. English power was such that it was only during periods of English civil conflict, such as the Percy rising of 1403, that it was possible for Welsh opponents to make much headway. At other times, the weight of English resources told. Had Glyndŵr been more successful, it would have exposed Wales to decades of incessant conflict and the Welsh to deep divisions. Like many leaders, he was more useful as a dead symbol for posterity.

The rising was not followed by new governmental arrangements. The marcher lords remained the crucial political figures; the Welsh second-class subjects. The penal laws of Henry IV forbade the Welsh to hold land in boroughs and the marriage of Welsh men and English women. In the new charter that Lord Charlton of Powys gave Welshpool in 1406 great care was taken to keep the 'foreign Welsh' away.

Yet the penal laws were generally a dead letter after the revolt: Wales could not be governed without the leaders of the native community. Furthermore, from the fourteenth century, social changes were working to the emergence of a Welsh gentry class. The Black Death was instrumental in breaking down the old landowning patterns. Kindred patrimonies (*gwelyau*) and the equality of status that was their central feature declined in favour of individual ownership. Inheritance and tenurial changes, especially the expansion of primogeniture and greater freedom in the disposal of land, facilitated the development of freehold estates and landholders gained wealth through military or administrative service or marriage. They acquired Crown lands, built substantial dwellings and developed political pretensions within the framework of an English-governed Wales. The bards sustained a sense of Welsh identity, although not in anglicised regions such as South Pembrokeshire and Gower, but those who were politically significant did not see this identity in terms of independence. As the tribal clans broke up, patterns of identity altered. Within the principality royal authority had replaced that of the clan in the maintenance of law and order. As almost all of the march was now in the hands of magnates, Wales was involved in the Wars of the Roses, and Welsh leaders were moving on to a wider political stage.

LATER MEDIEVAL SCOTLAND

The wars of independence (1296–1357) secured the independence and territorial integrity of Scotland, and this helped develop a sense of national consciousness. A distinct Scottish ecclesiastical province was created by the Lateran Council of 1215. John Barbour's poem, the *Brus*, composed in Scots in 1375, was an anti-English national epic centring on Robert the Bruce and the 'freedom' of Scotland. Other late-medieval histories of Scotland – the *Chronicle of the Scottish People* by John Fordun (1380s), the *Orgynale Cronikil* by Andrew Wyntoun (1410s) and the *Scotichronicon* by Walter Bower (1440s) – were produced to show that Scotland was a distinct state with its own history. It was also a relatively successful state. Scotland was far poorer and less populous than England, its agriculture less developed and without an important export comparable to English wool or later cloth. Scottish government was less sophisticated than that of England; its armies were smaller. Local administration and justice was left to the nobility.

Some powerful magnates, such as the Earls of Douglas in the Borders, had increased their possessions and power during the wars of independence and this restricted royal authority. The Mac-Donalds, Lords of the Isles and Earls of Ross, were similarly powerful in west-coast Scotland. Yet in 1452–5 James II was able to crush the main branch of the Douglases, in 1476 James III gained Ross and in 1493 James IV destroyed the MacDonalds' position and extended his authority to the Hebrides. These gains were achieved with the help of most nobles, who did not see the kings as threats to their position.

England remained a problem for the Scottish monarchs, not least because their usual alliance with France, the Auld Alliance, brought them into conflict with her. James I was an English captive in 1406–24; James II died when a wedge blew out during the bombardment of English-held Roxburgh Castle in 1460; James IV was killed at the battle of Flodden when he invaded in 1513. Conflict and confrontation with England were expensive, for example the naval race of the early sixteenth century. The *Great Michael*, an enormous warship built for James IV in 1511, cost £30,000 Scots to construct and had running costs of £668 monthly at a time when annual royal income was less than £4,000 per year. There were no other foreign commitments. The Viking presence finally disappeared: James III gained Orkney and the Shetlands by his 1469 marriage to Margaret of Denmark.

It would be mistaken to exaggerate Scotland's political success. Its monarchs faced serious political challenges. James I, who had only gained power in 1425 by destroying the power of the former regent, his uncle the Duke of Albany, was murdered in an attempted coup in 1437. His reign and that of his successors saw a fair number of judicial executions of opponents, such as Albany, or the Livingstones in 1450. James II personally stabbed William, Eighth Earl of Douglas to death in 1452 while the Earl was under the king's safe-conduct. James III faced serious aristocratic opposition from 1479 led by his royal brothers. In 1488, unable to muster sufficient support, he was killed shortly after his defeat at Sauchieburn at the hands of a rebel force under the standard of his own son, then still a minor. The rebels took over the government, and in turn had to face rebellion in 1489. Given such problems at the centre, the stress on local control of much administration was prudent. Yet in Scotland, as in England, the striking feature of most fifteenth-century violence was the attempt to seize control of the central government, generally in the person of the monarch. Political instability essentially arose not from challenges to the power of the state but rather from the emergence of two rival factions within the royal family which competed with each other for dominance in government from 1384. There was no doubt of the integrity of the state, and this national political consciousness was fortified by the frequency with which Parliament met in Scotland. James IV substantially increased the royal revenues, remained popular and brought considerable harmony to Scottish politics, although he used his position to follow an ultimately unsuccessful attempt to increase his international standing. There was a renaissance of the Scottish court under James IV and James V.

ECONOMY AND SOCIETY IN FIFTEENTH-CENTURY ENGLAND

The difficulties of the agrarian economy following the Black Death created problems for most landlords until the 1470s. Rents fell, serfdom declined, villages were abandoned and the lynchets that permitted the cultivation of steep slopes were deserted. The trade of most markets and fairs declined. Economic problems led to places being allowed a reduction of their tax assessments. However, the scarcity of labour resulting from endemic plague brought advantages to those of the peasantry that were able to exploit it, not least because of the decline of serfdom. The labour-rent of unfree peasants was generally commuted into money payments, and they were thus integrated directly into the money economy. Several foreign visitors commented on the prosperity of England as a whole, not just of London. Labour shortages also encouraged a shift to pastoral farming, which needed fewer workers. Landlords enclosed their land for sheep farming, leading to rural depopulation in counties such as Lincolnshire. The severity of this situation was such that conversion of tilled land to pasture was made an offence by Parliament in 1489.

The spread of pasture led to a growth in wool and then in cloth exports. The English had developed breeds of sheep with particularly good wool, much sought after by the cloth-manufacturing centres of Flanders, and the wool trade had grown during the thirteenth century, bringing prosperity to towns such as Shrews-bury. From the fourteenth century, however, the wool was increasingly exported in the form of cloth. Great Yarmouth, for example, was responsible for three-quarters of the country's exports of worsted cloth, 12,000 worsteds passing through it in the tax year 1400–1. The growth in wool and cloth exports brought wealth to such East Anglian cloth centres as Hadleigh, Lavenham and Long Melford and was reflected in their substantial churches. Economic shifts also accentuated social differentiation. Thus in Suffolk in 1327 there were only 28 parishes where one person contributed 30 per cent or more of the total tax paid; by 1524 there were more than 180.

Wool and cloth exports also helped to keep England's trade in balance, were vital to governmental finances and helped to finance English participation in the Hundred Years War. In addition they helped to accentuate the relative wealth of south-eastern England, increasingly the centre of power.

MEDIEVAL ENGLISH CULTURE

Cultural links after 1066 were very much with France. The conquest moved England from the Scandinavian to the western continental cultural sphere. Yet it would be wrong to neglect Norman adaptability. If buildings begun between 1066 and 1100 displayed distinctly Norman features, while few of the Anglo-Saxon decorative traditions were continued, the situation altered after 1100 with the revival of Anglo-Saxon workshops and styles and the creation of a vibrant Anglo-Norman style.

It was not until the fourteenth century that vernacular (English or Scots, not French or Latin) literature developed. This led to major works in English: the anonymous *Gawain and the Green Knight*, Geoffrey Chaucer's *Canterbury Tales* (c.1387), William Langland's *Piers Plowman* (1362–92), and Thomas Malory's *Morte d'Arthur* (1469), as well as ballads, carols and mystery plays. The Scottish poet Robert Henryson wrote a number of fine works in the vernacular, including the *Testament of Cresseid*. Much literature, however, continued to be written in Latin.

There were other aspects of vitality. A native architectural style, the Perpendicular, was predominant from c.1370 until the mid-1500s, and was seen in soaring works with large windows and fan vaulting, such as the chapel of King's College Cambridge. A distinctive style of English music, with composers such as William Cornish, John Dunstable and Walter Frye, attracted continental attention. Minstrel performances and itinerant troupes of players offered a secular counterpart to religious 'mystery plays'. The first known example of the former in Lancashire occurred in 1352–3. England was still very much part of an international cultural world, but it was playing a more active role within it.

RELIGION IN MEDIEVAL ENGLAND

The Norman Conquest had brought England into the mainstream of western Christendom, exposing it to the new religious impulses of the eleventh and twelfth centuries, such as new monastic orders and the crusades. The English Church was subject legally, and to a large extent in practice, to the papacy. The clergy owed loyalty to two masters, the king and the pope. International religious links led to clerics following careers abroad and their counterparts doing so in the British Isles. The spread of new monastic orders and of the friars affected the British Isles: the Dominicans and the Franciscans arrived in England in the 1220s. A less attractive aspect of Britain's role in Western Christendom was anti-semitism, which flourished on the Continent from the 1090s. The first reference to Jews in England is later, in the early twelfth century, but thereafter anti-semitism became a feature of English life, culminating in Edward I's expulsion of the Jews in 1290. William of Norwich in 1144 may be the first instance of a child whose murder was falsely blamed upon Jews. Anti-semitism reflected a hostility to aliens that became a readily apparent feature of medieval society.

Several kings clashed with papal pretensions. John's refusal to accept the pope's choice of archbishop of Canterbury led to England being placed under an interdict, with all church services suspended in 1208. There was hostility to foreign ecclesiastical jurisdiction and to the movement of funds abroad, and legislation in the fourteenth century was designed to establish limits on papal rights: the Statutes of Provisors (1351) and *Praemunire* (1393).

Anti-clericalism was exploited by the Lollard movement, which was inspired by John Wycliff (d. 1384), a radical Oxford theologian who denied the need for priestly intercession between God and man, the pope's temporal authority and the doctrine of transubstantiation. Wycliff emphasised the authority of scripture and criticised the wealth of the monastic orders. He was condemned by the pope and the English Church. Lollardy was persecuted after Wycliff's death, especially after the failure of a Lollard conspiracy in 1414. The Church played a central role in society, not least as the crucial source of education, health and social welfare. Medieval hospitals were, for example, primarily religious institutions, offering warmth, food and shelter rather than clinical treatment.

The popularity and vitality of the late-medieval English Church are controversial issues. Some historians stress its popularity and vitality and argue that the Reformation was therefore widely unpopular; other scholars are not so sure. The liturgy of the faith can be seen as central to people's lives, giving them meaning and beauty, or anti-clericalism can be stressed. It is possible to emphasise the corporate nature of worship, especially the mass, or to stress the argument that it was becoming more individual, with private prayers directing attention from the Latin liturgy enunciated by the priest. Traditional practices and beliefs were supported by a host of verbal and visual narratives, including carols, mystery plays, stained-glass windows, statues and wall paintings. That was why their subsequent abolition and destruction during the Reformation were so important. What is clear is that fifteenth-century English Christianity was still very much part of an international church, and that disquiet about some aspects of its position and about the existence of the Lollard heresy increased the sense of unease of the period.

HENRY IV, 1399–1413

Henry IV had moved boldly to seize the throne, but once he had replaced and then murdered Richard II he was confronted by a number of acute problems. The most serious at first was Owain Glyndŵr's rising in Wales, but Henry also faced the fragmentation of the English position in Ireland, French attacks on the English possessions in Aquitaine, difficulties with Scotland and serious opposition in England. Henry's seizure of the throne was helped by Richard II's childlessness, but his claim to the throne was debatable, certainly far worse than that of Edward III when Edward II was removed.

Henry was challenged within England by a mighty magnate family, the Percys, who wielded great power in the north. The Percys had backed Henry's seizure of the throne, but, angry with his refusal to do as they wanted, they rebelled in 1403 and allied with Glyndŵr. Henry IV responded vigorously, defeating and killing the Percy heir, 'Hotspur', Sir Henry Percy, at the battle of Shrewsbury and forcing his father, the Earl of Northumberland, to disband his forces. In 1405 Northumberland organised a new rebellion with Glyndŵr, Archbishop Scrope of York and Edmund Mortimer, Earl of March, who had a good hereditary claim to the throne as he was descended from Edward III's third son, compared to Henry's descent from the fourth. Glyndŵr, Northumberland and March agreed to divide England in three, but Henry quelled their rebellion, as he quelled that by Northumberland in 1408. The Earl was defeated and killed on Bramham Moor. These years of conspiracy and rebellion indicate the problems created by Henry's seizure of the throne: royal prestige had been greatly lessened. It is also clear that it is misleading to think of later medieval English politics in terms of the progressive extension of the role of Parliament. Indeed, in the fifteenth century Parliament was far less important than aristocratic factionalism.

HENRY V, 1413–22

Henry IV's eldest son, the dynamic Prince Hal, took a leading role in the fighting of his father's reign, both in England and Wales. As ruler, Henry V was a warrior king. He easily crushed a Lollard conspiracy organised by Sir John Oldcastle (1414) and an attempt organised by the Earl of Cambridge to proclaim the Earl of March king (1415). Rather than trying to advance English interests in Ireland or Scotland, Henry then turned to the more glamorous goal of conquering the parts of France recognised as Edward III's by the Treaty of Brétigny. After careful preparations, he invaded Normandy in 1415, captured the port of Harfleur and then set off to march overland to Calais. A far larger French army sought to block him at Agincourt, but, as at Crécy in 1346, the English archers smashed the successive advances of the French cavalry, mounted and on foot, inflicting crippling losses.

Agincourt helped to make Henry and the war popular in England, and he followed it up by conquering Normandy in 1417–19.

This led Henry to renew the claim to the French throne. The French were affected by civil war and in 1419 the powerful Duke of Burgundy joined Henry. The following year Henry's victories led to his betrothal to Catherine, the daughter of Charles VI of France. By the Treaty of Troyes (1420) Charles recognised Henry as his heir and as regent during his reign. Henry V wanted to be accepted by the French as their ruler, not as a conqueror. Charles's son, the Dauphin, continued, however, to resist and Henry died in 1422 on campaign near Paris, possibly of dysentery. It is unclear what he might have achieved had he lived, but his ambitions are a useful reminder of the danger of assuming that the future state structure of western Europe was clear. Indeed Parliament expressed anxiety about keeping the two crowns separate and preventing England from becoming a satellite of a France ruled by the same monarch. Henry brought medieval English kingship to a peak of achievement and fame, successfully operating not only as a military leader, but also in relations with the nobility and clergy, in the restoration of public order, as a manager of Parliament and as an active administrator. Henry had far fewer problems with Parliament than his father. He was concerned to maintain justice and order, and was devoted to the Church. Henry viewed the Lollards as both heretical and seditious. The king's heroic image reflected not only his martial character and achievements, but also his promotion of English nationhood: Henry emphasised England's history and role, supported the cult of English saints and furthered the official use of the English language.

HENRY VI, 1422–61, 1470–1

Henry V's death left his son, Henry, king, though only nine months old. Later in 1422 he was also proclaimed king of France on the death of his grandfather, Charles VI. One uncle, John, Duke of Bedford, became regent and sought to maintain Henry V's impetus and to defeat another uncle, Charles VI's son, now Charles VII. The English had much success by 1429, winning for example a major victory at Verneuil (1424). French resistance revived, however, when a charismatic peasant girl, Joan of Arc, inspired Charles VII. In 1429 an army led by Joan lifted the English siege of the strategic fortress of Orléans, and Charles was crowned at Rheims.

In response Henry was crowned at Paris in 1430, and the captured Joan was burned as a witch (1431). It was too late. The balance of military success had moved. Once the English cause faltered opposition to the war increased in England and allies wavered in France. The Burgundians had handed Joan over and had secured English control of Paris, but in 1435 they abandoned Henry VI. The English lost Paris the following year. After Bedford's death in 1435, the English suffered from poor leadership and were driven back by the French. Maine was lost in 1444. In 1449–51 Normandy and Gascony fell rapidly to Charles VII's stronger army, not least his impressive train of artillery. This brought victory in battle over English archers (Formigny, 1450) and the speedy fall of fortified positions. An English counter-offensive was crushed by the French at Castillon (1453).

France was lost. Calais was held until 1558 and the Channel Islands are British to this day. The claim to the French throne was only abandoned in the reign of George III (also, although more realistically, the last king in America), but these were faint echoes of a centuries-long link. A crucial precondition of the modern history of the British Isles was the more insular character of England after 1453. It was to be one of the keys to its subsequent domestic and international development.

WARS OF THE ROSES, 1450–87

The civil conflicts of late-fifteenth-century England are given a misleading coherence by being called the Wars of the Roses. This is an unhelpful term, both because the 'Lancastrian red' rose and the 'Yorkist white' were not the sole identifications employed and also because the struggle between the families of Lancaster and York for the throne was but one theme in the conflict of the period. Violence began not in 1455 when Richard, Duke of York attacked nobles close to Henry VI and his wife, Margaret of Anjou, at the battle of St Albans, but five years earlier when the chief minister, William, First Duke of Suffolk, was murdered on a boat in the English Channel, having been impeached in Parliament and banished, and when a major uprising took place in Kent. The two events reflected the political crisis of Henry VI's government. Suffolk was a court favourite, unpopular because he had monopolised patronage. Cade's Rebellion reflected widespread discontent at a government seen as corrupt at home and defeated abroad. Before being crushed, the rebels defeated a royal army at Sevenoaks, captured London and executed hated officials. There were also widespread disturbances in south and west England, including the killing of the bishop of Salisbury and attacks on Church property in Hampshire, Wiltshire and Dorset.

Henry VI was a poor leader; incompetent and ineffectual, he eventually went mad. He lacked the vigour and success that had enabled his two predecessors to overcome the weak Lancastrian claim and in the Duke of York he faced a determined exponent of a rival and better dynastic claim to the succession of Edward III: York was descended from Edward's third son. Henry's partisanship in disputes between nobles compromised his royal status so that the royal government could not provide unity among the nobles, and thus stability and peace; and his vicious wife was a determined supporter of faction.

Distrust within the elite was exacerbated by violence, creating blood feuds, for example between the houses of Beaufort and York, or the struggle for dominance in the north between the Nevilles and the Percys. The price of failure was often death. After the battle of Wakefield (1460) Richard of York's severed head, adorned with a paper crown, was publicly displayed. Henry VI's only child, Edward, Prince of Wales, was killed by the Yorkists at the battle of Tewkesbury (1471). Failure could also lead to loss of power, privilege, property and influence. It was not, therefore, surprising that there was a determination to win, a conviction of the importance of seizing power. This affected the claimants to the throne, as well as powerful nobles, such as Richard Neville, Earl of Warwick, the 'kingmaker'; although it was also the case that some nobles did not take part in the wars, a group that was even larger in 1485 when Richard III and Henry Tudor fought for the throne.

The clashes of the 1450s became more serious in 1460 when the Yorkist victory at the battle of Northampton led York to claim the throne. Henry VI was captured, but Margaret and Prince Edward were still at large. York set out to defeat them, but was killed at Wakefield. His ambitious eldest son, Edward, realising that compromise with Margaret was impossible, then claimed the throne. Margaret followed her victory at Wakefield by defeating Warwick, then a Yorkist, at St Albans (1461), and releasing Henry VI; but

London defied her and she then retreated north in the face of Edward's advance. The two sides clashed at Towton (1461), the battle with the most combatants yet fought on English soil. The Lancastrians were heavily defeated and Edward IV (1461–83) then reigned with few problems until he fell out with Warwick in 1469. The two differed over Edward's growing independence, both in foreign policy and over his favour for his wife's relations, the Woodvilles. Warwick defeated Edward at Edgecote (1469) and gained power, only to lose it in 1470 and flee to France. He was there reconciled to a fellow exile, Margaret, and committed himself to restoring Henry VI.

With French help, Warwick and Edward IV's discontented brother, George, Duke of Clarence, invaded in 1470. An outmanoeuvred Edward fled into exile and Henry was restored. In 1471, however, Edward invaded and defeated Warwick in thick fog at the battle of Barnet and Margaret at Tewkesbury. Warwick was killed at Barnet. Edward's position was further secured when Henry VI was killed while imprisoned in the Tower of London. Thereafter England was more stable under Edward IV than it had been under Henry VI, but there were problems both from Lancastrian supporters and within the royal family. Clarence had betrayed Warwick in 1471 but was killed in the Tower in 1478 for plotting against Edward, according to contemporaries drowned in a butt (barrel) of malmsey wine.

Edward died at 40, too early to allow his young son, Edward V, to establish himself on the throne. Edward IV's surviving brother, Richard, Duke of Gloucester, had his nephews declared bastards, became king as Richard III (1483–5) and sent the young princes to the Tower where they swiftly disappeared. They were probably murdered, though the subject is still controversial. Richard III was very capable, but widely distrusted. He divided the Yorkists by seizing the throne, had only a narrow base of support and couldn't trust the uncommitted. The Woodvilles rebelled unsuccessfully in 1483, as did Henry, Duke of Buckingham, who had played a crucial role in Richard's seizure of the throne. Having abandoned his new master, Buckingham was captured and executed.

In 1485 the lottery of military fortune and dynastic extinction brought Henry Tudor to the throne of England. Henry was a quarter Welsh. His grandfather, Owain, from the Tudors of Penmynydd, a leading Welsh family of officials and earlier the leading servants of the rulers of Gwynedd prior to 1282, had married Henry V's widow; his father, Edmund, had married Margaret Beaufort, the heiress of the cadet Lancastrian line. The main line had been cut short with the deaths of Henry VI and his son Edward, and Henry Tudor was thus the unlikely bearer of Lancastrian hopes against the house of York.

In 1485 Henry Tudor invaded with the help of French troops. The unpopular Richard III was only supported by a few nobles, and crucial betrayals at the battle of Bosworth gave Henry victory and the throne. Henry himself had even less aristocratic support than Richard; indifference and fear characterised a country exhausted by civil war. Had Richard triumphed he might have been able to consolidate his position: despite his unpopularity, he would have faced no strong Lancastrian claimant. However, the death of the childless Richard at Bosworth and the earlier deaths of the princes in the Tower and of Clarence gravely weakened the Yorkists and helped Henry to establish the new Tudor dynasty.

Nevertheless, Bosworth did not end the Wars of the Roses. Lambert Simnel and Perkin Warbeck claimed, respectively, to be Clarence's son, Edward, Earl of Warwick, then held in the Tower, and the younger of the sons of Edward IV who had in fact died in the Tower. They were supported by domestic and foreign opponents of Henry, who had to fight to retain the throne. Simnel's army was defeated at Stoke (1487), the last battle of the Wars of the Roses, and Warbeck, a major nuisance around whom malcontents congregated, was captured (1497) and hanged (1499). Yorkist plots continued, centred on the de la Pole family, but the situation was more stable than it had been for decades. Henry's marriage in 1486 to Elizabeth of York, daughter of Edward IV, helped to unify the two factions, a process symbolised by the replacement of the roses of Lancaster and York by the Tudor rose.

HENRY VII, 1485–1509

Like Charles II in 1660–85, Henry's essential aim was to avoid having to go on his travels again. He manoeuvred skilfully, both at home and abroad, and improved the effectiveness of the existing governmental machinery. Henry took an active role, personally supervising the administration and reasserting monarchical control over the nobility. The Crown's feudal rights and judicial authority were both reasserted, as was its position in the localities. Henry ruled with vigour: rebel estates were confiscated, he was unwilling to delegate his authority and he placed people under bonds for good behaviour. Governmental finances were dramatically improved, so that Henry VII left a modest fortune on his death, and law and order were enhanced. The private armed forces of nobles were limited. Henry was careful not to get involved in lengthy hostilities abroad. A short war with France was ended on satisfactory terms in 1492, and thereafter Henry negotiated to some effect, enabling England to become an important, albeit second-rank, power in European diplomacy.

When Henry had landed at Milford Haven in 1485 he had promised to restore the Welsh to their liberties and free them from 'miserable servitudes'. His victory at Bosworth appeared to vindicate the prophecies of the bards about Welsh greatness and had a great psychological importance to the Welsh; there was a feeling that Llywelyn had been avenged and that new doors of opportunity had opened. Changes were indeed made: there were extensive concessions of the benefits of common law to the Welsh, while some Welshmen were appointed as bishops and took a major role in civil administration. In 1489 the title Prince of Wales was revived for Henry's son, who was significantly named Arthur (he predeceased his father). Following a precedent of 1471, a council covering Wales and nearby counties under Arthur was established at Ludlow, although it was dominated by English administrators. Nevertheless, a political focus that was more immediate than distant London had been created for Wales. Opportunities were created for ambitious Welshmen, thus serving to develop an alliance between the Crown and the more active gentry.

NEW MONARCHY?

Yet major change in Wales, as elsewhere in Britain, awaited the Reformation crisis. The England of the Yorkists and Henry VII is often seen as one of the 'new monarchies', experiencing a similar development to the France of Louis XI (1461–83) and the Aragon of Ferdinand (1479–1516). It is, however, unclear how far new monarchy was really novel and based on a plan for establishing stronger royal authority and a more effective centrally directed administrative system, or whether it was substantially a matter of re-establishing royal power after a period of disruption; for France, Aragon, Castile and Scotland also experienced civil conflict at the same time as the Wars of the Roses. Certainly the process by which municipal, county and Crown officials gained authority, leading to more effective social control, was very long-term, dating back to the stabilisation of government from the reign of Henry II on. The 'new monarchs' in Britain needed their nobility: they might break individual nobles but there was no anti-aristocratic policy. It is appropriate not to exaggerate change within the period 1460–1560 prior to the Reformation crisis, and instead to focus on the political problems and responses created by that crisis.

4

The Sixteenth Century

The sixteenth, like all centuries in the modern history of the British Isles, was a century of significant change. The particular importance of the period was that it witnessed a new emphasis on religious division, one that created serious problems at home and abroad, and that there was a related stress on relations between the parts of the British Isles. It is also significant in the long term that England developed trans-oceanic interests and ambitions, not least in the New World. First, however, it is appropriate to turn to the condition of the people.

SOCIAL AND ECONOMIC DEVELOPMENTS

The central fact affecting the lot of the British in the sixteenth and early seventeenth centuries was that there were more of them. The population of Wales, for example, rose from about 226,000 in the 1540s to about 342,000 in 1670; that of Scotland to about one million by 1650. The biggest increase was in England – the population more than doubled from under 2.5 million to about 5 million by 1651, thus increasing England's strength within the British Isles. The large size of the Irish population helped to underline its threat in English eyes. The population increase was due largely to a fall in mortality, though by modern standards mortality was still very high; while a rise in fertility due to a small decrease in the age of marriage was probably also important.

A rise in population led to a growth in economic demand. Former common land was enclosed, leading to riots, while the area of cultivation was extended. Yet economic expansion put pressure on living standards. The labour shortage, high wages and low rents of the late medieval period were replaced by a price inflation that had an even greater effect from its following a period that had known scant inflation. Much of the peasantry lost status and became little different from poorly paid wage-labourers. Enclosure reflected not just capitalist opportunity but also a decline in paternal responsibility on the part of landlords, for example in Norfolk gentry sheep farmers such as the Townshends benefited at the expense of tenants and lesser farmers. Although the impact of enclosure was very varied by region, in the sixteenth century it was generally designed to promote pastoral rather than arable farming.

Inflation in England was exacerbated by the debasement and increase in volume of the coinage. Rents and food prices rose faster than wages in England, and this pressed hard on tenants and on those with little or no land. Very little data is available for Scotland. The high prices that helped English landowners also hit the poor. This led to a growth in the number of paupers and vagrants which greatly concerned the Tudors. The 1495 Act Against Vagabonds and Beggars was only the first of a number of statutes, including a series of poor laws (1531, 1536, 1572, 1598, 1601). Compulsory poor rates were introduced in 1572, an act of 1597 encouraged the provision of 'Abiding and working Houses' and in 1598 the relief of poverty was made the responsibility of the individual parish; but the situation was harsh, particularly for able-bodied men unable to find work, who were treated as rogues and vagabonds. The Poor Relief Act of 1662 established that the right to relief was dependent upon the pauper being settled in the parish, a practice that led to the expulsion of paupers deemed nonresident. The system lasted until the Poor Law Amendment Act of 1834 which introduced the comprehensive workhouse system. In Scotland there was a licensed begging system, a blue badge granting the right to beg in one's home parish.

Economic pressure led to widespread malnutrition among the poor and to some starvation. Most folktales centred on peasant poverty and in many the need and wish to have an inexhaustible quantity of food is a central theme. Economic problems led to social pressure on the weaker members of the community and those judged most marginal, for example to measures against illegitimacy and bridal pregnancy, to the insistence on a formal church wedding as the sole source of marital legitimacy and to attempts in some parishes to prevent the poor from marrying. Churchwardens policed moral conduct. It was in this context of social tension and coercion that concern about alleged witchcraft developed.

The poor were harshly treated by man and nature alike. They ate less and less well than the wealthier members of the community, and their housing was of low standard. Everywhere the malnutrition of the poor reduced their resistance to ill-health. Whereas the wealthy might choose to seek compromise in their disputes with each other, they generally showed no such willingness in disputes with their social inferiors. Social, political, economic and moral intimidation were frequently the lot of the poor.

Unless through crime, charity or as servants, the poor were certainly cut off from the growing affluence and comfort of the wealthy, with their finer clothes and larger houses. Yet the highly public life of wealthy families made their affluence very visible to the poor: a powerful message of the nature of the social order. The gentry were an important source of employment and patronage, and wealth was also spreading down the social scale to the yeomanry. There were more clothes and furniture, more musical instruments and medicaments than a century earlier. Growing wealth had cultural and social consequences. There was much new building, particularly in brick in England. In Scotland there was much building in stone in the sixteenth century; bricks were only used in ports that traded with the Low Countries, such as Aberdeen where bricks were built into stone houses, particularly near the harbour. More material consumption was seen as a major cause of what was regarded with concern as a significant rise in crime. The breakdown of master–servant relations in a more volatile and less paternalistic society was also partly responsible.

The newly wealthy Welsh gentry built prestigious houses, entertained liberally, showed great interest in sometimes spurious genealogical studies and sought to adopt a code of aristocratic conduct. They were very interested in education, which secured their gentility, distinguished them from the rest of the community and provided valuable legal skills. Some discarded the Welsh language and ceased to patronise bardic culture, but many did not. The Celtic interest in lineage was matched elsewhere: this was a society that emphasised the connections and status of blood as well as inheritance.

In England and Scotland aristocrats and gentlemen built stately homes in new styles that reflected their wealth and status and also particularly in England, the more peaceful nature of the state English, and to a lesser extent Scottish, aristocratic homes wer no longer built like fortresses. Instead, houses such as Hardwick Hall, described by contemporaries as 'more glass than wall', and Longleat, had massive windows. Landscaping in gardens and park strengthened and reflected ideas of order and hierarchy. Hierarch and the control of the countryside was also reflected in the limita tions of rights to hunting by the English Game Acts of 1485 and 1604. Freeholders lost ancient rights to hunt on their own land thanks to the greater property qualifications introduced by th second act. Scottish social organisation remained more tradition ally feudal.

Printing brought books, offering the possibility of a more privat and individual culture than that provided by the conspicuous con sumption and display of court splendour, public ceremonial an elaborate buildings. The first book printed in England was pub lished by William Caxton in 1474. Scotland gained its first printin press in 1507. A new reading public bought books, includin religious literature, and helped to spur rising literacy. There wa also more money available for cultural and leisure activities. Th Theatre, the first purpose-built public playhouse in England, wa opened in London in 1576 and the Globe in 1599. The Lor Chamberlain's Men, a theatrical company in which William Sha kespeare (1564–1616) had a stake, produced plays at both theatre The degree to which theatrical companies were patronised b aristocrats such as the Lord Chamberlain and the Earl of Esse demonstrated the social leadership of the nobility. Theatre deve oped in Scotland, although essentially in a court setting, with work by, for example, Sir David Lindsay. Shakespeare himself responde to the possibilities offered by economic development, buying u local property and pursuing his debtors in court and possibl speculating in grain. Although the drama of the age is principall remembered in terms of his plays, the London market was larg enough to support other playwrights, including, in the late si teenth century, Thomas Dekker, Robert Greene, Thomas Kid and Christopher Marlowe and, early in the following centur Francis Beaumont, John Fletcher, Ben Jonson, Philip Massinge Thomas Middleton, William Rowley and John Webster.

The vitality of contemporary London was a major theme in their plays, as was the wealth and social pretension of groups in society. Urban growth was the most obvious aspect of population increase, not least because it reflected both natural increase and migration from the countryside. By 1665 about 20–25 per cent of the English population was urban. London's population rose from about 50,000 in 1500 to about 500,000 in 1700. It did so without serious unrest until the mid-seventeenth century, in part because of the cohesion of the city's elite and their willingness to respond to social ideals of reciprocal rights and obligations. Poor relief, though limited, thus contributed to social control in London. Urban growth fostered urban culture, as in the spread of theatre or the increase in the number and importance of town halls. Supplying the towns helped to fuel economic activity elsewhere in the country. Thus the coal industry in the north-east of England developed in the late sixteenth century in order to supply London. In the fifteenth century, 15,000 tons of coal were shipped annually from the Tyne; by 1625 400,000 tons. Both Gresham's Exchange and the Bourse were constructed in London, providing new focuses for economic activity. Edinburgh grew to about 30–35,000 people in 1700, certainly then the second city in Britain, if not well before.

Throughout the British Isles, though most obviously in England and Wales, the role of the market economy became more insistent and consistent and increasingly affected areas that had formerly been characterised by subsistence agriculture and poverty. Welsh cattle and sheep were driven to English markets, especially London. The scale of cattle droving, which had been a major source of wealth interchange between the Scottish Highlands and Lowlands, rose greatly. An increasing number of animals were to find their way to England, although it is possible to argue that in the sixteenth century the Scottish economy was still autonomous. More Welsh coal was mined and exported: Swansea's annual exports rose from about 1,800 tons in the 1550s to about 7,700 in 1640. Lead mining in Cardiganshire developed under Elizabeth I, while copper, iron and slate production also expanded in Wales. Regional variations in prices in the British Isles became less pronounced than in the medieval period. The enclosure of land in County Durham during the seventeenth century, so that it could be more easily cultivated and adapted to new agricultural methods, was a response to the rise in population associated with the development of lead and coal mining. Similarly, lead mining developed considerably in Derbyshire.

HENRY VIII (1509–47) AND THE REFORMATION

The growing extent to which a national economy was being created in England and Wales, feeding in particular the demand of the prosperous south-east of England, matched the greater political control being exercised by that region, both within England and in the British Isles. This owed much to the political dimensions of the Reformation crisis. Henry VIII greatly strengthened the state enough for it to survive the problems subsequently posed by the accession of a minor, two single women and a new, foreign dynasty. He sought both to gain and to exercise authority.

There was little sign at the accession of the young Henry VIII that his reign would be so dominated by religious issues. The Lollard heresy had had scant lasting impact, and, although criticism of the wealth and privileges of the church had long been widespread, there were also many signs of popular piety, including much church building and the active veneration of local saints.

Henry VII had gained his throne by conflict, but had little personal interest in warfare. Henry VIII, in contrast, saw himself as a warrior king. In his early years he devoted most of his energy to the highly competitive international relations of the period, a form of conspicuous display and dynastic pride rather than national interest. Henry campaigned in person against the French in 1513 and 1523, winning the battle of the Spurs in 1513. His leading minister, Thomas Wolsey, the clever and greedy son of an Ipswich butcher, rose simultaneously through Church and state thanks to Henry's favour, becoming Archbishop of York (1514), a cardinal (1515) and Lord Chancellor (1515–29). Wolsey was no sweeping innovator, but instead provided the funds for Henry's expensive foreign policy. Warfare, however, with its new costs of numerous cannon and attendant new fortifications and warships, created serious financial problems. In 1525 the attempt to levy an 'amicable grant' to pay for Henry's foreign policy, led to riots and the abandonment of the tax.

Henry's position was challenged more by dynastic concerns than by popular hostility. His failure to have a legitimate son posed serious problem for the continuity of the dynasty. Henry's first wife, Catherine of Aragon, had borne five children, but only a daughter, Mary, survived. In England, unlike France, rule by a woman was legal, but there was concern about how successful it might be. Henry was trying to end his marriage before he fell in love with Anne Boleyn. The papacy was unwilling to comply with Henry's demand for the annulment of his marriage because Catherine's nephew was Emperor Charles V, the most powerful ruler in Italy. Henry's mounting anger led first to the fall of Wolsey in 1529 and subsequently to the rejection of papal jurisdiction over the English Church. The preamble to the Act in Restraint of Appeals [to Rome] of 1533 declared: 'this realm of England is an empire, and so hath been accepted in the world, governed by one supreme head and king having the dignity and royal estate of the imperial crown of the same.'

This was the first claim of imperial status for the realm, rather than the Crown. By being declared an empire, England was proclaimed as jurisdictionally self-sufficient. The sovereignty of law made in Parliament was established by Henry. In 1534 the term 'majesty' appeared for the first time in statutes and proclamations, and, by the Act of Supremacy of that year, Henry became the 'Supreme Head' of the English Church. This supremacy reinforced Tudor government by its stress on obedience, and focused the impact of government on changing those aspects of church organisation and practice deemed hostile or unacceptable, for example shrines and pilgrimages. Becket's shrine at Canterbury – a symbol of opposition to royal authority – was destroyed. Henry's propagandists used the example of the Old Testament kings of Israel as their model. Already, in 1533, an English court had granted Henry an annulment of his marriage and he had both married Anne and had a daughter, Elizabeth. The Act of Succession of 1534 placed the children of his current marriage first in the succession by bastardising Mary. However, Anne's failure to produce a son endangered her position, and she succumbed to factional hostility motivated by concern about her allies and policies. Anne was tried and executed on the trumped-up charge of adultery in 1536 and her marriage declared void, thus bastardising Elizabeth. Henry then married the innocuous Jane Seymour. She produced a son, Edward, in 1537, but died soon after.

These shifts in direction interacted with a religious situation made volatile by the beginnings of the Reformation with Martin Luther's challenge to the papacy in Germany in 1517. Initially there had been few signs that England would respond. William Tyndale's translation of the New Testament from Greek into English, which was influenced by that of Luther, was printed in Germany in 1525–6 and smuggled thence into England; but Henry was doctrinally conservative. In 1521 he wrote a book, *Assertio Septem Sacramentorum*, against Luther, earning the title 'Defender of the Faith' from Pope Leo X. There were few Protestants in England until Henry VIII's break with Rome encouraged them and weakened traditional authority. The question of what would have happened had Henry not broken with Rome is necessarily speculative. Protestant opinion was rising, but was still very much that of a minority with limited political influence, although the success of populist legislation against clerical pluralism in 1529–30 indicated the acceptability of attacks on the pretensions of the Church. In Scotland there was significant Lutheran influence in the east-coast ports in the 1520s and subsequently. This may be the reason why the region was later to lean more to Episcopacy than to Calvinist Presbyterianism.

In the 1530s Henry's breach with the papacy and the growing influence of Protestantism in circles close to him led him to move in the direction of Lutheranism, though he himself was no Protestant and did not wish to see an abandonment of the Catholic faith. Furthermore, as a result of the royal supremacy, all religious questions became political; dissent a direct challenge to the Crown. The Treason Act of 1534 extended treason to words (not just deeds) and the denial of royal supremacy. The humanist intellectual Sir Thomas More, who had vigorously persecuted Protestants, resigned as Lord Chancellor (1532) in protest at Henry's divorce, was imprisoned for refusing to swear the oaths demanded under the Act of Succession, and executed for treason in 1535 after a rigged trial.

In the late 1530s English policy moved in a more Protestant direction, in part under the influence of Henry's chief minister, Thomas Cromwell. The first complete translation of the Bible to be printed in English, that by Miles Coverdale, was dedicated to Henry in 1535. Henry argued that the 'word of God' supported the idea of royal supremacy and this encouraged the translation of the Bible. An official English Bible was produced (1537) and every parish church was instructed to purchase a copy (1538). The availability of English Bibles changed reading habits and helped lead to a greater stress on personal piety rather than on the lives and intercession of saints. Monasticism, one of the most visible symbols and important parts of the Catholic ecclesiastical order, an institution moreover that was attacked by Protestant reformers and was a longstanding source of popular anti-clericalism, was destroyed in 1536–40: the 1536 Act dissolving the smaller monasteries and transferring their property to the Crown was followed by the dissolution of the rest of the houses.

The dissolution of the monasteries was very unpopular. Despite individual abuses, they still played a major role in the spiritual life of the population and were important in local economics. Furthermore, for a society that disliked change, such radical steps were very alarming. It also led to exaggerated rumours, for example in Lincolnshire that Henry intended to despoil the parish churches and to tax cattle and sheep. As a result, in 1536 there were major risings in Lincolnshire and Yorkshire, as well as the Walsingham conspiracy in Norfolk in 1537. These risings were weakened by the unwillingness of most to overthrow the king. In Lincolnshire the 'rebels' of 1536 clearly saw themselves as demonstrators: they administered an oath of loyalty, declared their loyalty to Henry and argued that he was being misled by evil ministers, particularly Cromwell. Unpersuaded, Henry sent troops under the Duke of Suffolk to suppress the movement. In Yorkshire, a large rebel force of over 30,000 led by Robert Aske, who called the rising the Pilgrimage of Grace, pressed for the end of monastic dissolutions, the removal of Cromwell, and the restoration of papal authority and of Mary Tudor to the succession. Henry's promise of pardon and concessions led the rebels to disband the rising, but it was never implemented and the rebel leaders were executed in 1537.

The extensive monastic estates might have served as a permanent gain of wealth and thus power for the Crown, but instead they became centres of aristocratic and gentry influence, because they were sold to pay for Henry's military preparations against and eventually unsuccessful wars with France and Scotland. Much of the land went to already established families, but the Crown was able to reward key supporters and make 'new men'. For example, John Russell, who served Henry as diplomat, official, admiral and general, received many of the lands of the abbey of Tavistock in

Devon from Henry, and Woburn Abbey in Bedfordshire from his successor, and was created Earl of Bedford in 1550. His successors, Dukes from 1694 to the present day, wielded political power in both Devon and Bedfordshire as a consequence of these grants. Thus, a new political geography, much of which was to last until the decline of aristocratic power in the late nineteenth century, was being created, and a vested interest, composed of many of the most powerful and talented members of the elite, created to defend the changes. The dissolution of the monasteries both symbolised and was an important aspect of the process by which the Reformation led to a major shift within society towards lay control.

Aside from governmental moves, the popular appeal of Protestantism was growing, though support was patchy. It proved easier to destroy or change the institutions and public practices of medieval Catholicism – to expunge much of its artistic medium, such as stained glass and wall paintings in churches, or to prevent pilgrimages, than to create a new and stable national ecclesiastical order, or national enthusiasm for Protestantism. Illiteracy, which prevented reading of the translations of the Bible; a shortage of qualified Protestant preachers; and a reluctance to abandon the old religion, all limited the spread of Protestantism, although its impact at Henry's court and in London gave it a role beyond mere numbers. Thomas Cranmer, a secretly married reformer, whom Henry had used to further his divorce from Catherine, was made archbishop of Canterbury in 1533 and actively backed Protestant measures.

In Henry's later years the king sought unsuccessfully to impose religious uniformity and heretics, such as Anne Askew in 1546, were burnt, but there was considerable uncertainty over the direction of royal favour. Moves against Protestantism, especially the restatement of Catholic doctrines in the Act of Six Articles (1539) and the speedy rejection by Henry of his fourth wife, the unappealing Anne of Cleves (1540), were linked to the fall and execution of Cromwell in 1540. Anne was never a Protestant; her brother was reforming Catholic, which was a major part of her attraction to Henry. Henry then married Catherine Howard, a member of the conservative Howard faction, but she was executed for adultery in 1542. At the end of his reign Henry, although faithful to many aspects of Catholicism, disgraced the Howards, leaving the succession to his only son, the young Edward VI, while power was left to Edward's uncle, Jane Seymour's brother, Edward, who became

Protector and Duke of Somerset. Together, they were to take England in a Protestant direction.

THE BRITISH DIMENSION

Henry VIII's changes had consequences both within and outside England. Within England, they helped to lessen the autonomy of distant regions. Between 1536 and 1569 the Tudors crushed a series of rebellions. Some, particularly Kett's in Norfolk in 1549 and Wyatt's in Kent in 1554, were in the south-east, the area of strongest royal authority and greatest national wealth. Others were more distant: in the north and in Cornwall. They reflected the determination and ability of the Tudor state to enforce national policies. The Reformation led to greater concern about security and lawlessness and more acute sensitivity to the nature of government in regions remote from the centre of power in southern England. The nature of religion was such that changes, such as the dissolution of the monasteries or new prayer books, had to be introduced on a national scale and this placed a great strain on the authority of the Crown. If the Reformation is seen, at least initially, as generally unpopular – and the thesis is a controversial one – then this has implications in terms of the strength of Tudor government. Changes in the parish churches were possible only because of the royal grip on the localities and on the elites who ran them. Though injunctions ordering liturgical change were disliked, they were normally obeyed, which means that the local elite saw that they were implemented. Thus, the Crown faced a challenge where the elite was recalcitrant.

The English Crown also faced major challenges in the British Isles. In part, these reflected the continuation of earlier trends, specifically the determination of independent Scotland not to follow the English lead and the lack of English control over much of Ireland.

ANGLO-SCOTTISH WARS

The first of these trends led to war twice in Henry VIII's reign. Scotland looked to France as England's principal opponent and therefore the power with the greatest vested interest in Scottish independence. Scottish contingents had been very helpful to France in the early fifteenth century. The Franco-Scottish alliance, renewed in 1512, brought Scotland and England to war in 1513 when Anglo-French hostilities broke out. James IV, irritated with his brother-in-law, Henry VIII, for a number of reasons, including disputes over raids across the border, fulfilled his commitment to France by invading England with the largest army that had hitherto marched south, 26,000 men, including a French force intended to encourage the use of new military methods. 20,000 English troops under the Earl of Surrey blocked the Scottish advance at Flodden. The Scottish pikemen were defeated by the more mobile English billmen. Flodden was a very significant battle for Scotland. James IV and at least 5,000, possibly as many as 10,000 of his subjects, were killed.

Negotiations in 1514 secured peace between England and Scotland until 1542, when Henry VIII attacked Scotland in order to cover his rear before a projected invasion of France. A Scottish counter-invasion was crushed at the battle of Solway Moss (1542), but at Ancrum Moor (1545) an English raiding force was in turn defeated. Nevertheless, English pressure continued, increasing under the Duke of Somerset, who wanted to establish both Protestantism and English influence in Scotland, and to block the French there. In September 1547 Somerset invaded at the head of 16,000 troops. Later that month, at the battle of Pinkie, the Scottish army, at least 25,000 strong, principally pikemen, was badly battered by English cannon and archers with at least 6,000 killed compared to around 800 English. The amateur Scottish army was poorly trained and lacked tactical flexibility. Somerset exploited the victory by taking a large number of positions where he established English garrisons, but this policy did not make English rule popular, proved ruinously expensive and had to be abandoned in 1549 in face of French intervention. Flodden and Pinkie together suggested that the Scots were not in a position to challenge the English field army. Their diverse armies lacked the ability to act as a coherent unit and some of the individual sections, especially the Highlanders, were disinclined to accept the discipline of remaining on the defensive under fire. The Scots also continued to have less firepower than the English. In addition to their customary inability to match English archery, the Scots lacked the resources, expertise and experience to match them in gunpowder weaponry.

Yet these disadvantages did not mean that Scotland was ripe for conquest: the English faced serious political and military problems north of the border, not least French intervention. There were considerable numbers of French troops there in 1545–60. Scotland was not to be conquered until 1650–2. Before then the history of Scotland and England had become further intertwined as a consequence both of Scotland's acceptance of the Reformation, following the Reformation Parliament of 1560, and of the union of the two crowns in 1603.

IRELAND

The acceptance of the Reformation by Scotland and Wales was crucial to their integration into a British consciousness and policy. Ireland, however, rejected the Reformation, a development that was central to the divergence of Ireland from the general model of British development. Henry VIII had sought to maintain his father's policy of increasing Tudor control in Ireland without major initiatives, but the Reformation altered the situation. In 1534 Thomas, Earl of Kildare rebelled, offering the overlordship of Ireland to the pope or the Emperor Charles V, in place of the schismatic Henry VIII, whose forces defeated him the following year. The castle of Athlone was regained as a military base for the Crown in 1537. The Reformation Parliament of 1536–7 acknowledged Henry as the 'supreme head' of the Irish Church, declared the succession to be in the heirs of Henry's marriage to Anne Boleyn, and, later, agreed to the dissolution of the monasteries. In 1541 the Irish Parliament accepted Henry as 'king of Ireland' rather than its lord. Gaelic nobles were offered English law and charters for their lands, an attempt to incorporate them peacefully into the structure of governmental control. Such a conciliatory policy was to be abandoned after Henry's death, but it already faced formidable difficulties given the precarious nature of control over much of the island.

WALES

The Welsh accepted the Reformation with little opposition which made changes in government easier. Wales was seen as exposed to

possible Spanish and Irish intervention, while the marcher lord
ships were regarded as badly administered. Henry VIII's legislation
of 1536–43, the Acts of Union, assimilated all Wales into the
English governmental system. The 1536 statute gave parliamentary
representation to the whole of Wales. Welsh subjects were made
equal to the English under the law, although the language of the
law was to be English. The marcher lordships were converted into
counties, and thus represented in Parliament. English inheritance
practices, justice and county institutions were all introduced. Welsh
land laws were abolished in 1543. The establishment of justices of
the peace in Wales in 1536 gave the Welsh gentry an important
measure of self-government.

Wales was not governed in precisely the same fashion as England
as the council in the marches continued, while from 1542 Wales had
its own system of courts, the Great Sessions, which lasted until
1830. Yet marcher independence had been destroyed, and a uniform system of government created for Wales. The Welsh had
identified themselves by their customary law, and when it was
abrogated the bards swiftly lamented the decline of 'Welshness'.
Equality of status, however, was the basis for a more mutually
beneficial relationship between the Welsh elite and the government.
The preamble to the Act of Union of 1536 declared its aim to
extirpate 'the sinister usages and customs' that caused differences
between England and Wales, and it was declared that no Welshman
could hold any post unless familiar with English, an objective that
would have concentrated power where it already was: in the hands
of gentry and clerics who could work with the English and were
educated accordingly. Upwardly mobile Welshmen had for long
been educated at Oxbridge or at the Inns of Court in London.

The Reformation had more of an immediate effect on the Welsh
population than did the administrative changes. Although they were
in serious eclipse by this time, the dissolution of monasteries and
chantries had an impact on landholding, substantially to the benefit
of the local gentry, and also disrupted the fabric of many communities. Education and poor relief were affected. Although enthusiasm for the Reformation was limited and areas of Catholicism
remained, there was no equivalent to the opposition that existed in
England, Ireland and Scotland. In addition, the translation of the
Bible into Welsh helped to sustain a sense of national identity. The
Welsh accepted the Reformation, but not the English language;

thanks to the acceptance of the former, Wales did not become a security problem and source of Protestant phobias and was spared the fate of Ireland. A translation of the Prayer Book and the New Testament was published in 1567 and William Morgan's readily comprehensible translation of the entire Bible appeared in 1588, although the metropolitan dominance of Britain was such that it had to be printed in London: by law only certain presses could publish Bibles anyway. In his Latin dedication to Elizabeth I, Morgan emphasised the value of official support of the Welsh language. Thanks to the translation, Welsh could be the official language of public worship and religious life in general, and the clergy had no need to catechise and preach in English. The Welsh language could develop from its medieval oral and manuscript characteristics into a culture of print. Morgan was subsequently an active bishop of first Llandaff and then St Asaph and his career testified to the energising possibilities of the Reformation. Other bishops, however, left a less happy reputation. Although not without merits, William Hughes, Bishop of St Asaph 1573–1600, became notorious for his pluralism, and was accused of corruptly leasing out episcopal lands, although his pluralism was in part due to the poverty of the diocese and to the control of its lands by the local gentry. Hughes's career illustrated the degree to which the literate Welsh now looked towards England. Educated at Cambridge, where he became a fellow of a college, he was for long chaplain to the duke of Norfolk and towards the end of his career he sought transfer to the bishopric of Exeter. If Welshmen sought careers in England with increasing success, many senior Welsh positions were still held by Englishmen. Thus Hugh Bellot obtained livings in Flintshire in 1584, and was Bishop of Bangor from 1585 to 1595.

MID-CENTURY CRISIS

The combined strains of the Reformation, weak monarchs, problems over the succession, aristocratic factionalism, regional particularism and foreign intervention plunged both England and Scotland into serious problems in the period c.1542–68. Like the French wars of religion (1562–98), they indicate the precarious nature of the achievement of the 'new monarchies', although the Reformation posed new challenges, not least in imposing uniformity, resisting foreign intervention and coping with the extent to which religious dissidence sapped obedience and encouraged opposition.

ENGLAND UNDER EDWARD VI, 1547–53

During Edward's reign England was open to the influence of continental Protestantism. Edward was strongly influenced by the Protestantism of his Seymour uncles. There was a surge of Protestant publishing and by 1553 there were about 10,000 foreigners in or near London. Peter Martyr Vermigli and Martin Bucer were appointed regius professors of divinity at Oxford and Cambridge. Allied with Archbishop Cranmer, the Duke of Somerset introduced Protestant worship by the Book of Common Prayer (1549). Parliament passed a Uniformity Act decreeing that the Prayer Book alone was to be used for church services, which were to be in English.

Hostility to religious change played a major role in the widespread uprisings in southern England in 1549, particularly in the south-west. There, the local gentry failed to suppress the rebellion and professional troops from outside the region were used by the government. Slaughter in battle and in execution claimed a high proportion of the region's male population.

In Norfolk the rising centred not on religion but on opposition to landlords, particularly their enclosure of common lands and their high rents, and to oppressive local government. One of the rebels' articles, 'We pray that all bond men may be free', was an attack on the harsh nature of the social system. The rebels, under the leadership of Robert Kett, a landowner willing to act against enclosures, seized Norwich and chose governors for the hundreds into which Norfolk was divided. The refusal of an offer of pardon turned the movement into a rebellion and troops were sent to suppress it. At the battle of Dussindale (1549), John Dudley, Earl of Warwick, using professional troops, including German mercenaries, cut the rebellion to pieces.

Protests and rebellions against Tudor government faced important political and military disadvantages. Peaceful protest was regarded as rebellion. Politically, ambiguity about the notion of rebellion ensured that there was an often-fatal confusion of purpose. Militarily, the untrained, amateur forces raised in the rebellions were no match for the troops the government could deploy. The rebels tended to lack cavalry, firearms and cannon; such forces could not challenge the government if it had firm leadership and the support of an important portion of the social elite. In Scotland the situation was different: the Protestant league formed by the Lords of the Congregation in the 1550s presaged a far higher degree of anti-monarchical militarisation than in England. In the 1560s Mary, Queen of Scots, a weak and discredited monarch, faced opposition from a group of powerful Protestant aristocrats and lacked the force to overcome them.

The English risings of 1549 were blamed in part on Somerset's opposition to enclosures and led to his being overthrown as Protector by the council (1549). John Dudley, one of the leaders of the council, became its Lord President (1550–3) and Duke of Northumberland (1551) and had Somerset executed in 1552.

Like Richard III, Northumberland was very able and determined, but self-serving and distrusted. This would not have mattered had he been successful and enjoyed a firm claim to government: Henry VIII had not lacked ambition, self-interest and cruelty. But, like Richard, Northumberland's faults helped to deprive him of success. He stretched the bounds of what was acceptable for a minister, trying to behave as a kingmaker in a political culture that did not want one; and, crucially, lacked both the weight given by the Crown and time to consolidate his position.

Northumberland pressed on headlong towards Protestantism. Continental radical Protestantism influence was especially strong in the Second Prayer Book (1552) and the statement of beliefs in the *Forty-Two Articles* (1553). The former expunged the remains of Catholic doctrine and practice: the bodily presence of Christ in the Eucharist was explicitly denied. The traditional trappings of Catholic religiosity – the special clothes of the clergy, the fittings of their churches, the religious rituals of calendarical festivity – were removed.

Northumberland was thwarted by Edward VI's deteriorating health. The succession became the crucial issue. Edward excluded his half-sisters, Mary and Elizabeth, claiming that they were illegitimate, and Lady Jane Grey, grand-daughter of Henry VII through his second daughter, was declared next in line. She was married to one of Northumberland's sons, and when Edward died was proclaimed queen (1553). Mary, however, proclaimed herself queen in

Norfolk and began raising troops. Northumberland set out to defeat her, but as support rallied to Mary, including London and the Privy Council, Northumberland surrendered. He and eventually Lady Jane were executed. If Northumberland had had the level of support Scots magnates in the 1560s opposed to Mary Queen of Scots were to command, a Protestant challenge might well have succeeded.

MARY, 1553–8

Mary, the daughter of Henry VIII and Catherine of Aragon, was a convinced Catholic; she restored papal authority and Catholic practice, although a papal dispensation allowed the retention of the former Church lands: their return would have alienated most of the propertied and the powerful. In 1554 Mary married her younger first cousin, Philip of Spain, a member of the leading Catholic dynasty, with the proviso that any child would inherit England and the Netherlands, and, if Philip's son by an earlier marriage died, the entire Spanish monarchy: England would thus have been closely linked to the Continent. Mary granted Philip the title 'King Consort'.

The marriage was unpopular and led to a rising in Kent by Sir Thomas Wyatt. Designed to block the wedding, it may also have been intended to make Elizabeth queen. London, however, refused to rise and the rebellion was crushed. This helped to give further impetus to the programme of re-Catholicisation. At least 280 Protestants, including Cranmer, Latimer and Ridley, were burnt at the stake, while others fled to the Continent. The Spanish marriage brought an expensive and unsuccessful war with France from 1557 that led in 1558 to the fall of Calais, England's last possession on the mainland of France. Mary died after long periods of dropsy, which appeared to some to be pregnancies. Philip had abandoned her for the Netherlands and she was more a tragic figure than a tyrant.

Mary had no child and was therefore succeeded by her Protestant half-sister Elizabeth. Re-Catholicisation had had scant time to take root. Yet Protestantism had had only limited popular support when Mary came to the throne, and Mary met with little resistance to her religious legislation in Parliament. The reformers' earlier destruction of the old ways was a crucial limitation on the chances of successful re-Catholicisation, but, had Mary had a Catholic heir who had lived long enough to reach maturity, England might well have been a triumph for the Counter-Reformation. The altars and statues that had been destroyed under Edward VI were difficult to replace, but under Mary most stone altars were nevertheless reinstated.

SCOTLAND

The succession also created major problems in Scotland. Born in 1512, James V died young after the Scottish humiliation at the battle of Solway Moss in 1542. His French alliance had led to two marriages, with Madeleine of France (1537) and Mary of Guise-Lorraine (1538), and, by the second wife, in 1542 he had a daughter Mary, who became Queen of Scots on his death. James V had resisted Protestantism, seeking in the Parliament of 1541 to protect Catholicism, although he favoured a measure of reform. His death gave the Protestants an opportunity for action, but war with England, French influence, and from 1554 the regency of Mary of Guise, led to opposition to Protestant activity. Mary, Queen of Scots was sent to France in 1548, and in 1558 married Francis, the Dauphin (heir to the French throne), who became Francis II in 1559. Scotland therefore appeared firmly in the French camp.

This situation ended in 1560. The accession of Elizabeth in 1558 gave rise to hope of English support for Scottish Protestants, and led to the Anglo-Scottish Treaty of Edinburgh in 1560. In 1560 Mary of Guise died, the French troops were expelled and Francis II also died, leaving Mary a childless widow. A Parliament dominated by Protestants abolished papal authority and the Mass and introduced Protestant theology.

Mary, who returned to Scotland in 1561, did not accept these changes, but she lacked the political ability to reverse them and to build up a strong body of support in the complex and bitter world of Scottish baronial factionalism. The Lords of the Congregation and their successors united against a Catholic monarch and the French alliance. Mary's second marriage to her cousin, Lord Darnley (1565), was unsuccessful and in 1566 he played a role in the murder of her favourite, David Rizzio. Mary possibly then con-

spired with the brutal James, Earl of Bothwell, who murdered
Darnley and married her (1567). This was an unpopular step and
in 1567 Mary was forced to surrender to the Protestant lords and to
abdicate in favour of the infant James VI, her son by Darnley.
Mary escaped the following year but was defeated at Langside and
fled to England to the mercy of Elizabeth.

ELIZABETH I, 1558–1603

Queen for forty-four years, Elizabeth was the longest-reigning
English monarch since Edward III. Her longevity and personality
played a major role in determining the political and religious
character of Tudor England. Born in 1533, Elizabeth was the
longest-living English monarch hitherto and was not to be surpassed until George II. Avoiding marriage and the perils of childbirth were clearly helpful, but her longevity was still remarkable;
although in Scotland William the Lion lived from 1143 until 1214
and Robert II from 1316 until 1390. Had Elizabeth lived only as
long as her half-brother, she would never have become queen; if she
had matched her half-sister or her grandfather she would have died
before James VI's mother, Mary, Queen of Scots, unless she had
had Mary executed earlier than 1587.

Elizabeth's caution and political adeptness were very important
in restoring a measure of political stability after the confusion of
mid-century, which was important both for the succession and for
the religious settlement. The fact that Elizabeth did not marry
revived uncertainty over the succession, but thanks to the execution
of Mary, Queen of Scots in 1587 there was a generally acceptable
Protestant succession in the shape of James VI of Scotland (born
1566), great-great-grandson of Henry VII through his elder daughter, Margaret, who had married James IV; although Elizabeth was
reluctant to commit herself to James.

Elizabeth had benefited from a humanist education, an upbringing in which she had been obliged to accommodate two different
regimes and reversals of fortune; she was no fanatic. She lacked the
religious zeal of her half-brother Edward and her half-sister Mary
and would have preferred a compromise religious settlement that
was closer to her father's Catholicism: without pope, monks and
some superstitions. But a lack of strong political support for such

an option forced her to go further. Nevertheless, Elizabeth introduced a Protestant settlement that was more conservative than that of Northumberland. There were limits to her Protestantism, as she showed in her own religious practice, and in her concern for ceremonies and clerical clothes. She accepted those aspects of Protestant doctrine and practice which were consistent with order and rejected those aspects which were not. This settlement was an appropriate one for a people among whom many could recall the old religious traditions. It was not until the 1580s that the Reformation gained general acceptance; that the old religion was dead for most people in most (not all) parts of Britain, and that Protestantism became identified with national survival in the war against Spain. Elizabeth was also determined to keep royal control over the Church, its bishops, doctrine and liturgy, and once the Elizabethan church settlement had been introduced, she was unwilling to respond to pressure for further reformation. This was to lead to tension with the more radical Protestants, who are termed Puritans.

Elizabeth became the most experienced politician in her kingdom, keen on maintaining the royal prerogative, but knowing when to yield, dexterous in making concessions without appearing weak, a skilled manipulator of courtiers who was able to get the best out of her ministers. She had favourites, but was prepared to sacrifice them for political advantage. Elizabeth did not condemn the contemporary stereotype of women as inferior to men, but instead claimed that she was an exceptional woman because chosen by God as his instrument. She was reasonably successful in coping with divisions among her advisors, but found it difficult to control her military comanders. She was intelligent and generally pragmatic, but found it difficult to adjust to change.

Elizabeth's Protestant settlement aroused Catholic concern. About 500 clerics refused to accept it and a number went into exile on the Continent where they established seminaries to train missionaries to proselytise for Catholicism in England. The most famous was Douai, founded in the Netherlands, then ruled by Philip II of Spain, in 1568. The same year Mary, Queen of Scots, who was next in line in the succession, fled to England where she was imprisoned. Her presence and capacity for self-dramatisation acted as a focus for discontent.

In 1569 there was a conspiracy at court to replace Elizabeth's leading minister, William Cecil, and to marry the Duke of Norfolk, a leading religious conservative, to Mary, Queen of Scots and acknowledge her as heir to the throne. This conspiracy was thwarted at court, but triggered a rising in the north by its supporters, particularly the earls of Northumberland and Westmorland, whose local positions were endangered by a lack of royal favour. The earls marked the start of the rising by occupying Durham Cathedral and celebrating Mass. Roman Catholic worship was restored in many churches. The earls, however, were unable to reach and release Mary when they marched south and they subsequently fled when the more powerful royal army advanced. Northumberland was executed, while the titles and honours of the house of Neville, the family of the earls of Westmorland, were extinguished. Over 200 rank-and-file supporters were hanged in retribution in County Durham, a policy advocated by Elizabeth, while their homes were plundered. The wealthier rebels were better treated, and, as one commentator noted, 'the common people say the poor are both spoiled and executed, and the gentlemen and rich escape'.

The Northern Rising was followed by the papal excommunication and depostion of Elizabeth in 1570 and by a number of conspiracies on behalf of Mary, particularly the Ridolfi (1571–2), Throckmorton (1582) and Babington (1586) plots. Elizabeth was reluctant to try Mary, a fellow sovereign and a relative, but in 1586 the interception of Mary's correspondence indicated that she had agreed to Elizabeth's assassination in the Babington plot. As a result Mary was convicted of treason, a questionable charge since she owed Elizabeth no allegiance, and beheaded at Fotheringay Castle (1587).

By then England was involved in a major war. Elizabeth's support for the largely Protestant Dutch rebellion against her former half-brother-in-law, Philip II of Spain, particularly the dispatch of troops, under her favourite, the Earl of Leicester, after the Treaty of Nonsuch with the rebels (1585), and her apparent connivance in raids on Spanish colonies and trade, led to war from 1585.

THE SPANISH ARMADA

The limited English commitment of troops made little difference to the conflict in the Netherlands, but it led Philip to decide on a major attack on England. Philip, however, failed to coordinate adequately two different plans: that of an amphibious invasion of England from Spain (the king of which was also King of Portugal from 1580 until 1640), and that for a crossing of the narrow Straits of Dover by the Spanish army in the Netherlands under Alessandro Farnese, Duke of Parma. The Spaniards were also delayed by the immensity of the necessary preparations and by Sir Francis Drake's successful spoiling raid on the main Spanish naval base of Cadiz in April 1587. The following year the Armada, a massive force of 130 ships and 19,000 troops, left Lisbon, instructed to proceed up the Channel and then cover Farnese's crossing. Storm-damage led to refitting in Corunna and in July the slow-moving fleet appeared off the entrance to the Channel. As they headed for Calais the Spanish warships, maintaining a rigid formation, were harried by long-distance English bombardment, but it did little damage and during nine days of engagements the Spaniards retained their formation. The English, however, had an advantage not only in superior sailing qualities, but also because their guns were mounted on compact, four-wheeled truck carriages, and therefore could be readily reloaded, while the Spaniards lacked such equipment.

When the Spanish fleet anchored off Calais, it was discovered that Parma lacked the shipping necessary to embark his forces. The Spanish formation was disrupted by a night-time English attack with fireships and the English fleet then inflicted considerable damage in a battle off Gravelines. A strong wind blew the Armada into the North Sea and it returned painfully to Spain via the north of Scotland and the west coast of Ireland, suffering heavy losses from storms and shipwrecks.

The loss of so many trained and experienced men was a serious blow, but the fleet was rebuilt and Spain was able to send fleets against England in 1596 and 1597. Both were stopped by storms, but the English themselves found it difficult to win a lasting naval victory. In 1589 Drake mounted a successful attack on Corunna, destroying Spanish warships, but thereafter the expedition was a failure. Drake was a poor naval strategist, Lisbon could not be taken and the attempt to intercept the Spanish treasure fleet from the New World off the Azores was unsuccessful. The English were driven back by storms, suffering much damage in the process. The Armada and the 'Counter-Armada' both therefore illustrated the limitations of naval power in this period, not least vulnerability to storms, the difficulties of combined operations and the major supply problems posed by large fleets.

THE PROBLEMS OF ELIZABETH'S LAST YEARS

The defeat of the Armada encouraged a sense of English national destiny that was reflected in the political language and the drama of the period. The winds that had helped were attributed to Providence. The expense of the long war, however, created difficulties. Royal fiscal policies, particularly the sale of monopolies to manufacture or sell certain goods, and also additional taxes, led to bitter criticism in the Parliaments of 1597 and 1601; and also failed to provide sufficient resources to bring success in war. Puritanism led to disputes in Parliament, especially in 1587 when Puritan MPs tried to legislate for a Presbyterian church settlement, an unsuccessful move that caused an angry dispute between Elizabeth, who opposed changes in religious matters, and some MPs. Elizabeth found it difficult to create a stable government after the ministers who had served her for so long – William Cecil, Lord Burghley; Leicester and Walsingham – died. The struggle with Philip II escalated, with Elizabeth sending troops to support the anti-Spanish side in the French Wars of Religion between 1589 and 1597. Expeditions to Brittany and Normandy were poorly executed, but were of some use in helping Henry IV consolidate his grip on the French throne. Philip, in turn, conspired in the British Isles, with Catholic aristocrats in Scotland, and in Ireland.

THE SUBJUGATION OF IRELAND

The attempt under Henry VIII to assimilate Gaelic Ireland was replaced under his successors by a policy of the 'plantation' of districts bordering the area under English control with English ('New English') settlers. This increased the security of the Crown's position, although the expropriation of Gaelic landowners was naturally unpopular. Begun under Edward VI, the policy expanded under Mary. From the late 1560s English rule became increasingly military in character and intention, leading to fresh attempts to extend and enforce control. Regional councils were established for

Connacht (1569) and Munster (1571) and, in the face of rebellions, the English resorted to the routine use of force. Authority was extended into outlying areas such as Sligo, Fermanagh and Monaghan. This was not a conducive environment for the expansion of Protestantism, and, as Catholic energies were revived by the Counter-Reformation, religious differences became a more important feature of the Irish situation, symbolising, reflecting and strengthening a political rift and the hatred felt between what were increasingly seen as conquerors and a subject population. The 'New English' enjoyed office and the benefits of government support; the Catholic 'Old English' felt alienated and excluded from office, the Gaels harshly treated by a corrupt and brutal rule. Elizabeth failed to devote the necessary attention to Irish affairs and allowed a more unaccommodating policy to be pursued there than she would have accepted in England. The Protestant Church did not minister successfully to the population. It proved difficult to find qualified Protestant clergy willing to serve the impoverished Church. One official reported in 1607 that the clergy of the archbishopric of Cashel were 'fitter to keep hogs than serve in the church'.

Gaelic resistance led to the Desmond rebellion of the 1580s and culminated in 1594 in a major and ably led rising by Hugh O'Neill, Earl of Tyrone. O'Neill raised an army of 10,000, substantial by the standards of Ireland, extended the rebellion from the north into Munster and also sought Catholic 'Old English' support. From mid-century, firearms, in the form of the arquebus, had been introduced into Ireland on a substantial scale, but in the 1560s, when he sought to dominate Ulster, Shane O'Neill's forces still relied on traditional weapons: axes, bows, javelins and swords. Hugh O'Neill's men, in contrast, used modern firearms, the musket and its smaller counterpart, the caliver, and were as well armed as the English. Many had served in the highly professional Spanish army, and O'Neill trained his entire force in the use of pikes and firearms. The wooded and boggy terrain of Ulster was well suited to guerrilla conflict and ambushes, and at Clontibret in 1595 O'Neill successfully ambushed an English army. Three years later, at Yellow Ford, another English force was badly battered when attacked on the march. In 1599 Elizabeth's arrogant favourite, Robert, Earl of Essex, failed to defeat O'Neill. This led to his disgrace and loss of royal favour. Heavily in debt as a result of the loss of his monopolies, Essex tried to stage a coup in January 1601 in order to seize Elizabeth and destroy his rival, the chief minister, Burghley's son, Sir Robert Cecil. Cecil outwitted the rash plan, the coup failed and Essex was executed. Not for the last time, Irish developments had had a crucial impact on mainland politics.

In 1600 the English sent a more effective leader to Ireland, the new Lord Deputy, Charles, Lord Mountjoy. He decided to campaign in the winter in order to disrupt O'Neill's logistical system, and also sought to immobilise the migrant herds of cattle which fed the Irish army on campaign. Enjoying numerical superiority, Mountjoy brought a new savagery to the conflict, but his attempt to invade Ulster was defeated at the battle of Moyry Pass (1600) by O'Neill's use of musketeers protected by field fortifications. English fears of foreign intervention were realised in September 1601 when Philip III of Spain sent 3,500 troops to Kinsale to support O'Neill Mountjoy responded by blockading Kinsale, but his force was rapidly weakened by sickness. O'Neill's relieving force, instead of blockading Mountjoy, decided to attack him. However, the night march on Mountjoy's camp was mishandled, and on the morning of 24 December O'Neill, unusually, lost the tactical initiative, allowing Mountjoy to move first. O'Neill also deployed his men in the unfamiliar defensive formation of the Spanish square (tercio), which proved cumbersome: the Irish had never mastered it. The English cavalry drove their Irish counterparts from the field, and the Irish infantry retreated, those who stood being defeated. The Irish lost 1,200 men, but, more seriously, the pattern of victory was broken. No more Spanish troops were sent and O'Neill was to surrender in 1603.

The Nine Years War in Ireland provides evidence of the strength of the Irish combination of traditional Celtic tactical methods and modern firearms, especially against an opponent unfamiliar with the former. It also reveals the folly of seeking to transform such a force into soldiers fighting on the standard western-European patterns, and, in particular, of requiring them to maintain the tactical defensive. Until 1601 O'Neill combined a defensive strategy – protecting Ulster – with a willingness to use offensive techniques. The switch in strategy in 1601 proved fatal. O'Neill was also up against a powerful state, with a more sophisticated military organisation and logistical system, and with naval support. The Irish could live off the land and use the terrain and they benefited from 'modernity' in the form of muskets, but their weak command structure reflected the problems of a people competing with a state. Furthermore, unlike the Scots in earlier conflicts, the Irish lacked the capacity to invade England.

By 1603 Ireland had been conquered. For the first time, the English controlled the entire island. Thereafter, Ireland was to be contested as a unit, and it was to be assumed that the loss of part would lead, if unchallenged, to that of the whole. As with the Romans and England, foreign conquest had brought a new decree of unity.

More immediately, the English victory was followed by the resumption and major extension of the policy of plantation. O'Neill and O'Donnell had been restored to their lands when they submitted in 1603, but the imposition of English law and custom in Ulster led them to flee to Italy in 1607, with many of their supporters. James I then confiscated their lands: 3,800,000 acres of Ulster were seized. Some of the less fertile portion was granted to the native Irish, but the rest was allocated to English and Scottish settlers, Crown officials, the established (Protestant) Church, and, in return for financial support for the plantation, the City of London. At the same time large portions of Antrim and Down in Ulster were granted as private plantations, and also settled largely by Scots. By 1618 there were about 40,000 Scots in Ulster. Other plantations were established further south in, for example, Wexford, Leitrim, Westmeath and Longford; these, however, had fewer Protestant settlers. Across much of Ireland, therefore, the native Irish landowners had been dispossessed in favour of Protestants, and in Ulster the native population as a whole saw their position deteriorate as large numbers of Protestants were settled. Discontent over land, religion and political status was to explode in the rising of 1641.

TRANS-OCEANIC EXPANSION

English power did not only increase in Ireland, though, having lost the vast bulk of their French possessions, the English did not immediately shift to trans-oceanic enterprise. They lacked both the 'stepping stones' provided to the Portuguese and Spaniards by the Azores, Madeira and the Canaries (as earlier Vikings had

had the Faroes, Iceland and Greenland), and the tradition of expansion at the expense of the heathen that the Portuguese and Spaniards had acquired from their long wars against the Muslims. Nevertheless, the English soon took part in expansion first across the Atlantic and then to southern Asia. Fishing expeditions from Bristol may have reached North America in the 1480s or 1490s but the first precise information relates to the Italian John Cabot, who sailed west from Bristol in 1497 hoping to reach the wealth of the East Indies and, instead, probably reached Newfoundland. This route was soon followed by numerous English fishermen, while other explorers probed icy seas searching for a north-west passage to the East Indies. Martin Frobisher, John Davis and Henry Hudson entered major bodies of water – Baffin Bay and Hudson Bay – but in the 1610s William Baffin, Luke Foxe and Thomas James established that these led to further shores not open ocean.

A north-east passage was also attractive. Sir Hugh Willoughby died on the coast of Lapland while searching for such a passage in 1553, but Richard Chancellor reached the White Sea and then travelled to Moscow opening up a tenuous trade route that was explored further by Anthony Jenkinson in 1558–62 when he travelled thence to central Asia and to Persia. A sea route to South Asia seemed a better prospect and in 1600 an East India Company was founded to trade there. It was to be the basis of Britain's Asian empire. The company was a chartered monopoly trading body that spread the considerable risks of long-distance trade among a number of investors and thus drew on the wealthy mercantile world of London.

Trade with South Asia challenged the control of much of India's trade with Europe enjoyed by Portugal, then ruled by Spain. English schemes had clashed earlier, as with unsuccessful attempts to break into Portugal's trade with West Africa in the 1550s and the attempt to take a share in the profitable slave trade between Africa and the Spanish New World in the 1560s. As tension rose in the 1570s, privateering attacks on Spanish New World trade and settlements became more common. Drake launched attacks in 1566–8 and 1570–3, and in 1577–80 became the first Englishman to circumnavigate the world, an expedition in which he sailed up the Californian coast and claimed it as 'Nova Albion' for Elizabeth.

The English also sought to establish a colony on the eastern coast of New America, called Virginia in honour of the unmarried

Elizabeth. In 1585 108 colonists were landed on Roanoke Island in what is now North Carolina, but they found it difficult to feed themselves and were taken off the following year. Another attempt was made in 1588, but when a relief ship arrived in 1590 it found the village deserted: disease, starvation or Indians may have wiped out the colonists. It was not until 1607 that a permanent colony was to be established in Virginia.

EARLY-MODERN WOMEN

The death of Elizabeth in 1603 is an appropriate place to review the position of women in the early-modern period. At the most elevated social level this was clearly in large part a matter of personality and politics, though the context was one of a male-centred if not misogynist culture. Thus, Elizabeth's court preachers emphasised traditional stereotypes of feminine weakness, and presented the queen as a woman rescued by God, rather than as a warrior queen. God was given masculine attributes, unsurprisingly so as all clergy were men. Elizabeth herself was no passive recipient of such nostrums, no more than her great-grandmother, Margaret Beaufort, who, having become pregnant by her second husband at the age of 12, intrigued strongly for the succession of her son, Henry VII, and then in 1485 took the unusual step of having herself declared by Parliament a *femme sole* (independent woman), able to hold property and act like a widow, even though her fourth husband, the Earl of Derby, would live for another twenty years.

Yet cultural pressures were hostile to such independence and were represented in the legal system. Much was traditional, for example the different standards applied to male and female premarital and extra-marital sex. Elizabeth had to cope with slanderous and politically compromising rumours about her preferences for men. The status and wealth of women continued to be derived from their husbands and fathers and thus defined by them. Margaret Tyler, the translator of *The Mirrour of Knighthood* (1578), criticised the traditional practice of arranged marriages to no effect. Wives were not normally allowed to make wills. Wealthy spinsters and widows, however, could be of considerable importance, as was indicated by educational and religious bequests, for example to several Oxbridge colleges.

There were also changes. Among the elite, changes in inheritance practice led to daughters and widows receiving less, to the benefit of more distant male relatives. The Reformation offered new opportunities to female spirituality and women were able to both claim and exercise a right to conscience and self-determination in religious matters. These opportunities, however, did not fully transcend gender limitations. The attitudes of Protestant sects reflected traditional social ideals and practices and few women rose to positions of authority within them. Convents, which had provided women with a world with some autonomy, were dissolved. Nuns were probably the group that lost most from the Reformation.

However, the Reformation did lead to a more sympathetic attitude towards marriage and sexual love within marriage, one that was reflected and strengthened by the fact that clergy now could be married. Yet concern about the disruptive nature of sexual desire focused on single and adulterous women. There was an important shift from regarding moral misdemeanours as matters for the Church courts to bringing them under secular authority, so that prostitutes and women of ill-repute were increasingly dealt with by the justices of the peace, a process that preceded but was furthered by the Reformation and that matched the concern with social control expressed by moves against vagrancy. The sexual standards of the day, however, reflected female as well as male views, suggesting that women to some degree supported the maintenance of patriarchy. It was considered morally, as well as aesthetically, preferable to use boys for female theatrical roles, rather than to have actresses.

After the Reformation, there were no major changes until the Civil War, which threatened to loosen Church controls over family behaviour. A new civil wedding ceremony was introduced in 1653, but traditional religious rites and social assumptions tended to prevail, and after the Restoration in 1660 there was a re-imposition of earlier norms. Margaret Fell's defence of the right of women to preach in churches, made in 1666, was singularly inappropriate in its timing. Four years earlier, a Dutch visitor to London had witnessed the treatment of a woman convicted of murdering her husband, a crime treated with great severity and scant consideration of provocation:

we saw a young woman, who had stabbed her husband to death
. . . being burned alive . . . She was put with her feet into a sawn-
through tar barrel . . . A clergyman spoke to her for a long time
and reproved her, and said the prayer. Then faggots [sticks] were
piled up against her body . . . and finally set alight with a torch
. . . and soon it was ablaze all round.

Women punished as witches by a male-dominated legal system also
suffered terribly. However, women were not simply the victims of
witchcraft accusations; they were also actively involved in bringing
prosecutions and acting as witnesses and searchers for marks supposedly revealing witches. Furthermore, there were also male
witches. In general, women were more active in the legal process
and thus had more control over their lives than patriarchal nostrums might suggest.

Similarly, women played a greater role in inheritance than was
legally essential. 55 per cent of the wills from the Archdeaconry of
Sudbury in 1636–8 named the wife as sole executrix (administrator
of the will). Many husbands showed confidence in their wives in the
phrasing of a will, and the interest in the well-being of widows
indicates the degree of matrimonial love. Nevertheless, whatever
their personal circumstances and legal position, hard work was the
fate of most women, commonly alongside their husbands, as in the
rural society and coalmines of Scotland.

5

1603–88

In 1603, for the first time, one individual came to power throughout the British Isles: James VI of Scotland and James I of England, Wales and Ireland. The male line of the Stuarts were expelled from Britain twice within the century, first in the British civil wars of the 1640s and early 1650s, generally known, inaccurately, as the English Civil War; and, secondly, in the civil war that began with the Glorious Revolution of 1688 and ended when the Stuart cause in Ireland capitulated in 1691. In retrospect, the period is usually so dominated by the (English) Civil War of 1642–6, its causes, course and consequences, that it is difficult to appreciate that both the war and its results were far from inevitable. The war was certainly a major struggle: more than half the total number of battles fought on English soil involving more than 5,000 combatants were fought in 1642–51. Out of an English male population of about 1.5 million, over 80,000 died in combat and about another 100,000 of other causes linked to the war, principally disease. Possibly one in four English males served in the conflicts. Hostilities and casualties in the related struggles in Ireland and Scotland in 1638–51 were even heavier. In Scotland, where many prisoners were killed on the battlefield, about 6 per cent of the population died; in Ireland an even higher percentage, greater than that in the potato famine of the 1840s. Bitter civil conflict was hardly without precedent, and more men may have fought at Towton (1461) than in any of the battles of the Civil War, but the sustained level of hostilities, the British scale of the conflict and the degree of popular involvement and politicisation were unprecedented. Attitudes were vicious. After the battle of Hopton Heath (1643) Sir John Gell, the parliamentary Governor of Derby, paraded the naked corpse of the Earl

of Northampton round the town. There was much looting, includ
ing a scarlet petticoat from Shakespeare's granddaughter. Trade
was disrupted and charitable provision collapsed. In addition, the
war came after a long period in which most of England, especially
the more prosperous south, had been peaceful. Town walls had
fallen into disrepair, castles into disuse.

The crisis of the mid-seventeenth century had a profound influ
ence in shaping values, fears and ideologies in the century-and-a
half after the restoration of monarchy throughout the British Isles
in 1660. There was urgency and fear after the Restoration, fear that
the world might again be turned upside down. What was crucial
then was the need to recreate the habits of thought and patterns of
the past, to destroy the work of the Civil War and exorcise its
divisive legacy.

Though crucial in its consequences, the Civil War, like the
French and Russian revolutions, was not inevitable either in it
causes or course. There had been serious political disputes during
the reign of James I and the early years of Charles I, but they had
been handled peacefully. Only marginal individuals resorted to
violence. A small group of Catholics put gunpowder in the cellar
under Parliament planning to blow it up when James I opened the
session on 5 November 1605, hoping that the destruction of the
royal family and the Protestant elite would ignite rebellion. The
attempt to warn a Catholic peer, Lord Monteagle, to be absent, led
however, to exposure of the plot and punishment of the conspira
tors. Guy Fawkes was tortured to force him to reveal the names of
his co-conspirators in the Gunpowder Plot of 1605, and then
executed. Twenty-three years later, George, Duke of Buckingham
Charles I's favourite and leading advisor, was assassinated; his
assassin, John Felton, was executed. Such events, however, were
far from typical.

JAMES I

James I (1603–25) was faced by factionalism at court, tension over
religious issues and the unpopularity of the pro-Spanish tendency
of his policies, and bitter criticism of his heavy expenditure and
consequent fiscal expedients. James's use and choice of favourites

were unpopular. A clever man, who lacked majesty and the ability to inspire or command support, but nevertheless had exalted views of his royal position and rights, James encountered problems similar to those of Elizabeth in her later years; but the Treaty of London with Spain (1604), his subsequent care to avoid war until persuaded into one with Spain in 1624, and the absence of conflict in Scotland and Ireland increased his political freedom of manoeuvre. With the exception of the brief Addled Parliament of 1614, which neither voted money nor legislated, James ruled without Parliament between 1610 and 1621. The Addled Parliament could not have encouraged him to seek parliamentary approval. The two houses quarrelled, while the Commons were prickly about their privileges and independence, fearing that some politicians had been undertaking to manage them for the king, and reluctant to vote supply until grievances had been settled. In response to demands in 1621 that Parliament should be able to debate any subject, James tore the Protestation from the Commons Journal and dissolved Parliament. The 1624 Parliament, however, provided the basis for war with Spain, successfully linking the redress of grievances to the grant of supply and helping to channel popular and political enthusiasm for the conflict to effect.

The political system continued to display serious strains in Charles I's early years. His favour for Buckingham was unpopular, while the steps taken to finance unsuccessful wars with Spain (1624–30) and France (1627–9) led to public discontent and parliamentary protests, especially the 1626 parliamentary complaints about unauthorised levies on trade and the Petition of Right (1628) which protested that imprisonment at royal will and taxes without parliamentary consent were illegal. The misuse of legal procedures in order to extend the Crown's lands was an example of an abuse that pressed hard on the elite. The House of Commons was particularly resistant to royal control. The tensions of the period led to a major revival of ringing bells for the accession day of Elizabeth I, recalling times past when the monarch had been clearly identified with the successful pursuit of what were generally seen as national interests. Yet there was nothing to match the crisis of 1638–42, no parallel to the serious problems that affected France and the Austrian Habsburgs in the 1610s and early 1620s. James I, and Charles I in his early years, did not have to campaign against their own subjects as Louis XIII and Ferdinand II had to do.

Not only did James succeed to the throne peacefully in 1603, bu
the union of the Crowns was reasonably successful during his reign
Despite James VI and I's hopes for a 'union of love', or at least a
measure of administrative and economic union between England
and Scotland, the union remained essentially personal, and Scot
land was governed by the Scottish Privy Council in a relatively
successful fashion. The Highlands were brought under greate
control from Edinburgh, and episcopacy was re-established. A
closer union was regarded with suspicion in England.

James's reign also saw the establishment of English colonies in
North America. The Virginia Company, chartered in 1606, estab
lished a colony in the Chesapeake region, while in 1620 the *May
flower* made a landfall at Cape Cod. Virginia and New England had
an English population of 26,000 by 1640. Henry Hudson entered
what became known as Hudson Bay in 1610. The English also
colonised Bermuda (1613), and in the West Indies, St Kitts (1624)
Barbados (1627) and Nevis (1628). Trans-Atlantic trade and fishing
grew, bringing new activity to ports on western coasts, for exampl
Bristol and those in north Devon.

CHARLES I's 'PERSONAL RULE', 1629–40

The situation in England eased in the early 1630s. Buckingham'
death, Charles I's decision in 1629 to rule without Parliament, and
the coming of peace with France and Spain helped to reduc
tension. Neutrality, while most of Europe was involved in th
Thirty Years War (1618–48), helped to bring a measure of prosper
ity. There was tension, however, over Charles's novel financia
demands as the king sought to deal with his serious financia
problems. The extension of ship money to support the navy to
inland areas in 1635 was particularly unpopular, though most di
not follow John Hampden in refusing to pay. The toleration o
Catholics at court, where the Catholic queen, Henrietta Maria, wa
a prominent supporter, was more serious, as was the Arminia
tendency within the Church of England associated with William
Laud, whom Charles made Archbishop of Canterbury (1633)
Arminianism, especially its innovations in worship and church
services, was seen as crypto-Catholic by its critics. For example
the moving and railing in of communion tables was regarded as a

reversal of Protestant practice. Charles lacked common sense, was untrustworthy and could be harsh towards critics. He believed in order, sought to maintain the dignity of kingship, and was a keen supporter of Laud's religious policies. He supported needlessly provocative measures such as the Laudian *Instructions* of 1630 which forbade the appointment of clergy as chaplains by nobles unless strictly in accordance with a law of 1530. In practice the instruction was unenforceable and provoked Puritan nobles. Charles was authoritarian, intolerant and no compromiser. Prerogative courts under royal control, especially Star Chamber and High Commission, could give out savage penalties. Nevertheless, despite differences over constitutional questions, such as the relationship between the monarch and the law, few in England wished to overthrow Charles I. There was considerable public attachment to the role of parliaments and to the principle of parliamentary taxation, but the system of government was generally believed to be divinely instituted, and if Charles was a bad ruler God would punish him in the next world, not man in this, though religion was seen by some as providing justification for resistance. Rebellion and civil war were regarded by most as akin to plagues in the body of the nation, and looked far from predictable in the mid-1630s.

THE CAUSES AND COURSE OF CIVIL WAR

The outbreak of civil war in England was the immediate result of political crisis in 1641–2 stemming from risings in Scotland (1638) and Ireland (1641). In Wales there was criticism of the policies of Charles I in the 1620s and 1630s, and in particular of the activities of the Council of the Marches, but it was far less serious than that elsewhere.

In Scotland, the absentee Charles's support for episcopacy and liturgical change and his tactless and autocratic handling of Scottish interests and patronage led to a Presbyterian and national response which produced a National Covenant (1638) opposed to all ecclesiastical innovations. Episcopacy was abolished and when Charles responded in the Bishops' Wars (1639–40), he was defeated. Charles's folly of threatening violence in 1639 was followed by making good that threat in 1640 without the means to sustain it. He made a poor choice of commanders and inadequate finance wrecked logistics. The English army was unpopular, poorly prepared and deployed and therefore collapsed when attacked by the large, professionally officered Scottish army in 1640.

As with the last military commitment, the wars with Spain and France of the 1620s, the Bishops' Wars weakened Charles, first by undermining his finances, and then because he was unsuccessful. They also altered the relationship between Crown and Parliament in England. Charles's 'Personal Rule' had failed. Rulers of England lacked the resources to fight wars, unless they turned to Parliament. To raise funds, Charles summoned the 'Short Parliament' in April 1640, but, as it refused to vote them until grievances had been redressed, it was speedily dissolved. The Treaty of Ripon (October 1640) ending the Bishops' Wars, however, left the Scots in occupation of the north of England and in receipt of a daily payment by Charles until a final settlement could be negotiated. Charles was therefore forced to turn to Parliament again, and this 'Long Parliament', which met in November 1640, was to survive, albeit with many interruptions and changes of membership, until 1660, longer than Charles.

Initially Parliament was united in the redress of grievances. It represented a sense of national identity and interest beside which the king's views appeared unacceptable. Parliament used the weapon of impeachment against Charles's much-feared ministers. Thomas, Earl of Strafford, the autocratic Lord Deputy of Ireland, was attainted and executed (1641) for planning to bring Charles's Irish army to England, and Laud was imprisoned (he was executed in 1645). Restrictions on the Crown's power were even more important, and Charles's opponents thought them crucial. One, Lord Saye and Sele, subsequently wrote that it was necessary to resist Charles because he had determined 'to destroy the Parliament of England'. They wanted to restore what they saw as the government of Elizabeth I: a system of clearcut Protestantism at home and abroad, and both Parliament and the aristocracy through the Privy Council playing a major role. A Triennial Act decreed that Parliament was to meet at least every three years. Other acts forbade the dissolution of the Long Parliament without its own consent, abolished Star Chamber, High Commission and ship money and limited the Crown's financial power.

Though these changes raised serious points, and the obstinate Charles was hostile after the execution of Strafford, they were accomplished without causing the division that religious issues created at the end of 1641. The retention of episcopacy, traditional order and discipline in the Church proved very divisive, while the need to raise forces to deal with a major Catholic rising in Ireland in 1641 led to a serious rift over how they were to be controlled and to an escalating crisis. Charles resorted to violence, invading Parliament on 4 January 1642 in order to seize his most virulent opponents, including John Pym, but they had already fled by water to the City of London, a stronghold of hostility to the king. As both sides prepared for war, Charles left London in order to raise forces, a crucial move as the history of civil conflict up to and including the Jacobite rising in 1745 was to show that control of the resources and legitimating institutions of the capital was to be vital.

In 1642 many sought peace, and local neutrality pacts were negotiated, but determined minorities on both sides polarised the nation. Compromise and conciliation proved impossible, the product of the tensions and fears created by Charles I's policies and apparent intentions. Although it is dangerous to adopt a crude socio-economic or geographical determinism in explaining the divisions between the two sides, and it is clear that each had support in every region and social group, it is also true that parliamentary support was strongest in the most economically advanced regions: the south and east of England, many of the large towns, especially London and Bristol, and in industrial areas; while that for Charles I in England and Wales was most pronounced in less advanced regions: the north, Wales and the west. Thus, religious and political differences were related to socio-economic situations, though not dependent on them. For example, the Derbyshire lead miners were split. Charles's supporters feared religious, social and political change, and were motivated by concepts of honour and loyalty. The sweeping parliamentary powers and reformation of the Church demanded by Parliament in the Nineteen Propositions of June 1642 seemed excessive to many moderates.

Fighting began at Manchester in July 1642, and at Nottingham the following month Charles, who lacked any military experience, raised his standard. He advanced on London, narrowly winning the battle of Edgehill (23 October), but failed to follow up after the battle and was checked at Turnham Green just to the west of the

capital in November 1642. An irresolute general, he failed to pres
home an advantage in what were disadvantageous circumstance;
and retreated to establish his headquarters at Oxford. His bes
chance to win the war had passed. In 1643 the royalists made gain
in much of England, particularly the West Country where Bristc
fell, but Charles's truce with the Irish rebels, which freed the roya
forces in Ireland, was more than counteracted by the Solem
League and Covenant between the Scots and the parliamentarian;
The Scots accordingly entered England the following January, an
at Marston Moor near York on 2 July 1644 they and a parliamer
tary army under Sir Thomas Fairfax and Oliver Cromwell crushe
the royalists under Prince Rupert and the Duke of Newcastle. Th
north had been lost for Charles I.

The following year the parliamentary forces were reorganise
with the creation of the New Model Army, a national army with
unified command under Fairfax, with Cromwell as commander c
the cavalry. The army was more cohesive and professional an
better cared for than other forces. Its initial effectiveness was i
part due to it being paid with remarkable regularity for more tha
two years. In 1645 this force defeated the royalist field armies, wit
the victory at Naseby (14 June) being especially decisive. Charles
had only 7,600 men to Fairfax's 14,000. Rupert swept the parli¿
mentary cavalry on the left from the field, but then attacked th
baggage train, while Cromwell on the parliamentarian right de
feated the royalist cavalry opposite and then turned on the royalis
infantry in the centre, which succumbed to the overwhelmin
attack. The superior discipline of the parliamentary cavalry thu
played a major role in the victory. By the end of the year, th
royalists were reduced to isolated strongholds, and in May 164
Charles I gave himself up to the Scots.

Parliamentary victory in England was due to a number of fa¿
tors, including the backing of the wealthiest parts of the countr;
the support of the Scots, London, the major ports and the nav;
and the religious zeal of some of its followers. Cromwell sa
himself as God's chosen instrument destined to overthrow religiou
and political tyranny, a potent belief. On the other hand, th
parliamentarians also suffered from lacklustre and unsuccessf¿
commanders, such as the Earls of Essex and Manchester and S
William Waller, the leading generals in 1642–3; they aroused ho
tility by high taxation, and initially had far less effective caval¿

than the royalists. The royalist army developed into an impressive force with good officers and sound infantry, and in 1644 an acceptable peace for Charles was not an impossible prospect. As with the collapse of royal power in 1639–40, the defeat of Charles I owed much to the Scots, and it is not surprising that they played such a major role in the politics of the late 1640s, nor that England only became really stable when a government acceptable to the Commonwealth was installed in Scotland in the early 1650s. The union of the Crowns ensured that the political fate of the two countries could not be separated. The Cromwellian conquests of Scotland and Ireland were the consequence, and they prefigured the Restoration of Stuart monarchy throughout the British Isles in very different circumstances, in ensuring the end of any successful attempt by Scotland and Ireland to chart a different political trajectory to that of England.

THE WAR IN WALES

The royalist cause was also defeated in Wales and Scotland. When the civil war broke out the overwhelming majority of the Welsh were loyal; support for Parliament was strongest in Pembrokeshire, an English area. The Welsh gentry were overwhelmingly royalist and there was no large urban environment within which support for Parliament and Puritanism could develop. Wales produced large numbers of men and much money for Charles, and Welsh troops, especially infantry, played a major role, both in operations against nearby targets, particularly Gloucester, which was besieged unsuccessfully in 1643, and in more distant fields.

Initially fighting within Wales was confined to the south-west. Tenby and Haverfordwest fell to the royalists in 1643, but Pembroke was reinforced by a parliamentary fleet in 1644 and much of the county was retaken. Parliamentary forces then advanced to capture Cardiganshire and Carmarthen, from which they were in turn driven in the summer of 1644. Fighting swayed to and fro until, in late 1645, the impact of parliamentary success elsewhere helped to produce triumph in south-west Wales.

In November 1643 much of north Wales was overrun by the parliamentary forces, but they were driven back by troops from Ireland and it was not until the summer of 1644 that the parlia-

mentarians made a major impact again in north-east Wales. Th
fall of nearby royalist bases in England, Shrewsbury, Bristol an
Chester between February 1645 and February 1646 was crucia
Royalist confidence in Wales was undermined, as was the Wels
economy, and in the autumn of 1645 the royalist position in sout
Wales collapsed, with mass defections. The castles were left i
royalist hands but they fell to the remorseless pressure of superic
parliamentary forces, Harlech finally surrendering in March 164'

THE WAR IN SCOTLAND

After the Scots entered England in January 1644, Charles se
James Graham, Marquis of Montrose, to invade Scotland. H
did so with a small army in April 1644 but, having capture
Dumfries, had to retreat in face of a more numerous oppositic
force. Invading again in August he routed Lord Elcho's larger arm
at Tippermuir (1 September): Montrose won a firefight and fo
lowed this up with a successful charge on an already beaten oppc
nent. On 13 September 1644 another victory was won outsic
Aberdeen. At Inverlochy (2 February 1645) Montrose's men d
layed firing on Argyll's Highlanders until the last moment and the
followed up their devastating volley with a successful charge. A
with the other Scottish battles, the bulk of the fighting was borr
by Irish or Lowland infantry, and the Highlanders were used 1
rout an already defeated opponent. More casualties were als
caused in the pursuit than in the battle. Montrose took Elgin (1
February) and Dundee (4 April), before retreating in the face (
more numerous opponents. At the battle of Auldearn (9 Ma
1645), Montrose's ability to respond decisively to the unpredictab
nature of the battle won victory, as it did for Cromwell at Naseb
A successful counter-attack brought victory over a larger force. A
Alford (2 July) victory in the opening cavalry-battle left the oppo
ing infantry exposed to attack in flank and rear; and at Kilsyth ('
August) the main government army in Scotland under Gener
William Baillie was defeated, Montrose's cavalry again playing
decisive role. Glasgow and Edinburgh were then briefly occupie
but Montrose's army shrank as the Highlanders returned hom
The Scottish army in England under General David Leslie marche

north and at Philiphaugh (13 September 1645) Montrose's outnumbered army was surprised and defeated. Montrose fled back to
the highlands, his prestige shattered. After guerrilla action that
winter, Montrose failed to take Inverness, although another royalist, the Marquis of Huntly, stormed Aberdeen on 14 May 1646.
Both then dispersed their troops when Charles I, having surrendered to the Scots, ordered them to lay down their arms.

Montrose was often at fault for neglecting to arrange effective
reconnaissance, and he failed to gain control of an area of any size
for long enough to establish himself and recruit substantial numbers of men. He was, however, a brilliant tactician, a master of the
flank victory and subsequent destruction of the opponent's centre;
and as a commander very successful in welding together militia and
regulars.

CIVIL WAR IN IRELAND, 1641–9

In 1641, driven by anger at their treatment by Protestant overlords
and settlers and under economic pressure, the Catholic Irish rose
and slaughtered many of the Anglo-Scottish settlers. Their leader
Rory O'More defeated government forces at Julianstown (29 November 1641) and then allied with many of the Old English landowners of the Pale. Ulster was overrun by the rebels. Protestant
churches were desecrated and bibles burned. The Scots sent an
army to reimpose Protestant rule and it landed at Carrickfergus
in April 1642. There was then a three-way struggle between Scots/
Parliamentarians, royalists under James Butler, Earl of Ormonde,
and the Catholic confederacy of Kilkenny: the Irish rebels. The last,
under Owen Roe O'Neill, crushed the Scots army at Benburb (5
June 1646). In 1647, with Charles I imprisoned, Ormonde surrendered Dublin to Michael Jones, a parliamentary colonel. His position there was challenged by the Catholic confederates under
Thomas Preston, but at Dungan Hill (8 August, 1647), Jones
heavily defeated Preston, capturing all his artillery. The parliamentary cause deteriorated in 1648 when the Second Civil War led
Ormonde to return from Scotland. In 1649 he took Drogheda and
Dundalk, and in June 1649 besieged Jones in Dublin. A sortie by
Jones defeated Ormonde at Rathmines (2 August). Cromwell
landed at Dublin 13 days later.

THE SECOND CIVIL WAR

As so often, victory led to disunity. Parliament, the army and the Scots were divided. There were crucial divisions over Church government, especially the establishment of a presbyterian system which the Scots demanded and many English parliamentarian opposed, and over negotiations with Charles, who was handed over by the Scots when they left England in 1647. Radical social and political changes were advocated by the Levellers, who had considerable support in the army, and the army, disaffected by the attitude of Parliament and the failure to pay its arrears of wages increasingly took a political role. Charles was seized by the army in 1647, but he rejected Cromwell's proposed settlement. Cromwell disenchanted with both the presbyterians in Parliament and the Levellers, whose mutiny in the army he had crushed, played the crucial role in ending the Second Civil War (1648). This stemmed from royalist risings and a Scottish invasion on behalf of Charles I who had agreed in return to introduce a Presbyterian system. The risings were crushed. Cromwell advanced into south Wales and his opponents were defeated at St Fagan's. Fairfax moved into Kent and disrupted the royalists there in June. The royalists then concentrated at Colchester, resisted assaults by Fairfax and waited for news of the Scots.

Having taken the surrender of Pembroke (11 July), Cromwell moved to intercept the Scots who, under the Duke of Hamilton entered Cumberland on 8 July and pushed south. Cromwell advanced into Yorkshire and decided to attack the flank of his opponents' advance at Preston. Hamilton ignored warnings from the royalist Sir Marmaduke Langdale and his uncoordinated forces were spread out when Cromwell pushed back Langdale's men and captured Preston on 17 August. The Scots surrendered.

Determined to deal with Charles, and thanks to religious zeal not intimidated about confronting their anointed king, the army purged Parliament in Pride's purge on 6 December 1648. Those who were left, the 'Rump', appointed a court to try Charles for treason against the people. Parliament argued that Charles had given his word of honour not to fight again, and that he had broken it when he encouraged the Second Civil War. Charles refused to plead, arguing that subjects had no right to try the king and that he stood for the liberties of the people. He was found guilty and

executed on 30 January 1649 at the centre of royal power, outside
the Banqueting Hall in Whitehall.

REPUBLICAN ENGLAND

The formal trial and public execution of Charles I were markedly
dissimilar to the killing of medieval kings. England was declared a
republic, the Commonwealth, and the House of Lords abolished.
Feudal dues had already been abolished in 1645. The Church of
England was effectively disestablished. The republican regime in
England was, however, faced with very different governments in
Scotland and Ireland, and could not feel safe until these had been
overthrown. In a tremendous display of military power that contrasted with the indecisiveness of much conflict on the Continent,
the republican forces conquered both Scotland, a success that had
eluded many English monarchs, and Ireland, as well as the remaining English royalist bases in the Channel Islands, the Isles of Scilly
and the Isle of Man.

THE CROMWELLIAN CONQUEST OF IRELAND, 1649–52

Cromwell crossed to Ireland and conquered most of the east and
south in 1649, a task that was completed with the overrunning of
the whole island by mid–1653. Cromwell's campaign, especially the
capture of Drogheda and Wexford in 1649, has since become
proverbial for cruelty and as such plays a major role in the anglo-
phobic Irish public myth. In fact, many Irish fought the royalists in
what was an Irish civil war as much as an English invasion;
massacres during conflicts in Ireland or in continental Europe were
far from new, the Catholic uprising of 1641 in particular beginning
with a widespread slaughter of Protestants; and at both Drogheda
and Wexford there were no attacks on women or children. At
Drogheda, however, where Cromwell's superb train of siege artillery enabled him to fire 200 cannonballs in one day, the garrison of
about 2,500 was slaughtered, the few who received quarter being
sent to work the Barbados sugar plantations. After Wexford,
Cromwell captured Ross, Carrick, Clonmel and Kilkenny, and
on 26 May 1650 he left for England. His successor, his son-in-

law Henry Ireton, defeated his opponents at Scarrifhollis (21 Jun
1650) and captured Limerick (27 October 1651). Galway fell th
following year. Conquest, however, led, as a result largely (
famine, plague and emigration, to the loss of about 40 per cer
of the Irish population, and was followed, especially in 1654–5, b
widespread expropriation of Catholic land, as the Anglo-Iris
Catholics lost power and status. The Gaelic schools, in which bard
were trained, were closed, a blow to the native cultural traditio
and the island was subjected to the Westminster Parliament.

THE CONQUEST OF SCOTLAND

Scottish quiescence was crucial to the early stages of the conques
of Ireland, but in 1650 Charles I's eldest son, Charles II, came t
terms with the Scots. In response, Cromwell invaded Scotland o
22 July 1650. He could not, however, breach the Scottish fortifie
positions around Edinburgh and, outmanoeuvred by David Leslie
had to retreat to Dunbar. Cut off from retreat to England by
force twice as big, Cromwell launched a surprise attack that de
feated the Scottish cavalry and then forced much of its infantry t
surrender (3 September). Edinburgh was then captured.

The following summer Cromwell used his command of the sea t
outflank the Scots at Stirling and occupy Perth, but Charles the
marched south into England, hoping to ignite a royalist rebellion
He reached Wigan on 15 August, but, short of recruits, decided t
head for the Welsh borders and not march directly on London
Shrewsbury, however, resisted Charles and when he reached Wor
cester on 22 August he had few additional men. His opponent
concentrated on Warwick on 24 August and then advanced o
Worcester, winning a crossing over the Severn at Upton. Th
parliamentarians under Cromwell, about 30,000 strong, drove o
Worcester on 3 September from a number of directions. Th
royalists, about 12,000 strong, launched an initially successfu
frontal attack on Cromwell's position, but numbers told and th
royalist army was overwhelmed. Hiding in an oak tree and sup
porters' houses *en route*, Charles II fled to France, but the royalis
cause had been crushed. By the summer of 1652 all Scotland ha
fallen. Heavily garrisoned and governed by commissioners sen
from England, Scotland faced many difficulties in the 1650s. Th

nobility were deprived of their hereditary jurisdictions, the people were heavily taxed and a Highland rising was crushed in 1654.

THE COMMONWEALTH

The strength, vitality and determination of the Commonwealth government was further displayed by its aggressive policy towards foreign powers. Commercial rivalry with the Dutch and suspicion of their political intentions led to the First Anglo-Dutch War (1652–4). The strength of the Commonwealth navy and the skill of its admirals, especially Robert Blake, led to success at sea, though the war was very expensive. Military strength and success, and war on the Continent, helped to win the republic international recognition. Unlike Reformation England, it was clear that the republic would not have to fear foreign intervention; its principal challenges lay at home.

There were indeed serious divisions within the republican camp. Clashes over religious issues were related to disputes over the position of the army and the nature of the constitution. Having changed the latter thanks to the use of force, it was difficult to prevent further desire for change and recourse to force. Evidence of social and religious radicalism, however small-scale its support might be, was deeply disturbing to many supporters of the Commonwealth. A variety of sects, groupings and tendencies, including Muggletonians, Diggers, Quakers and Ranters, supported a variety of radical changes, including the communalisation of waste land, abolition of the Church and of lawyers, proclaimed the superiority of personal revelation over scripture, and argued that the second coming of Christ was imminent.

OLIVER CROMWELL

Disputes led Cromwell, now head of the army, to close the purged 'Rump' Parliament in April 1653. A new, overwhelmingly military, council of state to administer the country, and a nominated 'Parliament', better known as the Barebone's Parliament after a radical member, Praise-God Barebone, were both appointed. This Parliament was the first to have representatives from Scotland and Ireland, mostly Englishmen serving there. Most members were not from the traditional ruling elite, but were instead minor gentry. If anything, though, they were less representative than the usual parliamentarians, as they were not elected by any process, but chosen by the council of officers. In the sole systematic reform of the electoral system before the First Reform Act of 1832 rotten boroughs (constituencies with very few electors) were replaced by more county seats and separate representation for expanding industrial towns, such as Bradford, Leeds and Manchester. The franchise (right to vote) was extended. Divorced from the bulk of the population, both elite and otherwise, the regime was, however, taking no steps to end this unpopularity.

Barebone's Parliament was divided between radicals, who wished, for example, to abolish tithes and the right of patrons to appoint clergy to livings, a property right and a source of gentry influence, and those who were less radical; and this led to the collapse of the Parliament in December 1653, creating a vacuum that Cromwell, as commander in chief, was obliged to fill. He did so by becoming Lord Protector. For a man born into the Huntingdonshire gentry who had had no tenants and who had worked for a living, this was possibly the most dramatic example of upward social mobility in British history, though it was a side-effect of the most sweeping political revolution in that history. Cromwell told MPs in 1657 that he had taken on his position 'out of a desire to prevent mischief and evil, which I did see was imminent upon the nation'. Until his death in 1658, Cromwell ruled even if he did not reign, but he faced difficulties with the Parliaments that were called and in the localities the decision in 1655 to entrust authority to major-generals instructed to preserve security and create a godly and efficient kingdom was unpopular. It also made it harder to demilitarise the regime. Cromwell's willingness to sacrifice constitutional and institutional continuity and his distrust of outward forms were not generally welcomed; nor were the religious 'reforms' of republican England, such as the introduction of civil marriage, attacks on the churching of women after childbirth, changes in baptism practices, the readmission of the Jews (expelled by Edward I in 1290), and the toleration of a range of sects and practices that were anathema to many. Parliament had already banned the eating of mince pies and Christmas pudding on Christmas Day in 1646.

Political, social and religious conservatism were both strong and strengthened by the experience of the 1650s. The 'godly' were neither numerous nor united: some of their preachers compared England to Israel after Moses, ungrateful for the gifts of God. Repression of popular rituals deemed superstitious, popish or profane, such as Christmas and dancing round the maypole, led to antipathy: Daniel Defoe was later to claim that 6,325 maypoles were erected in the first five years after the monarchy was restored in 1660. In the 1650s hostility to Puritanism fused with resentment towards the repressive, radical and illegal regime. War with Spain (1655–9) led to the capture of Jamaica, but hopes of gaining Cuba and Hispaniola proved wildly over-optimistic and the cost of the conflict caused a financial crisis.

In Wales, the royalist defeat was followed by the creation of a new ruling order in which the attempt to spread radical Puritanism played a major role. Under an Act of 1650 for 'the Better Propagation of the Gospel in Wales', seventy-one Commissioners were instructed to organise the evangelism of Wales. 278 Anglican clerics were dispossessed, their tithes and livings placed at the disposal of the commissioners, who helped themselves to some of this income, and itinerant Puritan preachers were appointed. One of the more prominent was Vavasor Powell, who received a bullet wound during the war and then thought himself called by a heavenly voice: 'I have chosen thee to preach the gospel.' As in England, the interregnum was a period of great uncertainty. Radical political and religious ideas, such as those of the Quakers, aroused widespread antipathy and most of the Welsh remained attached to the Anglican Church. Such allegiance could take ugly forms. The Quaker evangelist Alice Birkett was stripped naked and stoned in Llandaff churchyard. This conservatism was to ensure that the Restoration of Charles II in 1660 was generally popular.

Cromwell died on the anniversary of his great victories of Dunbar and Worcester, but he was not an Alexander cut short in his prime. When he died the unpopularity and divisions of the regime were readily apparent, and there was, in Charles II, a legitimate pretender still threatening the stability of the system. Cromwell had neither led the latter-day children of Israel to the promised land, as he had sought to do, nor created a stable government that would maintain and further his achievements. Cromwell's support for legal and educational reform was, however, forward-looking. His successor as Protector, his son Richard, was unable to command authority, but in his last months, Oliver's leadership had also been faltering.

Parliamentary, army and financial problems crippled Richard's protectorate. Deposed in 1659 as a result of a military coup, he was followed by a restoration of the Rump Parliament and the Commonwealth, but the Parliament was dismissed by the army (October 1659), and, with anarchy apparently imminent and the army divided, the commander in Scotland, George Monck, marched south, restored order and a moderate Parliament, and this paved the way for the return of monarchy (1660). Charles II was invited to return from exile. The Puritan attempt to reform society and worship, to force their moral imperatives upon society, had failed. English society was to be much more conservative as a result.

RESTORED MONARCHY

The Restoration Settlement brought Charles II (1660–85) to the thrones of England, Ireland and Scotland. He was an appropriate figure to preside over the reconciliation and, still more, the stabilisation required after the 1640s and 1650s. Able and determined on his rights, Charles was nevertheless flexible and his ambition was essentially modest, the preservation of his position, rather than centring on any creation of a strong monarchy. He lacked the autocratic manner of his second cousin, Louis XIV of France, who assumed personal power in 1661. If there was to be a royalist reaction, it would not be led by the king, although it was claimed that he told his trusted advisers in 1669 that he planned an autocracy. Charles's charm was also a definite asset and, if he was not trusted by all and was seen as a tyrant and a rake by some, he was able to avoid the reputations and fates of his father, Charles I, and his brother, James II.

Apart from those who had signed Charles I's death warrant, all parliamentarians and Cromwellians were pardoned. Royal powers were to be fewer than they had been in 1640, but greater than in late 1641, let alone later in the 1640s. Charles II was given a reasonable income and control over the army, but the prerogative taxation and jurisdictional institutions of the 1630s, for example ship money and Star Chamber, were not restored. There was to be no substantial landed estate under Crown control that might enable the monarch to maintain his financial independence. Proposals advanced in the 1650s for the reform of Parliament, the law and the universities, were certainly not welcome in the conservative atmosphere of the 1660s. Bradford, Leeds and Manchester lost their parliamentary seats. The monarch might again reign by divine right, and a very different right from the providentialism claimed by Cromwell, but he was to rule thanks to Parliament: this was intended to be a parliamentary monarchy. The loss of prerogative powers and the need for parliamentary taxation ensured that Charles would also rule through Parliament, as was shown in 1661–2 when Charles II's hopes of a broadly based established Church incorporating as many Protestants as possible, with toleration for the rest, were rejected by the 'Cavalier Parliament' (1661–79). The Corporation Act (1661) obliged town officials to accept an Anglicanism that clearly differentiated itself from nonconformity, while the Test Acts (1673, 1678), excluded Catholics from office and Parliament and Dissenters from office. Thanks to the Act of Uniformity of 1662, Presbyterian clergy were ejected from their parishes, and worship with five or more people was forbidden unless according to Anglican rites. 130 ministers lost their livings in Wales, and in England the Baptist preacher John Bunyan was convicted of preaching without licence to unlawful assemblies and began writing *The Pilgrim's Progress* in prison. Fear as well as revenge conditioned the Restoration Settlement. A sense of precariousness, especially fears about republican conspiracies which indeed existed, led to treason and militia acts. Nevertheless, much of the legislation was undermined when Puritan gentry evaded it: gentry JPs often colluded in this evasion. Ejected Puritan clergy were frequently employed by Puritan gentry as private chaplains and tutors.

In Ireland the Cromwellian land settlement was put into only mild reversal. In Scotland Parliament, episcopacy and aristocratic power and influence were restored. About a third of the Scottish parish ministers were unwilling to accept the new religious settlement. Nonconformist conventicles acted as centres of defiance, and government attempts to suppress them led to unsuccessful rebellions in 1666, 1680 and, more significantly, 1679. John, Duke of Lauderdale, the Secretary for Scottish Affairs, maintained royal power.

Charles II was unhappy with the religious settlement and with attempts to restrict his freedom of manoeuvre. This became more serious as a result of his Catholic leanings. He was the ruler on whom the fictional King Bolloximian of *Sodom: or, the Quintessence of Debauchery* was modelled:

> Thus in the zenith of my lust I reign;
> I eat to survive and survive to eat again
> . . . And with my prick I'll govern all the land.

Vice and corruption at court were bad enough to many, but a Catholic as ruler was totally unacceptable. In a culture that knew little of religious toleration such a king appeared to imperil national independence, Church and society. Anti-popery and fear of arbitrary government were as important in the second half of the century as in the first. Yet, as later with George III, it would be unwise to exaggerate the king's unpopularity. Charles II touched a large number of people for the King's Evil (scrofula), evidence of faith in and demand for the curative powers of kingship.

Failure in the Second Anglo-Dutch War (1665–7), including an humiliating attack on the English fleet in the Medway (1667), was followed by the Secret Treaty of Dover with the most powerful Catholic monarch, Louis XIV (1670). Charles, in broad terms, promised to declare his conversion to Catholicism and to restore the religion to England. The two monarchs were to unite in attacking the Dutch, the leading Protestant power. This was the real Popish Plot, and suspicion about Charles's intentions helped not only to bedevil the rest of his reign, but also to ensure that his successor, his Catholic brother James II (1685–8), came to the throne in an atmosphere in which suspicion about Catholics had been both heightened and crucially linked to Louis XIV, whose moves against Protestants in France, culminating in the revocation of the Edict of Nantes (1685), were an apparent warning that Catholic rulers could not be trusted and would always be bitterly anti-Protestant.

THE POPISH PLOT

The Third Anglo-Dutch War (1672–4) was unsuccessful and it led to the fall of Charles's ministry, the Cabal. Such political storms could, however, be mastered by the adept Charles, always ready to sacrifice ministers to secure his own position, but the Popish Plot of 1678 attacked Charles at his weakest points. Though he was the father of at least fourteen male bastards, the succession was a major problem for Charles. There were no legitimate children by his

marriage to the somewhat unappealing Portuguese princess, Catherine of Braganza (who had brought Bombay and Tangier as her
dowry in 1661), so his brother James, Duke of York, was his heir.
The Popish Plot stemmed from claims made by the adventurer,
Titus Oates, of the existence of a Catholic plot to assassinate
Charles and replace him by James. The murder of Sir Edmund
Berry Godfrey, the magistrate who took the evidence, and the
discovery of suspicious letters in the possession of James's former
private secretary, Edward Coleman, inflamed suspicions and led to
politics by orchestrated paranoia, a series of show-trials in which
Catholics were convicted and then executed. The revelation by
political rivals that Charles II's leading minister, Lord Treasurer
Danby, had been negotiating with Louis XIV, fanned the flames.
Danby fell from office and court power collapsed.

THE EXCLUSION CRISIS

The Popish Plot became an attempt to use Parliament to exclude
James from the succession and to weaken Charles's government:
the Exclusion Crisis (1678–81). Its leading advocate, Anthony, Earl
of Shaftesbury, created what has been seen as the first English
political party, the 'Whigs', an abusive term referring to Scottish
Presbyterian rebels, originally used by their opponents, though the
party should rather be seen as a faction held together by informal
ties, ambition and ideology, not by party discipline and central
control. The Whigs produced a mass of propaganda. The first
unlicensed newspaper made clear its didactic nature in its title,
'The Weekly Pacquet of Advice from Rome . . . in the process of
which, the Papists arguments are answered, their fallacies detected,
their cruelties registered, their treasons and seditious principles
observed'. Mistrust of the court wrecked the possible success of
an alternative to exclusion in the shape of the limitation of James's
power.

   Anti-Catholicism could help create a crisis that the Whigs could
exploit, but they suffered from the determination of most people to
avoid rebellion and a repetition of the chaos of the Civil War; the
strength of Charles's position in the House of Lords and the king's
right to summon and dissolve Parliament as he thought fit, both of
which blocked exclusion in a legal fashion; the lack of a generally

agreed alternative to James; and Charles's fixed determination. With Scotland and Ireland securely under control after the Covenanter rising of 1679 in Scotland was suppressed, Charles II did not face a crisis comparable to that of 1638–42, and he avoided foolish moves such as his father's attempt to arrest the Five Members. In reaction to the Whigs, the 'Tories' developed as a conservative and loyalist grouping, supporters of the king and the Church of England. In Scotland the Test Act of 1681 obliged all ministers and office-holders to repudiate Covenants. James was based in Edinburgh in 1679–82 and Holyrood Palace in Edinburgh was rebuilt as a court centre in the northern kingdom.

Whig failure to secure exclusion in 1681 led to a reaction that was eased by Charles's negotiation that year of a subsidy from Louis XIV that enabled him to do without Parliament for the rest of his reign. Whig office-holders were purged and Whig leaders fled or were compromised in the Rye House Plot (1683), an alleged conspiracy to assassinate Charles and James. This led to executions and stimulated an attack on Whig strongholds. Corporation charters, for example that of London, were remodelled in order to increase Crown influence, and Dissenters (Protestants who were not members of the Church of England, many of whom were Whigs) were persecuted.

JAMES II, 1685–8

Thanks to the reaction against the Exclusion Crisis, James II (James VII in Scotland) was able to succeed his brother with little difficulty (1685). His situation was strengthened that year by the defeat of rebellions in Scotland and England. Charles II's most charismatic bastard, James, Duke of Monmouth, who had pressed a claim to be Charles's heir during the Exclusion Crisis, arguing that Charles had really married his mother, Lucy Walter, landed at Lyme Regis on 11 June 1685. Monmouth won widespread support in Dorset and Somerset, and, at Sedgemoor on the night of 5/6 July, in a surprise attack on the royal army he nearly succeeded. His force was, however, routed with heavy casualties. Monmouth was executed and some of his supporters transported to the colonies or hanged after biased trials in the 'Bloody Assizes' of the West Country by Chief Justice George Jeffreys. A parallel rising in

Scotland under the Duke of Argyle was also crushed and Argyle was executed.

Like Cromwell, victory gave James a conviction of divine approval, and the rebellion led him to increase his army, but Parliament was unhappy about this and especially with the appointment of Catholic officers. James prorogued Parliament in November 1685 and it never met again in his reign. With less constraint, he then moved towards the Catholicising of the government. This made him unpopular. The changes necessary to establish full religious and civil equality for Catholics entailed a destruction of the privileges of the Church of England, a policy of appointing Catholics, the insistent use of prerogative action, and preparations for a packed Parliament. James took steps to develop the army into a professional institution answerable only to the king. And yet there was no revolution in the British Isles. Unlike in 1638–42, the Stuart monarchy was now strong enough to survive domestic challenges, and there was no breakdown of order in Scotland and Ireland.

The birth of a Prince of Wales on 10 June 1688 was a major shock to those unhappy with James's policies. 'It could not have been more public if he had been born in Charing Cross', noted the future Bishop Atterbury, but unhappy critics spread the rumour that a baby had been smuggled in in a warming pan. Hitherto James had had no surviving children from his fifteen-year long second Catholic marriage, but had two daughters, Mary and Anne, living from his Protestant first marriage. Mary was married to James's nephew, William III of Orange, who was the leading Dutch political figure and a Protestant. A male Catholic heir threatened to make James's changes permanent. Nineteen days later, in an enormously popular verdict, Archbishop Sancroft of Canterbury and six bishops were acquitted on charges of sedition for protesting against James's order that the Declaration of Indulgence granting all Christians full equality of religious practice, a move that challenged the position of the Church of England, be read from all pulpits.

THE 'GLORIOUS REVOLUTION', 1688

The more volatile and threatening situation led seven politicians to invite William to intervene in order to protect Protestantism and traditional liberties. Motivated rather by a wish to keep the British Isles out of Louis XIV's camp, William had already decided to invade. In many respects his invasion was a gamble, dependent on whether Louis XIV decided to attack the Dutch, on the policies of other powers, the winds in the North Sea and Channel, and the response of the English fleet and army. After his initial invasion plan had been thwarted by storms, William landed at Torbay on 5 November 1688. He benefited from a collapse of will on the part of James, who had an army twice the size of William's. James had been a brave commander earlier in his life, but in 1688 he suffered from a series of debilitating nose-bleeds and failed to lead his army into battle. There was also a haemorrhage of support, culminating with the flight of Lieutenant-General John Churchill from James's camp at Salisbury to William's side and that of Princess Anne from London. As James's resolve failed a vacuum of power developed. Most people did not want any breach in the hereditary succession, and William had initially claimed that he had no designs on the Crown. However, as the situation developed favourably, especially when James had been driven into exile, William made it clear that he sought the throne. This was achieved by declaring it vacant and inviting William and Mary to occupy it as joint monarchs. All Catholics were debarred from the succession.

6

. . . .

1689–1815

What was to become known as the Glorious Revolution was both the last successful invasion of England (and one that was largely bloodless) and a coup in which the monarch was replaced by his nephew and son-in-law, though William III's success also depended on an absence of extensive opposition in England, an absence reflecting apathy, reluctant compliance and a measure of active enthusiasm in his favour. The change of monarch led to war with Louis XIV of France, who gave James II shelter and support; and the need for parliamentary backing for the expensive struggle with the leading power in western Europe helped to give substance to the notion of parliamentary monarchy. The financial settlement obliged William to meet Parliament every year, the Triennial Act (1694) ensured regular meetings of Parliament, and, by restricting its life-span to three years, required regular elections, thus limiting potential for the management of Parliament by corruption. William's was truly a limited monarchy.

The Glorious Revolution was to play a crucial role in the English public myth, to be seen as the triumph of the liberal and tolerant spirit, the creation of a political world fit for Englishmen, the taproot of the Whig interpretation of history. This interpretation never made much sense from the Scottish or Irish perspective and it has recently been seriously challenged. What was for long seen as an irresistible manifestation of a general aspiration by British society for progress and liberty, can now be seen as it was by contemporaries, as a violent rupture, an ideological, political and diplomatic crisis. The cost of William's invasion was not only a civil war that brought much suffering to Scotland and Ireland, but also a foreign war that created considerable stresses within Britain.

143

James II was resolved to regain his throne and the Glorious Revolution was thus responsible for Jacobitism, as the cause of the exiled Stuarts came to be known from the Latin for James, Jacobus. Initially, James had French backing, controlled most of Ireland and had considerable support in Scotland. This situation looked back to the last period of Stuart dispossession, the English civil wars and interregnum, and there was no certainty that James would not be restored as his brother Charles II had been in 1660. This was a precedent that offered hope to the Jacobites. However, William III, like Cromwell before him, was to succeed in having the Stuarts and their supporters driven from Scotland and Ireland, thus forcing them to become reliant on foreign support that was offered in accordance with a diplomatic and military agenda, timetable and constraints that rarely suited the Jacobites.

James's standard was raised in Scotland in April 1689 by John Graham of Claverhouse, who was backed by the Episcopalians, the supporters of a Scottish Church controlled, like that of England, by bishops. This had been the established form, but in Scotland the Glorious Revolution entailed the establishment of its Protestant rival, Presbyterianism, which also enjoyed the support of about half the population. At the battle of Killiecrankie on 27 July, Claverhouse's Highlanders routed their opponents with the cold steel and rush of a Highland charge, but their leader was killed and the cause collapsed under his mediocre successors. Most of the Highland chiefs swore allegiance to William in late 1691.

WAR FOR IRELAND

The decisive battles were fought in Ireland, the Williamite conquest of which demonstrated the ability of a powerful and well led military force to overcome a hostile population. Ireland was more accessible than Scotland to the major French naval base of Brest. James's supporters controlled most of Ireland in 1689, although Derry, fearing Catholic massacre, resisted a siege and was relieved by the English fleet in July 1689. The following month William's forces, mostly Danes and Dutch, landed and occupied Belfast and Carrickfergus. Naval power thus offered William military flexibility and prevented James from controlling all of Ireland.

Arriving in Ireland in June 1690, William marched on Dublin to find the outnumbered Jacobite and French army (21,000 to 35–40,000) drawn up on the south bank of the River Boyne. Louis XIV's failure to attach the importance to Ireland that William III did was also crucial in terms of the resources available to the combatants. Having beaten the Jacobites at the Boyne on 1 July, William easily took Dublin, though he failed to take Limerick the following month. John Churchill, then Earl of Marlborough, captured Cork (September) and Kinsale (October). On 12 July 1691 Hugh Mackay turned the Jacobite flank at the last major battle, that of Aughrim, by leading his cavalry across a bog on which he had laid hurdles, and the Jacobite force broke, their infantry suffering heavy casualties in the rout. Galway fell and the Jacobite position collapsed with the capitulation of Limerick on 3 October. The war had done much damage. For example, the east town of Athlone was burnt in 1690, while the west town was badly damaged in 1691, receiving 12,000 cannon shot and 600 bombs from William III's artillery.

EIGHTEENTH-CENTURY IRELAND

By the Treaty of Limerick (1691) the Jacobites in Ireland surrendered, many, the 'Wild Geese', going to serve James in France. Ireland was then subjected to a Protestant ascendancy, which further entrenched the Protestant position in Ireland. The Catholics had held 59 per cent of the land in 1641 and 22 per cent in 1688. By 1703 this had fallen to 14 per cent, by 1778 to 5 per cent. Catholic officials and landowners were replaced and parliamentary legislation against Catholics was passed. Catholics were prevented from freely acquiring or bequeathing land or property by legislation of 1704. They were also disfranchised (lost the vote) and debarred from all political, military and legal offices and from Parliament. Acts forbade mixed marriages, Catholic schools and the bearing of arms by Catholics. The Catholic percentage of the population did not diminish, however, because serious repression was only episodic, not consistent, while the Catholic clergy, wearing secular dress and secretly celebrating mass, continued their work, sustained by a strong oral culture, the emotional link with a sense of national identity, by hedge-school teaching and by a certain amount of tacit government acceptance, and support from parts of Catholic Europe.

As a result of the transfer of land ownership, absentee landlords became more common, with money thus drained from the rural economy. Jonathan Swift, no Catholic but the Church of Ireland (Protestant) Dean of St Patrick's, Dublin, the leading Irish writer of the period, bitterly denounced the situation. In his *A Proposal for the Universal Use of Irish Manufacture . . . Rejecting and Renouncing every Thing wearable that comes from England* (1720) Swift attacked landlords, who, he alleged, had 'reduced the miserable People to a worse Condition than the Peasants in France'. The government tried to suppress the pamphlet. Swift's *A Short View of the State of Ireland* (1728) was a bitter account of the impact of English dominance on the Irish economy. A lack of economic activity was linked to poverty, so that tenants 'live worse than English Beggars'. In *The Intelligencer* of December 1728 Swift argued that Irish impoverishment would lead to emigration to America. His *Maxims controlled in Ireland*, written in 1729, again attacked absentee landlords and claimed that the condition of the poor was so bad that death was welcome.

Much of Ireland's economy remained basically pre-industrial. However, as it was drawn more fully into the market economy, its agricultural sector experienced growing diversification and commercialisation. Textile production developed markedly, while communications improved with the turnpiking of roads and development of canals. Recent scholarship has emphasised that Catholics of the period should be seen not as an amorphous mass of down-trodden victims, but as a more flexible group that interacted not only with civil disabilities but also with a growing economy. However, a combination of social stresses and agrarian discontents led to sporadic outbreaks of organised violence in certain parts of Ireland in the later eighteenth century: the Whiteboys of 1761–5 and 1769–76, the Oakboys of 1763, the Steelboys of 1769–72 and the Rightboys of the 1785–8. The American War of Independence provided the spark for a reform movement on the part of Protestant nationalists and weakened government opposition, so that in 1782 the Dublin Parliament, then a Protestant body, secured legislative independence from the Westminster Parliament.

ENGLISH DOMINATION OF THE BRITISH ISLES

The Glorious Revolution had profound consequences for patterns
of government in the British Isles, even if they were unintended. It
led to English domination of the British Isles, albeit domination
that was helped by and shared with important sections of the Irish
and Scottish population: Irish Anglicans and Scottish Presbyterians. The alternative had been glimpsed in 1689 when James II's
Parliament in Dublin had rejected much of the authority of the
Westminster Parliament. This path had, however, been blocked.
Jacobitism, and the strategic threat posed by an independent Scotland and Ireland, pushed together those politicians in the three
kingdoms who were opposed to it. The union of 1707 between
England and Scotland arose essentially from English concern about
the possible hazards posed by an autonomous, if not independent,
Scotland. There was only limited support for the measure in Scotland. Its passage through the Scottish Parliament depended in part
on corruption. The Scottish Privy Council, the main instrument of
absentee government for the past century, was also abolished in
1708, ensuring that greater stress had to be placed on the non-
institutional management of Scottish politics.

   In the early eighteenth century there was some support for union
with England among Irish Protestants, but it was unsuccessful. The
preservation of a Parliament in Dublin enabled Ireland's Protestant
politicians to retain a measure of importance and independence,
but legislation in Westminster, the result of protectionist lobbying
by English interests, hindered Irish exports, particularly to English
and colonial markets, while the granting of Irish lands and pensions to favoured courtiers exacerbated the problem of absentee
landowners and revenue-holders, with a consequent drain of money
out of the country.

   England clearly dominated the British Isles after 1691, but, for
the politically involved groups at least, a sense of separate identity
and national privileges continued to be important in Ireland and
Scotland, though less so in Wales. Ireland retained its Parliament
until the Act of Union of 1800; Scotland had a different national
Church – 1689 bringing a Presbyterian establishment – and legal
and educational systems. It continued to be governed by Scots and
yet the sense of separate identity was weakened, especially at the

level of the elite, by the decline of the Gaelic and Scots languages, and the growing appeal, at least among the elite, of English cultural norms and customs and the English educational system. Welsh, Irish and Scots sought to benefit from links with England. The Union brought access to a greatly expanded network of patronage. Scots came to play a major role in the expansion of empire, not least through service in the army and in the East India Company. Protestantism, war with France and the benefits of empire helped to create a British nationhood, which developed alongside the still strong senses of English, Scottish, Irish and Welsh identity.

EIGHTEENTH-CENTURY SOCIETY

The nature of British society in the period 1689–1815 has been a matter of some controversy. It is possible to stress modernity, to see a rising middle class and an age of reason, a polite and commercial people, aristocratic ease and elegance, urban bustle and balance, a land of stately homes and urban squares: Castle Howard, Blenheim, Bath, the West End of London, Dublin and the New Town of Edinburgh. 'Georgian buildings', constructed in a new style, embellished the expanding towns of the period: buildings with large windows were built in a regular 'classical' style along and around new boulevards, squares and circles: in stone in Scotland and brick in England. Parks, theatres, assembly rooms, subscription libraries, race-courses, and other leisure facilities were opened in many towns. The first theatre in Lincolnshire, for example, was built, in Stamford, soon after 1718. Others followed in Lincoln (*c.* 1731), Spalding (*c.*1760), Gainsborough (1775), Boston (1777), Grantham (1777), Louth (by 1798) and Sleaford (1824). As elsewhere, most of the gates and walls of Newcastle were demolished, and the city gained assembly rooms (1776) and a theatre (1788). Such development served an increasingly urban population: it rose from about 5.25 per cent of the English population in 1500 to about 27.5 per cent in 1800, much of the growth being in London. New construction was not restricted to England. In Carrickfergus in Ulster the wooden bridge was replaced in stone in 1740, a new market house was constructed in 1775 and a new county court-house and gaol in 1779. Whereas earlier buildings in the town had been defensive in character, there was no sense of menace in the new urban landscape. Carrickfergus benefited from the development of the Ulster linen industry and many artisan houses were rebuilt in brick or stone with slate roofs.

Different images and views can also, however, be stressed. Serious disease played a major role in what was a hostile environment. The plague epidemic of 1665–6, which killed over 70,000, was the last in England (bar a small outbreak of plague in Suffolk in 1906–19): mutations in the rat and flea population were probably more important in preventing a repetition than were clumsy and erratic public-health measures and alterations in human habitat thanks to construction with brick, stone and tile, and a move away from earthern floors. There were still, however, other major killers, including a whole host of illnesses and accidents that can generally be tackled successfully in modern Europe. Smallpox, typhus, typhoid, measles and influenza were serious problems. 38 per cent of the children born in Penrith in 1650–1700 died before reaching the age of 6. Smallpox epidemics there were superimposed on the pre-existing cycle of mortality which was linked to movements in grain prices. This led to corresponding fluctuations in susceptibility to smallpox, thereby exacerbating the oscillations in child mortality. This, of course, is a modern analysis. Contemporaries lacked such knowledge and to them disease was a subject of anxiety and bewilderment.

The year could be divided by the prevalence of different diseases: smallpox in spring and summer, dysentry in spring and autumn. Primitive sanitation and poor nutrition exacerbated the situation. Glasgow had no public sewers until 1790 and the situation thereafter remained totally inadequate for decades. The limited nature of the housing stock led to the sharing of beds, which was partly responsible for the high incidence of respiratory infections. In London the stock of accommodation available to the bulk of the population declined in quality and shrank in quantity in the 1720s–50s as buildings deteriorated and there were few housing starts. Thus, the effective density of population increased, with all that that implied for potential exposure to infection. The substantial geographical variation in London's epidemiological regime was related to wealth. Problems of food storage and cost ensured that the bulk of the British population lacked a balanced diet even when they had enough food. Poverty remained a serious problem. The Workhouse Test Act of 1723 encouraged parishes to found workhouses to provide the poor with work and accommodation, but too few were founded to deal with the problem, especially as the population rose from mid-century. Gilbert's Act of 1782 gave JPs the power to appoint guardians running Houses of Industry for the elderly and infirm. Workhouses, however, remained less important than 'out relief': providing assistance, and sometimes work, to the poor in their own homes. Under the Speenhamland system of outdoor relief introduced in 1795, although never universally applied, both the unemployed and wage-labourers received payments reflecting the price of bread and the size of their family. Payments to families were made through the man.

The majority of children did not attend school, the distribution of schools was uneven and the curriculum of most seriously limited. It was generally argued that education should reflect social status and reinforce the status quo, and thus that the poor should not be taught to aspire. The educational opportunities of women were particularly limited. Illiteracy was widespread, being more pronounced among women than men, and in rural than in urban areas. Belief in witchcraft nevertheless markedly diminished, although there were still episodes. *Lloyd's Evening Post, and British Chronicle* of 2 January 1761 carried a report from Wilton in Wiltshire, not a remote 'marginal' environment:

> A few days ago, one Sarah Jellicoat escaped undergoing the whole discipline usually inflicted by the unmerciful and unthinking vulgar on witches (under pretence, that she had bewitched a farmer's servant maid, and a tallow-chandler's soap, which failed in the operation) only by the favourable interposition of some humane gentlemen, and the vigilance of a discreet magistrate, who stopped the proceedings before the violence thereof had gone to a great pitch, by binding over the aggressors by recognisance to appear at the next assizes, there to justify the parts they severally acted in the execution of their pretended witch law.

The Reverend Robert Kirk, Episcopalian minister in Aberfoyle, Perthshire, published in 1691 his *The Secret Commonwealth; or an Essay on the Nature and Actions of the Subterranean (and for the most part) Invisible People heretofoir going under the name of Faunes and Fairies, or the lyke, among the Low Country Scots, as they are described by those who have the second sight.* For revealing this knowledge he was allegedly abducted by the 'little people' in 1692.

The painter William Hogarth (1697–1764) depicted the vigorous, if not seamy side of life in London, a thriving metropolis where crime, prostitution and squalor were ever-present, venereal disease and destitution much feared. Crime was linked to hardship: in Lincolnshire, the bad winter of 1741 led to a doubling of the theft figures. The criminal code decreed the death penalty, or transportation to virtual slave labour in British colonies, for minor crimes (although not in Scotland for nearly so many); the game laws laid down harsh penalties for poaching and permitted the use of spring guns by landlords. Under the Transportation Act of 1718, passed in order to deal with the rise of crime in perfunctorily-policed London, 50,000 convicts were sent to America from England and Wales by 1775 for seven or fourteen years or life; the loss of America was followed by consideration of transportation to Africa and finally, in 1788, the establishment of a convict settlement in Australia. The Scots began deporting criminals to America in 1766. Many who were transported died under the harsh conditions of their long journeys, a British counterpart to the cruel treatment of Africans sent to the New World as slaves.

A feeling of insecurity helps to explain that, in so far as there was an aristocratic and establishment cultural and political hegemony, it was in part bred from elite concern, rather than from any unchallenged sense of confidence or complacency. Aristocratic portraits and stately homes in part reflected a need to assert tradition and superiority and to project images of confidence against any potential challenge to the position of the elite. There were bitter political and religious disputes. The succession to the throne was a cause of division and instability until the crushing of James II's grandson, Charles Edward Stuart, 'Bonnie Prince Charlie', at the battle of Culloden in 1746. The disestablishment of Episcopalism in Scotland after the Glorious Revolution, and the sense of 'the Church in danger' from Dissenters and Whigs in England and Wales, fed tension. The Toleration Act of 1689 gave Dissenters (but not Catholics) freedom of worship in licensed premises in England and Wales. Though William III (1689–1702) and, to a greater extent, the first two Hanoverian rulers, George I (1714–27) and George II (1727–60), relied heavily on the Whigs, the continued existence of a popular and active Tory party was a challenge to the practice of Whig oligarchy, as was the existence of vigorous traditions of urban political activity. Political division was echoed in culture: the politeness of much early-eighteenth-century Augustan literature was co-extensive with the sometimes savage satire of writers like Alexander Pope and Jonathan Swift, much of whose work is spiked with bitterness and sometimes savage satire. The impulse for order which has been seen as a dominant motif of the age should not be regarded as a simple reflection of some political and social reality. Rather, the commentators, writers and artists of the period stressed the need for order because they were profoundly aware of the threats to that order around them.

Likewise, far from being a secular age as it is sometimes presented, the eighteenth century was one in which religious concerns still constrained and influenced the content of much cultural activity. This was a volatile and varied cultural world in which politics and religion were far from placid, and in which much that might seem today irrational was far from marginalised. By no means a cool age of reason, it saw the religious enthusiasm that led to the foundation of Methodism, as well as almanacs, and millenarian and providential notions that were not restricted to a superstitious minority. Methodism was initially a movement for revival that sought to remain within the Church of England, but after its founder, John Wesley, died in 1791 it broke away completely, and his decision to ordain his own ministers in 1784 marked a point of division between Methodism and the Church of England. Intellectual advances were also affected by religion. Isaac Newton, 1642–1727, from 1703 president of the Royal Society, a body established in 1660 to encourage scientific research, discovered calculus, universal gravitation and the laws of motion, but also searched for the date of the Second Coming and argued that comets, which he and Edmund Halley had analysed, should be seen as explaining the Deluge. Newton argued that God acted in order to keep heavenly bodies in their place. He was believed to act through the normal laws of physics; not to break them. Science was not therefore to be incompatible with the divine scheme. There was a widespread interest in alchemy.

There was a profound sense of disquiet about the very nature of society coming not so much from radicals as from clergy, doctors and writers concerned about moral and ethical values. Morality was a central cultural theme. Hogarth's moral satires were a considerable success. The engravings of his series *A Harlot's Progress* sold over 1,000 sets and were much imitated. The plays of Colley Cibber, George Colman, George Lillo and Oliver Goldsmith, who had a good acquaintance with the street culture of his native Ireland, propounded a morality opposed to vice and indulgence. The etiquette of the period condemned dishevelment and slovenliness in clothing. Samuel Richardson's *Pamela* (1740), the first of the sentimental novels, was a very popular work on the prudence of virtue and the virtue of prudence. Few contemporaries were as convinced as later historians that theirs was an age of stability. For them stability in culture and politics was perhaps regarded as something which had existed in the past and was now increasingly lost, or as something which should be worked towards; it was hardly something which had been achieved in the present, or, if so, could only be maintained through constant vigilance.

EIGHTEENTH-CENTURY WOMEN

One measure of the position of any group in society is provided by crime and punishment. In late-eighteenth-century Dublin women suffered greatly as victims of crime. Girls were raped and wives murdered and battered, without the judicial system taking much action. In comparison with the substantial number of hangings for theft there were very few convictions for rape. Some women sought to respond by bringing prosecutions. Other women, however, were active participants in the world of crime, not in committing violence but in organising shoplifting and handling stolen goods.

Crime reflects both the basic dynamics of human interaction and more specific circumstances. The women involved in committing crimes responded to the opportunities created by the growth of wealth in society. More generally, the growth of wealth also provided the context for women's lives. There was still much poverty, not least in regions that were marginal to economic growth, and the rising population of the second half of the century placed much demand on available resources. Yet there were also more material goods and a slowly changing material fabric of life. This was most obvious in the cities, but it was not restricted to them. The process was a long-term one that can certainly be traced back to the sixteenth century. The probate inventories of the village of Stone-leigh in Warwickshire in 1500–1800 present a picture of a community that steadily added to its material comfort and from time to time renewed its buildings. From 1600 there was a marked increase in housing. After 1600 the number of beds in large farms increased sharply: improved comfort and privacy may have led to more people having their own bed. Around 1700 goods appeared which were produced for mass distribution; Ticknall-ware for the dairy and tin dripping-pans for the hearth. There was a growth of separate rooms for separate functions, such as dining rooms. Thus the domestic space in which many women lived was changing and they were increasingly gaining differentiated space for their own purposes. Women also played an active role in the 'public spaces' of eighteenth-century society. Actresses such as Mrs Siddons were prominent on the London stage. Women played an important role in the debating societies that developed in London from the late 1770s, although less so in enlightened societies in Scotland. Less 'genteel' activities were also patronised. On 5 September 1759 *Lloyd's Evening Post, and British Chronicle* reported,

> On Monday night was fought at Stoke-Newington [London], one of the most obstinate and bloody battles between four noted bruisers [boxers], two of each sex; the odds, before the battle began were two to one on the male side; but they fought with such courage and obstinacy, that at length the battle was decided in favour of the female.

The emotional position of many women was difficult. Love did not always feature in matrimony and the portrayal of marriage to a callous husband as imprisonment offered in Thomas Southerne's play *The Wives' Excuse* (1691) was not fanciful: Mrs Friendall, the perceptive and wronged protagonist, declared, 'But I am married. Only pity me.' Prior to 1750 the majority of actions for divorce brought in the London Consistory Court were brought by women against their husbands for cruelty. After *c.*1750 the notion of romantic marriage and domestic harmony came to prevail among the prosperous and the ideal of divorce for incompatibility arose. It was still, however, a long and difficult process and the custody of any children was invested in the father so that separated and divorced women lost contact with them.

THE BRITISH ISLES AS PART OF EUROPE

There were obvious differences between society in Britain and on the Continent. These included the demographic and economic prominence of the capital, London, and the high percentage of the English labour force not engaged in agriculture. Common legal rights and penalties were more widespread in Britain than in most continental states, where the currency of privilege was more defined in the legal system. The rotation of crops and use of legumes that increasingly characterised East Anglian agriculture, and the growing use of coal, were not mirrored across most of Europe. Urban mercantile interests were more politically significant than in other large European states. And yet it would be inappropriate to focus on such differences and to suggest that therefore it is unhelpful to consider Britain in a European context. 'Progressive' features of British agriculture and industry were matched elsewhere. The agricultural techniques of East Anglia owed much to those of the province of Holland, while coal was already used for industrial processes in a number of continental regions, such as the Ruhr and the Pays de Liège. Industrial development was not restricted to Britain, but was also important in a number of continental regions, such as Bohemia and Silesia.

The major variations between, and indeed within, regions within the British Isles were such that it is more pertinent, as in more recent times, to note common indicators between individual British and continental regions than to stress the divide of the Channel. In socio-economic terms, it is possible to stress similarity, rather than contrast, between Britain and the Continent, particularly in the first half of the century. This is more problematic as far as politico-constitutional aspects are concerned. The 'Glorious Revolution' led to a contemporary emphasis on specificity and uniqueness that has been of considerable importance since. The Whig tradition made much of the redefinition of parliamentary monarchy in which Parliament met every year, of triennial elections, the freedom of the press and the establishment of a funded national debt. The Revolution Settlement, the term applied to the constitutional and political changes of the period 1688–1701, was seen as clearly separating Britain from the general pattern of continental development. Indeed, to use a modern term, it was as if history had ended, for if history was an account of the process by which the constitution was established and defended, then the Revolution Settlement could be presented as a definitive constitutional settlement, and it could be argued that the Glorious Revolution had saved Britain from the general European move towards absolutism and, to a certain extent, Catholicism. For fashionable intellectuals on the Continent, Britain offered a model of a progressive society, one that replaced the Dutch model that had been so attractive the previous century, though there was also criticism of aspects of British society. Many eighteenth- and nineteenth-century French and German historians and lawyers looked to Britain (by which they tended to mean England) as culturally and constitutionally superior, and thus as a model to be copied. With time, Britain also became more important as an economic model and a source of technological innovation.

Many foreign commentators underrated the divisions in eighteenth-century British society. Politics, religion, culture and morality, none of them really separable, were occasions and sources of strife and polemic, and the same was true not only of views of recent history, most obviously the Revolution Settlement, but also of the very question of the relationship between Britain and the Continent. Alongside the notion of uniqueness as derived from and encapsulated in that settlement, there was also a habit, especially marked in opposition circles, of seeking parallels abroad. Thus, *Fog's Weekly Journal*, a leading Tory paper, could suggest in 1732 that the Parlement of Paris, an essentially judicial body, was readier to display independence than the Westminster Parliament. This habit was accentuated from 1714 by the Hanoverian connection, for under both George I and George II the contentiousness of that connection led to a sustained political discourse about the extent to which Britain was both being ruled in accordance with the foreign interests of her monarchs and being affected in other ways, especially cultural. Different British attitudes to the relationship with continental Europe reflected internal political divisions, for example Tory hostility to the Dutch and to Protestant Palatine refugees.

THE GROWTH OF THE EMPIRE

Britain was not the only European maritime and trans-oceanic imperial power, though her naval strength and colonial possessions had grown considerably since the mid-seventeenth century. Her control of the eastern seaboard of North America north of Florida had been expanded and consolidated with the gain of New York from the Dutch (1664), the French recognition of Nova Scotia, Newfoundland and Hudson Bay as British (1713), and the foundation of colonies including Maryland (1634), Pennsylvania (1681), Carolina (1663) and Georgia (1732). Possibly 200,000 people emigrated from the British Isles to North America during the seventeenth century, far outnumbering the French settlers in Canada and Louisiana, and the settlements founded included Charleston (1672), Philadelphia (1682), Baltimore (1729) and Savannah (1733). The English also made a major impact in their West Indian islands where they developed a sugar economy based on slave labour brought from West Africa; British coastal bases there included Accra (1672). The East India Company, chartered in 1600, was the basis of British commercial activity, and later political power, in the Indian Ocean. Bombay was gained in 1661, Calcutta in 1698. Scottish colonisation – directed in Nova Scotia and independent in the unsuccessful Darien scheme (an attempt to establish a colony in central America (1698–1703)) – played a major role in the background to union between England and Scotland.

Trade outside Europe became increasingly important to the British economy, and played a major role in the growth of such ports as Bristol, Glasgow, Liverpool and Whitehaven. Trade with the North American colonies grew greatly from the mid- seventeenth century. The mercantile marine grew from 280,000 tonnes in 1695 to 609,000 in 1760, the greater number of experienced sailors providing a pool from which the navy could be manned, in part by the dreaded press gangs.

POWER STRUCTURES

The Glorious Revolution is crucial to the Whig interpretation of British history, central to the notion of British uniqueness. This concept can, however, be queried by comparing Britain and the Continent in the post–1688 period in both a functional and an ideological light. Functionally, the crucial relationship in both was that of central government and ruling elite, a term that in the British Isles should be taken to include the peerage, the more substantial landed gentry, higher clerics and leading townsmen: the elite was more open to social mobility than was the case elsewhere in Europe. Members of the elite owned and controlled much of the land and were the local notables, enjoying social prestige and effective governmental control of the localities. Central government meant in practice, in most countries, the monarch and a small group of advisors and officials. The notion that they were capable of creating the basis of a modern state is misleading. Central government lacked the mechanisms to intervene effectively and consistently in the localities. In addition, in what was, in very large part, a pre-statistical age, the central government of any large area lacked the ability to produce coherent plans for domestic policies based on the premise of change and development. Without reliable, or often any, information concerning population, revenues, economic activity or land ownership, and lacking land surveys and reliable and detailed maps, governments operated in what was, by modern standards, an information void. The contrast with the established Churches of the period is instructive. Thanks to their possessing a universal local system of government and activity (the parochial structure), and an experienced and comprehensive supervisory mechanism in the episcopal structure, the churches were able to operate far more effectively than secular government, not least in collecting information.

Lacking the reach of modern governments, those of the early-modern period relied on other bodies and individuals to fulfil many functions that are now discharged by central government, and they reflected the interests, ideology and personnel of the social elite. Whatever the rhetoric and nature of authority, the reality of power was decentralised and consensual. Religion, education, poor relief and health were focused on the parish, which represented the interrelationship of Church and state at the local level. On a local level the parish was dominated by the laity and gentry, but this imbalance was far less marked on the national scene, in which the state needed the sanction of the established churches.

Social welfare and education were largely the responsibility of ecclesiastical institutions or of lay bodies, often with religious connections, such as the Society for the Promotion of Christian Knowledge, established in 1698, which encouraged the foundation of charity schools in the early eighteenth century. Education in England had to be paid for by the pupil's family, which was generally the case in the grammar schools, mostly sixteenth-century foundations, or by a benefactor, dead or alive; it was not supported by taxation, although in some parishes there was some free schooling. In Scotland there was a stronger tradition of obligation: an Act of Parliament of 1496 made education compulsory for the eldest sons of men of substance. An Act of the Privy Council of 1616 decreed that there should be a school in every parish. After the Reformation schools and universities in Scotland came under the control of local authorities.

The regulation of urban commerce and manufacturing in Britain was largely left to town governments. The colonels of regiments were often responsible for raising their men, and for supplying them also, as the administrative pretensions of the early-modern state in military matters were generally unrealised, especially in so far as land forces were concerned, though the British navy was administratively, as well as militarily, impressive. Most crucially, the administration of the localities, especially the maintenance of law and order and the administration of justice, both in Britain and elsewhere in Europe, was commonly left to the local nobility and gentry, whatever the formal mechanisms and institutions of their authority. When James II had intervened and appointed Catholics as Lords Lieutenant of the counties this had been of limited value to him as the new men lacked the stature and connections of traditional aristocratic holders of the office.

Despite the constitutional differences between the British Isles and most continental states, the shared reality at the local level was self-government by the notables and their supporters, and at the national level a political system that was largely run by the elite; although this dominance was qualified as far as politics and parliamentary rule were concerned, by strong traditions of popular independence, especially in the major towns. In the sixteenth canto of his ironic poetic epic, *Don Juan* (1824), the Romantic poet Lord George Byron (1788–1824), stressed the dominance of electioneering by the elite, whatever their theoretical political differences: 'the "other interest" (meaning / The same self-interest, with a different leaning)'. As the radical Thomas Spence claimed in 1800, 'Are not our legislators all landlords?' He continued by stating, 'It is childish to expect ever to see small farms again, or ever to see anything else than the utmost screwing and grinding of the poor, till you quite overturn the present system of landed property.' Much urban and industrial property was also owned by aristocrats. For example, most of the town of Kildare belonged to the earl of Kildare.

The key to stable government in the British Isles, as on the Continent, was to ensure that the local notables governed in accordance with the wishes of the centre, but this was largely achieved by giving them the instructions that they wanted. For the notables it was essential both that they received such instructions and that they got a fair share of governmental patronage. This system worked and its cohesion, if not harmony, was maintained, not so much by formal bureaucratic mechanism, as by the patronage and clientage networks that linked local notables to those wielding national influence and enjoying access to the monarch. The strength and vitality of the British aristocracy in the post–1688 world is readily apparent, not least because there was no sharp divide between them and the wealthy commoners, mostly landed, who, in large part, dominated and comprised the House of Commons. At the local level, the gentry, as justices of the peace, were the dominant figures. They had been entrusted with much of the business of government in the localities from the fourteenth century, and their role continued whoever directed affairs in London. Law and order depended on the JPs and in Hanoverian Britain they were also the crucial figures in the local allocation of the land tax. Wales was particularly dominated by its gentry because, compared to England and Scotland, the peerage was sparse and relatively unimportant. The JPs played a smaller role in Scotland. The sheriff courts of Scotland, until 1747 heriditable jurisdictions, were increasingly staffed with professional lawyers. The Orkney and Shetland islands were ruled by the earl of Morton who held the lordship of Orkney and Shetland and by the lairds (gentry) who sought to gain the property of the udallers (freeholders) and change them into tenants.

The system of aristocratic and gentry control cohered through patronage and personal connection, leaving copious documentation about such matters in the private correspondence of prominent politicians, such as Thomas Pelham, Duke of Newcastle, Secretary of State, 1724–54, and First Lord of the Treasury, 1754–6, 1757–62. Aside from this 'functional' similarity between Britain and the Continent, there was also an 'ideological' counterpart in the form of a shared belief in the rule of law and of government being subject

1. The 'Long Man of Wilmington', Sussex

The presence of baffling giant hillside figures, often impossible to date – some very ancient, some possibly more recent – reflect the limitations of the available information for understanding much of ancient British history. The 'Long Man' is an enormous figure: the two poles or spears he carries are each 250ft high. The figure could be Bronze Age or Nordic or even medieval; in any event the motives of his builders are utterly mysterious.

2. Head of Mithras

The extension of Roman rule and the decline of belief in the traditional Roman pantheon of gods led to a proliferation of new religions, the effects of which were felt in Britain. Of these Christianity ultimately proved the winner, but it initially had to beat off strong competition. The male cult of the Middle Eastern god Mithras was a particularly strong influence on Roman soldiers. Temples to Mithras have been uncovered around England, dating from the third century AD, including several on Hadrian's Wall. This striking head was housed in a temple in the Walbrook area of the City of London.

3. A detail from *The Book of Kells*

The Book of Kells was probably started in around 800 by Irish monks on Iona, a small island in the Inner Hebrides. The monks fled Viking raids and settled in Kells, County Meath, where the work was completed. Irish monks played a major role throughout western Europe both in scholarship and missionary activity. They were particularly important at Charlemagne's court and in spreading Christianity in Germany. This flourishing Irish cultural and intellectual life was shattered by the Viking occupation.

4. 'Scissors' arch, Wells Cathedral, Somerset

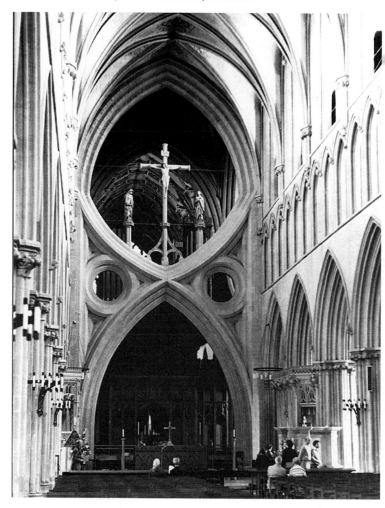

Medieval English architecture was in many ways highly derivative of French models. Many quintessentially 'English' buildings such as Durham and Canterbury cathedrals were built by French architects working for Norman or Angevin masters. However, just as the rulers became in some measure anglicized so an authentically English Gothic tradition grew up, most spectacularly in cathedrals such as Wells. The results were often startlingly impressive and original – for example, in these functional yet superbly decorative fourteenth-century 'scissors' arches.

5. The Battle of Agincourt, 1415

art of British imperial history the Battle of Agincourt always held an important place, but
nd of the Empire in the twentieth century and the martial attitudes that surrounded it
left the battle with perhaps less contemporary resonance. Agincourt was a crucial
, both in traditionally marking the emergence under Henry V of a self-consciously
ish (rather than Norman or Frenchified) court, and as a further stage in the unsuccessful
of the Hundred Years War to unite England and France under a single monarch. This
was ultimately a complete failure and the English kings were ejected even from long-
possessions such as Bordeaux, but the war was important in helping solidify English
French) senses of nationality, and its demands for money, men and supplies were partly
nsible for the precociously centralized and effective government of England.

6. The 'Darnley Portrait' of Elizabeth I, attributed to Federigo Zuccaro

Queen for 44 years, Elizabeth was the longest-reigning English monarch since Edward III. Her longevity and personality played a major role in determining the political and religious character of Tudor England. She was intelligent and generally pragmatic, but found it difficult to adapt to change. Elizabeth did not condemn the contemporary stereotype of women as inferior, but instead claimed that she was an exceptional woman because chosen by God as his instrument.

The Stuart disaster. The father provokes and loses a civil war (1642–6) and is executed, the son (as James II) so mishandles his reign that the country is invaded in 1688; he is exiled and then replaced by his daughter, Mary, and her Dutch Husband, William III.

8. Christ Church, Spitalfields

The reign of Queen Anne (1702–14) saw the apogee of Tory Anglican triumphalism, with the building of many superb churches such as Nicholas Hawksmoor's masterpiece in east London. The astonishing scale and expense of these buildings was quite out of proportion to the size of the congregations, but in this case the church initially served an important function as a focus of worship for the French Huguenot (Protestant) immigrants who made Spitalfields a highly successful weaving and clothing centre – a tradition continued in the area in the late twentieth century by Bengali immigrants.

James II's exile meant that the direct line of the royal family had been subverted. With the deaths of his daughters (Mary and Anne) and the coronation of the only distantly related (but Protestant) George I in 1714 a genuine crisis of conscience affected many in the British Isles, particularly in Scotland. Sympathy first for James III, then his son ('James II') and grandson ('Bonnie Prince Charlie' or 'Charles III') led to serious security problems for eighteenth-century Britain, with conspiracies and rebellions of varying seriousness down to 1745–6. Ingenious means were found to reflect hidden Jacobite loyalties, pride of place perhaps going to this apparently messy old drinks tray which, with the correct positioning of a cylindrical mirror, becomes a portrait of Bonnie Prince Charlie.

10. The Peterloo Massacre, Manchester, 1819

Early nineteenth-century Britain was ravaged by disturbances caused by the dislocation of the economy resulting from the end of the Napoleonic wars and the pressures of rapid industrialization. The Peterloo massacre was one of the most notorious clashes. A crowd of 60,000 gathered in St Peter's Field, Manchester, to attend a reform meeting addressed by 'Orator' Hunt. Local authorities panicked and the crowd was cleared by troops who killed several people and wounded many others. The period raised the possibility that Britain might turn to violent politics on the French model.

11. **Bargoed Coal Mine, Glamorganshire**

The Industrial Revolution fundamentally altered the nature of the British Isles. Previously 'underdeveloped' and inaccessible areas became, through the presence of coal, astonishingly vigorous and dynamic. Coal was central to the production of energy (steam power), to transport (railways) and to new industrial processes (for example, iron smelting) and Britain produced the most coal in the world.

12. The Easter Rising, 1916

The Irish Question dominated late nineteenth- and early twentieth-century British politics and continues to be important today. The irreconcilable demands of Irish Unionists for continued membership of the United Kingdom and Irish Nationalists for independence came to a head in 1914 in threats by Unionists to rebel if faced with Home Rule and, most dramatically, in 1916 in the Dublin rising which led to thousands of nationalists fighting British troops throughout the city. The ferocity of the fighting can be seen in this photo. Harsh reprisals from British military officials preoccupied with the First World War made continued British rule difficult and created further support for Nationalism. The civil war that led to the transfer of power from Westminster to an Irish Free State in 1922 marked a fundamental change in the relations between the different parts of the British Isles.

13. **Painting of the South Downs by Frank Newbould, commissioned as a Second World War civilian war effort poster**

A potent element in twentieth-century English life has been an obsession with a particular kind of romantic landscape, reflected, for example, in the popularity of the poetry and novels of Thomas Hardy, the music of Ralph Vaughan Williams and in the success of ramblers' clubs. This led particular edge to government 'recruitment' of the landscape itself into war posters. The confusing use of 'Britain' to refer to a landscape quite alien to, say, a Welshman is an ancient one.

14. The Royal Scots Fusiliers in Burma, 1944

Although seen as a modern event, the fighting of the Second World War was quite foreign to contemporary British experience. For example, these Scottish soldiers were fighting alongside Indian, Caribbean, West African, Australian, Egyptian, Kenyan, Ceylonese, English and New Zealand troops, all under British command, in a great imperial crusade to defeat the Japanese invaders of British-ruled Burma. Fifty years later, Britain is a medium-sized member of the European Union on the verge of relinquishing its last significant colony, Hong Kong. The circumstances that led to Scots fighting in the jungles of Burma, a country with which contemporary Britain has no important links or influence at all, have completely disappeared. Burma itself was given independence in 1948, a year after the independence of India destroyed the logic of Britain's presence in South Asia.

George Square, Glasgow, 1995

striking feature of contemporary Britain has been the changing role of major cities.
eir industrial bases have been largely destroyed and, after a period of severe decay,
ny city centres are in the midst of renewal projects encouraging resettlement and
rism and attempting to renew civic pride. Glasgow was often seen as the quintes-
tial insanitary and violent industrial city but is now, despite continuing high unem-
yment, establishing itself as a beautiful and dynamic European city. A perverse side-
ect of deindustrialization has been that, for the first time since George Square was
lt in the early nineteenth century, it is now possible to see it unencrusted with soot
d dirt and through clean air.

16. The Mandir Temple, Neasden, 1995

Despite the refusal of much of Britain's population to believe this, Britain continues to benefit enormously from wave upon wave of immigrants – as has been the case throughout its history. A spectacular recent example is the East African Asian community which settled in the 1960s and 1970s. A mark of its success and confidence is the Mandir Temple in Neasden, northwest London, the largest Hindu temple outside India. The many different woods and marbles were shipped from around the world to Gujarat in western India, where specialized craftspeople carved the extraordinarily elaborate details and shipped the vast 'kit' to London for assembly. A totally unimagined consequence of nineteenth-century policies to colonize British East Africa with South Asians, the Mandir temple is both a marvellous building in its own right and a symbol of Britain's continuing creative and modern engagement with its own past.

to it. The constitutional mechanisms by which this should pertain varied, but there was a common opposition to despotism.

Thus, the public myth of uniqueness that played such a major role in the Whig inheritance (by the 1770s most politicians could see themselves as Whigs), can be qualified and indeed was by domestic critics who charged, with reason, that the Whigs had abandoned their late-seventeenth-century radical ideas, and denied that the British system was different from and better than those across the Channel. Particular attention was focused on the way in which the 'executive' or central government had allegedly subverted the freedom of Parliament by corruption. What was in fact being witnessed was the re-creation of a measure of stable government in Britain by means of a new consensus, in which patronage and the avoidance of radical changes were dominant, smoothed by practices that lessened the chance of unpredictable developments. Therefore, despite the role of a permanent and quite effective Parliament, the ministerial Whigs could be seen as having created a stable state which, its critics claimed, bore comparison with both strong continental monarchies and that attempted by the Stuarts. Such comparisons, voiced during the years of Whig hegemony in 1714–60, were also to be pressed home in the 1760s and early 1770s when George III (1760–1820) broke with the tutelage of the 'old corps' Whigs, who had dominated politics under Georges I and II, and allegedly sought to create a stronger monarchy. Contemporaries searched for parallels in the crown-backed Maupeou 'revolution' in France (1771) and in Gustavus III's coup in Sweden (1772), both seen as measures designed to subordinate 'intermediate institutions' to Crown authority, and in the Swedish case a *coup d'état* for the monarchy.

The stately homes of the period were, in part, a testimony to wealth, confidence, agricultural improvement and greater political and, to some degree, social stability after the restoration of Charles II. Such building activity revived after the Restoration, and flourished in the eighteenth century, with houses such as Sir Robert Walpole's mansion at Houghton. Sir John Vanbrugh (1664–1726), the exponent of the English baroque, displayed at Blenheim, Castle Howard and Seaton Delaval a degree of spatial enterprise similar to the architects of princely palaces on the Continent. Robert Adam (1728–92), a Scot, rebuilt or redesigned many stately homes, including Culzean, Kenwood, Luton Hoo, Mellerstain House, and Syon House, his work redolent with classical themes. Landscape gardening, inescapably linked to wealthy landed patronage, flourished and was influential abroad. The architect William Kent (1684–1748) developed and decorated parks (grounds of houses) in order to provide an appropriate setting for buildings. Lancelot 'Capability' Brown (1716–83) rejected the rigid formality associated with continental models, contriving a setting that appeared natural, but was nevertheless carefully designed for effect. His landscapes of serpentine lakes, gentle hills and scattered groups of newly planted trees represented a less insistent conquest of nature by man and swiftly established a fashion in a world where the small number of patrons and their interest in new artistic developments permitted new fashions to spread swiftly, while their wealth enabled them to realise and develop the new fashions. Brown's ideas were developed further by Humphry Repton (1752–1818) in accordance with the concept of the 'picturesque', which stressed the individual character of each landscape and the need to retain it, while making improvements to remove what were judged blemishes and obstructions and to open up vistas. A growth in privacy was inherent in the emergence of landscaped estates; they reflected a growing separation of the aristocracy from rural society.

JACOBITISM

By the reign of George III there was no question about who should be king, only about his powers. The situation had been very different earlier in the eighteenth century. The principal political threats to the Protestant succession and the Whig system were seen as coming from Jacobitism until mid-century, and from France. James II was succeeded in 1701 as the claimant to the throne by the 'warming-pan baby', 'James III', and, though the latter's attempt to invade Scotland with French support in 1708 was unsuccessful, his claim was a threat to the Hanoverian succession. The childless William III (1689–1702) had been succeeded by his sister-in-law Anne (1702–14), none of whose many children survived to adulthood. Under the Act of Succession (1701), she was to be succeeded by the German house of Hanover, descendants of James I's daughter Elizabeth. The Act of Security passed by the Scottish Parliament directly contradicted the settling of the crown on Hanover and this led to the Union and the forcing of the Act of Succession on Scotland by incorporation. The unexpectedly peaceful accession of George I in 1714 was a major disappointment for James, but the consequences were not completely unhelpful to his cause, for George's enthusiastic support of the Whigs alienated the Tories whom Anne had favoured in 1710–14 and helped to revive Jacobitism. Tories were excluded from most senior posts in government, the armed forces, the judiciary and the Church, and their role in county government was lessened.

THE '15

In 1715 the Jacobites planned three risings. 'James III' was to follow William III by landing in the south-west of England, where there was to be the major rebellion, followed by a march on London, while there were also to be risings in the Highlands and the Border counties. The rising in the south-west was nipped in the bud in September 1715 as a result of prompt government action on the basis of intelligence, and Jacobite indecision. However, on 6 September John Erskine, Earl of Mar, raised the Stuart standard at Braemar. Perth was seized and the royal forces under the Duke of Argyll were heavily outnumbered. Indecision on Mar's part, however, allowed the loss of valuable campaigning time. Mar should have attacked Argyll as soon as possible so that Scotland could have been a base for assisting the risings in the borders and the north of England. Instead he did not march on Edinburgh until November. On 13 November he fought Argyll at Sheriffmuir, north of Stirling. Unaware of the dispositions of the other, each general drew up his forces so that their right wings overlapped the other's left. The left wings of both armies were defeated, but Mar failed to exploit his superior numbers. The indecisive battle was in practice a victory for Argyll as Mar needed a triumph in order both to hold his army together and to help the Jacobites in the borders.

Rising there in October, the Jacobites had decided that Dumfries, Newcastle and Carlisle were too strong to attack, and had instead resolved to invade Lancashire, an area with many Catholics whom they hoped to raise. There were about 1,100 active English Jacobites in the '15. The Cumbrian militia offered no resistance, and on 9 November the Jacobites entered Preston, but it was to prove as unfortunate for them as it had been for the invading Scots in August 1648. Thomas Forster failed to defend the line of the Ribble against advancing government troops, though a government assault on the town, which had been hastily fortified with barricades, failed on 12 November. However, instead of attacking the besiegers or trying to fight their way out, the Jacobites allowed their enemies to surround the town on the 13th and the weak Forster unconditionally surrendered on 14 November. Archbishop Wake and the bishops ordered declarations for George I to be read in all churches.

'James III' arrived at Peterhead on 22 December and Scone, where his coronation was planned, on 8 January 1716. Yet, freed of concern about England, where the battle of Preston marked the end of the Jacobite rising, Argyll had now been provided with a far larger army, including 5,000 Dutch troops. Despite the bitterness of the winter and a Jacobite scorched-earth policy, Argyll marched on Perth on 21 January. The Jacobites were badly affected by low morale and desertion and James abandoned Perth, throwing his artillery into the Tay. The army retreated to Montrose, but, rather than defending it, James and Mar sailed for France on 4 February and their abandoned army dispersed.

WALPOLEAN GOVERNMENT

In 1722 the Atterbury Plot, a Jacobite plan to seize London, was blocked by prompt governmental action, including the effective use of espionage and the creation of a large army camp in Hyde Park. The 1720s and 1730s were bleak years for the Stuart cause, because the leading minister, the venal but able Sir Robert Walpole (1721-42), followed policies that were less aggressive and objectionable than his predecessors and crucially kept Britain at peace for most of the period, thus denying the Jacobites foreign support. He was unwilling to support any further improvement in the legal position of Dissenters, a measure that threatened the position of the Church of England and its Tory supporters in the localities. Walpole was certainly corrupt and his ministry a Whig monopoly of power, but he caused offence principally to those who took a close interest in politics, rather than to the wider political nation, whose position was eased by his generally successful determination to reduce taxation, especially on land. This policy was helped by his preservation of peace, although in 1733 the attempt to shift the burden of taxation from land to goods led to the Excise Crisis, a political storm that forced him to withdraw his financial plan. However, he survived pressure both in Parliament and at court and went on to win the 1734 general election.

The Walpolean system broke down in his last years. The collapse of Anglo-Spanish relations over vigorous Spanish maritime policing of what they claimed was illegal British trade with their Caribbean possessions, symbolised by the display to a committee of the House of Commons of the allegedly severed ear of a merchant captain, Robert Jenkins, led to war with Spain, the War of Jenkins' Ear (1739–48), a war that Walpole had sought to avoid. He did very badly in the general election of 1741, in part as a result of the support for the opposition of Frederick, Prince of Wales, who had fallen out with his father, George II, and his father's ministers; rather as George himself had done in 1717–20 while Prince of Wales. Walpole sought to maintain his position, but declining majorities in the House of Commons created a crisis of confidence in the winter of 1741–2, and Walpole resigned in February 1742 after he lost his majority. He was made Earl of Orford by George II, who was very reluctant to lose his services, and opposition attempts to prosecute him for corruption were thwarted. The ministry which replaced Walpole's, in which the dynamic John, Lord Carteret was a leading figure, sent British troops to the Continent in 1742 in order to resist French advances at the expense of Austria.

WAR WITH FRANCE

Britain had already fought France in 1689–97 (War of the League of Augsburg or Nine Years War) and 1702–13 (War of the Spanish Succession). These wars were designed both to prevent Louis XIV's domination of western Europe and to safeguard the Protestant Succession. William III had only limited success in the 1690s, as he struggled to resist the French conquest of the Spanish Netherlands (modern Belgium), but in the second war, John, Duke of Marlborough, the husband of Queen Anne's cantankerous favourite, Sarah Churchill, won a series of crushing victories (Blenheim 1704, Ramillies 1706, Oudenaarde 1708) which drove French forces out of Germany and the Low Countries. Marlborough was dismissed by the Tory ministry of 1710–14 because they sought peace, but it was largely thanks to his victories that the government was able to negotiate good terms by the Treaty of Utrecht (1713). This accepted the British position in Newfoundland, Nova Scotia and Hudson Bay and the capture of Gibraltar (1704) and Minorca (1708). The French also recognised the Protestant Succession in Britain, while Louis XIV accepted a territorial settlement in western Europe that ended fears of French hegemony for a generation.

George I was able to negotiate an alliance (1716–31) with the regency government that followed Louis XIV, committing France to support the Hanoverian succession, and Walpole kept the peace with France. His successor's abandonment of this policy led to French support for Jacobitism. Carteret believed that Britain must resist French gains in Germany, and in 1743 the British defeated the French at Dettingen, George II being the last British king to command in battle, but in 1744 the French responded with an attempted invasion of England on behalf of the Jacobites, only to be thwarted by Channel storms. Britain then formally entered the War of the Austrian Succession.

THE '45

The following year 'James III's' eldest son, Charles Edward (Bonnie Prince Charlie), evaded British warships and landed in the Western Isles. He quickly overran most of Scotland, despite the reluctance of some Jacobite clans to rise for a prince who had brought no soldiers, and the antipathy of the many Scots who were not Jacobites. The British force in Scotland received very little local support, and fell victim to a Highland charge at Prestonpans outside Edinburgh (21 September 1745). Crossing into England on 8 November 1745, Charles Edward took Carlisle after a brief siege, and then, without any resistance, Lancaster, Preston, Manchester and Derby, which was entered on 4 December. The British armies had been outmanoeuvred and, if few English Jacobites had risen to help Charles, his opponents were affected by panic. But the lack of promised English and French support weighed most heavily with the Scots, and the Jacobite council decided on 5 December to retreat, despite Charles's wish to press on. There had been a crucial breakdown of confidence in the prince among his supporters, arising from the failure of his promised support. The Scots considered themselves to have been tricked into a risky situation.

Had the Jacobites pressed on, they might have won, capturing London and thus destroying the logistical and financial infrastructure of their opponents. By retreating they made defeat almost certain, not least because, in combination with bad weather and the British navy, the retreat led the French to abandon a planned supporting invasion of southern England. Charles evaded pursuit, retreated to Scotland successfully and on 17 January 1746 beat a British army at Falkirk. However, George II's inexorable second son, William, Duke of Cumberland, brought up a formidable army and on Culloden Moor near Inverness on 16 April 1746 his superior firepower smashed the Jacobite army. Cumberland's army included a substantial Scottish contingent. Cumberland recorded of his opponents that 'in their rage that they could not make any impression upon the battalions, they threw stones at them for at least a minute or two, before their total rout began'. He had secured the Protestant Succession established by William III.

SCOTLAND AFTER THE '45

The aftermath was harsh. The Hanoverian regime had been overthrown in Scotland, the army humiliated, and the government was determined to ensure that there was no recurrence of the '45. The Highlanders were regarded as barbarians, and Cumberland's successor, the Earl of Albemarle, offered his solution for 'the bad inclination of the people in most of the northern counties and their stubborn, inveterate disposition of mind . . . nothing could effect it but laying the whole country waste and in ashes, and removing all the inhabitants (excepting a few) out of the kingdom'. The 'pacification' of the Highlands was to be characterised first by killings, rapes and systematic devastation, and secondly by a determined attempt to alter the political, social and strategic structure of the highlands. The clans were disarmed, and the clan system broken up, while roads to open up, and forts to awe the highlands were constructed. Hereditable jurisdictions were abolished, the wearing

of Highland clothes prohibited. Those Scottish MPs in the Westminster Parliament who did not agree with this policy had little
choice but to acquiesce in its implementation since they had no
national and autonomous powerbase from which to oppose it. The
rebellion and its suppression therefore gave cause and opportunity
for the sort of radical state-directed action against inherited privilege, especially regional and aristocratic privilege, that was so rare
in Britain. More long-term political changes were also important.
In effect Scotland, like many dependent parts of multiple kingdoms
or federal states, was losing its capacity for important independent
political initiatives. This affected both the Highlands and the
country as a whole. Yet, it was not a case of English pressure on
an unwilling people, for political changes profited, and were in part
shaped by, local politicians. Many Scots, particularly the numerous
Presbyterians, were firm opponents of the Stuarts and supporters
of the Protestant Succession. London relied not on Englishmen but
on Scottish politicians to govern Scotland, such as the third Duke
of Argyll and, at the close of the century, Henry Dundas. Clerics,
burgesses and provosts conducted a great deal of local administration. The Scottish professional classes and minor lairds who stayed
at home contributed a great deal to the administration and character of their country.

The '45 both revealed the vulnerability of, and led to the firm
establishment of, the Hanoverian regime. It thus closed a long
period of instability and provided the basis for a fundamental
recasting of British politics in which Toryism lost its Jacobite
aspect, thus facilitating the dissolution of the Whig-Tory divide
over the following 17 years. Attempts to conciliate opponents and
comprehend them within ministerial ranks, and expectations concerning the future behaviour of the heir to the throne, first Frederick, Prince of Wales, who died in 1751, and then the future George
III, along with the behaviour of the latter after he came to the
throne in 1760, compromised the cohesion and identity of the
Tories, and brought some of them into government. In addition,
the relationship between England and Scotland became essentially
one of the willing co-option of the powerful Scots through patronage, with no alternative Jacobite or nationalist focus of loyalty and
with a diminishing emphasis on coercion. This process was helped
by the great economic expansion of central Scotland, particularly
the area round Glasgow, that began in the third quarter of the

eighteenth century. Urbanisation in Scotland was more telescoped and abrupt than in England. The urban population there grew by 132 per cent in 1750–1800 and Aberdeen, Edinburgh and Glasgow were the setting for a major explosion of intellectual life known as the Scottish Enlightenment. Many new ideas about government, society and science were advanced. The most famous individual work was Adam Smith's masterpiece of free-market economic analysis, *The Wealth of Nations* (1776). James Hutton's *Theory of the Earth* (1785) was the foundation of modern geology. The New Town proposals of Sir Gilbert Elliott and Lord Provost Drummond sought to make Edinburgh a fitting metropolis for the chief city of North Britain.

Scotland after the Union of 1707 and the suppression of Jacobitism retained a distinctive structure of local government, a different legal system and a different established Church, but the Scots came to play a major role in the expansion of empire, a policy actively pressed by Dundas who rose to be Home Secretary, Secretary of State for War, President of the Board of Control for India, First Lord of the Admiralty and Viscount Melville. The political elites of England and Scotland turned together against the domestic radicalism inspired by the French Revolution, leading from 1793 to a repression that suppressed demands for a more democratic political system. The avoidance of revolution in Scotland was not, however, only due to repression. Radical sentiment was limited, while paternalism in the form of a more responsive poor law and subsidised grain prices helped to lessen discontent. The Scottish Enlightenment had been politically conservative and aristocratic dominance of society was still strong, helped by the extent to which Scotland was still an overwhelmingly agrarian society.

THE SEVEN YEARS' WAR, 1756–63

The unification of Britain helped her in conflict with France. The decisive struggle was the Seven Years' War (1756–63). It ended with the Thirteen Colonies on the eastern seaboard of North America, and the British possessions in India, secure, with Canada, Florida, and many Caribbean islands acquired, and with Britain as the leading maritime power in the world, thus fulfilling what James Thomson had seen as the national destiny in his ode 'Rule Britannia' (1740): 'Rule Britannia, rule the waves: / Britons never will be slaves'. This was the achievement of the ministry of William Pitt the Elder and the Duke of Newcastle (1757–61), and of a number of able military leaders, including Wolfe, Clive, Hawke and Boscawen. Robert Clive's victory at Plassey, over the vastly more numerous forces of the Indian Prince, Surajah Dowla, in 1757, laid the basis for the virtual control of Bengal, Bihar and Orissa by the East India Company. The French were subjugated in India in 1760–1, and Britain emerged as the most powerful European state in the Indian subcontinent. The French attempt to invade Britain on behalf of the Jacobites was crushed by the British naval victories of Lagos and Quiberon Bay (1759). That year, British troops also beat the French at Minden in Germany, while, after a hazardous ascent of the cliffs near Quebec, that city was captured, General James Wolfe dying at the moment of glorious victory on the Plains of Abraham. The bells of victory rang out across Britain: the ringers at York Minster were paid four times between 21 August and 22 October for celebrating triumphs, beginning with Minden and ending with Quebec. The victories were also a tribute to the national unity that had followed the defeat of Jacobitism: Scots played a major role in the conflict. In 1762 British forces campaigned round the globe. They helped the Portuguese resist a Spanish invasion, fought the French in Germany and captured Martinique from the French and Havana and Manila from the Spaniards, an extraordinary testimony to the global reach of British power, particuarly naval power, and the strength of the British state.

EIGHTEENTH-CENTURY WALES

Britain was an imperial state, one of developing maritime and economic power. This growth, however, was achieved without political and social revolution, and was regional in its impact. It is instructive to consider the situation in Wales. Until the impact of industrialisation, Wales was a particularly conservative part of Britain, overwhelmingly Anglican, strongly royalist under the restored Stuarts, and keenly Tory until the mid-eighteenth century. Its quarrelsome gentry elite was more closely identifying itself with a sense of British identity. At their level there was a decline in the use of Welsh, and English cultural norms and customs had a growing appeal. The Welsh gentry increasingly intermarried with their English counterparts, while a greater number of heirs were educated in England.

At the same time, although possibly 80, or even 90 per cent of the population used Welsh as the medium of communication, Wales lacked centralising institutions, or social, ecclesiastical or legal arrangements corresponding with its linguistic distinctiveness. There was, however, a clear sense of identity, expressed in part through hostility to outsiders. Thus, in 1735 John Campbell of Calder (Cawdor), MP for Pembrokeshire and possessor of estates there and in Scotland, wrote to his son:

On Sunday there came here . . . two Highlanders in highland clothes without breeches, with long swords and each a pistol stuck in his girdle, they brought your uncle Philipps eight dogs . . . The Highlanders came by Shrewsbury, through Montgomeryshire and Cardiganshire. The people in England were very civil to them and pleased with their dress, but when they came some miles into Wales the people were afraid of them and the folks of the inns would not have given them lodging. They were forced when they came into an inn to say that they would pay for what they had and to behave themselves civilly and so doing, they would not be turned out of a public house, saying this with their pistols in their hands frighted the folks into compliance, or else they must have lain under the hedges, and may be got no victuals, but this was among the Wild Welsh; in our part of the country (Pembrokeshire) they know a little better.

In 1776 Jabez Fisher, an American traveller, recorded of Shropshire, 'Call the People in this country Welsh and you offend them: go into Wales and you can offer them no greater insult than to call them English. Is this Patriotism? Tis Love of one's own Country.' In the eighteenth century scholars and antiquaries were carving out a Welsh identity in terms of the ancient language and history of Wales; some of their claims were totally spurious.

This clear sense of identity, based on the Welsh language and on the sense of the Welsh past, had no political expression or consequences. Wales was not treated in any distinctive fashion and presented no particular problems for London ministries. There was no nationalist movement. There were also no particular agencies for the government of Wales and new initiatives, such as income tax and the census, were introduced without qualification. London-based institutions such as the customs and the excise encompassed Wales. There was nothing to match the distinctive Scottish legal and religious system. Wales was also of scant importance in political terms. Its twenty-four MPs were far fewer than those from, say, Cornwall, and formed only a small portion of the 558 MPs elected after the union with Scotland; they also do not seem to have acted as a group. The Welsh electorate, fewer than 19,000 in 1790 though significantly larger than the Scottish electorate, was relatively docile and during the Jacobite crises Wales was essentially quiet: there was certainly nothing to compare to the Scottish risings of 1715 and 1745. No monarch visited Wales in the eighteenth century, but then none visited Ireland, Scotland or the north of England either. Wales, especially north Wales, also saw very little of the army. Minor detachments from regiments stationed in England were usually found only at Carmarthen, Aberystwyth and Aberdovey, and their major function was to support the customs and the excise.

The major developments in eighteenth-century Wales were religious. Evangelicalism was linked to efforts to spread education and reform society. Anglicans and Dissenters waged campaigns against Catholicism, drunkenness and profanity, and for salvation and literacy. The use of the Welsh language was controversial. Some clerics and squires sought to suppress it, as did the charity schools. The Reverend Griffith Jones (1683–1761) was much abused and denounced as a secret spreader of Methodism because from the 1730s he stressed the need to use Welsh as the medium of a popular literacy campaign and to catechise in it. In 1737 alone he opened thirty-seven schools and he was partly responsible for the edition of the Bible and Prayer Book in Welsh issued by the Society for Promoting Christian Knowledge in 1746. Religious radicalism also flourished, while the Great Revival of the mid-eighteenth century led to the rapid growth of a distinctly Welsh form of Methodism that was centred on Calvinistic theology. This was to be the characteristic creed of the Welsh-speaking areas of north and west Wales in the nineteenth century. The south Wales valleys were also strongly Nonconformist. Independent and Presbyterian roots in the south are important as they correct the common idea that the Calvinistic Methodists suddenly conquered the whole country in c.1800.

Socio-religious developments in the eighteenth century – education, religious revival and the campaign against illiteracy – were to have a more fundamental impact on the future of Wales than did the corrupt political system under the Hanoverians. They were central to Welsh historical memory and laid the foundations for the culture of nineteenth-century Wales, though the actual 'conquest of the countryside' was really in c.1790–1820. This began a critical stage in the Nonconformist cultural hegemony. Between c.1810 and 1840 a new Welsh reformation hit hard at everyday life, destroying the traditional culture of Wales, with its plays, fairs and feasts, and creating the culture of the chapel. Furthermore, the emergence of radical thought on the part of religious Dissenters in the period surrounding the War of American Independence and the French Revolution was to be the basis of Nonconformist radicalism in the nineteenth century. There was growing division between English-speaking, English-oriented Welsh gentry and Welsh-speaking, Welsh-focused professionals and working people.

ECONOMIC DEVELOPMENT

Britain was to have to defend the maritime and colonial position it gained in the mid-eighteenth century from serious challenges in the period 1775–1815: rebellion in America and Ireland, war with Revolutionary and Napoleonic France. The society that did so was changing both socially and economically. After a century of limited growth, if not stagnation, population growth rates shot up, leading to a rise in the population of England and Wales from, in millions, 5.18 (1695), 5.51 (1711), 5.59 (1731), 6.20 (1751), 6.97 (1771) to 8.21 (1791), with the growth rate being highest in 1781–91 at 0.83 per cent per annum. The Scottish population rose from 1.26 million in 1757 to 1.6 million in 1801. As the labour force expanded, Britain had to import grain to feed the growing numbers and real wages were put under pressure, although they remained roughly stationary until the 1790s. The rising population was sustained and high growth rates continued. A decline in the death rate was less important than an increase in fertility from the 1780s to the 1820s. Rural fertility triumphed over urban mortality, for the towns were particularly dangerous as incubators and spreaders of disease, and their population increased only as a result of migration from rural areas. In London, however, infant mortality fell greatly with different methods of infant care and feeding. Agricultural improvement, the construction of canals and better roads, and the development of industry and trade led to a growth in national wealth and a different economy. Thus the percentage of the male labour force employed in industry rose from 19 (1700) to 30 (1800), while that in agriculture fell from 60 to 40, though agricultural productivity increased, thanks in part to the use of lime as a fertiliser; the limekilns were fired by coal. In 1790 the Oxford Canal linked Oxford and the Midlands, creating the final link in a network joining the rivers Trent, Mersey and Thames. The opening of the Monkland Canal in 1793 stimulated the development of the Lanarkshire coalfield to serve the rapidly growing Glasgow market. Scientific advances were made in a number of fields. William Brownrigg (1711–1800) formulated the concept of a multiplicity of chemically distinctive gases. Joseph Black (1728–99), professor of chemistry at Glasgow and later Edinburgh, discovered latent heat and first fixed the compound carbon dioxide. Henry Cavendish (1731–1810), a master of quantitative analysis, was in 1766 the first to define hydrogen as a distinct substance and in 1781 the first to determine the composition of water by exploding a mixture of hydrogen and oxygen in a sealed vessel. Joseph Priestley (1733–1804) discovered a number of gases and oxides, and electricity.

The spread of fodder crops, such as clover, coleseed and turnips, helped to eliminate fallow and to increase the capacity of the rural economy to rear more animals, sources of the 'roast beef of old England', woollen cloth and crucial manure. The percentage of enclosed land increased greatly: during the century about 21 per cent of England was affected by enclosure acts. They were especially common during the 1760s and 1770s when the heavy clay soils of the Midlands were enclosed and there was widespread conversion from arable to pasture, and again during the long war with Revolutionary and Napoleonic France in 1792–1815 when high prices brought an extension of arable cultivation particularly to unused or lightly used land. Hedges became even more characteristic of lowland Britain.

Enclosure did not necessarily raise efficiency, and it also created work. Agriculture remained very labour-intensive because agricultural labour was very cheap. In addition there are examples of unenclosed areas that witnessed agricultural improvement. Enclosure, however, made it easier to control the land through leases, was often linked to innovation and frequently accompanied by a redistribution of agricultural income from the tenant farmer to his landlord. Progressive landowners disrupted traditional rights and expectations and the enclosure of common lands led to particular bitterness. Enclosure was helped by the extent to which, unlike in continental Europe, peasant ownership of the land was limited. The system of tenure in Britain helped to perpetuate landlord control. To underline the theme of regional variety, it is, however, worth noting that the social context of enclosure varied: in some areas, such as Northamptonshire, landlords secured parliamentary acts to further their interests, but in others, for example Hampshire and Sussex, enclosure was by private agreement and caused less tension. The rise in population combined with war with France led to a boom in agriculture from the 1790s to the 1810s. This led to more rental income, which was reflected in extensive building by landlords: the Georgian houses for which much of particularly rural England is still noted. Substantial stately homes were also constructed in Scotland and Ireland, for example Culzean and Inveraray in the former. There were, however, also many losers from agrarian change. From the early 1790s the Highland clearances in Scotland reflected the move to an agricultural system imposed by landlords that required fewer people. The Countess of Sutherland cleared 794,000 acres of clan land in 1814–20. In Ireland, intensive cultivation of the potato supported a major expansion of the population.

Even if the rate of industrialisation was less impressive than used to be believed and was restricted to only a few sectors, the qualitative impact of economic change was obvious to contemporaries. A sense of economic change and the possibilities of progress was powerfully present amongst many people in the later eighteenth century. There were important changes in the intensity of work, the organisation of labour and in material conditions. The impression was of Prometheus Unbound, of extraordinary opportunities offered by technological innovation. John Kay's flying shuttle of 1733, which was in general use in Yorkshire by the 1780s, increased the productivity of handloom weavers. James Hargreaves's spinning jenny (1764–5), Richard Arkwright's waterframe (1769) and Samuel Crompton's mule (1779) revolutionised textile spinning. In 1769 James Watt patented a more energy-efficient use of steam engines. Steam pumping got water out of deep coalmines. Steam-powered winding engines were introduced in coalmines in the early 1790s. Coal, iron and lead production grew rapidly in Wales, helping to turn the interest of many gentry families to industry and mineral exploitation. The Welsh landscape was already changing. In 1776, Jabez Fisher found at Tintern not only the spectacular ruins of the medieval Cistercian abbey, but also

> a great Manufactury of Wire, the Iron being manufactured from the Ore, a furnace to make it into Barrs from whence it is taken to the tilting Mill, where it is lengthened out into long rods. It is then drawn thro the holes of the different sizes till it be reduced to the desired fineness. The whole operation is performed by water by the addition of very little Labor.

Fisher also visited the copper-smelting site at White Rock near Swansea founded in 1737:

> Here are 43 Furnaces constantly in Blast, all employed in their proper departments, and 150 Men who appear like what we might conceive of the Inhabitants of Pandaemonium. The greatest decorum is however preserved; they all move like a Machine.

Economic growth was linked to Britain's wars and the burgeoning demands of her empire, to home demand and to changing foreign markets. Metallurgical industries, especially gun founding, developed, and ironmasters were keen to adopt new technological developments. Canals and waggonways were built to move coal. For example the fourth Duke of Portland built a new harbour at Troon on the west coast of Scotland in 1808 and linked it to his coalpits at Kilmarnock by a waggonway which in 1839 carried over 130,000 tons of coal.

TRANSPORT AND THE PACE OF CHANGE

Greater ease of communication helped to unify the elite, facilitating education, socialising and travel for business or political reasons.

Many turnpike acts were passed in the late eighteenth century, enabling local trusts to take over sections of roads and finance improvements through tolls. The Edinburgh–Glasgow road, for example, was turnpiked in the 1780s. The introduction from the 1780s of the macadamised and cambered road gave a harder and drier surface and thus permitted greater speeds for horse-drawn carriages. Bridges were also built, replacing fords and ferries. London newspapers were sent to the provinces in increasing numbers, and postal services improved considerably, Royal Mail coach services starting in 1784, to the benefit of the expanding banking system as well as to the letter writer, that central character in two recent and rapidly developing literary forms, the novel and the magazine.

Many of the social features that were to be associated with economic transformation were already common. Far from the British Isles being a rural Elysium, lacking only a Boucher to depict plenty and languorous calm, but all too soon to be ravaged by industrialisation, the rural world had already in the fifteenth and sixteenth centuries witnessed massive disruptions of land and labour. Neither enclosure, sweeping changes in land use, rural proletarianisation nor the social and economic changes wrought by industrialisation, technological change and the rise and decline of specific areas and economic activities were new. They were, however, both to increase in scale and pace from the late eighteenth century, and never to cease to do so thereafter. This process of continual change, more than anything else, marked the birth of modern times.

GEORGE III, 1760–1820

For those few who wielded power, however, political challenges were foremost. The Whig-Tory two-party alignment that had played a major role since the beginning of the century gradually gave way in the 1760s to a number of essentially personal political groups, the rivalries of political leaders and the changing preferences of George III fostering instability. As much as any continental ruler who did not have to face a powerful representative institution, George was determined to reject what he saw as the politics of faction, to thwart the efforts of unacceptable politicians to force their way into office. As did other rulers, George found it most difficult to create acceptable relationships with senior politicians at his accession, when he had to persuade those who had had a good working relationship with his predecessor, and those who had looked for a dramatic change, to adjust to his wishes. George broke with William Pitt the Elder in 1761 and with the Duke of Newcastle in 1762 and made his favourite, John, third Earl of Bute, First Lord of the Treasury in 1762, only to see the weak-willed Bute resign in 1763 in the face of bitter domestic opposition. George complained to the French ambassador in 1763 about 'the spirit of fermentation and the excessive licence which prevails in England. It is essential to neglect nothing that can check that spirit'. George was determined to uphold the Revolution Settlement as he understood it, but the ambiguity of a number of constitutional points, such as the collective responsibility of the cabinet and the degree to which the monarch had to choose his ministers from those who had the confidence of Parliament, exacerbated the situation, as did the volatile political atmosphere in London. Dissatisfaction there, part of which stemmed from economic difficulties after the end of the Seven Years' War, was exploited by a squinting anti-hero, John Wilkes, an entrepreneur of faction and libertine MP, who fell foul of George as a result of bitter attacks on the king in his newspaper the *North Briton*. Not until 1770 did George find a satisfactory minister who could control Parliament: he was Frederick, Lord North.

THE LOSS OF AMERICA

The discontent and divisions of the 1760s over the determination of George III to pick ministers of his own choice paled into insignificance, however, beside the collapse of the imperial relationship with America. The determination to make colonies, not represented in Parliament, pay a portion of their defence burden was crucial, though so also was the increasing democratisation in American society, a stubborn rejection of British authority, concern about British policy in Canada, and the borrowing of British conspiracy theories about the supposed autocratic intentions of George III. The Seven Years' War had left the British government with an unprecedently high level of national debt and it looked to America to meet a portion of the burden. The Americans, however, no longer felt threatened by French bases in Canada and were therefore unwilling to see British troops as saviours. The Stamp Act of 1765 led to a crisis as Americans rejected Parliament's financial demands, and thereafter relations were riven by a fundamental division over constitutional issues. The fact that Britain's most important colonies in the western hemisphere, those in the West Indies, did not rebel, despite the sensitivity of their elites on questions of constitutional principle, suggests, however, that there was no inevitable crisis in the British imperial system, but rather that factors particular to the American colonies were crucial. Similarly there was no rebellion in Ireland.

Fighting broke out near Boston in 1775 as a result of the determination of the government of Lord North to employ force, and the willingness of sufficient Americans to do likewise. An ill-advised attempt to seize illegal arms dumps led to clashes at Lexington and Concord, and the British were soon blockaded by land in Boston. Their attempt to drive off the Americans led to very heavy losses at the battle of Bunker Hill. The Americans declared independence (1776) and the British were driven from the thirteen colonies but held Canada (1775–spring 1776), before counter-attacking to regain New York (1776). The British seizure of Philadelphia was matched by defeat at Saratoga (1777), and, after the French entered the war on the revolutionary side (1778), the British lacked the resources necessary for America and were pushed onto the defensive in a world war. Spain joined France in 1779 and at the end of 1780 the Dutch were added to the list of Britain's enemies in what became a global conflict.

Though the Franco-Spanish attempt to invade England failed (1779), and the British held onto Gibraltar, India and Jamaica, defeat at Yorktown (1781) was followed by a collapse of the will to fight on and by the acceptance of American independence. This split the unity of the English-speaking world. America, inhabited by an independent people of extraordinary vitality, was to be the most dynamic of the independent states in the western hemisphere, the first and foremost of the decolonised countries, the people that were best placed to take advantage of the potent combination of a European legacy, independence, and opportunities for expansion and growth. America was to play a crucial role during the First and Second World Wars helping to ensure the success of the alliances that included Britain; and also ensured that aspects of British culture, society and ideology, albeit in altered forms, were to enjoy great influence, outside and after the span of British empire.

THE MINISTRIES OF WILLIAM PITT THE YOUNGER, 1783–1801, 1804–6

As so often in British history, defeat led to the fall of the government. Lord North's resignation in 1782 was followed by a period of marked ministerial and constitutional instability. Forced to accept ministers whom he disliked, George threatened abdication, and in 1783–4 breached several fundamental political conventions in engineering the fall of the Fox-North ministry and supporting that of the 24-year-old William Pitt the Younger, the severe but sometimes drunk second son of Pitt the Elder, although it lacked a Commons majority. Pitt's victory in the 1784 general election was also, therefore, a triumph for George and it began a period of largely stable government that lasted until Pitt's resignation in 1801. Like Walpole and North, Pitt understood the importance of sound finances, and, although he was interested in electoral reform, he did not push this divisive issue after it had been defeated in 1785. The War of American Independence more than doubled the national debt, but Pitt's prudent financial management and reforms and a dramatic growth in trade, not least with America, stabilised the situation. As so often in a monarchical state, continuity was, however, threatened by the succession, for George, Prince of Wales, later George IV, was not only opposed to the frugality, virtue and duty of his father, but also to Pitt, preferring instead the latter's chief opponent, Charles James Fox, who, unlike the prince, had talent, but, like him, lacked self-control. When in late 1788 an attack of porphyria led to the conviction that George III was mad and near death, the resulting Regency Crisis nearly produced the fall of the government, but fortunately for Pitt the king recovered in early 1789.

Defeat at the hands of America had led to reform, especially in the Royal Navy, and this was to help Britain in the more serious challenge that lay ahead. She bounced back from the loss of the Thirteen Colonies, Florida and various Caribbean islands (Treaty of Versailles, 1783), to establish the first British foothold in Malaysia (Penang, 1786) and the first European colony in Australia (1788), and to thwart Spanish attempts to prevent her from trading and establishing settlements on the western coast of modern Canada (Nootka Sound crisis, 1790).

WAR WITH FRANCE

Though buffeted seriously during the war with Revolutionary and then Napoleonic France (1793–1802, 1803–14, 1815), most worryingly with the Irish rising of 1798 and the threat of invasion by Napoleon from 1803, Britain survived, thanks in particular to a series of naval victories, culminating in Horatio Nelson's triumph at Trafalgar (1805). The war against Revolutionary France had revealed, however, that the British were unable to defend the Low Countries, and subsequent expeditions there – the 1799 landing in Holland under George III's son Frederick, Duke of York (now best remembered in a nursery rhyme for marching troops up and down hills), and the 1809 attack on Walcheren – ended in failure. Napoleon's domination of the Continent was a major challenge to British interests. He sought in the Continental System, which was inaugurated in November 1806, to bring Britain to her knees by economic means. The Berlin Decrees declared Britain blockaded and banned trade with her. Napoleon's extra-European interests were also a threat to Britain. His invasion of Egypt in 1798 had been gravely weakened when Nelson destroyed the French fleet at the battle of the Nile in Aboukir Bay, but thereafter Napoleon remained interested in the prospect of weakening the British in India, possibly in cooperation with Russia, and of establishing new French colonies.

The war placed a major strain on British resources, and defeats led to or exacerbated political problems. Pitt the Younger discovered that wartime leadership was considerably more difficult than the period of reform and regeneration he had earlier helped to orchestrate, and he died, worn out, in office. The cost and economic disruption of the war pressed hard throughout society, leading to inflation, the collapse of the gold standard under which paper currency was met by the Bank of England (1797), the introduction of income tax (1799), the stagnation of average real wages and widespread hardship, especially in the famine years of 1795–6 and 1799–1801. The real wages of Lancashire cotton weavers fell by more than a half in 1792–9. There was a nationalist dimension to radicalism in both Ireland and, to a lesser extent, Scotland. Radicals found their activities prohibited or limited, while trade unions were hindered, though not ended, by the combination acts of 1799 and 1800 which made combinations of employees for improved pay or conditions illegal. Further economic difficulties arose from the war with the United States of America (1812–14) over the British regulation of neutral trade. The British burnt Washington D.C. and defended Canada successfully, but were defeated outside New Orleans.

That conflict, the only war Britain fought with the United States after 1783, was only a diversion, however, from the struggle with Napoleon, and the British were fortunate that they fought the Americans after the French navy had been defeated and when Napoleon's system was beginning to collapse. Eventual triumph over Napoleon came as part of an alliance to which Britain contributed money (£66 million in subsidies and armaments to her allies) and the Duke of Wellington's victories in the Peninsular War (1808–13) in Portugal and Spain, such as Vimeiro (1808), Talavera (1809), Salamanca (1812), and Vitoria (1813). The disciplined firepower of the British infantry played a major part in these triumphs. Wellington never had more than 60,000 British troops under his personal command and was always outnumbered in both cavalry and artillery, but he was a fine judge of terrain and, as at Vimeiro, the well-positioned British lines succeeded in blunting the attacking French columns. British commitment culminated in the major roles taken by Britain at the peace congress of Vienna (1814–15) and, under Wellington, on the battlefield of Waterloo (1815). Though British troops composed less than half of the Anglo-German-Dutch force that Wellington commanded, they played a decisive role in stopping the successive advances of French cavalry and infantry, until finally Napoleon's veteran guard units were driven back. Their major role at Waterloo sealed the rehabilitation of the Highlanders and made possible the 1822 pageant in Edinburgh to welcome George IV.

UNION WITH IRELAND

The Act of Union with Ireland in 1800 was a response to the rising of 1798. Increasing Catholic wealth in the second half of the century and divisions among the Protestants were important to the long-term process by which the Catholics came to play a more central role in politics and a more active role in society. The harnessing of Irish manpower for war with France also strengthened pressure for improvement in the position of Catholics. Concern about the possible impact of the French Revolution led the government in London to improve the legal position of Catholics. The French Revolution had radicalised Irish discontent and provided the possibility of foreign support for a rebellion. When in 1791 Wolfe Tone founded the United Irishmen, until 1796–7 largely a Presbyterian Ulster movement, he put forward a programme advocating manhood suffrage, equal electoral districts and annual parliaments which, if implemented, would have destroyed the oligarchical regime at Dublin. Pitt the Younger overruled the Lord Lieutenant, the Earl of Westmorland, and the wishes of the Protestant Ascendancy in Ireland, and placated the Catholic agitation by granting better off Catholic freeholders the vote in 1793. The Place and Pensions Act and the Catholic Relief Act allowed Catholics to bear arms, sit on juries and hold minor civil and military office. Pitt was already thinking about the possibility of a parliamentary union between Britain and Ireland. The Irish Catholic Church, concerned about the hostility to the Catholic Church, and indeed to Christianity, of the French revolutionaries, preached the religious duty of obedience to the government of George III.

Important initiatives were, however, blocked. Earl Fitzwilliam, Lord Lieutenant 1794–5, sought to remove the remaining legal disabilities barring Catholics from Parliament and government office, but was disavowed and recalled. Fitzwilliam had believed that concessions were necessary in order to prevent the spread of revolutionary sentiment and his failure helped in the alienation of Catholic opinion, and confirmed radicals in the view that the only means to achieve their aims was revolution. The United Irishmen, who had been banned in 1794, had reformed as a secret society that was openly republican and increasingly Catholic, and had already begun to plot revolution. Tone had sought support in America and France. He managed to persuade the French to mount a major invasion attempt in 1796, but it was thwarted by adverse winds. When the French fleet reached Bantry Bay in December 1796 it failed to land any of the 12,000 strong force it carried. The United Irishmen developed a military organisation but the British army disarmed its Ulster cells in 1797. As the United Irishmen increasingly sought to win Catholic backing, they alienated Protestant support. Rising sectarian violence culminated in rebellion in 1798. The arrest of the Leinster provincial committee of the United Irishmen and of the organisers of the projected uprising in Dublin gravely handicapped the rebels, who were only able to mount a serious military challenge in Wexford where the local garrison was weak. The rebels won a victory at Oulart Hill but were smashed at Vinegar Hill. More people were killed in Ireland that year than during the revolutionary Terror in France. The rebellion, which was supported by an unsuccessful French invasion of Connacht, was firmly suppressed by Cornwallis, who had been defeated by the Americans and their French allies at Yorktown in 1781.

   This rebellion demonstrated that the Ascendancy could not keep Ireland stable, and encouraged the British government to support union. The Act of Union of 1800 abolished the separate Irish Parliament in return for Irish representation at Westminster. The House of Commons had to be enlarged to accommodate 100 new MPs, although a number of Irish 'rotten' boroughs lost their seats. Four spiritual lords and twenty-eight temporal lords were added to the House of Lords. The established churches were combined into one Protestant Episcopal Church called the United Church of England and Ireland, although this Nnion never amounted to much. However, Pitt's attempt to follow Union by admitting Catholics to Parliament and to most public offices was thwarted by George III, who argued that this would breach his promise in his coronation oath to protect the position of the Church of England. Catholics could not become MPs in the new Parliament until 1829. The marginalisation of Catholics was demonstrated by the ecclesiastical geography of Ireland. In the town of Kildare, for example, where the overwhelming majority of the population were Catholics, the sole place of Catholic worship was a chapel in a remote part of the town. Nevertheless, Catholics had more rights than ever before. In the medium term (or even the 1820s at any rate) the insistence on Protestantism and civil rights going together may have undermined the Union, but a fair share of informed high political opinion thought it could go forward on that narrow basis.

EXPANSION OF THE EMPIRE

Naval power permitted Britain to dominate the European trans-oceanic world during the Revolutionary and Napoleonic wars.

Danish, Dutch, French and Spanish naval power were crippled; Britain was left free to execute amphibious attacks on the now-isolated centres of other European powers, and to make gains at the expense of non-European peoples. The route to India was secured: Cape Town was captured in 1795 and then again, after it had been restored in 1802, in 1806; the Seychelles in 1794; Réunion and Mauritius in 1810. The British position in India and Australasia was consolidated, while her gains at the Congress of Vienna included Ceylon, the Seychelles, Mauritius, Trinidad, Tobago, St Lucia, Malta, Cape Colony and Guyanna. The Pacific became a British rather than a Spanish lake, while India served as the basis of British power and influence around the Indian Ocean.

The nature of the British empire and of the European world both altered dramatically. In 1775 the majority of British subjects outside Britain were white (though the population of the West Indian colonies was predominantly black slaves), Christian, of British or at least European origin, and ruled with an element of local self-government. By 1815 none of this was true. By then most of the trans-oceanic European world outside the western hemisphere was British; by 1830 this was true of the vast majority of all European possessions abroad. The situation was not to last; indeed 1830 was the date of the French occupation of Algiers, the basis of their subsequent North African empire. Nevertheless the unique imperial oceanic position that Britain occupied in the Revolutionary, Napoleonic and post-Napoleonic period was to be of crucial importance to its nineteenth-century economic and cultural development. France was to become a great imperial power again; Portugal and the Dutch were to make gains, Germany, Italy, Belgium (and the United States) to become imperial powers, but for none of these was empire as important, as central a feature of public culture, as it was for Britain, by the late-Victorian and Edwardian period. The rise in British imperial power had a great influence on the British economy, on the British elite, who were provided with a new sense of role and mission and, in many cases, with careers, and on British public culture. Service in the colonies, particularly in India, came to be prestigious, more so than anything similar in France or Germany. Sir Walter Scott referred to India, where many Scots pursued a career in the army, administration and commerce, as the 'corn chest for Scotland'. The sense of Britain playing a major role in resisting challenges to the European system, which had characterised opposition to Louis XIV, the Revolution and Napoleon, ebbed, as empire, especially from the mid- and late 1870s, set the themes of Britain's role and identity, a process that was furthered by the development of widespread emigration to certain colonies. The establishment of the British imperial position owed much to success in war, and it was not surprising that the pantheon of imperial heroes defined and depicted in the nineteenth century was largely composed of military figures, such as Nelson. Wellington was the only former general in British history to become Prime Minister (1828–30).

7

Age of Reform and Empire, 1815–1914

THE INDUSTRIAL REVOLUTION

The rise of Britain to become the greatest imperial power in history was not alone responsible for the divergence between her and the other European powers. Economic development and the rise of nationalism further constituted and accentuated the process of divergence. The harnessing of technological change led to an economic transformation of the country, not least as a consequence of the benefits of readily available capital and labour and the burgeoning markets of growing home, colonial and foreign populations. The Wheal Virgin steam engine of 1790, produced by the Birmingham partnership of Boulton and Watt, could do the work of 953 horses. Widespread use of the abundant and easily-worked British supplies of coal to fuel mechanical power freed the economy from its earlier energy constraints, reducing costs and increasing the availability of heat energy. This was exploited in a host of industries such as soap production, glass-works and linen bleaching. The rate of growth in coal mining substantially increased in mid-century as demands from the iron industry grew. As a mobile source of energy, the steam engine permitted the concentration of industrial production in towns and was also responsible for a growth in the range of products for the growing middle class.

Alongside major changes, however, it is also appropriate to stress the two-tier, gradual and evolutionary nature of the Industrial Revolution. Technological change was generally slow in the early decades of the century and there was great variety within industries.

Handloom weaving, for example, persisted on an appreciable scale in Lancashire into the 1840s; London and Birmingham were primarily cities of workshops, not factories; water rather than coal continued to provide much of the power for Scottish industry before 1830. Despite the railway, much of Britain remained a horse-drawn society. The chronologies of the growth in the use of steam power and in urban population do not tally. Despite these factors, the notion of an Industrial Revolution is still justified. The potential and character of much of British industry changed dramatically. Many of the fastest-growing cities of the early nineteenth century were centres of industrial activity, for example Bradford, Dundee and Merthyr Tydfil.

The Industrial Revolution gave Britain a distinctive economy. The annual averages of coal and lignite production for 1820–4, in million metric tons, were 18 for Britain, 2 for France, Germany, Belgium and Russia combined. The comparable figures for 1855–9 were 68 and 32, and for 1880–4, 159 and 108. Raw cotton consumption in thousand metric tons in 1850 was 267 for Britain and 162 for the rest of Europe, and in 1880, 617 and 503. The annual production of pig-iron in million metric tons was in 1820, 0.4 for Britain, the same for the rest of Europe, in 1850, 2.3 and 0.9, in 1880, 7.9 and 5.4; of steel in 1880, 1.3 for Britain, 1.5 for the rest of Europe. The British population (excluding Ireland) rose from an estimated 7.4 million in 1750 to 29.7 in 1881, and much of this growing population lived in the shadow of mill, mine and factory. For example, the population of Manchester and Salford grew more than five times between 1801 and 1891. The 1851 census showed that, for the first time, the English urban population exceeded its rural counterpart.

THE TRANSPORT REVOLUTION

The Great Exhibition of the year 1851 was a tribute to manufacturing skill and prowess, as was the evolution from the stationary to the locomotive steam-engine and the consequent railway revolution. The Stockton and Darlington Railway was opened in 1825; the Liverpool to Manchester in 1830. The locomotive that began services on the Stockton and Darlington Railway had a speed of twelve to sixteen miles an hour. When Goldsworthy Gurney's steam-jet (or blast) was applied to George Stephenson's *Rocket* locomotive in 1829, the engine reached a speed of twenty-nine miles an hour. In the following two decades a national system developed, albeit one constructed and run by competing companies. Services from London reached Southampton in 1840, Bristol in 1841, Exeter in 1844, cutting the journey time from twenty-one to less than six hours, Norwich in 1845, Lincoln in 1846, Plymouth in 1847, Holyhead, the postal port for Ireland, in 1850, cutting the journey time from forty to nine-and-a-half hours, and Truro in 1859. By 1850 the network covered most of the country apart from north Scotland, south-west England and most of Wales. The railway network subsequently spread throughout the British Isles and was far more extensive than the canals. In 1911 there were 130 manned stations in Devon and Cornwall alone. Canals were not immediately eclipsed by the railways. Their cheaper tariffs still made them an attractive prospect where heavy goods did not need to be moved rapidly and as feeders for railways. Yet in the end the railways largely consigned them to decay.

The railways brought new sounds and smells, the dramatic engineering of bridges, such as Brunel's across the Tamar (1859), and the Forth Bridge (1890), viaducts and tunnels, such as the Severn Tunnel (1886), and transported goods and people round the country. The number of passenger journeys rose from 60 million miles in 1850 to near 300 in 1870. The manufacture and maintenance of trains became an important aspect of Britain's industry with major workshops at towns that were founded or greatly expanded, such as Crewe, Doncaster, Swindon and Wolverton. Even towns that are no longer noted for their railway works could be heavily dependent on them. In Brighton and Gateshead, for example, the railway was the largest employer.

Economic patterns changed, not least the nature of marketing. Small market centres collapsed and the position of towns in the urban hierarchy altered. Railways competed with coastal shipping, supplanting it in the crucial movement of coal from the North-East to London and East Anglia. Trains were used to move perishable goods, such as fruit, flowers and milk, to the major cities: over 15,000 tons of Cornish broccoli annually by 1900; a special daily refrigerated van carrying Devon rabbit carcasses to London before World War Two. Use of the railway from the 1840s enabled the brewers of Burton-upon-Trent to develop a major beer empire.

Train travel encouraged the growth and popularisation of domestic tourism, not least the development of the seaside resorts that changed much of coastal Britain, such as Newquay, Ramsgate, Bournemouth, Hove, Eastbourne, Margate, Southend, Yarmouth, Skegness, Cleethorpes, Bridlington, Scarborough, Morecambe and Blackpool. The very building of the railways, with large gangs of migrant workers moving across rural Britain, disrupted local social patterns and assumptions. The cultural impact of change in transportation was also dramatic. It brought the 'standardisation' of time and a new speed to news and changing fashions. 'Local' trends and towns were eclipsed by metropolitan fashions.

SOCIO-ECONOMIC CHANGE

In Britain the nineteenth century was an age of dramatic economic change, possibly most so in Bradford, whose population climbed from 16,012 in 1810 to 103,778 in 1850 as the city became the global centre of worsted production and exchange. Factory horsepower in the town rose 718 per cent between 1810 and 1830. Mechanisation there brought profit, larger factories and a wave of immigrants. Innovation was continual. The mechanisation of yarn spinning was followed in 1826, despite riots by hostile workers, by that of worsted weaving. By 1850 the work formerly done in Bradford by thousands of handloom weavers, working in the countryside, was now performed by 17,642 automatic looms contained in factories and mass-producing women's dress fabrics.

Mechanisation was crucial to uniformity, the production of low-cost standardised products. As a result, brands of mass-produced goods, such as chocolate and soap, could be consumed and advertised nationally. Though factory production did not predominate until the second half of the century, industry and trade changed the face of the nation and the life of the people: 'many a weary hand did swelt / In torched mines and noisy factories' (John Keats, Isabella, 1820). The consequences of economic growth were varied. At the great seaport of Liverpool about 30,000 sailors were ashore at any one time, leading to a major rise in prostitution: there were about 300 brothels in 1836, 538 in 1846, and in 1857 there were at least 200 regular prostitutes under 12. The Bradford Sanitary Committee visited over 300 houses in 1845 and found an average of three people sleeping per bed. As the British Isles had a number of regional economies and not a national one, industrial growth was far from uniform across the country. It was concentrated in areas with coal: the North-East, the Midlands, southern Lancashire, the West Riding of Yorkshire, South Wales, Fife and Strathclyde. 1910 was the peak year for the number of collieries in South Wales: 688 in all. Heavy industries such as iron and steel, engineering and shipbuilding, were attracted to coal and iron-ore fields. Thus Workington on the Cumbrian coast developed as a major centre of iron and steel production from 1857 on. Railways built in the 1840s and 1850s created ready access to nearby iron-ore fields and to the coke supplies of Durham. Many of the migrant workers for the town came from Ireland. Middle-class professions developed to 'service' these new industries: new professions such as accountants emerged, as did new 'industries' such as leisure and tourism. Conversely previously important areas, such as East Anglia and the South-West, suffered de-industrialisation, in part because they lacked coal, and depopulation. Norfolk, once a county with an important textile industry, saw this collapse from the 1790s in the face of competition from factory-produced cottons. Many small market towns, such as Diss and Swaffham in Norfolk, had little growth and were not to change greatly until they expanded again from the 1960s.

AN AGE OF ENTREPRENEURS

The wealthy businessmen of the industrial areas purchased landed estates, patronised the arts and increasingly sought political and social influence. One of the greatest was William Armstrong (1810–1900), and his career epitomised the opportunities of the Victorian age, the intertwined forces of technology and industry. Grandson of a Northumberland yeoman farmer and son of a Newcastle corn merchant, he became a solicitor, but was also an amateur scientist, with a particular interest in hydroelectrics. His development of the hydraulic crane led him to establish an engineering works at Elswick (1846). Armstrong subsequently expanded into both armaments and shipbuilding, his Elswick Ordnance Company becoming one of the largest engineering and armaments concerns in the world. The 110-ton, nearly 44-foot long, Armstrong breech-loaders manufactured for *HMS Victoria*, which was launched in 1887, were the largest and most powerful guns in the world. Warships were also built for a host of foreign powers, including Japan, Italy, Argentina and Chile. When he died, Armstrong was employing 25,000 people.

Armstrong was at the forefront of technological application, responsible for the installation of the world's first hydroelectric power station, and the mock-baronial stately home he built at Cragside was in 1880 the first house to be properly lit by lightbulbs. Armstrong supplied the hydraulic equipment to raise Tower Bridge, opened in 1894 and a potent symbol of empire. He was also responsible for the hydraulic lifts that were necessary if the London underground railway system was to expand with deep stations. A great local benefactor, who helped provide Newcastle with a better water supply and supported local education and health, Armstrong gained great wealth and became a peer in 1887. He was president of the Arts Association and a purchaser of the works of contemporary British painters, such as Dante Gabriel Rossetti. It was appropriate that in 1894 this greatest of the Victorian, or indeed modern British, warlords should have purchased Bamburgh Castle, the centre of Northumbrian power for much of the Anglo-Saxon period, and a great medieval royal fortress.

Isambard Kingdom Brunel (1806–59) was less successful than Armstrong, but shared his desire to apply technological innovations. Brunel's formidable engineering triumphs, the Clifton suspension bridge, his achievements as chief engineer on the Great Western Railway 1833–46, and his large iron-clad steamships, the *Great Western* (1838), *Great Britain* (1845) and *Great Eastern* (1858), reflected his work at the forefront of technical innovations, on, for example, screw propellers. The *Great Western* was, when launched, the largest steamship afloat and it was the first to sail regularly to America; the *Great Britain* the first large ship using a screw propellor; the *Great Eastern* the largest steamship yet built, and one constructed by new methods. Not all entrepreneurs came from outside the landed order. In 1859 Rowland Winn began developing the iron industry on his family's Lincolnshire estates. This supplied an iron and steel industry in Scunthorpe. In 1885 Winn, by then Lord St Oswald, replaced manual labour in his mines with grab cranes. By 1917 the St Oswald mines were supplying one-twelfth of Britain's output of iron ore.

Financial links played a major role in British imperial expansion which in economic terms was expressed by investment and shipping, as much as the export of manufactured goods. Thus London, the centre of finance and shipping, grew in economic importance, and the values of the metropolitan elite that controlled it were different to those of the factory owners of the north and more akin to the 'gentlemanly' lifestyle of the traditional landed elite. The structure of wealth in the country was only partly changed by the growth of industrial capitalism.

A GLOBAL ECONOMIC POWER

Economic growth did not, however, mean that there were no fears of continental economic competition. France was much feared as an industrial rival down to the 1840s, while concern about German competition was a major reason for the repeal of the Corn Laws which kept the price of grain high for the benefit of British agriculture. In the parliamentary debates of February–March 1839 on the Corn Laws, in response to the depression, almost every speaker was aware of the threat from foreign manufacturing, especially because of the German *Zollverein* (customs union) of 1834. Confidence was most developed in the 1850s and 1860s, which were abnormally prosperous decades, and even then it was not unqualified.

Nevertheless, it was not simply the scale of British economic development that was of importance, but also the links that, literally, were being forged. As a result of the end of protection for British agriculture with the repeal of the Corn Laws (1846) and of the technological changes, including steamships, barbed wire, long-distance railways and, in the 1880s, refrigerated shipholds, which led to the development of agricultural production for the European market in other temperate climes and to the ability to move products rapidly without spoilage, Britain became, from the 1870s and 1880s, part of a global agrarian system. She was looking to empire, both formal and informal, rather than to Europe; grain from Germany, Poland and Russia was only bought in significant quantities in some years. Some continental agricultural products were important, most obviously fruit and vegetables such as German sugar-beet. By the end of the century Danish bacon and eggs were the staple of the British breakfast. Nevertheless, it was North American grain, Argentine beef and Australasian wool and mutton that were crucial, all, ironically, opened up by British technology, particularly railways, and helped by British finance. In combination, these imports led to the end of the golden age of 'high farming' and, instead, to a severe and sustained agricultural depression from the 1870s which badly affected farm-workers and rural craftsmen, and led to high rates of rural depopulation until the end of the century, and to a general stop in the construction of mansions by landlords. The spread of new technology, for example combined reaping and mowing machines, also affected the rural labour force. The total area devoted to agriculture in Britain fell by half a million acres between the 1870s and 1914. The cheap food that fed the growing work-forces of the industrial north of England, helped to lead to a sustained depression throughout much of the more agrarian south, a regional disparity that was to be reversed the following century. Sunderland, today a city with many urban problems, was in 1850 the greatest shipbuilding town in the world, with high wages and a high rate of owner-occupation of housing. Thanks to cheaper food, industrial workers were able to spend a lower proportion of their wages on food than hitherto, thus becoming important consumers, as well as producers, of manufactured goods.

EMPIRE

Britain was the leading imperial power in the nineteenth century. At the end of the century she ruled a quarter of the world's population and a fifth of the land surface. Between 1860 and 1914 Britain owned approximately one-third of the world's shipping tonnage and by 1898 about 60 per cent of the telegraph cables, a crucial aspect of imperial government and defence planning. In 1890–1914 she launched about two-thirds of the world's ships and carried about half of its marine trade. In *Cargoes* (1903), John Masefield was able to present the three ages of marine trade through a 'Quinquireme of Nineveh', a 'Stately Spanish galleon', and lastly, a 'Dirty British coaster' carrying a cargo of British exports: 'cheap tin trays', a mass-produced product. Investment abroad ensured that overseas income as a percentage of UK gross domestic product rose from 2 in 1872 to 7 in 1913: an ability to export finance was crucial to Britain's economic position in regions such as South America.

These were also years of still-spreading territorial control. Britain gained the most important share of the two leading colonial carve-ups of the period, the scramble for Africa and the seizure of hitherto unclaimed island groups. She became the leading power in east and southern Africa: successfully invaded Egypt in 1882, defeated the Mahdists of Sudan at Omdurman (1898), a battle in which the young Winston Churchill served, gained what was to become British Somaliland, Kenya, Uganda, Zambia, Malawi and Zimbabwe, and eventually defeated the Afrikaner republics of southern Africa, the Orange Free State and Transvaal, in the Boer War of 1899–1902. The war proved far more difficult than had been anticipated, but the ability of Britain to spend £250 million and deploy 400,000 troops was a testimony to the strength of both its economic and imperial systems, while her unchallenged control and retention of the South African ports allowed her to bring her strength to bear. On the other hand, many contemporaries were deeply worried by the army's performance and the war was followed by a budgetary crisis.

British strength spread throughout the oceans of the world. Between 1850 and 1914 her list of island possessions was enlarged by the Andaman, Nicobar, Gilbert and Ellice, Kuria Muria, South Orkney, South Shetland and Cook islands, Malden, Starbuck, Caroline, Pitcairn, Christmas, Phoenix, Washington, Fanning and Jarvis islands, Fiji, Rotuna, the Solomons, Tonga, Socotra, and South Georgia. British naval power was supported by the most numerous and wide-ranging bases in the world, a testimony to the global reach of the British state. In 1898 these included Wellington, Fiji, Sydney, Melbourne, Adelaide, Albany, Cape York (Australia), Labuan (North Borneo), Singapore, Hong Kong, Weihaiwei (China), Calcutta, Bombay, Trincomalee, Colombo, the Seychelles, Mauritius, Zanzibar, Mombasa, Aden, Cape Town, St Helena, Ascension, Lagos, Malta, Gibraltar, Halifax (Nova Scotia), Bermuda, Jamaica, Antigua, St Lucia, Trinidad, the Falklands and Esquimalt (British Columbia). The peacetime army was always overstretched to meet the numerous commitments of empire, but it grew in size to 195,000 men in 1898, and this force was supported by a substantial body of native troops in the Indian army, the basis for a powerful expansion of British power in southern Asia in the

Victorian period. Sind was conquered in 1843, Baluchistan and Kashmir became British vassals in 1843 and 1846 respectively, the Punjab was annexed in 1849 and by 1886 all Burma had followed. The Indian Mutiny of 1857–8 was a severe shock, and the Afghan tribes successfully resisted invasions during the wars of 1838–42 and 1878–9, but in co-operation with the landlords and native princes the British governed India with considerable success. British explorers, particularly James Bruce, David Livingstone, Mungo Park and John Speke, explored much of Africa. Others explored Australia and Canada, while the Royal Navy charted the oceans of the world.

Empire was not simply a matter of power politics, military interests, elite careers and an ideology of mission and purpose that appealed to the propertied and the proselytising. It also had relevance and meaning throughout a society affected by the growth of popular imperialist sentiment. This was reflected in the jingoistic strains of popular culture: the ballads of music hall and the images depicted on advertisements for mass-produced goods; though, on the other hand, many of the workers appear to have been pretty apathetic about imperialism, and many Liberal politicians, including William Gladstone, Liberal Prime Minister 1868–74, 1880–5, 1886, 1892–4, were critical of jingoism, of imperial expansion for its own sake, and of many advances of British power, for example into Uganda. Empire reflected and sustained the widespread racist assertions and assumptions of the period, both of which were amply demonstrated in the literature and press of the period. Empire provided the occasion and stimulus for a new concept of exemplary masculinity focusing on soldier heroes such as Wolseley, Gordon, Roberts and Kitchener, who were presented as national icons in a fusion of martial prowess, Protestant zeal and moral manhood. Their victories were gained at the expense of numerous non-Europeans, often slaughtered by the technology of modern weaponry, as in Kitchener's victory at Omdurman (Sudan) in 1898. Charles Gordon, who died defending Khartoum in 1885, was presented as a quasi-saint resisting a vast force of Muslims. The impact of such controversial imperial events was enough to threaten prominent politicians such as Gladstone. The sieges of the Indian Mutiny (1857–8) and the Second Boer War (1899–1902) offered drama for the entire country. Imperial clashes were re-enacted in open-air spectacles in Britain: the tableau and pageant became art forms. Army service was a glorious route out of the slums for many working-class men. Newspapers spent substantial sums on the telegraphy that brought news of imperial conflict. The Protestant and Catholic churches of Britain devoted their resources to missionary activity outside Europe, particularly, though not only, within the empire which they endorsed as a means of facilitating Christian missions, not to proselytism on the Continent.

BRITAIN AND EUROPE

With the succession of Queen Victoria in 1837, the dynastic link with Hanover was broken: only men could succeed there. Britain's global responsibilities meant that she took a view of the world in which Europe was simply one element, though it was a very important element. The concepts of the 'Concert of Europe' and 'the Balance of Power' indicate how central the Continent was in the conduct of British foreign policy. Prominent Foreign Secretaries, such as George Canning, 1807, 1822–7, Prime Minister 1827, and Henry, Viscount Palmerston, Foreign Secretary 1830–41, 1846–51, Prime Minister 1855–8, 1859–65, were extremely concerned with continental international relations, for example in Iberia, Greece and the Near East. In addition, imperial issues could have a European dimension, most obviously with 'the Eastern Question', the problem created by Russia's growing influence and ambitions in the Balkans as the Turkish empire declined. Furthermore, the absence of challenges on the Continent could free Britain for imperial ambitions.

British governments worried about the plans and actions of their continental counterparts. Invasion by France, including through a planned Channel tunnel, was feared in 1847–8, 1851–2 and 1859–60, while Russian moves in the Balkans led Britain to go to war with her: the Crimean War (1854–6). This was the last war that Britain fought with a European power until the First World War broke out in 1914, an unprecedented length of time. The Crimean War was characterised by administrative incompetence, heavy losses in manpower and a series of military misjudgments, most famously the Charge of the Light Brigade into the face of Russian artillery at Balaclava in 1854, an action that was as outmoded and unsuccessful as the attempt to defend rotten boroughs in 1832. An imperial power that could conquer much of the world lacked the military strength, crucially a large European army, to compete effectively in European power politics. Nevertheless, the war also indicated Britain's continued ability to project her power around the world, naval attacks being mounted on Russian coasts as far as Kamchatka on the Pacific, and in this she was assisted by technological advances. The warships sent to the Baltic in 1854 were all fitted with steam engines, and also benefited from Brunel's work on gun-carriages.

More generally, educated Victorians were acutely aware of what they shared with other European peoples as a result of a common culture based upon Christianity and the legacy of Greece and Rome. Gladstone published three books on the classical Greek writer Homer. The growing number of public schools made the classics the centre of their teaching. Those who could afford to do so performed and listened to German music, read French novels and visited the art galleries of Italy. The British were involved, intellectually and at times materially, for most of the century, in what was happening on the Continent. This was obviously true of the Napoleonic and Crimean (1854–6) wars in which Britain participated, but, in addition, the Greek War of Independence and the *Risorgimento* (Italian unification) aroused enormous interest, more so than many of the British minor colonial wars and acquisitions of colonial territory. The manner in which the Italian hero Garibaldi was mobbed by working-class crowds when he visited England in 1864 testified to the way in which Victorians of all social classes were able to relate many of the events taking place on the Continent to their own struggles and aspirations. In 1876 Gladstone was able to embarrass Disraeli's ministry seriously over the massacre of Bulgarians by the Turks. Continental news remained very important in the British press, though more attention was devoted to imperial questions from the 1870s.

A major difference between Britain and continental countries, especially in the mid-nineteenth century, was that Britain traded abroad far more than they did, and far more widely. Continental economies were more self-sufficient; what foreign trade they did was mainly with other European countries. So Britain was dependent on foreign trade, and on the wider world outside Europe, in a way they were not. From this followed many aspects of Britain's difference from the Continent: Britain's outward-looking perspective and internationalism; her interest in peace, which was believed to create the best conditions for trade, and which determined her diplomatic isolation from the Continent (except during the Crimean War) – to avoid being dragged into European wars; and her opposition to a large and expensive army.

BRITAIN AND AMERICA

The British attitude towards America was ambivalent and vice versa. Many Victorians wrote about it, for example Charles Dickens, Anthony Trollope and James Bryce, all of whom were taken by its energy and drive, yet often shocked by its 'vulgar' (populist) politics. A standard means of criticising a politician was to accuse him of the 'Americanisation' of British politics, and Gladstone and Joseph Chamberlain both suffered accordingly. There was also much downright hostility between the two states: over the Crimean War, when the British, being very short of troops by 1855, tried to recruit American mercenaries; the American Civil War, when the British were considered too favourable to the South; and in disputes over clashing imperial interests in the New World and the Pacific, for example involving Venezuela in the 1890s. The Civil War divided British public opinion fairly widely. The South sought to win diplomatic recognition, a step that would have legitimated secession. The Foreign Secretary, Lord John Russell, and the Chancellor of the Exchequer, Gladstone, were sympathetic, but fears that recognition would lead to war with the Union prevented the step. It was not only power politics that led to hostility. There were also cultural and economic rivalries, for example over copyright law in the 1850s. On the other hand, despite disagreements over the Maine frontier and, more seriously, tension over the fate of modern British Columbia, the British and the Americans managed to agree the course of the long Canadian border without war. Similarly, cross-border raids on Canada by the Fenians, American-based Irish terrorists, did not trouble relations for long. There was massive British investment in America, particularly in railways, the transfer of British technology, again in railways, and important cultural and social links. A number of American women married peers or their heirs in 1870–1914, some bringing great wealth, as when Consuelo Vanderbilt married the duke of Marlborough in 1895.

MORAL POLITICS

Empire was a crucial component of British nationalism, especially towards the end of the century. The imagery of government fuelled this: Victoria was made Empress of India in 1876, the journal *Punch*, an influential creator of images, popularised empire in its cartoons, and public buildings were decorated with symbols of empire. The expansion of empire was seen as furthering moral, as well as national, goals by spreading what was seen as liberal government and the rule of law, and providing opportunities for Christian proselytism. A sense of the strengths of the British constitution was another major aspect of nationalism. Though political expedients, compromises and the search for short-term advantage played a major role in the details of political reform, a sense of idealism was also important, the 'moral economy' of eighteenth-century paternalism and crowd sentiment being replaced by the 'moral politics' of the nineteenth century. The erosion of the 'moral economy' at the same time as 'moral politics' emerged is one of the paradoxes of Victorian culture. The social location and ideological context of much activism became more 'respectable'. Moral campaigns, for example against slavery, cruelty to animals and alcohol, aroused widespread support, fuelling a major expansion in the voluntary societies that were such a characteristic feature of Victorian Britain. The numerous hymns of the period meanwhile made clear the commitment to a Christian society: faith was far from being a matter of personal salvation alone. The role of the moral crusade had different focuses, ranging from the Anti-Corn-Law League through to the moral purity campaigns in the 1890s.

RADICALISM

Though domestic radicalism had initially been encouraged by the French Revolution (1789), the growing violence and radicalism of the Revolution led, especially from 1792, to reaction, a rallying to Church, Crown and nation, with which the name of the politician-polemicist Edmund Burke will always be linked; although he was more liberal on slavery and on British policy in America, India and Ireland. This conservative surge helped to see Britain through years of defeat at the hands of France, but serious economic strains and social discontent did not end with the war, and were indeed exacerbated from 1815 by postwar depression and demobilisation. Population growth led to under-employment and unemployment and thus low wages and poverty both for those in and for those without work. Unemployment, which also owed something to new technology and thus inspired Luddites to destroy new industrial machines in Yorkshire in 1811–12, the unbalanced nature of industrial change and the economic problems it caused, poor harvests and agitation for political reform, produced a volatile post-war atmosphere. Parliament, dominated by the landed interest, passed the Corn Laws, which prohibited the import of grain unless the price of British grain reached 80 shillings a quarter. Thus the price of the essential component of the expenditure of the bulk of the population was deliberately kept up. The result was food riots amongst hungry agricultural labourers, with attacks on farmers and on corn mills, and demands for wage increases. Threshing machines, which replaced the hand-flailing of cereal crops, also led to anger and there were outbreaks of machine-breaking, for example in south Norfolk in 1822. Income tax, seen as an emergency wartime measure, was repealed in 1816. William Cobbett (1762–1835), a leading political writer, denounced 'The Thing' – the Anglican, aristocratic establishment that dominated society, politics, religion and learning by means of patronage.

Luddism was not only about destroying machinery. It was, in areas such as Nottinghamshire, about strengthening the wage-bargaining position of trade unions, but governmental attitudes in the 1810s were hostile to the aims of numerous sections of the labouring classes and not conducive to the development of popular activism outside the context of self-consciously 'loyalist' activity. Discontent and violence led to repressive legislation, most prominently the Six Acts of 1819; although by the standards of modern totalitarian regimes there was no police state. The Peterloo Massacre in Manchester (1819), a panic charge by the Yeomanry (militia) ordered on by the over-excitable Manchester magistrates, on an enormous crowd gathered to support demands for parliamentary reform by speakers such as 'Orator Hunt', led to eleven deaths and many injuries. It inspired widespread revulsion. The radical poet Percy Bysshe Shelley (1792–1822) depicted *The Mask of Anarchy*: 'Trampling to a mire of blood / The adoring multitude' and called for a popular rising: 'Ye are many – they are few.' However, the radicals were divided and most, including Hunt, rejected the use of force after Peterloo, which received so much attention because it was untypical. A small group of London revolutionaries, under Arthur Thistlewood, plotted to murder the entire Cabinet and establish a government, but they were arrested in Cato Street in 1820. Thistlewood, who was hanged for treason, declared at the end of his trial, 'Albion [England] is still in the chains of slavery'. A rising in Huddersfield, also in 1820, was unsuccessful, while Hunt was imprisoned for his role at Peterloo. There was also tension in Scotland, culminating in the so-called 'Radical War' of 1820. The Glasgow Police Commission appointed 700 new constables in 1817 and in 1819 took the threat of rebellion seriously. The radicals there used the slogan 'Scotland Free or a Desert'. About 60,000 people went on strike in Glasgow and Strathclyde.

George IV, Prince Regent 1811–20 while his father, George III, was incapacitated by porphyria, and King 1820–30, was very unpopular, especially for his extravagance and, to a lesser extent, his conservatism: he thanked the Manchester authorities for their conduct at Peterloo. George's unpopularity climaxed in 1820 when he tried to divorce his separated wife, Caroline, and to remove her royal status. Her cause was taken up by public opinion and the government felt obliged to abandon its campaign against the queen, though she was successfully denied a coronation. Though his visits to Ireland and Scotland were very successful, *The Times* remarked in 1830, 'Never was there a human being less respected than this late king . . . what eye weeps for him?' Discontent was widespread in the 1810s and, though to a lesser extent, the 1820s, arson and animal-maiming frequent in rural areas, for example in Essex. The invention of friction matches in 1826 by the Stockton chemist John Walker, and their subsequent manufacture as 'strike anywhere lucifers', made arson easier.

THE FIRST REFORM ACT, 1832

Tensions eased during the prosperous years of the early-1820s, not least because the Earl of Liverpool's government became less repressive after 1822; but in the late 1820s an industrial slump and high bread prices helped cause a revival in popular unrest. In 1830 'Swing' riots affected large parts of southern and eastern

England. Machine-breaking, arson and other attacks often followed letters signed by 'Swing' threatening trouble if labour-saving, and thus job-destroying, machines were not removed. Over ninety threshing machines were broken in Wiltshire; there were at least twenty-nine cases of arson in Lincolnshire. The identity of 'Captain Swing', a pseudonym appropriated by the protestors, is unclear, and the riots probably spread spontaneously rather than reflecting central control. Some industrial machines were also attacked. Wage and tithe riots contributed to the atmosphere of crisis in 1830: in much of rural England it was the last episode of riot until the period of trade-union activity in the 1870s.

In 1830 there was also much pressure for reform of Parliament to make it more representative of the wealth and weight of the community. The Whig government of Earl Grey that took power after the elections of 1830 thought such reform necessary, though the House of Lords opposed it. Grey thought the situation 'too like what took place in France before the Revolution'. Commons majorities for reform and popular agitation, including riots in Bristol, Merthyr Tydvil and Nottingham, led to a political crisis, and William IV (1830-7), a former naval officer, eventually felt it necessary to agree that he would make new peers in order to create a majority for reform in the Lords. This led the Lords to give way. The First Reform Act (1832), described by its authors as final, fixed a more uniform right to vote that brought the franchise to the 'middle class', and reorganised the distribution of seats in order to reward growing towns, such as Birmingham, Bradford and Manchester, and counties, at the expense of 'rotten boroughs', seats with a small population that were open to corruption. Voting qualifications still differed between the boroughs and the counties, the size of electorate still varied greatly by seat, and women were still excluded from the vote, but about one-fifth of all English adult males could vote after 1832: the size of the English electorate increased by 50 per cent, without 'danger' to the constitution. The growth of the Scottish electorate was even more spectacular. The Municipal Corporations Act of 1835 reformed and standardised the municipal corporations of England and Wales. Elected borough councils, based on a franchise of rated occupiers, were given control over the local police, markets and street lighting. This made town governments responsible to the middle class and was a crucial precondition for a wave of reforming urban activism, although much of this was slow in coming, and there had also been considerable improvement before 1835.

Grey was to complain in 1837 that the Reform Act had made 'the democracy of the towns paramount to all the other interests of the state', which was not what he had intended. The following year, William Wordsworth (1770–1850), one of the greatest of the Romantic poets and initially a radical and a supporter of the French Revolution, revealed in his *Protest Against the Ballot* the extent of the conversion to reaction that was to help him gain a civil list (government) pension (1842) and the poet laureateship (1843). It began:

> Forth rushed from Envy sprung and Self-conceit,
> A Power misnamed the SPIRIT of REFORM,
> And through the astonished Island swept in storm,
> Threatening to lay all Orders at her feet
> That crossed her way.

Wordsworth continued by urging St George, patron saint of England, to stop the introduction of the secret ballot as it threatened to spawn a 'pest' worse than the dragon he had slain. Not one of Wordsworth's masterpieces, the poem underlines the hostility and fear that reform aroused in many circles, the sense that concessions to change had to be balanced by containment.

CHARTISM

Others, however, were dissatisfied with the limited extent of reform. The radical Henry 'Orator' Hunt, whose address had triggered the violence at Peterloo and who supported universal manhood suffrage (right to vote), opposed the First Reform Act because he feared it would link the middle and upper classes against the rest. Dissatisfaction led in the late 1830s to a working-class protest movement, known as Chartism, that called for universal adult male suffrage, a secret ballot and annual elections. The Six Points of the People's Charter (1838) also included equal constituencies, the abolition of property qualifications for MPs, and their payment, the last two designed to ensure that the social elite lost their control of the representative system. Chartism was also a strongly regional movement and contained a 'back to the land' element. Although Chartists disagreed over tactics, there was general support for the argument that peaceful agitation should be used. Many Chartists argued that force could be employed to resist illegal action by the authorities, but, in practice, there was great reluctance to endorse violent policies. The general Chartist Convention held in Birmingham in 1839 presumed that Parliament would reject the Chartist National Petition, and called on the people to refrain from the consumption of excisable goods, a means of putting pressure on the government and the middle classes, and pressed for the people to exercise a right to arm, which was seen as a preparation for a general strike or 'sacred month' for the Charter that was in fact not implemented due to disagreements over appropriate action and lack of preparedness. Parliament resisted Chartist mass-petitions (1839, 1842, 1848), and Britain did not share in the disorders of 1848, the year of revolutions on the Continent, although there was support for action in Scotland. Chartism collapsed as a result of its failure to achieve its objectives, and of growing prosperity: mass support for Chartism was apparent only in times of recession. Similarly, rural protest movements against heavy rent and tithe burdens did not change the situation in the countryside.

THE CONDITION OF THE PEOPLE

The pressure that economic circumstances placed on the bulk of the population is indicated by the decline in the height of army recruits in the second quarter of the century, although as Britain had a voluntary army this is only a limited guide to the physical stature of the population as a whole. The strains of industrialisation in the early nineteenth century caused much social and political tension. Unlike cotton textiles, many other industries were slow to experience technological transformation, with the result that general living standards only rose noticeably from mid-century. The unstable credit structure exacerbated slumps. Working conditions were often unpleasant and hazardous with, for example, numerous fatalities in mining accidents. Poor ventilation helped the build-up of gas, leading to explosions such as that at Haydock in Lancashire in 1878 which killed 189 men and boys. The manufacture of matches from yellow phosphorous contributed to jaundice, psoriasis, chronic diarrhoea and phosphorous rotted jaw. Food adulteration was a general problem in the period. In 1858 the accidental use of arsenic in the manufacture of sweets led to twenty deaths in Bradford and eventually the introduction of better methods of control. The Factory Acts regulating conditions of employment in the textile industry still left work there both long and arduous. The 1833 Act established a factory inspectorate and prevented the employment of under-9s, but 9–10-year-olds could still work eight-hour days (which by 1836 would also apply to those under 13), and 11–17-year-olds twelve hours. The 1844 Act cut that of under–13s to six-and-a-half hours, and of 18-year-olds and all women to twelve; those of 1847 and 1850 reduced the hours of women and under-18s to ten hours. There were still about 5,000 half-timers under 13 in the Bradford worsted industry in 1907.

If the bulk of the working population faced difficult circumstances, the situation was even worse for those who were more 'marginal' to the economy. Henry Stuart, who reported on East Anglian poor relief in 1834, found three main groups of inmates in the often miserable parish workhouses: the old and infirm, orphaned and illegitimate children, and unmarried pregnant women, the last a group that was generally treated harshly, far more so than the men responsible. The Poor Law Amendment Act (1834) introduced national guidelines in place of the former more varied parish-based system, but the uniform workhouse system that it sought to create was not generous to its inmates. Outdoor relief was abolished for the able-bodied and they were obliged to enter the workhouse where they were to be treated no better than the conditions that could be expected outside in order to deter all bar the very destitute from being a charge on the community. Bastardy and indigent marriage and parenthood were to be discouraged. The system was to be overseen by the Poor Law Commissioners in London. In Wimborne workhouse beds had to be shared, meat was only provided once a week, there were no vegetables other than potatoes until 1849, men and women were segregated, and unmarried mothers had to wear distinctive clothes. In general, expenditure was severely controlled, discipline was harsh and the stigma attached to poverty grew. There was some popular opposition to the workhouses. The one at Gainsborough was destroyed while it was being built in 1837 and there were also disturbances elsewhere, for example at Todmorden which was for many years the sole

English Poor Law Union area without a union workhouse. Opposition there owed much to John Fielden, a wealthy cotton manufacturer and radical MP. A degree of outdoor relief continued in many places.

Social differentiation also characterised the care of the insane. Ticehurst Asylum, founded in the 1790s to cater for the wealthy, followed a 'no-restraint' policy and offered pleasant surroundings, plentiful food, and permitted visits, as did the York retreat. Elsewhere the situation was far more bleak, although the Asylum Act of 1845 brought a measure of reform.

Social assumptions and conventions pressed harder on women than on men. Women, not men, were blamed for the spread of venereal disease. Under the Contagious Diseases Acts (1864, 1866, 1869), passed because of concern about the health of the armed forces, women suspected of being prostitutes, not men who also might have spread disease, were subjected to physical examination and detention, if infected, in garrison towns and ports. After an extended campaign, in which women acquired experience of acting as political leaders, in the Ladies National Association for the Repeal of the Contagious Diseases Acts, the acts were repealed in 1886. Charity could temper hardship, but it often entailed deference if not subordination for its recipients. Andrew Reed's charity established in 1813 for the education of orphans led to the foundation of schools at first Clapton and then Watford (girls and boys were, as was usual, educated separately). Subscribers to the charity were awarded votes and widows had to lobby them to gain entry for their offspring. Parliament made the first grants towards education in 1833, but the Newcastle Commission of 1858 showed that only one in eight children was receiving elementary education.

> Hell is a city much like London –
> A populous and a smoky city

Shelley's statement in *Peter Bell the Third* (1819) seemed increasingly appropriate. Fast-expanding towns became crowded and polluted, a breeding ground for disease. 8,032 of the 9,453 houses in Newcastle in 1852 lacked toilets. Mortality rates remained high, though, thanks in part to vaccination, smallpox declined. Infant mortality was especially high, in both town and countryside. In largely rural Norfolk one-quarter of all deaths in 1813–30 were of children less than one year old. Cholera, a bacterial infection largely transmitted by water affected by the excreta of victims, hit first in Britain in 1831, in slums such as the overcrowded east end of Sunderland. By 1866 about 140,000 people had died of cholera. Disease struck most at the poor living in crowded and insanitary urban squalor, but also threatened the rich. Edward, Prince of Wales nearly died of typhoid, another water-borne infection, in 1871; his father, Victoria's husband, Prince Albert, had been killed by it in 1861. Dysentry, diarrhoea, diphtheria, whooping cough, scarlet fever, measles, and enteric fever were significant problems and frequently fatal. The death or illness of breadwinners wrecked family economies, producing or exacerbating poverty and related social problems. Neither these, nor political discontents, however, led to revolution in 1848. There was no equivalent in Britain to the unsuccessful attempted insurrection by the Young Ireland nationalist movement. Instead, change came gradually. The year 1848 saw the Health of Towns Act which created a General Board of Health and an administrative structure to improve sanitation, especially water supply. The new Act enabled the creation of local boards of health. The one that was constituted in Leicester in 1849 was instrumental in the creation of a sewer system and in tackling other aspects of the urban environment, such as slaughter-houses and smoke pollution. Despite its limitations and the opposition that it encountered, the Act was a definite advance in awareness of and organisation for public health.

THE VICTORIAN ETHOS

The contrast with the violent nature of political development on the Continent led to a measure of complacency. Having suffered from defeat and colonial rebellion in 1791–1835, Britain's colonial and maritime rivals were to be absorbed in domestic strife and continental power politics over the following four decades. Meanwhile, as reform legislation was passed within Britain, so British imperial power spread throughout the world, and the two processes were fused as first self-government and later dominion status were granted to the 'white colonies'. New Zealand achieved self-government in 1852, Newfoundland, New South Wales, Victoria, Tasmania and South Australia in 1855, Queensland in 1859; the Dominion of Canada was created in 1867. It is scarcely surprising that an optimistic conception of British history was the dominant account in academic and popular circles. A progressive move towards liberty was discerned, a seamless web that stretched back to Magna Carta in 1215 and the constitutional struggles of the barons in medieval England and forward to the nineteenth-century extensions of the franchise. These were seen as arising naturally from the country's development. This public myth, the Whig interpretation of history, offered a comforting and glorious account that seemed appropriate for a state that ruled much of the globe, was exporting its constitutional arrangements to other parts of the world and could watch the convulsions on the Continent as evidence of the political backwardness of its societies and the superiority of Britain. The leading British role in the abolition of the slave trade and the emancipation of the slaves also led to self-righteousness and a degree of moral complacency, not least about the position of the poor in Britain, although even when there was moral concern, it was often hardly helpful to the poor. The extension of civil rights to those outside the established Church, most obviously with the repeal of the Test and Corporation Acts in 1828 and the Act for Catholic Emancipation in 1829, could be seen as another aspect of British reason and superiority. In addition, the nineteenth century was very much a period of evangelicalism, which was by no means confined to the middle class, and this further encouraged a sense of national distinctiveness and mission.

There was confidence in the present, faith in the future. In 1857 the painter William Bell Scott stated that 'the latest is best . . . not to believe in the 19th century, one might as well disbelieve that a child grows into a man . . . without that Faith in Time what anchor have we in any secular speculation'. His painting *The Nineteenth Century, Iron and Coal* (1861), was set in the major industrial city of Newcastle and sought to capture, as he stated, 'everything of the common labour, life and applied science of the day'. It depicted workers at Robert Stephenson's engineering works, one of the largest manufacturers of railway engines in the world, an Armstrong gun, the steam of modern communications, telegraph wires. The Victorians sought to provide and secure a stable civic order, based on the rule of law, through which liberties could be safeguarded, prosperity enjoyed and progress maintained. This required what was seen as responsible and rational conduct and the control of emotionalism.

The Britain of Queen Victoria (1837–1901) had a sense of national uniqueness, nationalistic self-confidence and a xenophobic contempt for foreigners, especially Catholics, unless they were anti-papist, for example Garibaldi and other supporters of the Italian *Risorgimento*. Nationalism played a major role in the contemporary sense of distance from the Continent, not simply because of a British rejection of foreigners and foreignness, and the loss of the cosmopolitanism that had characterised much of the eighteenth-century elite, but also because of the corresponding development of a sense of national identity, politically, economically, culturally, and ethnically, in the continental states of the period. The reign of Victoria was the age of the unification of Germany (1871) and Italy (1870). Moreover, political reform on the Continent ensured that by 1865 many European states had more extensive franchises than those of Britain. Whether they had a 'democratic' facet or not, continental states increasingly seemed better able to challenge British interests.

ECONOMIC AND IMPERIAL CHALLENGES

The process of late-Victorian expansion took place in a context of European competition that was far more serious, and gave rise to more concern than the position in 1815–70, worrying as that had been at times. The British economy remained very strong, and new industries, such as engineering and automobiles, developed. The pace of scientific advance and technological change was unremitting, and British scientists led in a number of fields. Michael Faraday (1791–1867), the son of a Surrey blacksmith, discovered electromagnetic induction in 1831, making the continuous generation of electricity a possibility. His work was expanded by two Scots, James Clerk Maxwell, the first professor of experimental physics at Cambridge, and Lord Kelvin. The development of commercial generators later in the century led to the growing use of electricity. New distribution and retail methods, particularly the foundation of department and chain stores, helped to create national products. The international context, however, was less comforting. This was due to the greater economic strength of the major continental powers, their ability to take advantage of new technology and their determination to make colonial gains in pursuit of their own place in the sun. These combined and interacted to lead to a relative decline in British power and to produce a strong sense of disquiet in British governmental circles.

The growth of German economic power posed the starkest contrast with the situation earlier in the century. The annual average output of coal and lignite in million metric tons in 1870–4 was 123 for Britain, 41 for Germany; by 1910–14 the figures were 274 to 247. For pig-iron the annual figures changed from 7.9 and 2.7 in 1880 to 10.2 and 14.8 in 1910; for steel from 3.6 and 2.2 (1890) to 6.5 and 13.7 (1910). The number of kilometres of railway rose in Britain from 2,411 (1840) to 28,846 (1880) and 38,114 (1914); in Germany the comparable figures were 469; 33,838; and 63,378. In 1900 the German population was 56.4 million, that of Britain excluding Ireland, 37, and including her, 41.5. In the Edwardian period, Britain's second most important export market, after India, was Germany.

The tremendous growth in German power posed a challenge to Britain, in whose governing circles there had been widespread support for German unification and a failure to appreciate its possible consequences. France and Russia were also developing as major economic powers, while American strength was ever more apparent in the New World and, increasingly, the Pacific. Given the importance of imperial considerations in governmental, political, and popular thinking, it is not surprising that British relations with and concern about the continental powers registered not in disputes arising from European issues, but from differences and clashes centring on distant, but no longer obscure, points on the globe, ranging from Fashoda in the forests of the Upper Nile, to the islands of the western Pacific. French and German expansion in Africa led Britain to take counter measures: in West Africa, the occupation of the interior of the Gambia in 1887–8, the declaration of the Protectorate of Sierra Leone in 1896, establishment of the Protectorates of Northern and Southern Nigeria in 1900, the annexation of the Gold Coast in 1901. German moves in East Africa led to the establishment of British power in Uganda in the 1890s. Suspicion of Russian designs on the Ottoman empire and French schemes in North Africa led the British to move into Egypt. This was confirmed in the late 1890s by the realisation that Britain could not defend the Ottoman empire against Russia, while the Franco-Russian naval threat made a base at Alexandria essential. Concern about French ambitions led to the conquest of Mandalay (1885) and the annexation of Upper Burma; while Russia's advance across Asia led to attempts to strengthen and move forward the 'north-west frontier' of British India and the development of British influence in southern Persia. The Russian advance was the biggest single on-going concern of British generals from the late 1870s and posed a military challenge which they never satisfactorily solved, until Russia's defeat by Japan solved it for them in 1905.

Specific clashes of colonial influence interacted with a more general sense of imperial insecurity. The idea of Social Darwinism, with its stress on inherent struggle as the context for progress, the survival of the fittest, had unsettling consequences in attitudes towards international relations. Pressing the case for imperial pre-ference, Joseph Chamberlain argued in 1903 that free trade threa-tened Britain's economic position: 'Sugar has gone; silk has gone; iron is threatened; wool is threatened; cotton will go.' In the 1880s there was concern about British naval weakness: in 1889 public pressure obliged the government to pass the Naval Defence Act, which sought a two-power standard, superiority over the next two largest naval powers combined. Expenditure of £21,500,000 over five years, a vast sum, was authorised. The importance of naval dominance was taken for granted. In the preface to his *History of the Foreign Policy of Great Britain* (1895), Captain Montagu Bur-rows R. N., Professor of Modern History at Oxford, wrote of 'this fortress-isle of Britain, safely intrenched (*sic*) by stormy seas, con-fronting the broadest face of the Continent, and, later on, almost surrounding it with her fleets, was and was not, a part of Europe according as she willed'. The myth of national self-sufficiency peaked in these years. Naval strength was a prerequisite of such an ideal. These were the years in which the British built battleships of the class of the *Magnificent*: the first ships carrying cordite-using big guns.

By the mid–1900s, it was Germany, with its great economic strength and its search for a place in the sun, that was the principal threat. British resources and political will were tested in a major naval race between the two powers, in which the British launched HMS *Dreadnought*, the first of a new class of battleships, in 1906. It was also the first capital ship in the world to be powered by the marine turbine engine, which had been invented by Sir Charles Parsons in 1884. A projected German invasion was central to *The*

Riddle of the Sands (1903), the novel by Erskine Childers that was first planned by him in 1897, a year in which the Germans were indeed discussing such a project. Military discussions with France following the Anglo-French *entente* of 1904 were to play a major role in leading Britain towards the First World War. From 1905 Britain began to plan seriously for war with Germany and to see her as a major threat to Britain's overall future (as opposed to the commercial challenge).

THE VICTORIAN PRESS

The state that was taking part in this growing confrontation with imperial Germany was different to that of the early years of Victoria's reign. Britain had become more urban and more industrial. Her population was more literate and educated and was linked by modern communications and a national press. Changes in the press were symptomatic of the modernisation of the country. One of the many ways in which Victorian London was at the centre of British life and that of the British empire was that of the provision of the news. Through its press, which laid claim to the title of the 'fourth estate' of the realm, London created the image and idiom of empire and shaped its opinions. Aside from this political function, the press also played a central economic, social and cultural role, setting and spreading fashions, whether of company statements or through theatrical criticism. In what was increasingly a commercial society, the press played a pivotal role inspiring emulation, setting the tone, fulfilling crucial needs for an anonymous mass-readership, and pandering to the lowest tone in the 'yellow press' of the 1880s. The press was itself affected by change, by the energising and disturbing forces of commercialisation and new technology. It was to be legal reform and technological development that freed the Victorian press for major development. Newspapers had become expensive in the eighteenth century, in large part due to successive rises in stamp duty. In the mid-nineteenth century these so-called 'taxes on knowledge' were abolished: the advertisement duties in 1853, the newspaper stamp duty in 1855 and the paper duties in 1861. This opened up the possibility of a cheap press and that opportunity was exploited by means of a technology centred on new printing presses and the continuous rolls or 'webs' of paper that fed them. A steam press was first used, by *The Times*, in 1814. Web rotary presses were introduced in Britain from the late 1860s. Mechanical typesetting was introduced towards the end of the century.

New technology was expensive, but the mass readership opened up by the lower prices that could be charged after the repeal of the newspaper taxes justified the cost. The consequence was more titles and lower prices. The number of daily morning papers published in London rose from eight in 1856 to twenty-one in 1900, of evenings from seven to eleven, while there was a tremendous expansion in the suburban press. The repeal of taxes also permitted the appearance of penny dailies. The *Daily Telegraph*, launched in 1855, led the way and by 1888 had a circulation of 300,000. The penny press was in turn squeezed by the halfpenny press, the first halfpenny evening paper, the *Echo*, appearing in 1868, while halfpenny morning papers became important in the 1890s with the *Morning Leader* (1892) and the *Daily Mail* (1896), which was to become extremely successful with its bold and simple style. The *Echo* peaked at a circulation of 200,000 in 1870. The papers that best served popular tastes were the Sunday papers, *Lloyd's Weekly News*, the *News of the World* and *Reynold's Newspaper*. *Lloyd's*, the first British paper with a circulation of over 100,000, was selling over 600,000 by 1879, over 900,000 by 1893 and in 1896 rose to over a million. The Sunday papers relied on shock and titillation, drawing extensively on police-court reporting.

In comparison an eighteenth-century London newspaper was considered a great success if it sold 10,000 copies a week (most influential papers then were weekly), and 2,000 weekly was a reasonable sale. Thus an enormous expansion had taken place, one that matched the vitality of an imperial capital, swollen by immigration and increasingly influential as an opinion-setter within the country, not least because of the communications revolution produced by the railway and better roads. The development of the railways allowed London newspapers to increase their dominance of the English newspaper scene. Thanks to them these papers could arrive on provincial doorsteps within hours of publication, although the provincial press remained very strong. Railways also led to the massive development of commuting in London.

REFORM

The press gave Charles Dickens (1812–70) early employment. His subsequent novels reflected many of the concerns of mid-Victorian society. Knowledge about prison conditions and other such social issues was spread by the Condition of England movement, which was linked to the cult of novels that was so strong from the 1840s on. Dickens himself was a supporter of reform in fields such as capital punishment, prisons, housing and prostitution. His novel *Bleak House* (1852–3) was an indictment of the coldness of law and Church, the delays of the former and the smugness of the righteous Reverend Chadband; *Little Dorrit* (1855–7) an attack on aristocratic exclusiveness, imprisonment for debt, business fraud and the deadening bureaucracy exemplified in the Circumlocution Office. Dickens's friend and fellow-novelist Wilkie Collins (1824–89) was criticised by the poet Algernon Swinburne for sacrificing his talent for the sake of a mission. Collins's novels dealt with issues such as divorce, vivisection and the impact of heredity and environment, the last a major concern to a society influenced by the evolutionary teachings of Charles Darwin and thus increasingly concerned with living standards. Darwin's *Origin of Species* (1859), which advanced the theory of evolution, aroused much attention.

Concern over the state of the population led to a determination to 'reform', i.e. change, popular pastimes. Leisure was to be made useful: drink was to be replaced by sport. The teetotal movement was well developed by 1833, and temperance excursions were developed by the Secretary to the South Midland Temperance Association, Thomas Cook, as the basis for an industry of organised leisure trips. Organised sport expanded, in part a response to the clearer definition of leisure time in an industrial and urban society, to the reduction in working hours, to the increase in average real earnings in the last quarter of the century, and to the role of the middle classes in developing 'rational recreations'. Professional football developed, becoming very popular. It drove out cricket in Scotland. Across Britain there was also a boom in middle-class sports, such as golf and lawn tennis, whose rules were systematised in 1874. Northumberland Cricket Club had a ground in Newcastle by the 1850s, while Newcastle Golf Club expanded its activities in the 1890s. By 1895 the *Daily News* covered racing, yachting, rowing, lacrosse, football, hockey, angling, billiards, athletics, cycling and chess. Less respectable traditional sports and pastimes, such as cockfighting, ratting and morris-dancing, lost popularity or were suppressed. The holiday trade also developed, although holidays reflected social divisions as did sport: few among the working class played golf, while the wealthy rarely watched football.

In mid-century reform was the leading divisive issue, reform of the protectionist system and reform of the franchise. The repeal of the Corn Laws (1846) by Sir Robert Peel, Tory Prime Minister 1834–5, 1841–6, split the Tories. It was followed by the repeal of the Navigation Acts (1849) and by Cobden's Treaty with France (1860), which cut duties on trade, as did Gladstone's free-trade budget of the same year. Free trade became a central theme of British policy. Reform was linked to the growth of middle-class culture and consciousness in the great northern cities such as Newcastle and Leeds; the civic gospel, expressed architecturally in their great town halls: Manchester's was opened in 1877. The basis of authority in such towns had moved greatly from traditional to innovative. Their newspapers played a major role in orchestrating opinion in favour of reform. Although Peelite conservatism appealed to an important segment of the middle class, the Anti-Corn-Law League was a symbol of middle-class aggression, while the mismanagement of the Crimean War helped to boost middle-class values of efficiency in politics at the expense of the aristocracy. This was linked to the movement of Whiggism to Liberalism in the 1850s and 1860s, as, in acquiring middle-class support, the Whigs became a party fitted for the reformist middle class. Reform was central to their appeal.

More active local government was an important source and instrument of reform with, for example, the public health movement from the 1840s, the laying out of public parks, especially following the Recreation Grounds Act (1859) and the Public Health Act (1875), and the building of libraries and art galleries for workers, though much was funded by charity or public subscription. Parks and other open spaces were seen as crucial to public health in offering fresh air. Thus Halifax opened the People's Park, paid for by Sir Francis Crossley, the MP and owner of the local carpet mills, in 1857; Leeds opened Roundhay Park in 1871; and Liverpool Corporation purchased farmland from the Earl of

Sefton and in 1872 the 265-acre Sefton Park was opened, typically by a member of the royal family, the Duke of Connaught. The 1862 Highways Act enabled the combination of parishes into highway districts in order to improve the roads.

A professional police force replaced the yeomanry and the sometimes incompetent constables and provided a much more effective check on working-class immorality: a powerful weapon of middle-class cultural dominance. As Home Secretary in 1822–7 and 1828–30, Peel believed that society could survive in turbulent times only if secular authority was resolutely defended. He was a determined supporter of the death penalty who eased and encouraged prosecutions. Peel's Metropolitan Police Act (1829) created a uniformed and paid force for London. This process was extended by acts of 1835 and 1839, and the County and Borough Police Act (1856) made the formation of paid forces obligatory. The new police largely replaced individuals as prosecutors in cases of criminal justice in England and Wales. The Hanoverian legal code was transformed. From the 1830s hanging was confined to murderers and traitors. The transportation of convicts to colonial dumping grounds ceased by the 1860s. Instead, prisons were built and reformatory regimes developed. From 1868 hanging was no longer carried out in public.

There was a great expansion of reading, and the expanding middle class also patronised a great upsurge in art, poetry and the performance or production of music, leading to popular art movements such as the Pre-Raphaelites: William Holman Hunt, John Millais and Dante Gabriel Rossetti, who enjoyed considerable popularity from the mid–1850s. Cities such as Glasgow, Liverpool, Manchester, Leeds, Newcastle and Birmingham founded major art collections, musical institutions, such as the Halle Orchestra in Manchester (1857), and educational bodies. Civic universities were created. Mason Science College, which eventually became part of the University of Birmingham established in 1900, was founded in 1880 by Sir Josiah Martin, a self-educated manufacturer of split-rings and steel pen-nibs. He spent part of his fortune on local orphans as well as on his new foundation which was designed to be especially useful for local industries. Men such as Martin set the tone of much of urban Victorian Britain. Their views and wealth were a tremendous stimulus to the process of Improvement, civic and moral, that was so central to the movement for reform.

Reform, however, did not only originate with the middle class. After Chartism failed and hopes of gaining political citizenship for the working class receded, there was a resurgence of interest in building up its own institutions, such as co-operatives and friendly societies (self-help sick and burial clubs), and in schemes for the improvement of the moral and physical condition of the working people through education and temperance. The Victorian age also witnessed the reform of most institutions, including the Church of England and public schools. Rational organisation, meritocratic conduct and moral purpose were the goals.

NINETEENTH-CENTURY IRELAND

The Union of 1801 ensured that the politics of Ireland were far more closely linked with those of Britain than heretofore. It is possible to write a brief survey of Ireland in this period centred on hardship and discord: the potato famine of 1845–8 and the struggle for Irish political autonomy. Both were of great importance. Yet, it is also important to recall that other themes can be advanced. Ireland remained within the empire, largely speaking English, there was no collapse into anarchy or civil war, and the Irish economy developed as part of the growing imperial economy, although the canal network was less extensive than in Britain and the railway system developed more slowly. Belfast developed as a great port and manufacturing industry, based on linen, shipyards and tobacco. Its expansion, however, saw the development of patterns of urban segregation based on religion. Throughout Ireland the closing decades of the century brought economic and social change, commercialisation, anglicisation and the dismantling of landlord power. By 1914 Ireland had gained a large share of its economic independence. Thanks to legislation in 1860, 1870, 1881, 1885, 1891 and 1903, landlords were obliged to settle the land question largely on their tenants' terms: farmers increasingly owned their holdings. The position of the Catholic Church markedly improved. In Kildare a convent was established, soon followed by a church and schools, and in 1889 a magnificent Catholic Gothic church whose spire dominated the town was opened. Ireland was more closely linked to Britain by economic interdependence and the rapid communications offered by railways and steamships, but its Catholic areas were at the same time becoming more socially and culturally distinct.

The reform process that characterised Britain was matched in Ireland. Thus, for example, the Municipal Corporation (Ireland) Act of 1843 replaced the traditional town governments, which had often been characterised by oligarchy and corruption, by elected municipal commissioners. The Irish Local Government Act of 1898 brought to Ireland the system of elected local councils introduced in England by acts of 1888 and 1894. Thus, alongside the far greater peasant proprietorship stemming from land legislation, local government was also transferred to the control of the largely Catholic bulk of the population. Landlords were a declining power economically and politically. In Ulster they also declined, but because of the power of local Unionists (unlike in the South, where Unionists were few) they managed to retain a foothold in politics. This, however, was shaky. The Belfast and East Ulster business classes took over the leadership of the Ulster Unionists from 1906, a year after the formation of the Ulster Unionist Council, and, although the landlords were a presence and had some influence, they were not a major force.

Nineteenth-century Ireland also had an important and growing nationalist movement. Part was violent, mounting terrorist attacks in Britain, Ireland and elsewhere. The Fenians, a secret organisation founded in 1858, tried to launch a rebellion in Ireland in 1867 and were responsible for terrorist acts in Britain and for an attempted invasion of Canada from the United States. The Fenians, reconstituted as the Irish Republican Brotherhood in 1873, continued to mount terrorist attacks, and in 1882 another secret society, the Invincibles, murdered Lord Frederick Cavendish, the Chief Secretary for Ireland, in Phoenix Park, Dublin, leading to new measures designed to maintain order. Some Irishmen served with the Boers against the British army.

Most Irish nationalism, however, was non-violent. Daniel O'Connell organised a party that in the 1830s and 1840s campaigned for the repeal of the Act of Union. The government responded by attempts to improve the lot of the population through reform and by firm action aimed at limiting extra-parliamentary agitation. The extension of the franchise in 1867 and 1884 greatly increased the number of Catholic voters and most of them supported home rule, which would have left an Irish Parliament and government in control of all bar defence and foreign policy. The Home Government Association of 1870 was followed by the Home Rule League (1873). Charles Parnell (1846–91) became leader of the MPs pressing for home rule in 1879 and this group became an organised and powerful parliamentary party with sixty-one MPs in 1880, eighty-six in 1885 and eighty-five in 1886. Their role in Parliament ensured that home rule came to play a major role in the political agenda.

IRISH MIGRATION

Earlier migration across the Irish Sea and to North America swelled in the mid–1840s as the potato blight drove hundreds of thousands to flee. The potato played a major role in feeding the expanding population of the early-nineteenth century, but reliance on one crop and over-population created a vulnerable situation. Crop blight began in 1845 and the 1846 and 1848 crops were disastrous. About 800,000 people died as a result of starvation or diseases made more effective by malnutrition. The government's attempts to bring relief were of little effect. Thanks also to emigration, mostly to the USA, the Irish population fell by 2–2¼ million. Migration was helped subsequently by the introduction of steamships which cut the time needed to cross the Atlantic from six weeks in the 1850s to one in 1914. Migration was one of the defining factors in the Irish experience in the nineteenth century.

IRISH IMMIGRATION TO BRITAIN

The Irish-born population of England and Wales rose to 602,000 in 1861, about 3 per cent of the total population. The equivalent statistics for Scotland in 1851 were 207,000: 7 per cent. Their impact was increased by concentration in a few cities, such as Glasgow, where 23.3 per cent of the adult population in 1851 were Irish-born, London, where the Irish were 5 per cent of the population in 1861, and Liverpool, where the percentage was near 25. Irish migration into Britain peaked in around 1860, declined until about 1870, rose again until 1877 and then fell until the end of the century. Overwhelmingly poor, and attractive as labour precisely because they were paid badly, the Irish migrants lived in the areas of cheapest rent, which were invariably the most crowded and least sanitary. Thus, in Newcastle where the percentage of Irish-born migrants rose from 5.73 of the population in 1841 to 8.02 in 1851, the majority were housed in poor living conditions in areas such as Sandgate. The men were generally employed as labourers or in other casual employment, the women as washerwomen, flower sellers or other poorly paid jobs. In Glasgow the majority of Irish immigrants did not gain jobs offering reasonable pay, conditions and status, and their position contrasted with that of migrants from the Scottish Highlands. However, an appreciable number of Irish emerged into the middle class.

Irish migrants focused and exacerbated anti-Catholic feelings, and sometimes undercut native workers, as in the Lanarkshire coalfield where they were used for strike breaking and wage reductions. In 1850 thanks to the acceptance of lower wages, they took over hoeing from women near Dunfermline, leading to an anti-Irish riot there in which migrants were brutally driven out. However, outside Lancashire such a violent response was unusual. Many Irish immigrants did not live in ghettos but were dispersed across working-class areas, and a certain number 'married out'.

GLADSTONE AND DISRAELI

Middle-class interests increasingly set the legislative agenda in late-nineteenth-century Britain, although aristocratic influences on policy making remained strong. The Second Reform Act, passed by a minority Tory government (1867), nearly doubled the existing electorate and, by offering household suffrage, gave the right to vote to about 60 per cent of adult males in boroughs. The Liberal victory in the following general election (1868) led to the first government of William Gladstone (1868–74) who pushed through a whole series of reforms, including the disestablishment of the Irish Church (1869), and the introduction of open competition in the civil service (1870), and of the secret ballot (1872). Bank holidays were created in 1871, providing holidays with pay and thus more leisure-time to the workforce. In 1872 the powers of turnpike trusts were ended and road maintenance was placed totally under public control. The 1870 Education Act divided the country into school districts and required a certain level of educational provision, introducing the school district in cases where existing parish provision was inadequate, though its provisions were resisted: in Ealing tenacious efforts by the Church of England to protect voluntary education and resist the introduction of public board schools, ignoring the implictions of rapid population growth, left 500 children unschooled twenty-five years after the act. The end of long-established distinctions, variations and privileges played a major role in the reform process. The Endowed Schools Commission established in 1870 redistributed endowments and reformed governing bodies. The Church of England underwent a similar change.

Gladstone was a formidable and multi-faceted individual of great determination and integrity, a classical scholar and theological controversialist, a hewer of trees and a rescuer of prostitutes. He had a library of 20,000 books. A Tory Treasury minister in the 1830s, he became the leading Liberal politician of the age, committed to reform at home and a moral stance abroad. His political skills bridged the worlds of Parliament and of public meetings, for under his leadership Liberalism became a movement enjoying mass support. Gladstone appealed from Parliament to the public and sought to gain mass support for his politics of action and reform. However, Liberalism as an *idea* did not remain the same; and after 1880 the Liberals only once again won an election outright.

The Tories or, as they were now called, Conservatives, came to power again in 1874 under Benjamin Disraeli, an opportunist and skilful political tactician who was also an acute thinker, able to create an alternative political culture and focus of popular support around the themes of national identity and pride, and social cohesion, that challenged Liberal moral certainty. Legislation on factories (1874), public health, artisans' dwellings, and pure food and drugs (1875) systematised and extended the regulation of important aspects of social welfare. The Factory Acts of 1874 and 1878 limited work hours for women and children in industry. The Prison Act (1877) established central government control. These were, however, less important for Disraeli than his active foreign policy which involved the purchase of shares in the Suez Canal (1875), designed to secure British control over the new short route to India, the creation of the title of Empress of India (1876), the acquisition of Cyprus (1878), and wars with the Afghans (1878–9) and Zulus (1879).

Economic difficulties, stemming from agrarian depression and a fall in trade, and political problems, skilfully exploited by Gladstone in his electioneering Midlothian campaigns (1879–80), led to Conservative defeat in the 1880 election. Imperial and Irish problems, however, affected Gladstone's second government (1880–5), with the unsuccessful First Boer War (1880–1) in South Africa, the occupation of Egypt (1882–3), the massacre of General Gordon and his force at Khartoum (1885), the Coercion Act, designed to restore order in Ireland (1881) and the murder of Lord Frederick Cavendish by the Invincibles (1882). In 1884 the Third Reform Act extended to the counties the household franchise granted to the boroughs in 1867, so that over two-thirds of the adult males in the counties, and about 63 per cent of the entire adult male population, received the vote. The Conservatives held office in 1885–6 but, as in 1868, were defeated in the first election held with the new franchise: many rural electors voted against their landlords.

The process of reform, both political and social, continued with the Redistribution of Seats Act (1885), which revised the electoral map; the Local Government Act (1888), creating directly elected county councils and county boroughs, and the London County Council; and the Workmen's Compensation Act (1897), obliging employers to provide compensation for industrial accidents. A collectivist state was developing, and in some respects it looked towards the later welfare state. State intervention in education helped in the decline of illiteracy. Greater social intervention by the new, more formal and responsive, mechanisms of local government encouraged a general expectation of state intervention in the life of the people, especially in health, education and housing.

The political situation was, however, complicated by the consequences of the economic downturn of the 1870s, by uncertainties stemming from the expansion of the electorate, and by the long-standing malaise over the Irish question. Fenian terrorism in Ireland, England and Canada led to casualties, and there was both pressure for land reform and agitation for home rule for Ireland. Proposals for home rule, introduced by Gladstone, were defeated in 1886 and 1893 at Westminster, where they helped to divide politicians. Conservatives led the resistance and the Conservative Party changed its name to the Unionist Party in 1886, but the defeat of the First Home Rule Bill in 1886 was due to the defection of ninety-three 'Liberal Unionists' from Gladstone's third government.

Home rule split the Liberals, not the first nor the last occasion when Ireland was of great significance for British politics. In Easter 1887 Gladstone wrote in his diary, 'now one prayer absorbs all others: Ireland, Ireland, Ireland'.

The political hegemony of the Liberals was destroyed in 1886 as the Conservatives, under the Third Marquis of Salisbury, won the general election. Though the Liberals, still under Gladstone, now elderly, half-blind and half-deaf, won the 1892 election, the Conservatives dominated the period 1886–1905 with the support of the Liberal Unionists. Salisbury (Prime Minister 1885–6, 1886–92, 1895–1902) and his successor and nephew, Arthur Balfour (1902–5), opposed home rule and followed a cautious policy on domestic reform. The cultural basis of Liberalism was under challenge and the mix of Conservative policies, attitudes and resonances were more attractive to the electorate. In 1900 Liberalism lost its overall majority of Scottish seats for the first time since 1832. Salisbury, a Marquis and owner of Hatfield House, one of the palaces the British domesticate as 'stately homes', derived most of his disposable income from urban property, including London slums. Two-thirds of his cabinet were peers, although it did nothing to advance the landed interest other than not passing budgets like the Liberal one of 1894 which had greatly increased death duties.

There was also, however, growing pressure for more radical political and social policies. Political opinion began increasingly to coalesce and polarise along social and class lines. The landed interest broke from the Liberals after 1886. Joseph Chamberlain's 'unauthorised' Liberal programme of 1885 called for land reform and was followed in 1891 by Gladstone's Newcastle programme which also called for home rule, Welsh and Scottish disestablishment, free education, a reduction in factory work-hours, electoral reform and the reform or abolition of the House of Lords. That year the Scottish Liberals called for land reform in the Highlands, an eight-hour day for miners and an extension of the franchise. The social order could be harsh as well as inegalitarian. In 1891 Tom Masters, a 13-year-old Northamptonshire farm labourer, was whipped by his employer for insolence. However, calls for a more radical Liberalism led to accusations that Liberalism was increasingly a threat to stability and a product of sectional interests. This encouraged a coalescence of opinion in defence of property and order in the shape of the Conservatives.

NINETEENTH-CENTURY WALES

Developments in Wales serve as a valuable prism through which wider processes can be understood. Growth there became more sustained from the 1790s and was also increasingly concentrated in coal- and iron-rich south Wales. The production of pig-iron there rose from 5,000 tons in 1720 to 525,000 by 1840; 36 per cent of the British total. The tremendous industrial expansion in Monmouthshire and east Glamorgan, at for example Ebbw Vale and Merthyr Tydfil, created numerous jobs and helped lead to a permanent demographic shift: Glamorgan and Monmouthshire had about 20 per cent of the Welsh population in 1801, 57.5 per cent in 1901 and 60–5 per cent from 1921. The growth in the south Wales coalfield was also important. Welsh coal was suited for coking for iron furnaces and for steamships, and Welsh anthracite coal was ideal for the hot-blast process for the iron and steel industry. The development of the port of Cardiff by the Third Marquis of Bute and the spread of the railways, especially the Taff Vale line between Cardiff and Merthyr Tydfil (1841), permitted the movement of large quantities of coal. Production (in million tons) rose from 1.2 in 1801 to 13.6 by 1870 and 57 by 1913. The majority was exported and the coal industry employed about a third of the Welsh male labour force. Coal furthered industrialisation, especially the emergence of Cardiff as the Welsh metropolis: its population rose from 10,000 in 1841 to 200,000 in 1921: that of the coalmining Rhondda from under 1,000 in 1851 to 153,000 in 1911. Economic growth changed the rest of the economy. New markets were created for Welsh agriculture. Coach services, droving and coastal shipping declined with the spread of rail, which in 1850 bridged the Menai Straits and in 1864 reached Aberystwyth. Economic and demographic growth in the industrial regions led to a decline in the relative importance of agriculture and rural Wales and played a major role in the reorientation in the standard images of Welshness and in the perception of national character and interest. Anglicans became outnumbered and the growth of Dissent played a major role in reshaping Wales culturally and politically. In place of the dominance of conservative Anglican gentry, the Liberal party, based on Dissent, was dominant from 1868 to 1918. The redefinition of 'Welshness' was a consequence of the growing presence of Nonconformity. The Nonconformist press played a significant role in the growth of radical nonconformity. The political and cultural affiliations of nonconformity were important in the growth of national feeling.

Industrialisation was not achieved without traumatic change, and the work that was required of people was back-breaking, dangerous and alienating. Even so, and in spite of the fact that it was a process of transformation from without, largely by wealthy English people, it met with relatively little violent resistance. Nevertheless, Merthyr Tydfil, the centre of early industrialisation, had a full range of industrial disputes in the early decades of the century, with particular bitterness in 1831. The Merthyr Rising collapsed in the face of military action and its own divisions, but at least twenty rioters were killed. Eight years later, a Chartist rising of over 5,000 men in Newport was stopped when a small group of soldiers opened fire and the rioters dispersed. The same year, the Rebecca Riots began in south-west Wales. The tollgates that handicapped the rural economy were attacked. The riots persisted until 1844 and extended their targets to include attacks on unfair rents and workhouses. 'Mother Rebecca', the symbolic leader of the protests, with a white gown and red or black face, was named from the Rebecca of Genesis, 'possessing the gates of those which hate them'. The 293 crowd attacks on tollgates in 1838–44 reflected considerable social alienation, the product of the industrial depression of 1839–42, the inflation of land rents during the Napoleonic War, and hostility to landlords, church tithes and the loss of common land through the widespread enclosures of 1750–1815, as well as to the high charges of the turnpike trusts. Hostility was also expressed by poaching and arson.

The Rebecca disturbances faded after an act of 1844 replaced turnpike trusts with highway boards in south Wales, but the following decades saw a series of serious coal strikes in Glamorgan. Nevertheless, it is necessary to put this militancy in context. Strikes were a natural response to a poorly regulated industry. What is more obvious is that the revolutionary sentiment that did exist did not lead to a full-blown revolution. There was nothing to compare with the Year of Revolutions (1848) on the Continent. Troops from the garrison at Brecon did play an important role in a number of disputes, but the number of regulars in South Wales in 1839 was only raised to 1,000. This scarcely compared with Habsburg forces in Hungary and Italy. Far from South Wales being 'held down', revolutionary sentiment was limited, while most industrial disputes were restricted to specific grievances. There was only a limited sense of worker solidarity and it was unusual for agitation to be far-reaching. Trade unionism emerged only slowly.

Political pressures, however, are not only expressed through violence. The new socio-economic order created through industrialisation was one that sat ill with traditional hierarchies, allegiance and practices. If this subverted secular and ecclesiastical hierarchies, it also challenged assumptions of Welshness, although these were of course always contingent. In part this was due to immigration. Industrialisation brought great demands for labour, particularly in the coalfields and iron works of south and north-east Wales, and this was exacerbated as coal mining expanded greatly in south Wales from the 1850s on. Initially, most of the necessary labour came from rural Wales, and migration to developing industrial regions eased rural poverty, although an appreciable Irish contingent also settled in Merthyr Tydfil. The Irish immigration also greatly affected Swansea and Cardiff after the initial impact upon Merthyr. The consequence is that the Catholic Church is important in modern Wales.

From the 1850s large numbers of English immigrants settled in south Wales. 11 per cent of Swansea's population in 1861 had been born in south-west England. Wales was unusual in Europe in having a net immigration rate in the nineteenth century. The immigrants had no commitment to Welsh culture which was anyway in a state of flux in the rapidly industrialising regions. English immigrants jumped into the melting pot, just like the people from the rural hinterland. As a result, the Welsh language came to be of far less consequence in the areas of Wales that were increasingly the centres of economic power and political representation; although over half the population of Wales still spoke Welsh in 1901 and the absolute number of Welsh speakers rose throughout the nineteenth century. Furthermore, despite immigration, industrial towns like Merthyr and Swansea were overwhelmingly the most important centres for Welsh culture throughout the nineteenth century. There was also an enormous Welsh-language press.

It was not only thanks to immigration, however, that the Welsh language became less widely used. Welsh was too much the language of religion, and was deemed to be flourishing when religion was flourishing. The use of English was encouraged throughout

Wales by members of the emerging middle class. Gentry land-owners were commonly English-speaking, but they had less of a linguistic impact than groups that were becoming more important as the economy of all of Wales was affected by economic growth and integration: cattle dealers and drovers, merchants, shop-keepers, master mariners. English was the language of commerce, the language in which financial records were kept. It was also the language in which the elite was educated.

As the use of English became more common, it also became more politically charged, a consequence in part of debates over the role and nature of public education. Furthermore, in the second half of the nineteenth century language came to play a role in a powerful political critique directed against Conservative landowners and the Anglican Church and in favour of Liberalism and Nonconformity, both of which were presented as truly Welsh. There was a parallel with the Irish home rule movement and the late-nineteenth century Gaelic cultural revival. Thus T.E. (Thomas) Ellis, elected as Liberal MP for Merioneth in 1886, declared in his election address his support for home rule for Ireland and Wales, the disestablishment of the Church of England in Wales, a revision of the land laws, and better educational facilities that were under the control of public, not Anglican, bodies. Welsh played a role in many of the schools established under the Welsh Intermediate Education Act of 1889.

There was also a greater interest in Welsh cultural history and identity, a growth in Welsh poetry, the development of choral singing and, in 1858, two years after the Welsh national anthem was composed, the 'revival' of the *eisteddfod*. This represented a success for the revival of the bardic craft by Edward Williams, Iolo Morganwg (1747–1826), a stonemason, shopkeeper, forger of an-cient manuscripts, charlatan, genius and poet, akin to a William Blake on opium. Iolo concocted much of the basis of the modern *eisteddfod* movement, including druidical ceremonies.

A range of new institutions, from University College Aberyst-wyth (1872) on, testified to a stronger sense of national identity, the institutionalisation of which created bodies that had an interest in its furtherance and that provided a vital platform and focus for those seeking to assert Welsh identities. Both the National Library and the National Museum were authorised by royal charter in 1907; the library opened in 1909, the museum was begun in 1910 but not opened until 1920. The *Cymru Fydd* ('Wales that is to be' or

'Young Wales') home-rule movement, launched in 1886, was very influential, but foundered in the mid–1890s on the antagonism between the south and north Welsh.

In political terms the assertion of Welsh identities was largely represented by Liberalism which increasingly swept Wales: all five of the Glamorgan constituencies were Liberal from 1857, twenty-three of the thirty-three Welsh seats after the 1868 general election, twenty-nine after that of 1880. Gladstone himself lived in Wales from 1839 to his death in 1898. Henry Richard won at Merthyr Tydfil in 1868 on an aggressively nationalist platform in which liberalism, Nonconformity and the 'Welsh nation' were fused. Landlord or landed-gentry political control had collapsed. This reflected the extension of the franchise, but even more the secret ballot, and was the product of a clash of class, religion, culture and language. Conservative control in the counties was swept away in 1868 and this was confirmed in 1874.

As so often with hegemonic concepts, the notion of Liberal Wales is in part misleading. Between 1880 and 1920 the Liberals commonly took only 45–55 per cent of Welsh votes, with 30–35 per cent backing the Conservatives; as the Welsh electorate was expanding (doubling to 127,000 as a result of the 1867 Reform Act and increasing to 1.17 million by 1918), this meant that Conservative support was rising substantially. Presumably many voters were unimpressed by the often tendentious oratory of the Liberals, while the Conservatives benefited from anti-Irish feeling. However, it was nearly always the Liberal candidate who was returned unopposed in the not-inconsiderable proportion of *uncontested* Welsh elections between 1880 and 1920; thus the true level of support for the Liberals must have been higher than 45–55 per cent.

Similarly, nearly half of the population attended no place of worship in 1851. 267,000 Welsh people signed the petitions leading to the Sunday Closing Act for public houses in Wales that was passed in 1881 with the support of twenty-eight Welsh MPs, but many of course did not. The act, the first since the 1650s to introduce different regulations in Wales, was nevertheless a testimony to the self-righteous determination of Welsh Nonconformity. Extended in 1921 to Monmouthshire, the act was qualified in 1961 when a new act allowed counties to vote whether they were to become wet or dry. The wet area was extended in each subsequent poll.

With David Lloyd George, Chancellor of the Exchequer 1908–15 and Prime Minister 1916–22, Welsh liberalism reached the apex of political power, but, as later with the Scot Ramsay MacDonald and Labour, this was as part of a British political consciousness. At the same time, there was a potentially uneasy relationship with the rise of Welsh cultural and political nationalism, although the key Welsh issues of the late nineteenth century – land, disestablishment and education – could be presented in radical Liberal terms and thus incorporated in British politics. In Wales radical liberals espoused national issues, particularly disestablishment, hostility to tithes, land reform and public education. Agitation over rents and tithes led to riots, particularly in 1887, but landlords were not shot: the Welsh wished to differentiate themselves from the more bitter contemporary agitation in Ireland. Bitter political disputes over disestablishment (first debated in the Commons in 1870), in 1909–13, led to the passage of an act in 1914, although, due to the war, it was not implemented until 1920. Welsh Liberals were bitterly opposed to church schools, especially to measures to provide public assistance to them. The 1902 act providing for finance for the schools from the rates led to non-compliance termed the 'Welsh Revolt', with county councils refusing to implement the act. In 1904 this led the Conservative government to transfer the operation of the act to the Board of Education, an unpopular measure that helped the Welsh Liberals to triumph in the 1906 elections. Religion was a crucial aspect of Welsh identity and passion, most obviously with the widespread religious revival of 1904–5.

NINETEENTH-CENTURY SCOTLAND

Much of Europe was inspired by nationalism, or, depending on one's perspective, suffered from it in the nineteenth century. Multinational empires, particularly Austro-Hungary and Russia, were challenged by the rise of nationalist politics and the same was true for Britain in Ireland and India. Yet in Scotland this was less the case, largely because of Scottish identification with the idea of Britain and the benefits of the British empire.

Scotland was affected by the same trends as England and Wales, not least the industrialisation, migration and urbanisation that reflected the development of coal-based industries and the new technology of steam. Thus steamships and the railway ended such centuries-old practices as droving (the driving of animals), while regions lacking coal, such as most of south-west Scotland, saw only limited growth. By 1861 the majority of the population were living in towns. Scotland was a powerhouse of innovation and entrepreneurs. Industrial growth was particularly rapid from the 1830s and was especially concentrated in Strathclyde, where it led to a major growth of population, largely due to migration from the countryside. Glasgow's population grew from 77,385 in 1801 to 274,533 in 1841 despite annual average death rates of 33 per 1,000 in 1835–9, the highest in Scotland. Thanks to industrialisation the percentage of the Scottish population in the central belt rose from nearly 40 in 1755 and nearly 50 in 1821 to 80 today. By the mid-nineteenth century less than 10 per cent of those employed in the central-belt counties of Lanark, Midlothian and Renfrew worked in agriculture, forestry and fishing. Despite a very high rate of emigration, Scotland's population as a whole rose from 1,265,380 in 1755 and 1,608,000 in 1801 to 4,472,103 in 1901.

As in England, urbanisation and poverty led to serious social problems. Dundee, for example, which, on the basis of imports of raw material from India, became the leading jute-working city in the world, suffered from slums, disease and high infant mortality. Glasgow was hit by a serious outbreak of cholera in 1832, and of typhus in 1817–18 and 1837. Economic growth encouraged immigration, mostly from Ireland. Yet Dundee also gained Polish Jews, Italians, Germans and Lithuanians. Change did not only take the form of industrialisation. Communications improved greatly. Edinburgh and Glasgow were linked by railway in 1841, and the railway provided Scotland with a network of rapid land communication to match coastal shipping. Service industries also developed, especially banking and life assurance in Edinburgh, which emerged as a major financial centre.

Change also pressed in more remote areas. Most of the population of the Highlands and Islands became bilingual in English and Gaelic. Gaelic alone was spoken only by a minority in the north-west and the northern Hebrides. The sentimentalised Highland landscape helped to bring the area to the attention of the outside world. Tourism flourished. In 1864 the original fort at Fort William was demolished to make room for the railway station through which English tourists reached the Highlands. Socially there had been a major shift in the region. The clan system had declined during the eighteenth century to be replaced by a more aggressively commercial attitude towards land tenure, social relations and economic activity, helping to lead to extensive emigration. After the Napoleonic wars the labour-intensive economy in which fishing, military employment and illicit whisky-making had played a major role was replaced by a more capital-intensive economy based on sheep-ranching, which required less labour. Most of the Highland population possessed no secure and long-term legal rights to land, and were therefore easily displaced in the 'clearances'. As in Ireland, there was a serious potato famine in the Highlands in the late 1840s. Hunger led to migration from the Highlands and Islands, a policy encouraged by landowners who did not wish to bear the burden of supporting the poor. Large numbers moved within Britain, but also to North America. Nearly two million Scots emigrated there and to Australasia. Those who remained reacted with increasing bitterness to the effects of change. In part the clearances were for leisure purposes: by 1884, 1.98 million acres, over 10 per cent of Scottish land, was reserved for deer and thus the hunting interests of a small minority. In the 1880s crofting MPs, opposed to clearances, won five seats in northern Scotland, while the 'Battle of the Braes' in Skye grew more intense. There was an Irish-type resistance to clearing: the Land League, modelled on the Irish Land League, had 15,000 members by 1884. The crisis led to the Napier commission and the Crofters' Holding Act of 1886 which established crofting rights and ended the major phase of the clearances.

The nineteenth century saw the development of a sense of national identity centring on a re-emergent cultural identity that did not involve any widespread demand for independence: kilts and literary consciousness but no home-rule party. The religious dimension, so obvious in Ireland, was lacking. Furthermore, the Highland peasantry were being evicted by their clan chiefs, rather than by English absentees. The National Association for the Vindication of Scottish Rights was launched in 1853. 2,000 people came to its first meeting at Edinburgh; 5,000 in Glasgow. It strongly urged Scottish rights, but was not *explicitly* nationalist. Later, some Scottish nationalists, such as Theodore Napier, identified with the Boers. The Scottish Patriotic Association, the Scottish Home Rule Association (SHRA) and other agitators all played a part.

The SHRA regarded the exerting of pressure on the most sympathetic political party as the best political strategy. In place of the notion of North Britain, which was rejected by the late nineteenth century, that of Scotland returned, although it was an increasingly anglicised Scotland. The Secretaryship for Scotland was restored in 1885.

WOMEN IN THE NINETEENTH CENTURY

Industrial urban society served women little better than rural society had done. Women were affected by social and ecological challenges similar to those of men, but they also faced additional problems. Like most men, most women had to cope with gruelling labour and debilitating diseases, but their legal position was worse, a reflection of a culture that awarded control and respect to men, and left little role for female merit or achievement. The restrictive nature of the work available to women and the confining implications of family and social life together defined the existence of the vast majority of women.

Social and economic pressures helped to drive women towards matrimony and also, whether they were unmarried or married, towards employment. Marriage offered most women a form of precarious stability, but the marital prospects of unmarried mothers were low, with the significant exception of widows with children of a first marriage, particularly if they possessed some property. As a result, unmarried mothers often became prostitutes or were treated as such. The absence of an effective social welfare system and the low wages paid to most women ensured that prostitution, either full- or part-time, was the fate of many. Part-time prostitution was related to economic conditions. Single women resorted to abortion, which was both treated as a crime and hazardous to health. Women, both single and married, suffered from the generally limited and primitive nature of contraceptive practices. Frequent childbirth was exhausting; and many women died giving birth, ensuring that many children were brought up by stepmothers. Joseph Chamberlain's first two wives died in childbirth, leaving him with responsibility for six children. Female pelvises were often distorted by rickets during malnourished childhoods, while there was no adequate training in midwifery. As a result obstetric haemorrhages were poorly managed and often fatal. It was not until the introduction of sulphominides after 1936 that mortality figures fell substantially. Birth control was, however, developing: in Scotland marital fertility declined appreciably between 1881 and 1901.

Employment for women was often arduous. A common form of work, the largest category of female employment in Wales in 1911, was domestic service. Household tasks, such as cleaning and drying clothes, involved much effort. It was possible in the hierarchy of service to gain promotion, but in general domestic service was unskilled and not a career. Wages were poor and pay was largely in kind, which made life very hard for those who wished to marry and leave service. The working conditions, however, were generally better and less hazardous than the factories of the age, where repetitive work for many hours was expected. Women often did very arduous jobs, such as coal-carrying in the mines, or work in the fields.

Women from the social elite came to have more opportunities. Higher education for women began in both Cambridge and Oxford, though they were not permitted to take degrees for many years. At Aberdeen University it was formally agreed in 1892 that women be admitted to all faculties, but none studied law or divinity, they were not offered equivalent teaching in medicine and there was unequal access to the Bursary Competition. Women students took no positions of influence and the student newspaper, *Alma Mater*, was hostile, presenting them as unfeminine or flighty and foolish: the men clearly found it difficult to adjust to female students, although their numbers and influence increased in the 1900s and especially during the First World War. By 1939 nearly a quarter of British university students were women.

The general notion of equality was one of respect for separate functions and development, and the definition of the distinctive nature of the ideal female condition was one that, by modern standards, certainly did not entail equality. Women's special role was defined as that of home and family, and was used to justify their exclusion from other spheres. To a certain extent such issues were meaningless for most women because their economic conditions and the nature of medical knowledge and attention ensured that their circumstances were bleak.

At the same time it is important to notice nuances and shifts: it is only from the misleading perspective of hindsight that Victorian society and culture appears as a monolith. Recent work, for example, has re-evaluated notions of Victorian sexuality in order to suggest that the image of universal repression was misleading. However, while sexual pleasure was given generally discreet approval within marriage, it was harshly treated, in the case of *women*, outside it. Thus some workhouses made 'disorderly and profligate women' wear distinctive yellow clothes, though the practice was stopped in the 1840s. The Foundling Hospital in London, founded in 1741 to deal with abandoned babies, only accepted in the nineteenth century infants from mothers who could prove that they had had sex against their will or on promise of marriage and were otherwise of irreproachable conduct, a policy designed to exclude prostitutes.

Social conventions, for example the prohibition of mixed bathing at the seaside, were often responses to behaviour deemed inappropriate, in this case the practice of nude male bathing, and were difficult to enforce. Local prohibitory regulations were anyway lifted from the 1890s. Social conventions were also affected by class behaviour. Thus, the attempts of Devon resorts to offer bathing with decorum were compromised by working-class male and female daytrippers, brought in large numbers by train, who bathed in the nude or semi-nude, either unaware of the regulations or unable to afford to hire swimming costumes.

Industrialisation ensured that more, predominantly single, women worked in factories, although it reduced rural opportunities, such as spinning. Women generally moved into the low-skill, low-pay 'sweated' sector as they were denied access to the new technologies. Female factory workers were generally worse treated than men, a practice in which the trade unions (male organisations) co-operated with the management. Both condemned the women woollen workers of Batley and Dewsbury for organising themselves in a 1875 dispute. Definitions of skills, which affected pay, were controlled by men and favoured them; skilled women, such as the weavers of Preston or Bolton, were poorly recognised. In contrast, women in the pottery industry were able to maintain status and pay despite male opposition.

A potentially important change was the institution of divorce proceedings in 1857. Before the 1857 Act, divorce required a private Act of Parliament, a very difficult process only open to the wealthy, or a separation achieved through the ecclesiastical courts, which did not allow remarriage. Even after the Act divorce still remained costly and therefore not a possibility for the poor. As a result, former practices of 'self-divorce' continued, while cohabitation was another option, though offering most women no economic security. Women suffered because marital desertions were generally a matter of men leaving, with the women bearing the burden of supporting the children: poverty made some men heedless of the Victorian cult of the family and patriarchy. Successive extensions of the franchise did not bring the vote to women, though they were socially less dependent than is generally assumed and than their legal situation might suggest.

THE RISE OF TRADE UNIONISM

Pressures for social reform from within the Liberal party were supplemented in the late nineteenth century by the development of more explicitly working-class movements, both political and industrial. The development of trade unions reflected the growing industrialisation and unification of the economy, the growth of larger concerns employing more people, and, by the end of the century, a new, more adversarial and combative working-class consciousness. Trade unionism, in turn, contributed to the politicisation of much of the workforce, although many trade unionists were not political activisits. The Trades Union Congress, a federation of trade unions, began in 1868, unionism spread from the skilled craft section to semi-skilled and unskilled workers, and there were major strikes in the London gasworks and docks in 1888–9. The 1890s were a crucial decade in the definition of 'mass' unionism. Keir Hardie, Secretary of the Scottish Miners' Federation, founded the Scottish Labour Party (1888) and the Independent Labour Party (1893). The latter pressed for an eight-hour day and 'collective ownership of means of production, distribution and exchange'. Six years later, the Trades Union Congress advocated an independent working-class political organisation, which led in 1900 to the formation of the Labour Representation Committee, the basis of the Labour Party. Some working-class militants looked to a marxist tradition: the Social-Democratic Federation pioneered the development of socialism in the 1880s and was Britain's first avowedly marxist party.

LATE-VICTORIAN SOCIETY

These developments reflected a situation of sustained doubt, if not a crisis of confidence, in late-Victorian society. This society did not seem beneficent to the growing numbers who were gaining the vote and becoming more politically aware; while many commentators were concerned about the relative weakness of Britain, economically and politically, compared to the leading continental states. British industries no longer benefited from cheaper raw materials, energy and labour. Foreign competition was responsible for closures, as in 1901 of the Tudhoe ironworks in County Durham which employed 1,500 men. There was less confidence that British institutions and practices were best. In the 1890s and early 1900s there was much interest in the German educational system, and much envy of its 'practical' orientation. Salisbury was not alone in being pessimistic on the future of the empire. These varied strands of disquiet were to lead to fresh pressure for reform and new political divisions in the period up to the First World War. The British could take pride in the spread of empire and the triumphalism of Queen Victoria's Gold and Diamond Jubilees in 1887 and 1897, but the divisions of the first half of the century, which had diminished or disappeared in its prosperous third quarter, were re-emerging, taking on new forms and being accentuated by new sources of tension. Economic change brought significant levels of social disruption.

There was persistent and justified concern about the 'state of the nation'. Infant mortality rates were high: in the north-eastern mining communities half the total deaths occurred in the range 0–5 years, and a high proportion in 5–15. Many families lived in only one room: about 7,840 out of the 20,000 in Newcastle in 1854. In 1866 43 per cent of the city's population was still living in dwellings of only one or two rooms; in 1885 30.6 per cent. Industrial pollution was a serious problem. Gastro-intestinal disorders linked to inadequate water and sewerage systems were responsible for Bradford's very high infant mortality rate. More generally, the supply of fresh cow's milk became badly infected in the 1880s and

1890s, leading to a serious increase in diarrhoea in inner cities in hot weather and a rise in infant mortality in the 1890s, especially as the practice of breast feeding decreased. In the Irish town of Kildare, although the water supply was improved in 1886, no adequate sewerage system was installed until 1900. Much of the town's population continued to live in thatched-roofed one-room cabins with overcrowding, lack of privacy and poor refuse disposal.

Poor urban sanitation, housing and nutrition were blamed for the physical weakness of much of the population. The army found this a serious problem at the time of the Boer War and the First World War, the Metropolitan Police thought their London recruits physically weak, and defeats at the hands of the visiting New Zealand All Blacks rugby team in 1905 led to discussion about a supposed physical and moral decline arising from the country's urban and industrial nature. The social surveys of Charles Booth in east London in the late 1880s and of Seebohm Rowntree in York in 1899 revealed that over a quarter of their population were living below what they saw as the level of poverty. There was concern at the apparent extent of atheism among the urban working classes. Liberal imperialists, such as Winston Churchill, emphasised the threat to imperial stability posed by social distress within Britain, and advocated reform as the best means of defence. William Booth had already founded the East London Revival Society in 1865; in 1878 it was reorganised as the Salvation Army. The Boy Scout movement was founded by Robert Baden-Powelll in 1908 in order to occupy and to revive the martial vigour of the nation's youth. The movement rapidly became a national institution.

'We are all Socialists nowadays', declared Sir William Harcourt, Liberal Chancellor of the Exchequer, in a speech at the Mansion House in 1895. He was referring to the creation of public utilities, 'gas and water socialism', and to the concern for social welfare that was such an obvious feature of late-Victorian values and that played a role in the amelioration of living conditions, especially the decline of epidemic disease. Urban and rural sanitary authorities and their districts responsible for the maintenance of sewers and highways were inaugurated in England and Wales by the 1872 Public Health Act following the recommendations of the report of the Sanitary Commission (1871). These districts were based on town councils and existing local boards of health in urban areas and boards of guardians in rural areas. The Rating and Local

Government Act of 1871 set up the central machinery, viz. the local government board. In respect of the local machinery of rural and urban sanitary authorities, the Public Health Act of 1875 was a consolidating measure.

The supply of clean water was improved or begun and London at last acquired a sewage system appropriate for the capital of a modern empire. In Glasgow the civic government was associated with the provision of pure water and with the individual purity of teetotalism. Typhus virtually disappeared by the 1890s, typhoid was brought under partial control and death rates from tuberculosis and scarlet fever declined. The provision of plentiful supplies of clean water was not only an engineering and organisational triumph, but also part of the process by which rural Britain was increasingly subordinated to the cities. Manchester, for example, looked to the distant Lake District to supplement supplies from the nearby Pennines. The Corporation purchased the Wythburn estate, stopped the local lead industry in order to prevent water pollution, and, despite overwhelming local opposition, gained parliamentary approval in 1877 for the drowning of the Thirlmere valley. The Public Health (Scotland) Act of 1867 established the appointment of sanitary inspectors.

Improved diet, thanks, in part, to a significant fall in food prices, played an important role in the decline in mortality rates, which in Newcastle fell from 30.1 to 19.1 per thousand between 1872 and 1900. Medical advances, not least the replacement of the 'miasma' theory of disease by that of 'germs', helped, though mortality contrasts between registration districts persisted: from 17.1 to 41.5 per thousand in Newcastle in 1881. There was a noticeable, though not invariable, relationship between life expectancy and population density and thus poverty: crowded cities, such as Liverpool, having very much higher mortality rates. Public health problems, however, also existed in small towns and rural areas. Edward Cresy reported to the General Board of Health on the small Sussex town of Battle in 1850, 'typhoid and other maladies have arisen here in consequence of putrescent matters having been retained too close to the dwellings of the poor from the want of a proper supply of wholesome water, and thorough ventilation . . .. the town is at present entirely devoid of proper sewers'. Reports on the situation in Bruton in Somerset in the 1870s and 1880s graphically described insufficient and defective toilet arrangements, in-

adequate sewerage disposal and a lack of clean water. A reluctance
to spend money ensured, however, that, as in mid-century London,
plans to improve the situation were delayed, and, though the
sewerage system was finally improved, Bruton did not construct
a water supply system in the Victorian period.

Social welfare was linked to the growing institutionalisation of
society that led to the construction of schools, workhouses and
asylums. The Wiltshire asylum was opened in Devizes in 1851,
replacing private madhouses run for profit. By 1914 a basic national network of infant and child welfare centres had been created.
Health-visiting was expanding. Educational authorities had been
made responsible for the medical inspection of schoolchildren.
Isolation, tuberculosis, smallpox and maternity hospitals and sa-
natoria were established by local authorities. Far from uncon-
strained capitalism, this was increasingly a regulated society.

Nevertheless, there were serious policy differences, reflecting
fundamental disagreements over Ireland, trade union relations
and the nature of the British political system. Ireland was the most
threatening issue, for the determination of the Ulster Protestants to
resist home rule took the country to the brink of civil war in 1914.
The formation of the Ulster Unionist Council (1905) and the Ulster
Volunteer Force (1913) revealed the unwillingness of the Ulster
Protestants to subordinate their sense of identity to Irish nationalism. They were assisted by the Conservatives, from 1912 the 'Conservative and Unionist Party', who did their best to resist the Home
Rule Bill introduced by the Liberal government in 1912. The bill,
twice rejected by the House of Lords, was passed in an amended
form in 1914 with the proviso that it was not to be implemented
until after the war. The crisis defined the political forces in Ireland
and gave a powerful impetus to the consciousness of the Ulster
Protestants. The authority and power of the British state was
challenged, in a fashion that was far more potent and threatening
than the imperial challenges of the Indian Mutiny and the Boer
War.

LIBERAL GOVERNMENT, 1905–15

After nearly twenty years in power, for most of the period 1885–
1905, the Conservatives were replaced by the Liberals, who from

1903 were allied with the new Labour party. Victors in the landslide 1906 election over the Conservatives, then divided over free trade, the Liberals governed until a coalition government was formed in 1915; although they lost their overall majority in both the 1910 elections and thereafter continued as a minority government dependent on Labour and Irish nationalist support. Some Liberals, particularly the dynamic David Lloyd George, Chancellor of the Exchequer 1908-15, were determined to undermine the power and possessions of the old landed elite, and keen to woo Labour and the trade unions. In 1906 the Liberals passed a Trade Disputes Act that gave unions immunity from actions for damages as a result of strike action, and thus rejected the attempts of the courts, through the Taff Vale case (1901), to bring the unions within the law. The Mines Regulations Act (1908) limited the number of hours that miners could spend underground. Lloyd George wished to move the Liberals to the left, and in 1909 announced a people's budget, introducing new taxes for the wealthy: land taxes, supertax and increased death duties. Lloyd George declared in a speech at Newcastle, not a town where the aristocracy were popular, that 'a fully equipped duke costs as much to keep up as two Dreadnoughts [battleships]', and that the House of Lords comprised 'five hundred men, ordinary men, chosen accidentally from among the unemployed'. His Liberal predecessors had never been so critical. The opposition of the Conservative-dominated House of Lords to this policy, only overcome in 1910, led to the Parliament Act (1911) which removed their right to veto Commons' legislation and weakened the self-confidence of the aristocracy. That year Lloyd George had also defused the first general railway strike. As the President of the Board of Trade (1908-10), Winston Churchill, a keen advocate of Lloyd George's budget, tried to improve wages in the 'sweated' trades where they were harsh and to develop unemployment insurance. As Home Secretary (1910-13), he attempted to reduce sentences for petty offences, although he dealt forcibly with both the militant suffragettes and labour unrest. In 1911 Lloyd George's National Insurance Act provided for all males eligible for insurance to be registered with a doctor who was to receive a fee per patient irrespective of the amount of medical attention provided. There were also provisions for unemployment assistance. Another Liberal, Herbert Samuel, was responsible for legislation extending governmental responsibility to all children, rather than only paupers or victims of cruelty. The birching of young boys was restricted, child imprisonment was ended and a national system of juvenile courts was created.

There were a number of major strikes in 1910–12, particularly in mining, transportation and shipbuilding; as well as the continued growth of the Labour Party and of trade-union membership, and a vociferous though largely middle-class suffragette movement demanding the vote for women. The militant tactics of the Women's Social and Political Union were designed to force public attention. Labour, which was associated with most of the leaders of the movement, officially endorsed women's suffrage in 1912. The situation seemed increasingly volatile. Labour won twenty-nine seats in the general election of 1906 and forty in that of 1910, though it was not until 1922 that it emerged as the second largest party. Although Labour benefited from a growing sense of class consciousness, the radical programme of 'New Liberalism' with its emphasis on state-directed social reform and the redistribution of wealth by taxation was more attractive to most electors outside Labour strongholds. Aside from the apparent imminence of conflict in Ulster, strikes also brought widespread violence in Britain. These took place against a recent history of often bitter labour relations. Workers were no longer prepared to accept the idea that their pay should fall during recessions. Instead, they were prepared to fight for what they perceived as a 'just' living wage. The growing socialism of the unions was a victory for the more militant elements among the working population, such as dockers and gasworkers.

Liberalism in its Welsh stronghold was challenged by the rise of Labour, which reflected the growth of trade unionism from the 1870s and particularly the 1890s. Bitter disputes over harsh terms of employment wracked the major North Wales slate quarry owned by Lord Penrhyn in 1900–3 and the South Wales coalfield in 1893 and 1898, and these helped to radicalise the workforce. *Llais Llafur* (*Voice of Labour*), the first Welsh-language socialist newspaper, appeared in 1897. Keir Hardie was elected for Merthyr Tydfil in 1900 and by 1910 there were five Welsh Labour MPs. That year, fresh industrial disputes reflecting the downward pressure on payments caused by more difficult economic circumstances led to violence in the form of sabotage and riots. At Tonypandy a miner was killed by police and troops were sent in by the Home Secretary, Churchill, to enforce order. The following year a rail strike led to sabotage at Llanelli, and troops killed two rioters. As with other such disputes, there was a potent mixture of workers dissatisfied with specific conditions and others seeking political transformation. Thus in South Wales in the early 1910s syndicalists and communists advocated public ownership.

In Britain in 1914, however, the Liberal party still displayed few signs of decline at the hands of Labour, while over 75 per cent of the working population were not members of trade unions and divisions existed within the workforce, between skilled and unskilled, between Protestants and Irish immigrants and between and within different regional economies. Much of the working class was, as in the Black Country and Scotland, prepared to vote Liberal or Conservative. Ethnic, religious, regional and occupational division were as important as class issues. Thus, in the cotton finishing industry, elite foremen engravers had little in common with poorly paid bleachers.

THE PERSISTENCE OF HIERARCHY

Britain, on the eve of world war, was still in many respects an hierarchical society. George V (1910–36) summoned 'My loyal subjects' to war. Hereditary monarchy was still important, though it had lost much of its power. Queen Victoria could influence but not control politics. In his *The English Constitution* (1867), Walter Bagehot claimed that 'a republic has insinuated itself beneath the folds of a monarchy' and argued that the monarchy was useful as an image rather than a source of authority: 'It acts as a disguise. It enables our real rulers to change without heedless people knowing it.' He stated that the monarch had three rights, none of them commanding: 'the right to be consulted, the right to encourage, the right to warn'. Society was obviously scarcely egalitarian. Third-class passengers were not allowed on Great Western Railway expresses until 1882. In 1880 over half of the fertile county of Norfolk was owned by landowners with more than 1,000 acres, and all those with estates there of more than 15,000 acres were members of the aristocracy, with the Earl of Leicester owning 43,000. In 1874 the Duke of Buccleuch owned 37 per cent of the land in both Selkirk and Dumfries and 25 per cent in Roxburghshire. Elected county councils following the Local Government Act of 1888 ended the oligarchy of JPs and squirearchy in favour of elected control of roads, housing and other functions, though the first elections for the new county councils led in 1889 to the Duke of Richmond and Lord Monk Bretton becoming chairmen of the West and East Sussex county councils respectively.

The aristocracy had survived as major players in political and social life until the very end of the nineteenth century, but thereafter they suffered major blows. Debts rose as a consequence of the economic problems of agriculture. Death duties were greatly increased in 1894. Greatly expanded institutions with a meritocratic ethos – the civil service, the professions, the universities, the public schools and the army – were all very significant in the creation of a new social and cultural establishment to replace the aristocracy in the late nineteenth century. This development had significantly taken place rather earlier in Scotland. The armed forces played a much less dominant role in Victorian Britain than in the leading continental states, where they served as a base for continued aristocratic, or at least landed, influence: the army in particular was not popular with politicians. In Britain the old landowning political elite had its dominance of the electoral process challenged in 1832, and thereafter a steadily decreasing percentage of MPs came from it. Mr. Merdle, the great 'popular financier on an extensive scale' in Dickens's *Little Dorrit* (1855–7), was 'a new power in the country . . . able to buy up the whole House of Commons'. This was an exaggeration, but reflected a sense of new economic forces and political interests. Joseph Chamberlain (1836–1914), a major Birmingham manufacturer of screws who employed 2,500 workers by the 1870s and became Mayor of Birmingham, sold his holdings in the family firm and became a professional politician, despising the amateurism and inherited privilege of aristocratic politicians such as the Marquis of Hartington, later Duke of Devonshire, who was Liberal leader in 1875–80; although he had to work with them. Moves against the game laws, by which rural sporting rights were controlled by the elite, reflected challenges to their position. The Game Act of 1880 reflected urban agitation and a different moral and socio-political world to that which had extended the privileges of the sporting interest by the Night Poaching Act of 1828 and the Game Act of 1832.

The aristocracy opposed the Liberal Party in the 1900s because they sought to preserve their political position, as well as to resist what appeared to be an entire ethos of change centring on the policies of the extension of the power of the state, collectivism and the destruction of the Union with Ireland. They grasped the danger that democracy might entail the poor plundering the rich, or, in the eyes of its supporters, the social justice of redistribution. Whereas Disraeli, an outsider, had acquired a country estate in 1848, the Liberal Herbert Asquith, a barrister, was in 1908 the first Prime Minister not to have his own country house, though he was to end up with one and an earldom. Asquith was more hesitant than his predecessors about accepting the claims of hereditary aristocrats to high office, although most of his cabinet came from the old upper classes.

RELIGION

The political, religious, intellectual and educational authority of the Church of England had been challenged. The role of the parish in education and social welfare declined in favour of new governmental agencies. Municipal and county government was better able than the Church to implement the aspirations of society for reform and control, and in many towns the prestige and authority held by the vicar passed to the mayor. Oxford and Cambridge, hitherto Anglican monopolies, where all the teaching was conducted by clerics, were to non-Anglicans by legislation of 1854 and 1856. The Church of Ireland was disestablished by Gladstone in 1869. Nevertheless, the Church of England still played a major role in a society which was still very much Christian in its precepts. There were numerous clergymen. The Church also reformed itself, rationalising its structure and revenues, and improving its pastoral care. In Lincoln Cathedral, for example, after a long period of nepotism and corruption under the Pretyman family from the 1780s to 1860s, there were attempts to improve the frequency of services, the care of the poor and education.

The principal challenge to the Church of England came not from atheism, but from the rise of Dissent. The vitality of Dissent led to many new congregations. Without the authority of an established church it was, however, difficult to prevent splits. Thus, for example, the Primitive Methodists formed in 1811 and the Wesleyan Reform Methodists in 1849. Six years earlier, in the Disruption of

1843, the Church of Scotland divided on the issue of lay patronage, a dispute that had a nationalist dimension because of the issue at stake.

The re-emergence of 'public' Catholicism, with the re-establishment of the Catholic hierarchy in England in 1850–1 and massive Irish immigration, caused tension. Between 1850 and 1910, 1173 new Catholic churches were opened in England and Wales, the largest number in London and Lancashire. The number of Catholics in Scotland, where the hierarchy was re-established in 1874, rose from about 146,000 in 1851 to about 332,000 in 1878, largely as a result of Irish immigration. Catholicism came to be accepted as part of the religious scene, albeit as clearly secondary to the established Church.

Although Jewish immigration increased greatly, the British Isles remained overwhelmingly Christian. Religion was an important prism through which the outside world was viewed, not least affecting attitudes towards foreign policy. In addition, racial pride was of considerable importance. The right of the British to rule over other peoples was still taken for granted, and Darwinism, with its stress on natural selection, seemed to give new force to it. Social Darwinism led to a view of the nation-state as a racial body that needed to grow if it was to avoid decline, an inherently aggressive attitude. The Primrose League, a popular Conservative movement launched in 1883, enjoyed much support in the 1880s and 1890s for its defence of Crown, Church, social system and empire.

SOCIAL CHANGE

There had also been major social change as both cause and consequence of the new mass electorate, universal compulsory primary education, and widespread urbanisation and industrialisation. These had brought widespread social dislocation, instability and fears. Deference and traditional social patterns, never as fixed as some thought, had ebbed, and the new and newly expanded cities and towns created new living environments in which the role and rule of the old world was far less. Only 10.4 per cent of the United Kingdom's workforce was employed in agriculture in the 1890s, compared to 40.3 per cent in France. Railways created new economic and social relationships, new leisure and commuting options.

Their construction destroyed or damaged many of the most prominent sites of the past, including Berwick and Newcastle castles and Launceston Priory, and wrecked the canal system. The geography and townscape of London was changed by the train, including underground railways, the tram, and new roads, such as Kingsway and Northumberland Avenue, which respectively destroyed a red-light district and the splendour of Northumberland House. In 1862 Gladstone joined the directors of the Metropolitan Railway on the first run over the full length of their underground railway in London. Glasgow also developed an underground system. By the early 1900s all bar 5 per cent of British rail passengers were travelling third class; an affordable system of rapid, mass transport had been created.

TECHNOLOGY

Technology was like a freed genie, bringing ever more changes. Railway and telegraphy were succeeded by motor car and telephone, electricity and wireless. The growth of the genre of 'scientific romance' testified to the seemingly inexorable advance of human potential through technology. In *The Coming Race* (1871), by Sir Edward Bulwer Lytton, one of the leading men of letters of his age and a former Conservative Secretary for the Colonies, a mining engineer encountered at the centre of the earth a people who controlled 'Vril', a kinetic energy offering limitless powers. The novel is largely forgotten, other than through Bo(vi-ne)vril. Science fiction played a greater role in the work of H(er-bert) G(eorge) Wells (1866–1946), who had studied under Charles Darwin's supporter, the comparative anatomist T. H. Huxley. Man's destiny in time and space was a central question for Wells, reflecting in part the intellectual expansion and excitement offered by the evolutionary theory outlined by Darwin in his *Origin of Species*, and by interest in manned flight. His first major novel, *The Time Machine* (1895), was followed by the *War of the Worlds* (1898), an account of a Martian invasion of England.

There was concern in some circles about what the poet Gerard Manley Hopkins termed 'the strokes of havoc' created by technological change and economic development. Similar views were expressed by such leading literary figures as Matthew Arnold,

William Morris and John Ruskin. Successful efforts were made to save some open spaces from development.

Developments were in fact less lurid than those outlined by Wells, but they still changed many aspects of human experience. The first demonstration of electric lighting in Birmingham was in 1882; the Birmingham Electric Supply Ltd. following seven years later. The electric lighting industry developed and spread rapidly: the installed capacity in the local-authority sector in Scotland rose from 6,332 kilowatts in 1896 to 84,936 in 1910. Electricity was also regarded as a means to improve the social environment. The first original, full-size British petrol motor was produced in 1895; the first commercial motor company was established at Coventry in 1896; motor buses were introduced in about 1898. In 1886 Parliament repealed the legislation that had obliged cars to follow a man carrying a red flag and, instead, allowed them to drive at up to 14 mph. 'Cinematograph Halls' showed films: by 1913 there were fourteen cinemas in Lincolnshire alone. The following year Manchester had 111 premises licensed to show films. The first successful flight by the American Wright brothers in 1903 led Lord Northcliffe to remark that 'England is no longer an island'.

The Motor Car Act of 1903 extended the rights of the motorist, the motor bus was introduced in London in 1905 and four years later the national Road Board was founded to lend energy and cohesion to road construction. Motor transport led to the widespread tarring of roads from the early 1900s, a major visual and environmental change. This process was largely complete by 1939. By 1914, there were 132,000 private car registrations. There were also 124,000 motor cycle registrations and 51,167 buses and taxis on the road. Cars ensured that bicycling, which had boomed following the development of the safety bicycle in 1885, descended the social and age scales. A new world of speed and personal mobility, with its own particular infrastructure, was being created. If cars were still a luxury, every such innovation contributed to a sense of change that was possibly the most important solvent of the old order.

8

The Twentieth Century, 1914–96

TECHNOLOGY, CHANGE AND THE STATE OF THE
NATION

War and the loss of empire framed the political experience of
Britain from the outbreak of the First World War (1914) to the
1960s, but the environmental, medical, social and economic con-
texts, as well as the nature of personal experience, were all to be
transformed totally as a result of technological innovation and
application. The nineteenth century had brought major changes,
but the contemporary age has truly witnessed revolutionary transformation in theoretical and applied science and technology in
most fields, whether transport, the generation and distribution of
power, medicine, contraception, agricultural yields, or the accumu-
lation, storing and manipulation of information. The wealth was
created and the means provided that would make it feasible to
suggest that man's lot on earth could be substantially improved.
Change would be so all-encompassing that fears about permanent
damage to the environment and to mankind itself would become a
major issue from the 1960s, though worried voices had been raised
earlier. In his *To Iron-Founders and Others*, the Yorkshire poet and
dramatist Gordon Bottomley (1874–1948) warned:

> When you destroy a blade of grass
> You poison England at her roots . . .
> Your worship is your furnaces,

. . . your vision is
Machines for making more machines.

In this brave and troubled new world, it was possible for people to travel and transmit ideas as never before, to create and destroy in new ways and on a scale hitherto only graspable in imaginative fiction, to synthesise and manufacture new substances, textures, tastes and sounds, and thus create from the fertile mind of man a world in which man himself, his desires, needs and imagination, seemed the sole frame of reference, the only scale.

For an elderly person in 1996 (a growing percentage of the population of the British Isles), it was not only the individual major technological innovations of their lifetime, whether atomic energy or contraceptive pill, television or microchip, jet engine or computer, bio-technology or artificial hip, that were of importance, in affecting, directly or indirectly, insistently or episodically, their life; it was also the cumulative impact of change. The past ceased to be a recoverable world, a source of reference, value and values for lives that changed very little, and became, instead, a world that was truly lost, a distorted theme-park for nostalgia, regret or curiosity.

Change was first a matter of displacement. Migration had always been important in British history, especially in the nineteenth century with mass movement to the new industrial areas and emigration to the colonies, but in the contemporary age the pattern of the people has changed even more radically. Rural England is now like a skeleton, without its people, a skeleton being clothed increasingly by commuters who live there but work elsewhere. In 1921–39 the number of agricultural labourers fell by a quarter, and the pace quickened after the Second World War. Horses were replaced by tractors, and local mills, both windmills and watermills, fell into disuse as they were replaced by electricity. Hand-milking was replaced by machines. Agriculture continues to shed workers, and has become increasingly a solitary activity. The bothies in which many male Scottish farm workers lived in claustrophobic and insanitary conditions, disappeared in the 1960s.

Other non-urban activities, such as forestry, mining and quarrying, have also either declined or dramatically cut their workforces. These changes have led to the depopulation of many rural regions, especially upland areas and those beyond commuting distance from towns, for example north Norfolk, the Lincolnshire Wolds and much of Cornwall and Wales. Many small rural schools have closed. This is not a case of the destruction of age-old lifestyles, for the rural world of 1900 was in many respects merely the result of the major changes of the period 1500–1900, while the depopulation of some rural areas had been a major problem in Tudor England and earlier. Change is and was constant, and yet, in terms of the sense of place and identity of the British population of this century, the past seemed more fixed and the scale of change therefore revolutionary. The countryside has become, for many of its inhabitants, a place of residence and leisure rather than of work, and urban attitudes have been introduced, as in complaints about the noise produced by farm animals and especially about the hunting of wild animals, principally foxes and stags, for sport. In much of rural England housing has become scarce and expensive as a result of purchase by commuters and buyers of second homes, while the problems of the agrarian economy have led to a large number of rural households living below the poverty line.

At the other end of the social scale, though the wartime boosts to production and state subsidies for agriculture under the 1947 Agriculture Act helped farmers and landowners, Lloyd George's tax changes and the disappearance of the vast labour force of cheap servants had already hit country-house life, and many country houses were demolished or institutionalised. Over 1,200 were destroyed or abandoned in 1918–75; many others were transferred to the National Trust, became reliant on paying visitors, or became schools. The dominance of much of rural England by the aristocratic estate became a thing of the past. Massive land sales after the First World War, in which many heirs to estates died, broke the traditional landlord-tenant relationship. For example, the Lincolnshire estate of the Earls of Yarborough, 60,000 acres in 1885, fell to about half after land sales in 1919, 1925, 1933, 1944 and 1948, although their links with tenants in north Lincolnshire remain close and extensive today. The growth of owner-occupation of farmland after 1918 ensured that the tenurial relationship upon which landowner control had rested became less important: the influence of landowners in the politics of agriculture was replaced by that of farmers. In so far as new country houses were built, they were essentially for rich businessmen or foreigners, who intended to play no role in local government and politics and did not wish to build up extensive landholdings, and not for landed families. Some families maintained control of their estates, but often they shrunk: more than half of the great estates in the East Riding of Yorkshire have sold much or all of their land. The aristocracy also lost their town houses. Again, these were demolished or converted to institutional use. In Scotland some traditional landholding patterns survive. The Duke of Buccleuch and Cameron of Lochiel each own major estates, but the number, extent and role of such estates are far less than in the past. The position of Anglo-Irish landowners collapsed due to land reform and civil violence in the first quarter of the century.

Visually and environmentally, the rural British Isles have also changed greatly. New crops have had an impact, most obviously the striking yellow colour of oil-seed rape and, in the 1990s, the pale blue of European Union – subsidised flax. Redundant farmsteads have fallen into ruin or been destroyed. Traditional occupations and activities that used and maintained habitats such as meadows have declined. The amalgamation of fields and bulldozing of hedges have led, since the 1950s, to the replacement, as in East Anglia, of the earlier patchwork of small fields surrounded by dense hedges, by large expanses of arable land, bounded often by barbed-wire fences. There are now fewer trees in heavily farmed lowland areas. These changes have had serious environmental consequences, as have changes in the use of more marginal lands. Marshlands have been drained and are now intensively farmed. Upland valleys, such as the North Tyne and the Durham Derwent and several in Wales, have been drowned for reservoirs. Other reservoirs are planned as water use and shortage becomes a more acute problem. Large plantations of coniferous trees have been planted on upland moors and on the Norfolk and Suffolk Breckland. Throughout the British Isles, pesticides are used extensively in agriculture, and enter the ground-water system. The conquest of nature has become ever more comprehensive and insistent.

People have not only moved off the land, but also away from declining industrial regions. Areas that were collectively the nineteenth-century 'workshop of the world' became industrial museums and regions of social dereliction, designated as problems requiring regional assistance, as under the Special Areas Act (1934), which in fact provided only limited assistance. During the slump of the 1930s, unemployment in Sunderland rose to 75 per cent of shipbuilders and half of the working population, and was associated with hardship and higher rates of ill-health. Jarrow, another ship-building town in north-east England, also had unemployment levels of over 70 per cent. People moved from such towns to areas of greater economic opportunity, mostly in the Midlands and south-east England. In addition, particularly since the Second World War, crowded inner-city areas have lost people as slums were torn down. Instead, people moved to new developments on 'green-field' sites in the countryside, or on the edge of older settlements. The former were new towns, the first garden city being Letchworth (1903), the latter suburban sprawl, the suburbia where a far greater percentage of the population now came to live. This was especially the case around major cities, particularly London, which expanded greatly in a contiguous fashion in the 1920s and 1930s, although far less so after Green Belt legislation was passed after the Second World War. The process is still continuing. In July 1992 the government indicated that it expected 855,000 new houses to be built in south-east England between 1991 and 2006. Many new and greatly expanded towns, however, for example Crawley, Basingstoke and Peterlee, translated old social problems to new sites, but also exacerbated them by destroying the 'old communities'.

Designed to allow the growing middle class to realise their earning potential, to escape from the crowded and polluted conditions of the city, and to join in the expanding hobby of amateur gardening, new housing was both cause and consequence of a massive expansion of personal transport. Commuting led to an increase in first train and later car use. In the 1920s and 1930s the development of the London 'tube' underground railway system allowed a major spread of the city to the north, while national private ownership of cars increased more than tenfold and by 1937 over 300,000 new cars were being registered annually. 'The sound of horns and motors', referred to in T. S. Eliot's poem *The Waste Land* (1922), was becoming more insistent and creating a national mass culture. The railways had often pioneered feeder bus services, but from the 1920s competition from road transport became serious for them. There were half a million road goods vehicles, nearly 2 million cars and 53,000 buses and coaches by September 1938. 240 miles of track and 350 stations were closed completely in the interwar period and another 1,000 miles and 380 miles to passenger traffic. Among the 'Big Four' railway companies the Southern Railway was alone in paying a regular dividend to shareholders before 1948.

After a fall in car ownership during the Second World War its rise accelerated rapidly, especially after petrol rationing stopped in 1953. In terms of thousand million passenger-kilometres, private road transport shot up from 76 in 1954 to 350 in 1974, an increase from 39 to 79 per cent of the total. This gain was made at the expense of bus, coach and rail transport. The percentage of goods traffic moved by road rose from 37 in 1952 to 58.3 in 1964.

Nationalised in 1948, the railways lost money from the late 1950s, and the Beeching report of 1963 led to dramatic cuts in the network. Freight and passenger services were greatly curtailed, the workforce cut, lines were taken up, many stations became unmanned halts or were converted to other uses. One of the major 'public spaces' of Britain, the railway, was thus greatly diminished in favour of the more 'individual' car. In 1991 Britain spent less per head on rail improvements than any other country in the European Union (EU) apart from Greece and Ireland, neither of which has a substantial network, and there is no effective long-term British plan for transportation investment. With the rise of leisure activities, several former railway trackbeds were turned into long-distance footpaths. Compared to America, however, rail transport still plays an important role in the British Isles, particularly in travel between the major cities and in commuting into them. Paradoxically, the relative decline of rail travel has not ended its grip on the popular imagination, although that has focused on the now-discarded system of steam trains. Preservation groups and other enthusiasts have re-opened a few lines and stations, while the storybook character 'Thomas the Tank Engine' is a figure of great popularity for children of about four, and some adults.

There were 12.2 million cars in Britain in 1970, 21.9 in 1990. Car ownership rose from 224 per 1,000 people in 1971 to 380 per 1,000 in 1994. Only 42 per cent of those who worked in Newcastle in 1971 lived in the city. Most of the rest commuted by car. Increased use of the car and the construction of more roads interacted. Trunk roads with dual carriageways were constructed, and a motorway system was created, beginning with the M6 Preston bypass, opened by Harold Macmillan (Conservative Prime Minister 1957–63) in December 1958. The latest, the Oxford to Birmingham M40, designed to supplement the overstrained M1 as a route between London and the Midlands, opened in January 1991. As road usage grew, it became necessary progressively to supplement existing roads. Every town soon required its bypass: Exeter's was opened in 1938.

The car, however, has led to many problems. Car exhaust emissions have led to environmental pollution, while by the early 1990s 45,000 children were being hurt on the roads every year and among those aged 5–15 two-thirds of deaths were the result of road accidents. In 1992, 4,681 people were killed in car accidents, compared to 499 by murder. Alarmist and often lurid reports about the latter feed popular concern about crime. In contrast, deaths and injuries due to cars arouse less public interest and concern and are treated as a fact of life.

Greater personal mobility for the bulk, but by no means all, of the population enabled and was a necessary consequence of lower-density housing and declining subsidies for public transport. Employment patterns have changed. In place of factories or mines that had large labour forces, most modern industrial concerns are capital intensive and employ less labour. They are often located away from the central areas of cities on flat and relatively open sites with good road links. A growing number of the rising percentage of the population who were retired left the cities to live in suburban, rural or coastal areas, such as Colwyn Bay and Worthing. New shopping patterns developed, with the rise of the supermarket in the 1950s and the hypermarket, mainly out of town, in the 1980s. By 1992 16 per cent of the total shopping space in Britain was made up of shopping centres, such as Brent Cross in north London, Lakeside Thurrock in Essex, the Glades in Bromley, Kent, Meadowhall in Sheffield and the Metro Centre in Gateshead, the last applauded by Margaret Thatcher, Conservative Prime Minister 1979–90. They are moulders of taste and spheres of spending activity at the centre of the consumer society. Almost all of their customers come by car, abandoning traditional high-street shopping with its gentler pace and more individual service. Related changes in location have also been of great importance in such areas as education and health. In 1971 14 per cent of junior school children were driven to school, in 1990 64 per cent. The percentage walking or going by bus has fallen markedly, again an aspect of the declining use of 'public space' and one surely related to the increase in obesity and unfitness among children. Parking space for cars has come to take a greater percentage of city space. Multi-storey carparks disfigure many townscapes, while the problems of parking have become a major topic of conversation.

Greater mobility for most, but not all, of the population has also exacerbated spatial segregation. The division of the population into communities defined by differing levels of wealth, expectations and opportunity is scarcely novel, indeed in most towns has developed greatly from the eighteenth century. It has become, however, more pronounced during the twentieth century, and an obvious aspect of what is termed the 'underclass', in both town and countryside, is their relative lack of mobility.

Consumerism and technology, the two closely related, have been crucial features of the contemporary age. Their impact has been very varied. Thus, the spread in the 1930s of large numbers of affordable cars with reliable self-starter motors, so that it was not necessary to crank up the motor by hand, led to a wave of 'smash and grab' raids as the criminal fraternity took advantage of the new technology. Greater mobility totally changed the pattern of crime. In response, London's Metropolitan Police experimented with mounting ship's radios in cars and was able to develop a fleet of Wolseley cars thus equipped with which to mount an effective response. The post-Second World War era was to see computer fraud, but also the use of computerised information and of sophisticated forensic techniques by the police. Traffic offences brought middle-class individuals into contact with the police and the courts. 'Flying pickets' (mobile groups of trade unionists) used cars to spread strike action, as in the 'Winter of Discontent' strikes of 1978–9 and the miners' strike of 1984–5. Labour-saving devices, such as washing machines and vacuum cleaners, reduced the burden of housework and replaced domestic servants, easing the struggle with dirt and disease, though they also ensured that household use of water increased considerably. The communication of messages has been revolutionised. Telephone ownership has risen to a high level; fax machines and mobile phones became important from the 1980s and the latter were the fashionable Christmas present in Britain in 1994. The growing numbers of personal and company computers have facilitated the use of electronic mail.

The number of radio and television channels has multiplied. Radio broadcasts began in 1922; the British Broadcasting Corporation, a monopoly acting in the 'national interest' and financed by licence fees paid by radio owners, was established in 1926; and it began television services in 1936. Commercial television companies, financed by advertising, were not established in Britain until 1955, and the first national commercial radio station, Classic FM, was not founded until 1992. Television ownership shot up in the 1950s, the numbers of those with regular access to a set rising from 38 per cent of the population in 1955 to 75 per cent in 1959. As a result, the cinema declined in popularity: by 1966 over half of those in the north-west of England had closed, although in the 1990s there was to be a significant resurgence of cinemas with multiplexes. Cinema admissions in Britain fell from a peak of 1.6 billion in 1946 to 54 million in 1974, before rising to 114 million in 1993. By 1994 99 per cent of British households had televisions (93 per cent in 1992) and 96 per cent had colour televisions. In the 1990s the larger number of regular television channels were supplemented for many by satellite channels, the receiving dishes altering the appearance of many houses as television aerials had earlier done. By 1992 over a million Sky Television dishes had been sold in Britain. Over 50 per cent of British households had video recorders, giving them even greater control over what they watched. The Japanese Sony Corporation alone manufactured 6 million television sets at Bridgend in the twenty years before Queen Elizabeth II (Elizabeth I of Scotland) formally opened for them a new colour television factory at Pencoed in Mid-Glamorgan in 1993.

Television has succeeded radio as a central determinant of the leisure time of many, a moulder of opinions and fashions, a source of conversation and controversy, an occasion of family cohesion or dispute, a major feature of the household. A force for change, a great contributor to the making of the 'consumer society' and a 'window on the world' which demands the right to enter everywhere and report anything, television has also become increasingly a reflector of popular taste. Just as radio had helped to provide common experiences – royal Christmas messages from 1932, King Edward VIII's abdication speech in 1936, the war speeches of Winston Churchill, heard by millions (as those in the First World War of Lloyd George could not be) – so television fulfilled the same function, providing much of the nation with common visual images and messages. This really began with the coronation service for Elizabeth II in 1953, a cause of many households purchasing sets or first watching, and thanks to television the royals have almost become members of viewers' extended families, treated with the fascination commonly devoted to the stars of soap operas. The *Royal Family* documentary of 1969 exposed monarchy to the close, domestic scrutiny of television. Indeed, both the 'New Elizabethan Age of optimism', heralded in 1952, and present discontents about the position and behaviour of the royal family, owe much to the media. Television is central to much else: the trend-setting and advertising that are so crucial to the consumer society, and the course and conduct of election campaigns. Parliament is televised and much of public politics has become a matter of sound bites aimed to catch the evening news bulletins. Television has increasingly also set the idioms and vocabulary of public and private life. Thus on 14 July 1989 the Prime Minister, Margaret Thatcher, was attacked by Denis Healey of the Labour party for adding 'the diplomacy of Alf Garnett to the economics of Arthur Daley', assuming that listeners would understand his references to popular television characters.

Technological change contributed to an economic situation in which the annual output of goods rose appreciably for most of the century, while personal output, consumption and leisure similarly rose alongside a major growth in British population: including Northern Ireland, up from 44.9 million in 1931 to 49 in 1951 and 55.5 in 1981. Despite the slump, for most of those in work the 1930s was a decade of improved housing, wider consumer choice and a better quality of life. It was a period of new and developing electrical goods, of cars, radio, television and the 'talkies'. Large numbers of cinemas were constructed: despite their relatively low population, Suffolk had forty in 1937 and Lincolnshire fifty-eight. Although the cinema provided escapism, the new electrical goods were of scant value to the unemployed, nearly 3 million in late 1932, and, despite a strong recovery in 1934–7, still above one million until 1941. Heavy industry was especially badly hit by the depression of the 1930s, although it had already encountered serious problems after the First World War. 238,000 tons of shipping were launched from shipyards on the Tyne in 1913, but less than 7,000 in 1933. More than a quarter of the Scottish labour force was out of work in 1931–3, as was about one-third of Derbyshire's miners, and the 1933 Derbyshire march of the National Unemployed Workers' Movement had such slogans as, 'We refuse to starve in silence . . . We want work schemes'. The decline of the Cornish tin industry was such that unemployment in Redruth in 1939 was 25 per cent; in Cornwall as a whole the percentage was 18–20.

Many of those who had work nevertheless faced low wages, a life of shifts and expedients, inadequate food and poor housing; but for many others the 1930s was a period of prosperity and this helped to account for the victory of the National Government in the 1935 British election. The same contrast was true of the recessions at the beginning of the 1980s and the 1990s. Alongside high unemployment, and social strains manifested in rising crime rates and urban riots, many of those in work had high living-standards. Average British disposable income rose by 37 per cent between 1982 and 1992. The real income of the bottom 10 per cent in Britain increased by 10 per cent in 1973–91 although the top 10 per cent gained 55 per cent, and average income differentials thus rose. Ownership of telephones, washing machines, dishwashers, cars and video-recorders all rose. In both recessions, however, the rising ownership of goods was in part met by increased imports, while British industry was harmed by the high exchange-rate of sterling as the interests of producers were subordinated to those of finance, not least due to a determination to reduce inflation.

Economic growth and changing political and social assumptions in Britain had led earlier to the development of national social security and educational provision and, from 1948, of a national health service, ensuring that the indigent and ill were offered a comprehensive safety net, while a range of services were provided free at the point of delivery to the whole of the population. Measures such as free school meals (1906), non-contributory old-age pensions (1908), labour exchanges (1909), the National Insurance Act (1911), the Education Act of 1918 which designated 14 as the minimum leaving age, and the creation of the Unemployment Assistance Board (1934), were limited but still an improvement on the earlier situation, and the establishment of antenatal screening in the 1920s was important. The Local Government Acts of 1929 abolished poor law unions, replacing boards of guardians by public assistance committees, which were committees of the counties and county boroughs, and encouraged local authorities to take over workhouses (since 1913 called poor law institutions) as hospitals. Philanthropy, mutual aid and voluntary activity, however, all remained important in the practice and policy of social welfare.

Further developments were widely supported in the three decades after the Second World War, a period when 'one-nation Toryism' and 'Butskellism' reflected a measure of continuity and consensus between Conservative and Labour policies. The Conservatives did not dismantle the National Health Service after they were returned to power in 1951. Both parties responded to Keynesian economic theory with its emphasis on economic stimulus, an expanding money supply and full employment. The creation of the welfare state reflected a conviction that social progress and economic growth were compatible, that indeed a major purpose of the latter was to achieve the former. The Education Act of 1944 obliged every local education authority to prepare a development plan for educational provision and the Ministry of Education imposed new minimum standards in matters such as school accommodation and size. The minimum school leaving age was raised to 15 and fees in state-supported secondary schools were abolished; legislation in 1947 extended the provisions to Scotland and Northern Ireland. Stable employment and social security were seen as important goals.

Following the 1915 Rent and Mortgage Interest Restrictions (War) Act, which owed something to the Clydeside rent strikes of that year, private landlordship became less profitable, tenants' rights more secure and renting from local authorities, 'council housing', more important. Partly due to the 'fair rent' system, which allowed rent officers to fix rents below the market level, supposedly to protect tenants from rapacious landlords, the private rental sector fell from an 80 per cent share of British housing in the 1940s to 8 per cent in 1988. The Housing Act of 1930 gave local authorities powers to clear or improve slum (crowded and substandard housing) areas, and after 1945 slums were swept aside and their inhabitants moved into new housing estates, reflections of the priority given to rehousing the masses and creating an acceptable living environment. Prefabricated methods of construction ensured that multi-storey blocks of flats could be built rapidly, and local councils, such as Glasgow in the 1960s, took pride in their number, size and visibility. Municipal housing policies helped in the consolidation of Labour's working-class base, for example in Clydeside and London. Extolled at the time and illustrated alongside castles and cathedrals in guidebooks of the 1960s, municipal multi-storey flats have subsequently been attacked as ugly, out of keeping with the existing urban fabric, of poor quality, and as lacking in community feeling and as breeders of alienation and crime. Alongside much unattractive and poor-quality municipal housing in the 1960s, there was also a brutal rebuilding of many city centres, for example Birmingham, Manchester and Newcastle. The Conservative governments of the 1950s fostered owner occupation and the Conservative government that came to power in 1979 felt little sympathy for public housing and under the 'right to buy' Housing Act of 1980 introduced a policy of the sale of council housing to tenants. This expanded opportunities for home ownership, but also depleted the stock of public housing. Whereas 29,290 new homes were built by local authorities in England and Wales in 1984, the figure for 1994 was only 528. Rent control was restricted in the 1950s, and after 1979 the 'fair rent' system was abolished. The number of private-renting households rose by 22 per cent in 1989–93.

There has been disagreement about the social and educational consequences of the comprehensivisation of British education, the abandonment, in the 1950s and especially from 1965, of streaming of children by ability into different schools after examination at the age of 11 (12 in Scotland). Grammar and secondary-modern schools were replaced by comprehensive schools, a policy actively supported by the 1964–70 Labour government and further implemented under the 1970–4 Conservative government. Labour politicians regarded grammar schools as elitist and favoured a more egalitarian approach. In practice, comprehensive schools varied greatly, often reflecting the social nature of their catchment area. Another major shift was away from single-sex and towards mixed schooling, by the 1990s overwhelmingly the norm in the state sector. Educational standards have been the cause of much controversy. The percentage of children in private (though not boarding) schools rose markedly in the 1980s before falling in 1991–4, and they continue to be perceived as both cause and consequence of class distinction.

Major expansions in higher education in the 1960s and early 1990s dramatically increased the percentage of school-leavers continuing in full-time education and thus eventually the graduate population. The number of students from lower-income families rose considerably. Nine new universities were founded in 1958–66 and the number and importance of polytechnics was increased. The

Robbins Report of 1963 recommended places in higher education for all suitably qualified candidates and the government responded. Students were also given free tuition, and help towards their maintenance in proportion to their parental income. The percentage of 18-year-olds entering university in the United Kingdom rose from 4.6 in 1961 to over 30 by the mid-1990s, by which time the polytechnics and several other colleges had also become universities. It is not clear that the hopes inspiring this process, especially those of fulfilling the economy's requirements for skills and widening opportunity, have been met. Similar uncertainty surrounds the attempt from 1989 to establish a national curriculum at primary- and secondary-school level in England and Wales.

The British National Health Service (NHS), established by the Labour government in 1948, brought about a fundamental change in the medical provision of the nation, and was for long regarded as one of the triumphs of social welfare policy. However, the NHS was harmed from the outset by the measures taken in order to win the consent of interest groups, especially doctors and dentists, and has subsequently suffered from the rising cost of medical treatment, a consequence of the greater potential for medical action and rising expectations of care. Private health-care has developed, with the percentage of the United Kingdom population having medical insurance rising from 8.7 in 1986 to 11.3 in 1992, and the state of the NHS was a major issue in the 1992 general election. Yet the NHS has been able to maintain the policy of treatment free at the point of delivery, so that many of the anxieties about the availability and cost of medical treatment that the poor faced earlier in the century have ended. It has established a much fairer geographical and social allocation of resources and skills than existed hitherto, and there has been a positive effort to develop medical education and specialised services spread across the regions rather than concentrated, as earlier, in a few centres, principally London.

Uniform health provision through the NHS has played a major role in the dramatic change in the medical condition of the population that has characterised this century, though other factors, such as improved diet, have also been of great importance. Britain has been in the forefront of medical research and development throughout the century, and as general medical knowledge has increased enormously, so the ability to identify and treat disease has increased exponentially. These improvements have touched the lives of millions and totally altered the condition of the people. In Norfolk death rates fell from about 22 to 12 per 1,000 people between 1851 and 1951.

The discovery of insulin in 1922 and its use from the mid-1920s enabled young diabetics to live. Britain has played a major role in the understanding and treatment of mental illness. The twentieth century has brought recognition of the importance of psychological and mental processes, and the diagnosis and treatment of mental illness has been revolutionised. The development from the 1940s of safe and effective drugs has helped in the treatment of major psychoses and depression, dramatically improving the cure rate. British scientists, such as Sir Alexander Fleming, the discoverer of penicillin, played a major role in the development of antibiotics in the 1930s and especially the 1940s. They were of enormous benefit for dealing with infections, which, of one kind or another, were a very common cause of death in the first half of the century. Tuberculosis was conquered thanks to the use from the 1940s of an American antibiotic, streptomycin, as well as to better diet, earlier diagnosis and the programme of mass BCG vaccination. It had killed one adult in eight at the beginning of the century (including, in 1930, the novelist D. H. Lawrence at the age of 44) and was still serious in the 1930s, particularly among the urban poor. Antibiotics also helped with other bacterial infections. Diarrhoeal diseases have diminished; while urinary infections and venereal diseases can be more readily treated. The common childhood diseases which caused high mortality and high morbidity in children in the early part of the century, such as measles, whooping cough, polio, diptheria, mumps and rubella (German measles), have been dramatically reduced by the post-war introduction of immunisation programmes for the entire child population. From the 1970s on there has been the introduction of population screening for the early detection and treatment of other diseases, such as breast and cervical cancer. The 1980s saw the increasing development and use of anti-viral agents for the treatment of viral infections. Health education has improved and become more important.

The range of surgical treatment has dramatically increased. The two world wars, especially the second, saw a major improvement in surgical techniques, with, for example, the development of plastic surgery. A major increase in anaesthetic skills, due to greater knowledge and the introduction of increasingly sophisticated drugs, has meant that complex surgical operations can be performed. Once serious operations, such as appendectomies, have become routine and minor. The range of research and development now encompasses skin grafts and artificial knee joints. There have been major advances in the treatment of the heart, and bypass and transplant surgery have been completely developed since the Second World War.

Medical advances have led to dramatic changes in the pattern of causes of death, although related developments in public health have also been of great importance. The poor, insanitary and overcrowded housing, low incomes and overcrowded maternity hospitals that were such serious problems as late as the 1930s, pushing up infant mortality rates and malnutrition among the poor and unemployed, lessened with post-Second World War social welfare policies. The Clean Air Act and other environmental measures, safety at work awareness and the Health and Safety at Work Act, as well as a growing understanding of the dangers of working in smoke-filled buildings and with asbestos, have all contributed to changes in health, not least to the decline of chest illnesses. The hazards of drinking to excess and, particularly, of smoking have become generally appreciated and been addressed by government action.

Large numbers of children died in the first half of the century, the United Kingdom infant mortality rate being 58 per 1,000 in 1937, and infections were then a major cause of death for the entire population. Today later-onset diseases, such as heart disease and cancers, are far more important, and infections generally only kill people who are suffering from associated disorders and are at the extremes of life. Birth in hospital has become the norm: in 1993 only one in every sixty-three births in England and Wales occurred at home. Infant mortality fell by nearly two-thirds between 1971 and 1994. Average life expectancy for all age-groups has persistently risen this century, the major exception being those aged between 15 and 44 during the 1980s. Average lifespan increased by an average of two years every decade in the 1960s–90s, so that projected mortality rates for 1996 were 74 for men and 79 for women compared to 67.8 and 73.6 in 1961. The rise in life expectancy has led to a new age structure, as a result of the increasing number of pensioners, and to problems of dependency posed by the greater number of people over 85. 12.6 per cent of Norfolk's population were over 65 in 1951; only 9.2 per cent a century earlier. But by 1990 the percentage was 19.6.

In addition, not all illnesses are in retreat. Possibly as a result of increasing car exhaust emissions, respiratory diseases, such as asthma, have definitely risen, and some others may also be increasing. Tuberculosis has made a comeback since 1987, partly due to refugees and immigrants from countries where it is more common. The massive increase in the importation, treatment and burying of hazardous waste in the 1980s has led to concern about possible health implications. A Department of Health survey in 1993 suggested that half the adult population was clinically overweight or obese helping to explain high rates of heart disease. Blood-pressure rates are especially high in the north and the west Midlands.

If the age-structure of the population has changed totally as a result of medical advances, so too have many aspects of people's lives. Contraceptive developments have dramatically increased the ability of women to control their own fertility and have played a major role in the emancipation of women, as well as in the 'sexual revolution', a change in general sexual norms, from the 1960s on. After 1921, when Marie Stopes founded the Society for Constructive Birth Control, it became increasingly acceptable socially for women to control their own fertility. The number of legal abortions in the United Kingdom reached a peak of 184,000 in 1990. Contraceptives are now widely available. The fertility of the approximately 20 per cent of couples who are infertile is changing thanks to new techniques such as *in vitro* fertilisation. Though AIDS (Acquired Immune Deficiency Syndrome) has developed as a new killer, leading to an emphasis on 'safe sex', antibiotics have dealt with most other sexually transmitted diseases. Pain is increasingly held at bay by more effective and selective painkillers, bringing relief to millions suffering from illnesses such as arthritis and muscular pain. Thus the condition of the people has really changed. They are healthier and longer-living. Nutrition has improved considerably, average height has increased for both men and women, and the country is affluent and health-conscious enough to emphasise the newly perceived problem of the overweight.

ECONOMIC PROBLEMS

Yet the modern age is also a period when Britain's relative economic performance has declined appreciably by comparison with
traditional and new competitors. Between 1960 and 1981 Britain's
annual growth in gross domestic product was lower than that of all
the other eighteen OECD countries. The average standard of living
fell beneath that of Germany, Japan, France and Italy in the post–
1960 period. There were serious problems with under-investment,
low industrial productivity, limited innovation, poor management
and obstructive trade unions. A sense of decline, pervasive at times,
was especially characteristic in the 1970s. The cover of the satirical
magazine *Private Eye* on 10 January 1975 showed the oil-rich king
of Saudi Arabia then visiting London, with the caption 'Britain
Sold Shock. New Man at Palace'. Ironically, the discovery of oil in
the North Sea in 1970 and its production from 1975 was to help
ease Britain's balance-of-payments problem, though it did not
prevent continued economic decline relative to competitors who
lacked that resource. By seeking, first informally and in 1990–2
formally through the European Monetary System, a fixed exchange
rate with the currency of the strongest European economy, Germany, British policy-makers surrendered the initiative over economic management and saw punishingly high interest rates, and in
September 1992 it proved impossible to sustain the policy. Britain
had to leave the system.

   In addition, longer-term structural changes in the British and
world economies created major problems, particularly widespread
unemployment (often to over 2 million and at times over 3 million
during the last fifteen years), a decline in manufacturing, particularly heavy manufacturing, industry with associated regional problems, and difficulties in maintaining a stable currency. For
example, the coal industry in mid-Glamorgan, which had employed
52,000 in 1947, provided jobs for fewer than 1,000 in 1992. The
postwar commitment to full employment was not met, and was
increasingly regarded as unrealistic.

   These problems interacted with aspects of the 'political economy', not least the rising power of trade unions with their generally
perceived determination to put sectional interests first, the conviction of politicians that they could improve the economy and a
variety of interventionist policies that have generally not had this

result. Trade union membership rose from 1½ million in 1895 to 13 million in 1978. The Union leaders such as Ernest Bevin, General Secretary of the Transport and General Workers Union 1921–40, Walter Citrine, Jack Jones, General Secretary of the Transport and General Workers Union 1968–78, and Hugh Scanlon, the engineers' leader, wielded great influence from the late 1930s until the Conservatives came to power in 1979. They played key roles in what was a corporatist state. During the Second World War, despite strikes, labour relations were far better than in the earlier world war and the institutional freedom of the unions was preserved alongside central planning and wage restraint. The postwar Labour government realised many of the unions' political aims, including nationalisation of much of industry (coal, steel, railways), universal statutory social services and the goal of full employment, and a wages policy was maintained until 1950. The unions' refusal to continue the wages policy helped lose Labour the general election in 1951, although it won more votes than the Conservatives (who won more seats in Parliament). In 1974 Jones forged a social compact (generally known as the social contract) with the Labour government of Harold Wilson (Prime Minister 1964–70, 74–6): the unions were to moderate wage demands in return for an acceptable legislative programme.

Relations between the unions and Conservative governments were more acrimonious, not least because political differences were matched by an absence of common assumptions, experiences and history. Strikes by the National Union of Miners, some of whose leaders were motivated by political hostility, defeated the Conservative government of Edward Heath in 1972 and, crucially, 1974; the strike in 1984–5 was only beaten by the government of the determined Margaret Thatcher after a long struggle, and then in part because the miners were divided and the weather good. In the 1970s, thanks to television and power cuts, people became accustomed respectively to the immediacy of picket-line violence and to taking baths in the dark.

Trade-union power and economic problems helped to discredit the postwar social democratic consensus, particularly the notion of the planned, corporatist state, and to lead to a reaction in the form of 'Thatcherism'. Unions engaged in wasteful demarcation disputes and many shop stewards adopted the language and attitudes of class warfare and economic conflict. A 'winter of discontent' in

1978–9, with strikes by hospital ancillary staff, ambulancemen and others in which 'secondary picketing' (disrupting work at concerns not otherwise involved in the dispute) had played a major and disruptive role, helped Mrs Thatcher to victory in 1979. She had little time for discussions with trade-union leaders, believing that they played too large a role in the economy, and she secured legislation to limit their powers, a task that Wilson had failed to achieve in 1969 when the bill based on the 'In place of strife' white paper (proposed legislation) was withdrawn due to trade-union and Labour-party opposition. Wilson told Scanlon, to 'get your tanks off my front lawn', but he could not control the unions. Under Thatcher, picketing and secondary strike action were greatly limited, pre-entry closed shops largely abolished, and unions forced to ballot members by post before strikes were called. Fixed-term contracts for employees became more common. In the late 1980s trade-union militancy became less common, and the level of industrial action (strikes) continued to fall in the early 1990s. By 1990 only 48 per cent of employees were union members and the number covered by closed-shop agreements had fallen to ½ million, compared to 4½ million a decade earlier. Trade-union membership fell to 7.3 million by January 1994. Far more wage negotiations were at a local level, there were fewer demarcation disputes and the spread of 'single-union agreements' eased industrial tension. Thanks to privatisation in the 1980s and early 1990s, fewer trade unionists are the employees of state-owned companies. Mrs Thatcher found it harder, however, to foster and manage economic growth.

Aside from difficulties with the unions, there has also been a lack of continuity in economic policy, for example over regional aid. The steel industry was nationalised in 1949 and 1967, and privatised in 1953 and then again after 1979, this time alongside gas, electricity, telephones, water and much else, as the Conservatives under Mrs Thatcher, and then (from 1990) John Major, strove to diminish the role of the state and to revive economic liberalism. Their success was limited: in 1995 one in five of the British workforce was still employed in the public sector. Despite the pursuit of a variety of economic policies since the Second World War, economic growth has not matched political expectations, leading to disagreement over expenditure priorities. A major increase in government expenditure and employment since 1914 has increased the importance of these disputes. The national budget has been unable to sustain the assumptions and demands of politicians on behalf of, for example, social welfare and defence. Thus, the devaluation of the pound by 30.5 per cent in 1949 was followed by public-expenditure cuts, leading to the introduction of prescription charges, and resignations by left-wing Labour ministers, especially Aneurin Bevan and Harold Wilson. Alongside the often unsuccessful management of the economy by politicians, notably the delay until 1967 by the Wilson government in devaluing sterling, there was also at times a serious neglect of aspects of the economy, symbolised by the remark of Sir Alec Douglas-Home, who renounced his earldom to become Conservative Prime Minister (1963–4), that his grasp of economics was of the 'matchstick variety'. Poor economic management and trade-union power, which thwarted the connection between high unemployment and low inflation, were in part to blame for high rates of inflation, which rose to an annual average of 15.8 per cent in 1972–5, and for the subsequent need to turn for assistance to foreign sources of finance, in the shape of the International Monetary Fund (1976). All postwar premiers, with the possible exception of James Callaghan (Labour, 1976–9), probably spent too much time on foreign policy and certainly found it difficult to abandon the expensive habit of seeing Britain as a major international player.

POLITICAL CULTURES

Higher living standards and an overall rate of economic growth are scant consolation to those with diminished experiences and disappointed expectations. And yet a striking feature of the domestic and international problems that Britain has encountered is that they have not led to a consistent or massive radicalisation of British politics. There have been exceptions. Strathclyde's militancy led to it being termed 'Red Clydeside' from the mid-1910s, and unrest there in 1919 led to tanks on Glasgow's streets. The British Communist Party was formed in 1920, and there was a general strike in support of the already striking coal miners in 1926. The 1930s saw the formation by Sir Oswald Mosley of the New Party, which subsequently evolved into the British Union of Fascists. Mosley, who had been successively a Conservative, Independent and then Labour MP, was a would-be dictator whose changing views revolved around a fixed point of belief in himself. He deliberately staged marches by his paramilitary Blackshirts in areas of Jewish settlement, particularly the East End of London and Manchester, in order to provoke violence. Mosley was discredited by his demagoguery, violence and links with Nazi Germany, and was imprisoned during the Second World War.

Some writers of the period expressed the fear that sinister conspiracies lay behind political and industrial problems, although this was only true to a very limited extent. This was the theme of the popular adventure novel *Bulldog Drummond* (1921) by 'Sapper' (Lieutenant-Colonel H. C. McNeile). John Buchan (1875–1940), a Scottish writer who served in intelligence during the First World War before becoming an MP and Governor-General of Canada, discerned in his popular adventure novel, *The Three Hostages* (1924), 'wreckers on the grand scale, merchants of pessimism, giving society another kick downhill whenever it had a chance of finding its balance, and then pocketing their profits . . . they used the fanatics . . . whose key was a wild hatred of something or other, or a reasoned belief in anarchy'. In *The Big Four* (1927) by the detective writer Agatha Christie (1890–1976), the best-selling author of all time, 'The world-wide unrest, the labour troubles that beset every nation, and the revolutions that break out in some . . . there is a force behind the scenes which aims at nothing less than the disintegration of civilisation'. Technology was at the service of this force: 'a concentration of wireless energy far beyond anything so far attempted, and capable of focusing a beam of great intensity upon some given spot . . . atomic energy', so that the Big Four could become 'the dictators of the world'. Such sinister threats facing Britain were to become a staple of spy thrillers, as in the novels of the former spy Ian Fleming (1908–64), beginning with *Casino Royale* (1952). Adventure stories, many of which testified to the imaginative potency of the new technology, Fleming's series of James Bond thrillers also revealed a sense of the nation under threat, an imaginative extension of the challenges facing the country.

Yet radicalism was to make little impact in Britain and the continuity of parliamentary government was not overthrown. Arguably the most successful radicals were the suffragettes. The largely peaceful general strike was defeated by the firmness of the Baldwin government and the resulting lack of nerve of the Trade-union leadership, and the combined total membership of the communists and the fascists never exceeded 38,000. The economic upturn of 1934 stemmed rising support for Mosley. Despite their subsequent reputation, far more Cambridge undergraduates of the 1930s were interested in sport than in communist activism.

The limited extent of radicalism was even more true after the Second World War. Nazi activities discredited the extreme right, while the policies and eventual failure of the Soviet Union struck successive blows at the credibility of the far left. Harry Pollitt, General Secretary of the British Communist Party 1929–56, became disillusioned with the stalinism he had served so faithfully after Krushchev's revelations about its nature. In 1968 the Communist Party of Great Britain condemned the Soviet invasion of Czechoslovakia. The Labour Party drifted to the left in the 1970s and was affected by 'entryism' by far-left groups, so that there was little to choose in the 1980s between the views of some Labour MPs and western European communists. Yet this helped to lead to four successive Labour defeats in the general elections of 1979, 1983, 1987 and 1992, the most unimpressive record of any major political party since the decline of the Liberals after the First World War, and one that was achieved despite serious economic difficulties for Conservative governments at the beginning of the 1980s and before the 1992 election. The attempt to create a collectivist society by means of state action, a new-model society planned in accordance with socialist principles, was rejected by the electorate, and in the late 1980s and early 1990s by the Labour Party itself under the leadership of Neil Kinnock (1987–92), John Smith (1992–94) and, from 1994, Tony Blair. The rising popularity of the party under Blair was directly linked to the espousal of policies deemed moderate. Similarly, successive public opinion polls in the 1980s and early 1990s revealed limited support for much of the agenda of the 'new right', with its emphasis on self-reliance and a limited role for the state and, instead, there was clear popular support for the welfare state, especially the National Health Service. The recessions of the early 1980s and early 1990s did not lead to a revival of left-wing radicalism, and the circulation of the communist daily newspaper, the *Morning Star*, fell below 10,000.

The relationship between the lack of sustained military defeat abroad and the absence of a successful challenge to the political system, or at least a major transformation of it, is unclear but suggestive. Germany, Japan, France, Italy and Austria all suffered serious defeat in the First and/or Second World Wars, leading to a political and institutional transformation which has been as important for the subsequent success of most of those societies as the rebuilding of economic systems on which attention is usually focused. No such process has taken place in Britain. Indeed, in several respects the essential features of the political system are still those of before 1914, a hereditary monarchy with limited, essentially consultative powers, albeit one that adopted the British name of Windsor in 1917 in place of that of Saxe-Coburg and Gotha, a bicameral Parliament, with the House of Commons being the most powerful and only elected chamber, national political parties with recognisably different regional and social bases of support, a largely two-party system, an absence of proportional representation, and a centralised British state without regional assemblies, or, still less, devolved or independent parliaments for Scotland and Wales. Britain remains in some respects an elective dictatorship, with the Prime Minister enjoying great power as head of both the executive and the leading party in the legislature, and national leader of that party. The social system is still markedly inegalitarian, and the political system, the civil service, the armed forces, the professions, the banking system, large companies and the universities are disproportionately dominated by those whose background cannot be described as working class. The Conservatives stressed the modest origins and difficult upbringing of John Major, Prime Minister from 1990, but neither circumstance is true of the bulk of his cabinet and parliamentary colleagues.

IRISH INDEPENDENCE

And yet, there have also been major changes, which can be summarised under the headings of Ireland, Empire, Europe and democratisation. War tore the guts out of the British empire, weakening it in resources and morale. The first major loss was Ireland. Half a million men of Irish descent, both Protestant and Catholic, volunteered to fight for King George V in 1914; fewer than 2,000 rose in the Easter Rising of 1916 in Dublin, an unsuccessful attempt to create an independent Irish Republic. The numerous soldiers' wives of Dublin, when informed by the rebels that the establishment of a republic meant that the payment of separation allowances had now ended, responded not with nationalist enthusiasm but with anger. Outside Dublin the planned nationalist uprising failed to materialise. The firm British response, however, served to radicalise Irish public opinion. Martial law was declared and a series of trials, executions and internments provided martyrs for the nationalist cause. In the 1918 general election 73 out of the 105 Irish parliamentary seats were won by the Sinn Fein party, nationalists under Eamonn de Valera, who refused to attend Westminster and demanded independence. They rejected the policy of 'home rule within the empire' which John Redmond (1856–1918), the leading prewar Irish politician, had supported and which had been the basis of the Home Rule Act in 1914. Redmond's brother, a home-rule MP, had died fighting for George V in the First World War.

Instead, in January 1919, a unilateral declaration of independence was issued by a new national assembly (Dáil Eireann) and the nationalist Irish Volunteers, soon to rename themselves the Irish Republican Army (IRA), staged their first fatal ambush. British refusal to accept independence led to a brutal civil war in 1919–21, followed by the Anglo-Irish Treaty of December 1921, which brought partition and effective independence for the new Irish Free State, which governed most of the island. The Irish Free State became a self-governing dominion within the British empire with a Governor-General appointed by the Crown. The Protestant unionists of the north refused to accept this and six out of the nine counties of Ulster opted out and became Northern Ireland, which remained part of the United Kingdom and was represented at Westminster by twelve MPs (increased after 1979 to seventeen). It was self-governed and became very much a Protestant state, its Catholic minority claiming to suffer discrimination, although the extent of this is controversial and claims that Catholics were worse treated in the allocation of public housing have been challenged. The partition was opposed by much of the IRA, which mounted a terrorist campaign in Ulster in 1921 and fought the newly independent government in the south in 1922–3, the latter a more bloody conflict than the so-called War of Independence. The IRA was beaten in both Ulster and the Irish Free State: IRA terrorism led to a vigorous response from the Irish government which executed 77 rebels and imprisoned 12,000. Thereafter IRA terrorism remained a minor irritant, in both north and south, until the late 1960s.

De Valera, who had been leader of Sinn Fein in 1917–26 and had rejected the Anglo-Irish treaty in 1921, won the 1932 election with the Fianna Fáil party he had founded in 1926, and was, thereafter, President of the Executive Council (1932–7), Prime Minister (1937–48, 1951–4, 1957–9) and President (1959–73). Much of the IRA was willing to accept his leadership and, indeed, he took some of its members into the government and the police. Others, however, wished to fight on for a united Ireland and this led them into conflict with De Valera, not least when they raided army bases, in order to gain arms, and took money and arms from Hitler. De Valera responded with imprisonment and executions, and, like the British government in Northern Ireland in the early 1980s, faced IRA hunger-strikers. He was unwilling to fight to push Ireland's territorial claim to Northern Ireland, although it was expressed in the 1937 constitution. Under that constitution the oath of allegiance to the Crown that MPs had been obliged to take under the Anglo-Irish treaty of 1921 was abolished. Vestigial British authority was extinguished by the Republic of Ireland Act (1948).

The IRA terrorist campaign of 1958–62 in Northern Ireland had no success, but, later in the decade, a civil rights movement essentially complaining about the position of Catholics led to a harsh and insensitive response and to violence, resulting in the intervention of British troops (1969) and the suspension of the Unionist regional government and its replacement by direct rule from London (1972). By September 1992 3,000 people had died in the 'troubles', many as a result of terrorism by the IRA, though with an increasing number killed by Protestant paramilitary groups determined that Ulster should remain part of the United Kingdom. IRA terrorism on the British mainland began in 1973, included attacks on the Conservative Party conference at Brighton (1984), and the cabinet (1991), and led to the deaths of three Conservative MPs.

THE FIRST WORLD WAR, 1914–18

The loss of Ireland revealed the weakness of the British empire when confronted by a powerful nationalist movement. The First

World War, in which Britain had played a major role on the victorious side, mobilising her resources of people and wealth as never before, was, however, followed by the expansion of the British empire to its greatest extent. The war began with pistol shots in Sarajevo, the assassination by Serbian terrorists of Archduke Franz Ferdinand, the heir to the Austro-Hungarian empire; it pitted a large coalition, in which Britain, France, Russia and, from 1917, the USA were the major powers, against Germany, Austria-Hungary, Bulgaria and Turkey.

The German invasion of Belgium, as a means to out-flank French forces, led Britain, which had guaranteed Belgian neutrality, to declare war on 4 August 1914. The German drive, first on Paris and then on the Channel ports, was thwarted, and late in 1914 both sides dug in across north-eastern France on Germany's 'western front'. The concentration of large forces in a relatively small area, the defensive strength of trench positions (particularly thanks to the machine gun) and the difficulty of making substantial gains even if opposing lines were breached, ensured that, until the collapse of the German position in the last weeks of the year, the situation was essentially deadlocked. British attacks, as at Neuve-Chapelle and Loos (1915), the Somme (1916), and Arras and Passchendaele (1917), led to unprecedentedly enormous losses of men with little gain of territory. Scottish losses were disproportionately high: 10 per cent of male Scots between 16 and 50, one in six of the imperial war dead. The war witnessed virulent patriotism in Britain, but the discontent of many soldiers with the situation led to thousands of court martials, while shell-shock affected large numbers. Some war poets produced bitter criticisms, though such views found no echo in public opinion or in the inscriptions on the numerous war memorials erected after the conflict. The unimaginative nature of British generalship, with its strategy of attrition, did not help. Douglas Haig, who was appointed to the command of the British army in France in December 1915, believed that the war would be won on the battlefield, and by determined leadership, superior morale and offensive operations. He saw the British as a chosen race who would be purified by victory. Haig had an anachronistic obsession with the potential of cavalry. In fact, though the blocking of German offensives in 1914, 1916 and 1918 were essential preconditions of victory, the war was in part won as a result of the collapse of Austria-Hungary and the exacerbation of the military, economic and domestic problems facing the Germans which destroyed their will to fight.

The western front dominated British strategy, not least because of concern about French stability, and was responsible for most of their 750,000 dead. There were also attempts to search out a weaker front and to strike at Germany's allies. These led to the disastrous expedition to the Dardanelles (1915), whose forceful advocate, the energetic First Lord of the Admiralty, Winston Churchill, resigned, and to failures in Iraq (1916) and at Salonika (1916), but also to Allenby's successful campaign in Palestine (1917–18). The German colonies were overrun. The threat from the German surface fleet was blocked at the indecisive battle of Jutland (1916), but their submarines took a heavy toll of British merchant shipping, until their impact was lessened by the use of convoys and the entry of America. The scale and duration of the struggle led to an unprecedented mobilisation of national resources, including, after over 2 million men had already volunteered to fight for king and country, the introduction of conscription (1916), and state direction of much of the economy. The war gave a tremendous boost to the role of the state and the machinery of government. The Cabinet Office was created in 1916. The allocation of resources by the new Ministry of Food led to a rise in civilian living standards and an improvement in the life expectancy of those of the worst-off sections of the prewar working class who were exempt from war service. State regulation increased in all spheres. The nature of rural socio-economic relationships was changed in 1917 with the introduction of statutory agricultural wage boards and control of agricultural rents.

The defeat of the German empire meant that its place in the sun was distributed among the victors, Britain gaining League of Nations mandates for Tanganyika, part of Togo and a sliver of the Cameroons, all in Africa, and Nauru Island in the Pacific. War with Germany's ally Turkey led to the annexation of Cyprus and Egypt (1914), and the gaining of mandates over Palestine, Transjordan and Iraq when Turkey's empire was partitioned at the end of the war. Ardent imperialists, such as Lord Milner and Leo Amery, pressed for the strengthening of the empire, partly in the hope that this would mean that Britain need never again be dragged into the continental mire. British influence increased in both Persia and Turkey, and British forces, operating against the communists in the Russian civil war that followed their coup in 1917, moved into the Caucasus, Central Asia, and the White Sea region and were deployed in the Baltic and the Black Sea. Lord Curzon, Foreign Secretary in 1919, suggested the annexation of parts of the Russian empire.

THE POLITICS OF THE 1920s

This high tide of empire was to ebb very fast. The strain of the First World War, the vast number of men lost, the money spent, the exhaustion produced by constant effort, left Britain unable to sustain her international ambitions, and this was exacerbated by political division. Lloyd George had split the Liberal Party when, in order to bring more decisive war leadership and further his own ambition, he had replaced Asquith as Prime Minister at the end of 1916, and he was dependent on Conservative support, a measure that strained postwar Tory unity. Thus, despite the major role that Britain played in the making of the Versailles Peace Treaty (1919) and Lloyd George's strutting on the global stage, there was an absence of stable leadership. In 1922 there was a Conservative revolt from below, by backbenchers, junior ministers and constituency activists: a meeting of the parliamentary Conservative Party at the Carlton Club, led to the decision to abandon the coalition. Lloyd George now fell, but so too did the Conservative leader Austen Chamberlain, who had sought continued support for the coalition. The new leader, Andrew Bonar Law (Prime Minister 1922–3), formed a totally Conservative government, and easily won the 1922 general election. Far from having broken the mould of British politics, Lloyd George was consigned to the political wilderness. When he had had power, he had been unwilling to support electoral reform, the proportional representation that would have helped the Liberals in the 1920s, and once out of power he certainly could not obtain such a change.

Liberal disunity helped in the rise of Labour, which became the official opposition after the 1922 election. The number of Labour MPs rose from 29 in 1906 to 288 in 1929. Its trade-union alliance allowed Labour to identify itself as the natural party of the working class and thus to benefit from the extension of the franchise, and the doubling of trade-union membership from 4 million in 1914 to 8 million in 1920. The party constitution of 1918 consolidated male trade-union domination of Labour. Liberalism survived best in areas such as Cornwall where trade unions were weak. The 1918 Reform Act gave the vote to men over 21 fulfilling a six-months residence qualification and to women over 30, increasing the electorate from 8 to 21 million. A Redistribution Act was based on the principle of equal size of constituency electorates, but the opportunity to introduce proportional representation was lost. The new electorate was not interested in such prewar Liberal Nonconformist causes as the disestablishment of the Church of England, the temperance movement and church schools.

The new larger electorate was potentially volatile, and winning its support posed a considerable challenge to politicians, similar to that which confronted Disraeli and Gladstone. Politics became more professional: the management of constituencies and political parties more a matter of full-time activity. Under Stanley Baldwin, Conservative leader 1923–37 and Prime Minister 1923–4, 1924–9 and 1935–7, the media were harnessed to create a political image for a mass electorate. Baldwin 're-packaged' himself energetically for the voters, and during the general strike of 1926 he used the *British Gazette* to spread government views.

The complex manoeuvres of three-party politics led to minority Labour governments under Ramsay MacDonald in 1924 and 1929–31, but the second was badly affected by the world economic crisis that began in 1929; it divided over the cuts that were believed necessary to balance the budget in order to restore confidence in sterling. A cut in unemployment benefit was rejected by the Trade Union Congress (TUC) and the bulk of the Labour Party, but MacDonald and a few supporters joined the Conservatives and some Liberals in forming a National Government which continued in power until the wartime coalition was formed in 1940. MacDonald was succeeded by Baldwin (1935) and Neville Chamberlain (1937), and the government won the general elections of 1931 and 1935. Labour lost working-class voters as a result of the economic problems of 1929–31, while the Conservatives benefited from the economic upturn of 1934 and from the consolidation of propertied and business interests into one anti-socialist party.

The 1920s were a period in which British governments drew in their horns. At home spending was cut, the 'Geddes Axe' – report of the Geddes committee (1922) – making cuts in education, housing and the armed forces. The homes that had been promised to those 'heroes' who had survived the mud and machine guns of the Somme and Passchendaele, and the other mass graves of humanity on the western front, were not all built, as the financial austerity of the Treasury thwarted some of the aspirations of the 1919 Housing Act. As Chancellor of the Exchequer (1924–9), Churchill, who had left the Liberals for the Conservatives in 1924, cut taxes and in 1925 put Britain back on the gold standard at the prewar rate with the dollar. This over-valued the pound, hit exports and harmed manufacturing. Britain had to abandon the gold standard in 1931 and the pound then dropped rapidly against the dollar.

The loss of most of Ireland in 1921 was not followed by any further reduction of cohesion within the British Isles. The Labour government failed to deliver on hopes of Scottish home rule in 1924 and elements in the Scottish Home Rule Association began to think that a national party would be more effective. The National Party of Scotland, founded in 1928, and the Scottish Self-Government Party, founded in 1932, united in 1934 to form the Scottish National Party, but it did not win a parliamentary seat until 1945.

Abroad, intervention in Russia against the communists had been a failure and was abandoned in 1919. In the Middle East, revolts in Egypt (1919) and Iraq (1920–1) led to Britain granting their independence in 1922 and 1924 respectively, while British influence collapsed in Persia (1921), and the British backed down in their confrontation with Turkey (1922–3), the last being a crucial factor in Lloyd George's fall. Unable to maintain Ireland or their extra-European pretensions in the 1920s, the British were also to fail to sustain the Versailles settlement in Europe and the League of Nations outside it. These failures were a consequence of what had already been obvious in the decades prior to the First World War: the problems created by the rise of other states and Britain's global commitments, and the particular strains that arose from that conflict and from subsequent developments. There was a lack of resources and will to sustain schemes for imperial expansion.

EMPIRE IN THE 1930s

And yet the empire was still very much a living reality in the interwar period. In some respects links developed further, a process given concrete form in the majestic buildings designed by Sir Edwin

Lutyens and Sir Herbert Baker for the official quarter in New Delhi, from where India was governed, and finished in the 1930s. Economic links between Britain and empire became closer. Imperial Airways, a company founded with government support (1924), produced new routes for the empire. Weekly services began to Cape Town (1932), Brisbane (1934) and Hong Kong (1936); in contrast, thanks to the problem of flying the Atlantic, they only began to New York in 1946. It took nine days to fly to Cape Town in 1936, and fourteen to Adelaide, but these were far less than sailing times. Commitment to the empire was demonstrated in a different form by the building of a major new naval base for the defence of the Far East at Singapore. Empire Day was important in the 1920s and 1930s.

The empire faced serious problems in the 1930s, not least pressure from the Indian National Congress and serious disturbances in Palestine, where there was violent Arab opposition to Jewish immigration. As with Ireland in 1914, it is not clear what would have happened in India had there not been war. The Government of India Act (1935), was bitterly opposed by Conservatives such as Churchill, who saw its moves towards self-government as a step towards the abandonment of empire, but was designed to ensure the British retention of the substance of power; however the provincial elections of 1937 were a success for Congress. Nevertheless, it was the Second World War that undermined the empire, even as it brought the British occupation of a little more territory, Somaliland and Libya, both formerly Italian, and led Churchill to consider the annexation of the latter, a move the American government successfully opposed.

THE SECOND WORLD WAR, 1939–45

The Second World War cost fewer British lives than the First, and the British army was spared from being put through the mangle of the trenches, but in several respects it was much more close-run for Britain. As in 1914, she went to war to resist German aggression and to fulfil the logic of her alliance politics, but in 1939–40 Hitler's Germany destroyed the system of British alliances. The eastern front was ended within weeks as Poland was defeated (1939), Stalin's Russia taking its share after it also had attacked Poland;

while the western front was rolled up in a German *blitzkrieg* that overran the Netherlands, Belgium and France and brutally exposed the military failure of the Anglo-French alliance (1940). Expelled from the Continent – though able by bravery, skill and luck to save much of the army in the evacuation from Dunkirk – Britain had the valuable support of its empire and control of the sea, but the first was challenged by Japan and the last by the potent threat of German airpower and still more by German U-boats (submarines). She appeared to have lost the war, and it is not surprising that several major politicians were willing to consider a negotiated peace with Hitler. In May 1940, Viscount Halifax, the Foreign Secretary, was ready, if Hitler made one, 'to accept an offer which would save the country from avoidable disaster', although it was clear from Hitler's conduct that he could not be trusted to respect any agreement. The occupation of the Channel Isles by vastly superior German forces in 1940 was followed there by compromise and collaboration and very little active resistance, not that the latter was practical. Hesitation in Britain was ended by the replacement of Neville Chamberlain, a Prime Minister identified with the appeasement of Germany in the late 1930s and with failure in war, by the egotistical but effective Churchill (1940). Churchill had warned about the dangers posed by Hitler long before the outbreak of war and had criticised appeasement. Convinced of the total rightness of the British cause and the utter untrustworthiness of Hitler, he was determined to fight on, however bleak the situation might be. He pinned his hopes on bringing the United States into the war. The blunting of German airpower in the Battle of Britain led Hitler to call off Operation Sealion, his planned invasion of Britain (1940), but British successes against the Italians in North Africa that winter were followed in 1941 by a German offensive there and by their conquest of Yugoslavia and Greece, the latter entailing the defeat of British forces in Greece and Crete.

The loss of Crete in May 1941 was the last major defeat for an isolated Britain. Hitherto her European allies had offered little as London had become a collecting house for governments in exile. The German assault on Russia (June 1941) and the Japanese attack on Britain and the United States, followed by the declaration of war on the Americans by Japan's ally Germany (December 1941), totally altered the situation. There were still to be serious blows, especially in early 1942, and the Battle of the Atlantic against U-boats was not won until early 1943, but Britain was now part of an alliance system, linked to the strongest economy and financial power in the world, and, as Britain and her new allies successfully blunted German and Japanese offensives in late 1942, the long and stony path to victory appeared clearer: the Russian victory at Stalingrad was crucial. In May 1943 the Germans surrendered in North Africa. In September 1943 the British and the Americans landed in Italy, and Italy surrendered unconditionally. The following June Anglo-American forces landed in Normandy and in May 1945 the Germans surrendered. As with the last campaigns against Napoleon, Russian strength had played a crucial role, but the Anglo-American achievement had also been considerable, not least because they were also bearing the brunt of the war with Japan, a conflict that ended with Japanese surrender in August 1945 just a few days after the dropping of American atom bombs. Nuclear weapons were the most spectacular application of technology to warfare, but in both world wars British technology, especially in metallurgy and electronics, had made major contributions to advances in weaponry, not least tanks in the First World War and radar in the Second.

THE LOSS OF EMPIRE

The war had fatally weakened the empire. Britain had lost prestige and resources, her dominion allies, especially Australia, had had to look to America for support, and there was a loss of confidence within Britain in the legacy of the past. The surrender of 'impregnable' Singapore to the Japanese on 15 February 1942, after a poorly conducted campaign in Malaya and the loss of the *Prince of Wales* and the *Repulse* to Japanese bombers, was either the most humiliating defeat in modern British history, or one to rank with Cornwallis's surrender at Yorktown in 1781. Cornwallis's army had marched out to the tune of 'The World Turned Upside Down', and its surrender had led directly to the loss of the American empire. The surrender of Singapore destroyed British prestige in Asia. Combined with the need for Indian support in the war against advancing Japanese forces, it spelled the end of empire in the Indian subcontinent, the heart of the British imperial experience. In 1942 the Congress Party was offered independence after the war in return for support during it, an offer that it spurned with its 'Quit India' movement. The Labour Party, which first and unexpectedly became a majority government in 1945 as a result of a reaction against the Conservatives as the party of privilege and prewar division and in favour of the collectivism and social welfare offered by Labour, was committed to Indian independence and this was achieved in 1947, though at the cost of partition and large numbers of deaths in Hindu–Muslim clashes.

Despite Indian independence, that of Burma (1949), and the ending of the Palestine mandate in 1948, Britain was still a major imperial power and the Labour government, especially its Foreign Secretary Ernest Bevin (1945–51), had high hopes of using imperial resources, particularly those of Africa, to strengthen the British economy and make her a less unequal partner in the Anglo-American partnership. Wartime conscription was continued. Bevin acted in a lordly fashion in the Middle East, but empire ran out in the sands of rising Arab nationalism and a lack of British resources, leading to a succession of crises starting with that in 1947 over sterling convertibility. The British faced a number of imperial problems in the early 1950s, including the Malayan Emergency (a communist uprising, which was tackled successfully), but it was the Suez Crisis of 1956, an attempt to destabilise the aggressive Arab nationalist regime of Gamul Abdul Nasser in Egypt, that exposed clearly their weakness.

Just as echoes of the appeasement of dictators in the 1930s were initially to be voiced when the Argentinians invaded the Falklands in 1982 and it was misleadingly thought that the British government would not respond, so in 1956 the Prime Minister, Anthony Eden (1955–7), who had resigned as Foreign Secretary in 1938 in protest at appeasement, was determined not to repeat its mistakes and accept Nasser's nationalisation of the Suez Canal. Secretly acting in concert with France and Israel, Eden sent British forces to occupy the Canal Zone. The invasion was poorly planned, but it was American opposition and its impact on sterling that was crucial to weakening British resolve and thus leading to a humiliating withdrawal.

A lack of American support has been seen by some historians as a major problem for the empire ever since the Second World War; in 1956 American anger made Britain's dependent status obvious. However, once the 'Cold War' with the Soviet Union began, the

Americans sought to sustain Britain's role as a world power. They were interested in preserving many of Britain's overseas bases, either to maintain Britain's utility as an ally or to have them ready for American use. Nor did they want premature decolonisation to result in chaos and perhaps communism. The Americans supported the continued British presence east of Suez in the 1960s and in the Suez Crisis itself saw themselves as rescuing a friend from a fit of madness. They sought to persuade Arab, Asian and African opinion that the USA was anti-imperialist in order to reduce the danger of Soviet exploitation of Suez, and of further Afro-Asian alienation from the West.

The fourteen years after Suez saw the rapid loss of most of the rest of the British empire. The British people might not have been European-minded after 1950; but neither were they imperial-minded, and after Suez many leading Conservatives, especially Harold Macmillan, Prime Minister 1957–63, and Iain Macleod, whom he appointed Colonial Secretary, became deeply disillusioned with the Empire and ready to dismantle it, a process that was hastened by colonial nationalist movements, though criticised by some right-wing Conservatives. Anticolonialism, however, was also a minority view. Empire was proving too expensive, too troublesome, and too provocative of other powers. Although in 1964 Wilson foolishly declared, 'We are a world power and a world influence or we are nothing', by 1969 none of Africa remained under British rule, and the east of Suez defence policy, supported by both Labour and the Conservatives, had fallen victim to the consequences of the devaluation of sterling in 1967. British forces withdrew from Singapore in 1971. Decolonisation was largely peaceful.

BRITAIN AND THE WORLD SINCE 1945

Britain's status as a major power was no longer territorial, no longer a consequence of empire, let alone economic strength, but rather a consequence of her being, from 1952, one of the few atomic powers, and of her active membership, both in American-led international organisations, especially NATO (the North Atlantic Treaty Organization of which she was a founder member in 1949) and, from the 1970s, in the EEC (European Economic Community), which she eventually joined in 1973.

NATO was designed to defend western Europe against the Soviet Union, for the defeat of Germany in the Second World War was followed by fears of Soviet plans and by a Cold War that lasted until the collapse of the Soviet Union in 1989. Already in mid-1944 planners for the Chiefs of Staff were suggesting a postwar reform of Germany and Japan so that they could play a role against a Soviet Union whose ambitions in eastern Europe were arousing growing concern. On 14 March 1946 the British embassy in Moscow asked if the world was now 'faced with the danger of the modern equivalent of the religious wars of the sixteenth century' with Soviet communism battling against western social democracy and American capitalism for 'domination of the world'. Denied American expertise, by January 1947 Clement Attlee, Labour Prime Minister 1945–51, had decided to develop a British nuclear bomb; the first one was exploded in 1952. In 1947 Britain and the USA signed a secret treaty for co-operation in signals intelligence. The Berlin Crisis (1948) made clear the vulnerability of western Europe and furthered dependence on the United States. It led to the stationing of American B–29 strategic bombers in Britain. British forces played a major role in resisting communist aggression in the Korean War (1950–3). In 1951 the Chiefs of Staff warned that the Russians might be provoked by western rearmament into attacking in 1952. Under American pressure, Britain embarked on a costly rearmament programme in 1951 that undid many of the economic gains that had been made since 1948, and helped to strengthen the military commitment that has been such a heavy economic burden on postwar Britain. Defence spending has taken a higher percentage of gross national product than for other western European powers. The anti-Soviet political and strategic alignment was continued by subsequent governments, both Conservative (1951–64, 70–4, 79–) and Labour (1964–70, 74–9). From 1960 American nuclear submarines equipped with Polaris missiles began to operate from the Holy Loch in Scotland and, by the Nassau Agreement of 1962, Macmillan persuaded President Kennedy to provide Britain with Polaris, which offered Britain a small but survivable, and therefore a not insignificant, submarine-based strategic nuclear force. That year *Dr No*, the first of the James Bond adventure films, had the hero of the British secret service saving American missile tests. In the 1980s, despite the protests of the Campaign for Nuclear Disarmament, American Cruise missiles were deployed in Britain, and American bombers attacked Libya from British bases.

Empire was replaced by NATO, Commonwealth and Europe. The dominion status given to the 'white' colonies was a preliminary to the establishment of the British Commonwealth as an association of equal and autonomous partners (1931). In 1949 the prefix British was discarded and it was decided that republics might remain members, a measure that enabled India to stay in. The Commonwealth was seen for a time as a source of British influence, or as the basis for an international community spanning the divides between first and third worlds, white and black, and its unity was fostered by a secretariat, established in 1965, and by heads-of-government meetings. Relations with South Africa, immigration policies and the consequences of British concentration on Europe have all led to differences between Britain and Commonwealth partners, but the absence of common interests and views has been of greater significance. Economic, military and political links with former imperial possessions have become less important. New Zealand and, even more, Australia now look to Japan as an economic partner, while Canada is part of a free-trade zone with the United States and Mexico. America replaced Britain as Canada's biggest export market after the Second World War, and as the biggest source of foreign investment there from the 1920s. The British share of this investment fell from 85 per cent in 1900 to 15 per cent in 1960, while the American rose from 14 to 75. The percentage of the Australian and Canadian populations that can claim British descent has fallen appreciably since 1945. Britain had little role to play as the Pacific became an American lake. In 1951 Australia and New Zealand entered into a defence pact with the United States. In the mid-1970s members of the former old sterling area largely switched their foreign reserves from pounds to dollars.

BRITAIN AND AMERICA

The United States has in some respects served Britain as a surrogate for empire, providing crucial military, political, economic and cultural links, and offering an important model. Part of the attraction is ideological. The American stress on the free market has appealed to more groups in British society, not least to commercial interests, than have the more statist and bureaucratic continental societies. In the last quarter-century, Anglo-American links have slackened, not least because anglophilia has become less important in America and Britain has had less to offer in terms of any special relationship. On the other hand, particularly through the role of American programmes on British television, American or American-derived products in British consumer society, the American presence in the British economy and the more diffuse, but still very important, mystique of America as a land of wealth and excitement remains very important to Britain, especially to British culture, in the widest sense of the word. Not least for linguistic and, to a certain extent, commercial reasons, postwar American cultural 'hegemony' has been stronger in Britain than elsewhere in Europe, and has thus accentuated differences. The Atlanticism of the 1960s led to the creation of schools of English and American studies in new universities such as East Anglia and Sussex, separate from those of European studies. Few Victorians would have thought it sensible to study their literature and history within this sort of a context. British film audiences have for long been under the sway of Hollywood, and American influence on television has been considerable. When 'J. R.', the leading character in the television series Dallas, was shot, it was reported on the BBC news, the fictional world displacing its less exciting real counterpart. America is the largest market for popular music, a field in which Britain leads. America also plays a very major role in the British economy, especially in car manufacture, oil drilling and refining, and electronics. In 1986 58 per cent of the foreign-owned manufacturing firms in Wales had American parent companies.

BRITAIN AND EUROPE SINCE 1945

The postwar movement towards western European unity reflected the particular interests of the participant states. Britain did not share the concern of Italy and Germany to anchor their new democracies, nor the willingness of France to surrender a portion of her sovereignty in order to restrict German independence, and so she was not one of the founding members of the EEC. The different nature of British commerce and investment was also important. Joining the EEC would be far more disruptive for Britain than it was for the other states, because their trade was overwhelmingly Euro-centric, while less than half of Britain's trade was. Thus, joining entailed a major economic dislocation; which for a country whose foreign trade was so vital was bound to make her adjustment to membership more difficult.

It soon became clear, however, that the EEC was going to be a success, and the costs of staying out seemed greater than those of joining. As a result, successive governments, both Conservative and Labour, applied to join in 1961 and 1967, only to be rejected by the veto of the President of France, Charles De Gaulle, who argued that Britain's claim to a European identity was compromised by her American links. Ireland, which had planned to join with Britain, did not pursue membership. De Gaulle's departure and a fresh application in 1970, by the Conservative government under Edward Heath (1970–4), led to the successful negotiation of British entry. Britain joined in January 1973 (as did Ireland). Division over the issue led the next Labour government to hold the sole national referendum ever held. 67.2 per cent voted to remain in the EEC (1975), though voters' interest in and knowledge of the issues was limited and they were more influenced by the support for membership displayed by most politicians. The only areas showing a majority against staying in were the Shetlands and the Western Isles, although only 59 per cent of the Scots who voted supported membership. Protestant suspicion of continental Catholicism was probably responsible for the very low pro vote in Ulster. In contrast, smaller percentages voted for devolution for Scotland and Wales in 1979, although they included the majority of those who voted in Scotland in 1979. Under the terms of the devolution referendum, which required a majority of the electorate (as opposed to votes cast), Scotland would have failed to vote yes to EEC membership in 1975; while under the terms of the EEC referendum, Scotland voted yes to Labour's devolution proposals in 1979 by a not very different margin. Thus, the English and Welsh, but not the Scottish, electorate of the 1970s appeared to favour both membership of a European body with supra-national institutions, rationale and pretensions and the retention of the configuration of the traditional British nation-state.

Concern about the European dimension has grown as the limited objectives of most of the politicians who constructed the EEC have developed in more ambitious directions, with the call to create

stronger institutions, to transfer a considerable measure of authority, and thus sovereignty, from the nation-states. Changing nomen-
clature has registered the perception of new objectives. The
European Union has developed from being an economic organisation, the EEC has become the EU. In response, the nature and
defence of national sovereignty have become important issues and
there has been much debate about the meaning of sovereignty.

The 'duality of ocean and continent' in British foreign policy,
discerned by Montagu Burrows and by a later Oxford professor of
modern history, Richard Wernham, depended on the 'defence of
insularity' and 'the shield of sea power', but as these were torn
away, by first airpower and then nuclear weapons, it was necessary
to rethink totally Britain's strategic situation and policy. This was a
crucial component in Anglo-American relations during the decades
of defence from the 1940s to the late 1980s. This defence was not,
however, simply bilateral, but part of a strategy for the whole of
western Europe. The largest sector allocation in the defence white
paper of May 1989, 39 per cent, was to the British forces in what
was then West Germany, positioned there to help resist any Russian advance across the North European plain. The close of the
Cold War may have brought an end to the decades of defence, and
writers of spy stories will have to search elsewhere than Moscow for
villains, but international uncertainty remains acute, and at present
the EU is neither intended nor able to meet Britain's international
and strategic requirements.

TWENTIETH-CENTURY WALES

The processes of change can best be grasped if studied in a particular area. Wales has certainly changed considerably from the
heavy industry and labour militancy of the start of the century.
Industrial and political militancy receded during the First World
War, in part because the government bought peace in the coalfields,
but in 1919 Lloyd George rejected pressure for nationalisation and
in 1921 the mines were returned to the coal owners and a major
dispute lost by the miners; once again troops were deployed in
south Wales.

Depression in the coal industry led the employers to cut wages in
1926 and 1931, and union resistance was unsuccessful. As a strong-

hold of coal, Wales played a major role in the general strike of
1926. Meanwhile, based on south-east Wales, the Labour Party was
becoming more prominent – taking ten Welsh seats in 1918, and
twenty-five in 1929. This was the new Wales that followed the First
World War: a Labour, not a Liberal, Wales that had to confront
significant economic change including major decline in important
and traditional industries. International competition, an over-
valued pound, inadequate investment and industrial problems hit
the coal industry: production fell from 56 million tons in 1913 to 48
in 1929 and 20 in 1945. The iron and steel and tinplate industries
were also badly hit. All the Cardiganshire lead mines were closed by
1931. Welsh unemployment rose to 37.5 per cent in 1932, and was
still 22.3 per cent in 1937. The effects of unemployment were local,
but, where it hit, gruesome in the extreme and for older people in
South Wales it is still a watershed experience.

Not everything was in decline. Deeside benefited from industrial
growth, by 1934 there was one cinema seat for every ten people in
south Wales, and that year it was considered worth rebuilding the
Olympia cinema in prosperous Cardiff. Nevertheless, decline in
particular industries affected much of the Welsh economy, while
unemployment and poverty sapped the population. Public health
was hit and tuberculosis became a more serious problem. About
450,000 Welsh emigrated between 1921 and 1939, mostly to expanding regions in southern England. The Earl of Plymouth, President of the National Industrial Council of Wales and Monmouthshire established in 1932, declared in 1938, 'the problem of
the Welsh industrial areas will never be overcome until we have
succeeded in finding a solution of the difficulties which confront
our great basic trade, the coal trade . . . to achieve a balanced state
in industry . . . essential we should have light industries'. Neither
solutions to the problems of coal nor light industries were to be
forthcoming in the interwar period and the hardship of those years
was to help cement an identity of Wales and Labour that persisted
in the postwar decades of economic growth. Whereas Lloyd George
was the dominant Welsh figure in British politics in the opening
decades of the century, in the 1940s and 1950s this role was
assumed by Aneurin Bevan, MP for Ebbw Vale, a radical socialist
who, as Minister of Health 1945–51, played the key role in the
foundation of the National Health Service. Labour enjoyed a
degree of electoral support greater than that of the Liberals during

their heyday. In addition taxation hit the great estates, and their decline influenced the society, economy and politics of rural areas: small freeholders became much more important.

Alongside Labour dominance, these were also years of growing, though still limited, activity on the part of nationalists. Plaid Cymru, the Welsh Nationalist Party, was formed in 1925 to campaign for self-government, but it had little impact. Its 'back to the land' policy extolled agriculture and sought to obtain cultural and economic integrity and political independence. The party was concerned primarily with the Welsh language and opposed to urban and industrial society, goals that were not shared by the bulk of the Welsh population, whose background was anglophone. Not only was self-government for Wales a minor issue in the interwar period, but institutions for distinct administration also made far slower progress than that for Scotland. The position of Secretary of State for Scotland, last held in 1746, was revived in 1885; and in 1934 the Scottish Office was created in Edinburgh. The Welsh equivalents were not created until 1964. In 1941 Councillor George Williams of Cardiff, Chairman of the National Industrial Council, complained that that body was 'the only organisation which can speak for the whole of the local authorities of the Welsh region on economic affairs'.

The severely depressed economy of interwar Wales, keen on financial support from the national exchequer, was not the best basis for widespread demands for home rule. Furthermore, radicals in the 1930s did not tend to look to constitutional reform. Thus from 1933 communist and left-wing Labour activists in the 'Little Moscows' of Wales proposed the formation of workers' defence groups or militias on continental lines to resist police activity, while some elements in Plaid Cymru looked to Mussolini and were denounced as neo-fascists. Indeed Welsh nationalism led Plaid Cymru to oppose Britain's role in the Second World War, which was seen as a clash of rival imperialisms. Some of its members were pacifists, products of a strong strain in Welsh Nonconformity, others refused to be conscripted, and several may have been German spies and saboteurs.

Wales remained a Labour stronghold until the 1960s, although a Liberal revival there played a key role in the national revival of the Liberal Party from 1945 onwards. The nature of Plaid Cymru's appeal was illustrated by the adoption speech made by Gwynfor

Evans in launching his parliamentary campaign in Merioneth in 1959:

> There is a great awakening in Merioneth and throughout Wales – the sound of chains and fetters breaking. Wales is experiencing an awareness of its nationhood, becoming proud of its ancestry, and gaining mental and spiritual freedom which will inevitably lead to national freedom . . . If we make a breach in this wall, we shall soon see the people following.

The electors, however, had little time for such rhetoric. Evans came bottom with 22.9 per cent, no real improvement on his performance in 1955. The seat was not to be won by Plaid Cymru until 1974.

In 1966–8 there was an upsurge in support for Plaid Cymru with their first parliamentary seat won, by Evans, at Carmarthen in 1966. In by-elections in 1967–72 Plaid Cymru also made an impact in English-speaking south Wales. This upsurge owed much to the unpopularity of Labour's economic policies, and was a consequence of disillusionment with Harold Wilson, as well as a reaction against the self-interested and occasionally corrupt dominance of most of Welsh local government by Labour.

Plaid Cymru won 175,000 votes in the 1970 general election and took three seats from Labour in 1974 (Carmarthen, Caernarfon and Merioneth), but thereafter support dipped in the 1970s and 1980s, although it won Yvys Mon (Anglesey) in 1987. When support revived in the 1992 election it did so in the Welsh-speaking heartland and not elsewhere. In 1992 Plaid Cymru's vote rose, although its share of the Welsh vote was still 2 per cent below that in 1974, and it won another seat – Ceredigion (Cardigan) and Pembroke North – from the Liberal Democrats, making four in total. The five seats where Plaid Cymru's vote increased by 5 per cent or more in 1992 were all amongst the ten Welsh speaking constituencies. In the top five of the latter, Plaid Cymru's vote was an average of 40.6 per cent (with a peak of 59 per cent in Caernarfon), but elsewhere Labour's strength led it to support the idea of an elected assembly for Wales when it returned to power in 1974. A Scotland and Wales Bill introduced in 1976 proposed an assembly with control over health, social services, education, development and local government, but with no taxation power and with the Westminster Parliament retaining the veto. The Bill met opposition from nationalists who felt that it did not go far enough but, more substantially, from Labour politicians, such as Neil Kinnock, and Conservatives. The unattractive consequences of regional dominance in an autonomous Wales was stressed, as was the danger of discrimination against non-Welsh speakers. In order to secure the passage of the Bill, the government had to concede a referendum in Wales. Held in March 1979, this found only 11.8 per cent of the Welsh electorate in favour of devolution, with 46.5 per cent voting against and 41.7 per cent not bothering to vote. Even in Gwynedd and Dyfed, the overwhelming majority of those who voted did so against devolution.

The ballot box was not the only medium in which the identity and future of Wales were contested. The Welsh Language Society, launched in 1936, sought to promote bilingualism and from 1963 painted out English names on signs. The Welsh Language Act of 1967 gave Welsh equal legal validity, though the percentage of Welsh speakers continued to decline: 40 per cent (1911), 30 per cent (1950), 25 per cent (1970) and about 18 per cent now. Welsh is spoken most in the rural areas that have been affected seriously by depopulation over the last century. In Anglesey, for example, Welsh-speaking is lowest in most urban and coastal districts and strongest in the rural inland parishes, which have not been centres of population growth.

Yet the declining use of the language is not the same as a loss of identity, although the latter is far from static: Welsh culture gets remade all the time. The religious life of south-east Wales remained Welsh-speaking even after Welsh ceased to be the common language. Older South Walians can sometimes discuss the doctrine of the atonement in Welsh yet can't talk about making tea in Welsh. On the other hand, the English-speaking culture of south Wales is a Welsh culture: it's certainly not English. Just because they spoke English, it would be wrong to argue that major politicians such as Aneurin Bevan and Neil Kinnock were not Welsh. The dominance of nonconformist values remains important. Temperance, for example, continues to be an emotive issue.

More violent nationalist groups used bombs to attack what they saw as alien presences, such as reservoir dams and pipelines taking water from drowned Welsh valleys to English cities, a cause that had first led to violent action in 1952. A rise in sporadic terrorist activity in 1966–9 was followed by a marked decline in the 1970s as devolution seemed a serious prospect, but its failure, and the un-popularity of the Conservative government elected in 1979, led to a fresh upsurge. Since 1979 Wales has been governed by a party which is in a very substantial minority there. Arson attacks on houses bought by outsiders, usually owned as second homes by the English, began in 1979. Terrorist activity in no way compares with Ulster and what is usually involved are little incendiaries in letters or burnings of empty cottages. A campaign of public protest forced the government to establish a Welsh-language television channel, S4C – yet another example of the extent to which Wales took a disproportionate share of national expenditure – although it could also be argued that Gwynfor Evans's threat to starve himself to death was a non-violent way to pressure the government into honouring its pledge to set up the channel.

SOCIAL CHANGE

The extent to which Britain is 'truly' part of Europe has vexed commentators since the Second World War. In some respects, Britain, Ireland and the societies of western Europe have been becoming more similar over the last twenty years. This is a con-sequence of broadly similar social trends including secularisation, the emancipation of women and the move from the land. Sexual permissiveness, rising divorce rates, growing geographical mobility, the decline of traditional social distinctions and the rise of youth culture are all shared characteristics. Deference, aristocracies, and social stratification have all declined, though differences in wealth, both capital and income, remain vast.

The role of the House of Lords in the United Kingdom has declined. In 1947 the Labour government was obstructed by the Lords in nationalising the steel industry. As a result, Attlee passed the Parliament Act (1949), which reduced the number of occasions on which the Lords can block legislation passed by the Commons before it becomes law from three to two, and reduced the delaying period of the Lords from two years to one. The aristocracy were also changed. The Life Peerages Act (1958) breached the hereditary principle of aristocratic status, by creating peerages that were not hereditary. The Peerage Act (1963) allowed peeresses to sit in their own right, and permitted the disclaiming of hereditary peerages.

The gradual virtual disestablishment of the Anglican Church in England, a process that really began with the Catholic Emancipation Act of 1829, has gathered pace in recent years, a parallel to the process of disestablishment that has already taken place on much of the Continent. The most influential clergyman of the interwar years, William Temple, Archbishop of York 1929–42 and of Canterbury 1942–4, had sought to reverse the decline of organised religion, and to make England an Anglican nation again and thus to justify the Church's claim to speak for it. But, although he strengthened the Church, he failed to give England a more clearly Christian character and his inspiration of the already developing role of the Church as a voice of social criticism and concern led to it being seen increasingly in a secular light. Only 10 per cent of British adults are active churchgoers, although in Northern Ireland, where communities are more tight-knit and religion a crucial expression of community identity, the percentage is 70, and in Scotland it is 16. Both the Church of England and the Scottish Episcopal Church have been particularly badly hit. The position of the established churches in the British Isles, especially England, has also been challenged by the rise of 'fundamentalist' Christianity, inspired from America, and also by 'new age' religions, while there has also been an appreciable number of converts to Buddhism.

In Britain, Ireland and the Continent, social paternalism, patriarchal authority, respect for age and the nuclear family, and the stigma of illegitimacy, have all declined in importance, while rights to divorce, abortion and contraception are established across most of western Europe (reducing the number of children available for adoption), and homosexual acts in private between consenting adults have been decriminalised, in Britain by the Sexual Offences Act of 1967. The profile of avowed homosexuals and lesbians in society has risen markedly. Cohabitation and one-parent families have each become more common, while the number of lifetime celibates has fallen. 31 per cent of live births in Scotland in 1994 were to unmarried mothers. Throughout the British Isles working hours and birth rates have also fallen; populations have 'aged', decreasing the economically active percentage.

Average rates of population growth in Britain as a whole were far lower in the inter-war period, when they fell to below replacement levels, than they had been in the nineteenth century. As a result, the number of children in an average family fell from three in

1910 to two in 1940. Despite a postwar birth-peak or 'baby boom' in 1947, and another in 1966, population growth-rates continued to decline in the 1950s and 1960s, to almost a standstill in the 1970s and early 1980s, before a slight upturn from the mid-1980s. The population of suburban, commuter and southern England has increased more rapidly than that of the north and of London.

IMMIGRATION

Immigration, especially from former colonies, has altered the ethnic composition of many continental societies. In Britain much of the immigration was from Europe: Irish after the potato famine of 1847–8; Russian and Polish Jews from the 1880s until the Aliens Act of 1905; and Poles and Ukrainians in the 1940s, after the Second World War; although there had also been substantial Chinese immigration at the end of the nineteenth and the start of the twentieth century, principally to sea-ports, such as London and Tyneside. There was a massive wave of Irish immigration during and after the Second World War.

From the 1950s large-scale immigration was from the 'New Commonwealth', especially the West Indies and the Indian sub-continent. A temporary labour shortage in unattractive spheres of employment, such as transport, foundry work and nursing, led to an active sponsorship of immigration that accorded with Commonwealth idealism, but for which there was little popular support. Concern about its scale and growing racial tension, particularly over jobs and public housing, led to Immigration Acts (1962, 1968, 1971) that progressively reduced Commonwealth immigration. The Commonwealth Immigrants Act of 1968 deprived East African Asians with United Kingdom passports of the automatic right to entry. Overt racism was a particular problem in the 1960s and early 1970s. In April 1968 a maverick Conservative MP, Enoch Powell, made a speech warning that immigration would lead to racial violence and pressed for the limitation of immigration. A month later a Gallup poll recorded that 74 per cent of Britons supported his views. In August 1972 the expulsion of 40,000 Ugandan Asians from Uganda and their admission into Britain fuelled fears of an immigration crisis. The racist National Front emerged in the years after 1970 as a potential force in British politics: although no NF

MP was elected, there were three NF councillors in London boroughs and race became a contentious issue.

Successive waves of immigrants in the nineteenth and twentieth centuries faced poor housing and took on the less attractive jobs, the 'sweated' trades, such as tailoring, and casual labour in the docks and the building trade. Social positions were crucial. Hannah Rothschild, from a wealthy Jewish banking family, could marry the future Liberal prime minister, Lord Rosebery, in 1878 – to the anger of a *Jewish Chronicle* opposed to mixed marriages. Herbert Samuel, also from a banking background, became in 1909 the first practising Jew to sit in the British cabinet, then a Liberal body; Disraeli was a convert to Christianity. However, most Jews faced much harsher conditions.

The impact of immigration has varied greatly. New Commonwealth migrants concentrated in London, the west Midlands and south Yorkshire; relatively few went to Scotland, Wales, Ulster, rural or north-east England. In 1971 the percentage in Bradford (Yorkshire) was 7.1 and in Birmingham 6.7, but it was only 1.3 in Newcastle. Within individual cities immigrants have concentrated in particular areas, influenced by a mixture of opportunity and self-segregation. Few immigrants re-migrate. The overwhelming majority of the Caribbean immigrants who arrived in the 1950s and early 1960s planned to save money in order to buy land in the West Indies and return, but they only gained low-paid jobs and never earned enough: only a tenth of these immigrants returned in the 1980s.

Some immigrants have sought assimilation. Thus the nineteenth-century Yiddish-speaking Jewish immigrants from eastern Europe were anglicised by the Jewish Board of Guardians and other institutions, so that their traditional language and culture were essentially lost. Their network of community facilities was, however, of great value in providing social welfare, so that, for example, rates of infant and maternal mortality among immigrant Jews in the poverty of east London were low. Many immigrant groups have striven to retain a distinctive identity, in certain cases linked to a lack of sympathy for generally accepted values. Over some issues, such as the mixed education of Asian Islamic women, this has created administrative and legal problems. Britain has both 'multi-culturalism' and a degree of racial tension, and though racial discrimination is illegal under the Race Relations Act (1977), racial violence has played a role in the harassment of non-whites, especially in attacks on housing estates. For both 'whites' and 'blacks' crime is a serious problem, with high rates of drug-dealing and muggings. Black hostility to what was seen as a discriminatory police force played a major role in the 1981 riots in south London and Liverpool and in subsequent violence. In October 1994 the 28,000-strong Metropolitan Police Force of London contained only 679 ethnic-minority officers; only one of the country's 384 chief superintendents was from the same group.

While the effects of immigration have become more of an issue in Britain, emigration has fallen. It was still a major factor in the first quarter of the century, and net emigration, rather than net immigration, was the situation until the 1930s and then again after the Second World War, though it is no longer the case.

BRITAIN AND THE EUROPEAN UNION

As increased numbers have travelled for pleasure, as a consequence of greater disposable wealth among the bulk of the population, the development of the package holiday, the use of jet aircraft and the spread of car ownership, so far more inhabitants of Britain than ever before have visited the Continent, and far more than ever before also make a regular habit of doing so. In 1991 there were 2.45 million British visitors to the USA, but a much greater number went to the Continent. If many visit 'little Britains' in nondescript Mediterranean resorts such as Benidorm, others do not. The metropolitan middle-class household that would have had servants sixty years ago may now have a second home in France, and *The Times* can carry regular articles on where and how best to purchase such properties. The opportunity of learning at least one foreign language is offered to all schoolchildren. Social differences, however, play a major role, both in language-learning and in leisure. More than a quarter of Britons have never holidayed abroad, regarding it as a luxury; and of the 56 million holidays taken in 1993 32.5 million were in Britain.

Economically and politically, Britain has become closer to the Continent. The societies of western Europe have felt threatened first by Soviet power and then by the chaos in eastern Europe that has followed the collapse of communism; their economies have been challenged by the staggering development of the 'dragon' countries of east Asia. Economically, Britain is more closely linked to continental markets and suppliers than she was in 1973, while her attraction for 'inward investment', especially from Japan, America and the other countries of the EEC, has largely arisen as a consequence of her access to what is now the largest trading system in the world. Such investment is of growing importance. In the north of England, for example, manufacturing employment in foreign-owned companies rose between 1979 and 1989 from 11.8 per cent to 17.1 per cent, and between January 1985 and June 1992 such investment there secured 34,388 jobs and an associated capital spend of £2.8 billion, much of it focused on serving EU markets. The passing of the Single European Act in 1987 committed Britain to remove all barriers to the creation of the Single European Market (SEM), and also altered the framework of British economic activity. The EU and the domestic market have been legally joined and it is necessary to comply with the SEM in order to operate in the EU and therefore in Britain. Politically, most British politicians proclaim their commitment to Europe and the EU even when criticising the practices or objectives of the latter.

And yet there are also important strains in the relationship. Affinity is not the only reason for closeness or union. Complementarity is also involved. That was certainly believed to be the case with the British empire in the later nineteenth century. The bases of imperial union were supposed to be twofold. There was a stress, sometimes misleading, on common British origins, customs, race, language and constitutions, but secondly an emphasis on the degree to which each complemented the others, especially economically. Thus the dominions and Crown colonies could exchange primary products for manufactured goods with industrial Britain, their common interests resting on the differences between the parts. This was also the relationship with trans-oceanic trading partners that were not part of the empire, most obviously South America. The EU was less amenable, because of the similarities between Britain and her neighbours, which made for a union of competitors rather than of partners.

There are also important political problems affecting the relationship. Scepticism about the notion of a European 'super state' and 'Euro-federalism' is widespread, and some of the support for the European ideal in 1980s was tactical and opportunistic, designed to attack Mrs Thatcher, who, though she signed the Single European Act, was not the most ardent admirer of European unity. Two very different indicators are the scarcity of the European flag in Britain, and the markedly patriotic response of the British public to the Falklands Crisis of 1982, when British forces drove out invading Argentine troops. In contrast, it is difficult to see much of a willingness to kill or be killed for Europe, and there has been little enthusiasm for the deployment of British troops in Bosnia. The EU was seen as irrelevant during the Gulf War of 1990–1 in which Britain took a major role. Political identity is still clearly national, not international. The British are reluctant to learn foreign languages. In 1991–2 their schools taught an average of only 0.9 languages per pupil, bottom of the EU bar Portugal. French is the commonest foreign language in Britain's secondary schools but it was studied by only 59 per cent of pupils in 1991–2; German was next at 20 per cent. The comparable percentages in Ireland were 69 and 24. The British were helped by the popularity of English in the EU. In 1991–2 83 per cent of secondary-school pupils in the EU were learning English as a foreign language, followed by French at 32 per cent.

DEMOCRATISATION

The ambivalent response to European unity has been matched, over a much longer time-span, by an ambivalence towards the democratisation of society. This has different sources and takes different forms. Few were as critical of democracy as the Earl of Halifax (1881–1959), an old Etonian who, aside from serving as Foreign Secretary (1938–40), was also Viceroy of India (1926–31) and Chancellor of Oxford University. He wrote to his father, 'what a bore democracy is to those who have to work it . . . I think it is a great pity that Simon de Montfort . . . ever invented our parliamentary system'. Hostility to democratic accountability has also been demonstrated, albeit in an implicit not overt manner, by the unwillingness of often self-defining elites, such as the judiciary or planners, to accept popular beliefs and pastimes as worthy of value and attention, and their conviction that they are best placed to manage society and define social values. Social and cultural condescension can thus be linked to contempt for popular views on such matters as capital punishment or immigration. Most institutions resist unwelcome pressures, while political parties temper their desire for popular support with their wish to maintain their ideological inheritance. The leader of the Conservative Party is elected exclusively by MPs rather than by all the members of the Party. Privilege continues to play a major role in society. The attempt to reform the House of Lords in 1968 was unsuccessful. All of the twenty-six judges appointed in 1993–4 had been to private schools and only three were women. This pattern is also found in the senators of the College of Justice in Scotland.

FEMALE EMANCIPATION

And yet, at the same time, there have been powerful forces democratising society. The most important has been the emancipation of women. Their legal and social position was limited at the beginning of the century, not least because most adult women did not have an independent income. In general, women lacked good jobs, and the employment rate among women with children was low, by modern standards. The change this century has been legal, economic and social.

Prior to the First World War, the suffragette movement won attention rather than support, as the Pankhursts, especially Emmeline Pankhurst who founded the Women's Social and Political Union in 1903, urged their followers to acts of violence; but the war saw a substantial increase in the female workforce as society was mobilised for total war. Men had been conscripted into the forces; and nearly 5 million women were in employment at the start of 1918, though their wages remained much lower than men's. That year, the vote was given to all men over 21 and to women over 30; a decade later the voting age for women was dropped to 21. Progressive changes in the law made divorce easier and removed the formal structure of discrimination. The Equal Pay Act (1970; implemented in 1975) was made more important by the major expansion of the female workforce from the 1940s. The expansion of the First World War had been partly reversed as men returned from the forces and women turned to domesticity, but that of the second conflict was not, and the economic shift from manufacturing to service industries helped to create more opportunities for women workers. Whereas previously most women had given up work when they married, older married women entered the labour force as clerical workers in large numbers from the 1940s. The number of married women entering the job market escalated from the 1960s. Clerical occupations are today the largest single occupational category for women, but they are generally poorly paid and are particularly vulnerable to changes due to new office equipment and practices. The banks, which employ many women, shed many staff in 1989–90 and 1993–5. Furthermore, an increasing percentage of female employment is part-time and much is in low-skill and low-pay jobs. Nevertheless, thanks to female employment (nearly 53 per cent of the workforce in 1994), the percentage of the population employed has increased since the 1920s; as, of course, has the possible number of unemployed. Rising female employment is possibly responsible for the increase in school attainment among girls, which has markedly risen at GCSE-level (examinations for 15–16-year-olds) since 1987, with the gap between male and female attainment also rising in the same period. Greater female participation in the workforce has hit some voluntary activities, such as party political membership. It is also partly responsible for women postponing having children and having fewer children. The average age for giving birth rose to 28 in 1993.

There was opposition to the expansion of opportunities for women. The National Association of Schoolmasters was founded in 1922 from a splinter group of male teachers opposed to the National Union of Teachers' support for equal pay, which was not achieved until after the Second World War. Its leaflets included such titles as 'Making our boys effeminate' (1927). The National Union of Foundry Workers only represented men during its history (1920–46), despite there being about 50,000 foundrywomen in the 1940s, a result of the entry of women into manufacturing during the war. More generally, the Labour Party and trade-union movement were reluctant to adopt issues pressed on it by female members, such as birth control and family allowances. In the 1920s Labour had only a quarter of the Conservatives' female membership. Family allowances were introduced in the 1940s; paid directly to the mother and thus giving her a measure of economic independence. The attempt by the Labour Party in 1994–5 to increase greatly the number of its female prospective MPs encountered particular resistance among conservative working-class branches of the party, although the party had a tradition of women in key roles.

Changes in the position of women cannot, however, be separated from other social questions. Class affected the recruitment for different tasks of women in both world wars. The mixture of classes in munitions work during the first war, though stressed in propaganda, was limited. Similarly, in the second war there was little mingling in the factories; social distinctions were maintained. 'Positive discrimination' in favour of hiring and promoting women in recent years has worked most to the benefit of middle-class women, and the practice of endogamy (marriage within the clan) may therefore ensure that social differences are thus fortified.

As with other movements lacking a centralizing structure, the 'women's liberation' movement of the 1960s and 1970s was a diverse one. It included pressure for changes in lifestyles and social arrangements that put women's needs and expectations in a more central position. The Abortion Act of 1967 was followed by a situation close to abortion on demand. Jobs and lifestyle became more important as aspirations for women, complementing rather than replacing home and family. The range of female activities expanded: the Women's Rugby Football Union was formed in 1983; the first Briton in space was Helen Sharman; in 1987 Elizabeth II amended the statutes of the most distinguished of British chivalric orders, the Order of the Garter, to permit the admission of women on terms equal to those of the Knights Companion of the Order. After considerable controversy, the first women were ordained priests in the Church of England in 1994; the Church of Scotland had women ministers from the late 1960s. English Congregationalists ordained women from 1919 and by the Second World War Congregationalists were quite used to women ministers, though they were not numerous.

While full-time male undergraduates at universities increased by 20 per cent between 1970 and 1989, women increased by 30 per cent. As with other developments of that period that led to pressure for change, the impact of the women's liberation movement diminished in the 1980s, which was ironically that of the first British woman party leader and Prime Minister, Margaret Thatcher. Her rise was a demonstration of the increasing equality of British society and showed that there was no ceiling of opportunity for women; her determination and success proved that a woman was easily capable of the job. Never rejected by the electorate, the confrontational Mrs Thatcher was, at the time she was toppled by disaffection among her overwhelmingly male MPs, fearing defeat in light of the government's unpopularity, the longest-serving prime minister of the century, and the Prime Minister with the longest consecutive period in office since Lord Liverpool (1815–27). The Conservatives retained their traditional lead over Labour among women voters: up from 4 per cent in 1987 to 8 per cent in 1992, although only 9.2 per cent of MPs were women after the 1992 general election, and the percentage of women in the higher levels of the establishment is low.

Legal changes continued to be of importance. Divorce has become considerably easier as a result of the Matrimonial Causes Act (1923), the Divorce Act (1937), the Legal Aid Act (1949) and the Divorce Reform Act (1969). The number of divorces more than doubled in 1971–92 and by 1992 there was one divorce for every two marriages. In Scotland there were 13,133 divorces in 1994 and 31,480 marriages, the latter the lowest figure since 1926. The Sex Discrimination Act of 1976 had considerable impact in the treatment and employment of women. The sexual harassment of women in the workplace now leads to extensive legal action. Equally, general social trends have been important. Alongside the stress on an eroticised vision of marriage, which was encouraged by Marie Stopes's successful book *Married Love* (1918), there has been an emphasis on the techniques of sexual pleasure and a rise in sex education. The former has become a major sphere of commercial activity; the latter one of educational policy, contrasting greatly with the ignorance of many, particularly women, earlier in the century.

By 1994 women, then 52 per cent of the population, accounted for almost half the number of total motorists in Britain and for 51 per cent of those under 35. They committed, however, far fewer motoring offences. Women were far more victims than culprits in cases of domestic violence, the rise in which accounted for much of the increase in violent crime between 1981 and 1993. This may reflect a greater willingness on the part of victims to report offences. Women also are more likely than men to feel unsafe going out at night – although in 1992 it was found that men are 70 per cent more likely to be attacked than women.

SOCIAL SHIFTS

Capitalism has been another force shaping the democratisation of society, for at the same time that the differing wealth and income of individuals ensures that their purchasing power varies, each is a consumer able to make his or her own purchasing decisions. This element of choice and the need to shape and cater to it have combined to ensure a whole range of social shifts, among which the most striking has been the emergence over the last forty years of the youth consumer and the development of cultural and consumer fashions that reflect the dynamism and volatility of this section of the market. The number of commercial radio stations rose dramatically in the 1990s. It is easy to focus on rock, pop and drug culture transmitted via the Beatles and the Sex Pistols, psychedelia and punk, but more significance can be attached to the wish and ability of youth first to create an adolescent identity – not to be younger copies of their elders – and secondly and more specifically to reject the opinions of their parents; pop culture is only one manifestation of this. The willingness to try different foods, to holiday in different places, to move away from parental religious preferences, to go on to higher education or to purchase property are as interesting and possibly more important. In 1968 the voting age was reduced to 18.

Certainly, the interrelationship between the aspirations of youth and socio-economic changes must be seen to play a role in the major expansion of the middle class that has been such a marked feature of the last three decades. In 1900 75 per cent of the labour force were manual workers, members of the working class. By 1974 the percentage had fallen to 47, by 1991 to 36. The manufacturing base has declined, the service sector grown. White collar has replaced blue collar (the fall in the working class hitting the Labour party), and average incomes for those in work have risen appreciably. Real disposable income for the average household rose 46 per cent between 1971 and 1992. Tax rates, which under Harold Wilson rose to a maximum of 98 per cent, have fallen substantially: direct taxation grew considerably in the 1960s and 1970s, but there was a shift to indirect taxation in the 1980s. The long-term impact of the social revolution of recent years, crucial aspects of which are falling union membership (the Trades Union Congress had more than 12 million members in 1979, fewer than 8 million in 1992), and rising home ownership (three-quarters of trade unionists by the late

1980s), is still unclear; but the basic lineaments of society for the foreseeable future are of a capitalist, consumerist, individualist, mobile, predominantly secular and urban, property-owning democracy, with a substantial and embittered underclass. Large numbers of beggars appeared on the streets, especially in London. Cases of tuberculosis among the homeless rose. Over 20 per cent of 18–25-year-olds had not registered to vote in 1992. Affluence and social fluidity have challenged notions of cohesion and collectivism.

'Who governs Britain?' was the slogan of the Heath government that, although it won more votes than Labour, was, nevertheless, defeated in February 1974. The defeat of the coal miners' strike of 1984–5 answered the question, and was followed by several years of boom and optimism. The substantial increase in individual and corporate debt in the 1980s as a consequence of the liberalisation of the financial system and government encouragement of the widespread desire to own property, combined with structural economic problems, have, however, ensured that many who are not in the underclass are in a vulnerable situation. Private household debt rose from £16 billion to £47 billion, mortgages from £43 billion to £235 billion in 1980–9. By June 1992 repossessions of houses by creditors were at an annual rate of about 75,000, while 300,000 mortgage-holders were six months or more in arrears.

A more general problem is posed by rising crime figures, the related perception of a more disorderly and lawless and less safe society, and the difficulties of policing. Between 1981 and 1993 the British crime survey showed a rise of 77 per cent in crime, with a 39 per cent rise in violent offences. It estimates that about 15 million crimes against households are currently committed each year. As a result of the Firearms Control Act of 1920 and its revision, the Firearms Act of 1968, it is necessary to show 'good reason' to own a gun and defence against crime is not acceptable. Thus, unlike in the USA, people are more dependent on the police in order to protect themselves. A perception of growing crime tempers public civility and lessens confidence in the use of public space. Northern Ireland, where crime rates and consumption of hard drugs are low, has other problems of lawlessness. Widespread refusal to pay the unpopular poll tax, introduced by Mrs Thatcher, indicated a willingness to reject laws deemed unfair. The unpopularity of the tax, combined with a worsening economic situation, helped to bring about the crisis of confidence in her leadership in the parliamentary Conservative party that led to her fall in November 1990.

Unlike during the late 1940s, there is now little confidence in central planning and limited support for state collectivism. More prefer to shop than to go to church on Sundays, and fewer of the population express their religious faith through the established churches than ever before. Traditional geographical loyalties were shaken by the Local Government Act of 1972 which, in the cause of 'rationalisation', totally reorganised local government in England, greatly altering county boundaries and abolishing several counties and the ridings of Yorkshire. The pattern of local government in Scotland and Wales was changed even more radically. Social differences remain, the working class eating less well, having poorer housing, more children, lower expectations and less access to higher education than the middle class. Class mortality differences have widened from the late 1950s. Nevertheless, although there are clear variations between and within regions in many fields, including political preference, crime patterns, nuptiality, fertility and house ownership, these are less marked than in the past. National broadcasting, state education and employment, nation-wide companies, unions, products and pastimes have all brought a measure of convergence that can be seen in the decline of dialect and distinctive regional practices, as in cooking. Wales and England appear indissolubly linked, nationalism has failed as yet to make much headway in Scotland, but the future of Ulster continues to be a major problem for its own citizens and for the British Isles as a whole. Britain is an active member of the European Union, and with a population of 58.2 million in 1994 it is its second most populous state after Germany; but the future trajectory of that body, and Britain's relations with it, are both unclear.

The threat of Russian power has markedly diminished, and, although many other regions of the world are unstable and pose challenges to British interests, western Europe appears safe for liberal democracy. The future of the environment is a growing concern, global warming and ozone depletion both being themes of the 1990s; but the British can look back on over four decades without a major war. The experience of serving or losing loved ones in the two world wars, which greatly affected such politicians as Attlee, Chamberlain, Eden and Macmillan, as well as millions of their contemporaries, is one that has not been repeated. History is

so often a story of the move from one crisis to another, and that of
modern Britain is no exception, but crisis can be seen as an integral
part of the functioning and development of any sophisticated
society. Despite its serious problems, British society still has many
attractive features and there is still a sense of national identity and
loyalty.

9

The British Isles Today

Throughout this book there has been stress on the importance of the physical environment. This, it is important to note, has also been greatly affected by human activity. Woods have been cleared, so that virtually none of the original virgin forest has survived. Since 1945 45 per cent of the United Kingdom's ancient semi-natural forest has been damaged or destroyed. Rivers have been deepened and straightened, coastlines altered. This has been a long process. The marshland of the Fens, for example, has been progressively drained from the Roman period to the present day, with particular activity in the seventeenth century and following the arrival of steam pumps from the 1820s. Yet at no stage has there been such pressure on the environment as in modern Britain. Other creatures are decimated by human activities: between 3,000 and 5,000 barn owls being killed on UK roads each year. Pine martens, members of the weasel family, were reported in 1995 to have vanished from England in 1994 and to be on the brink of extinction in Wales. On the other hand, the Welsh red kite has been brought back from the brink of extinction. Environmental concern is greater now than ever before. This has been institutionalised with the creation of national parks in England and Wales (1949) and areas of outstanding natural beauty, and the foundation of the Countryside Commission in 1968. There are conservation areas in towns, listed buildings, scheduled ancient monuments and sites of special scientific interest. More money is now spent on maintaining environmental standards, most obviously with payments – about £900 million in 1994 – under the Wildlife and Countryside Act 1981 to farmers to 'set aside' land from farming or to adopt less intensive farming methods.

The susceptibility of the environment to human pressure has become more dramatically apparent. There have been improvements: the toxicity of rivers such as the Thames and the Tyne has decreased: concentrations of heavy metal pollutants are declining. Yet cities that enjoyed far more sunshine hours from the clearer atmosphere after the declaration of smokeless zones have now started to notice a decline due to greater emissions from car exhausts. Building on greenfield sites is still more common than urban renewal. Purchasing power impacts on the environment. In 1971 food took one-fifth of the average family budget; in 1993 one-ninth, freeing disposable income for other forms of expenditure. In 1990 158 million tons of carbon dioxide were dispersed into the environment above Britain. Increased use of water, thanks in part to machines such as dishwashers, put great pressure on water reserves, and led to the depletion of natural aquifers and to restrictions on water use. In 1990 hosepipe bans affected 20 million customers. More material goods tend to mean a greater use of energy, although reliability and energy efficiency have risen. By 1991 90 per cent of households had a telephone, compared to 42 per cent in 1972: for washing machines the percentages are 88 and 66. 73 per cent of households own videos, 62 per cent microwave cookers. The consumer society continues to produce massive quantities of rubbish. Noise is another consequence of technological development, and the number of complaints about it rose by 390 per cent in 1978–92.

The deserted church or meeting house in rural Britain is one apt symbol of the nature of change. Once crucial to a sense of community, order, hierarchy and place, churches were increasingly declared redundant or demolished from 1950 on. For example in the Withern group of parishes in Lincolnshire there were thirteen parish churches in the Middle Ages, eleven in 1900 and only five in 1993. Empty churches symbolise the move from rural to urban, a process, intensified by transport policies, that was also marked by the closure of rural schools, shops, pubs and post offices. Only 2.5 per cent of the United Kingdom's workforce in the early 1970s was employed in agriculture. Commuters now dominate many villages, reflecting the appeal of an image of the countryside, but also reflecting and ensuring a shift in the nature of rural life and the effective erosion of any significant boundary between rural and urban society. Commuting into London increased 7 per cent in

1981–91; 18 per cent into Birmingham and 29 per cent into Manchester.

Deserted churches also reflect the increasingly sceptical and secular nature of society, the last a development that also affects members of other religions, such as Jews, Muslims and Sikhs, although Islam has become more active thanks to immigration. Such secularism has taken many forms. For example religious opposition, as well as public prejudice, delayed the development of cremation, a policy supported by some doctors and nonconformists, as opposed to earth burial. The first crematorium opened at Woking in 1885, but for long cremation was a minority option. In Manchester, where the first cremation was in 1892, cremation only became more popular from the 1940s. Now, in Britain, it is the usual way of disposing of bodies. Noise-abatement orders are now served on some churches by local authorities at the behest of people no longer happy to listen to church bells.

A different shift in national traditions is suggested by diet. Since the 1960s this has been increasingly affected by new ingredients and dishes introduced from foreign countries. Chinese, Indian and Italian meals dominate the restaurant trade. Supermarkets increasingly stock foreign dishes; in the 1990s there was growing consumption of continental-style breads. There has also been a widening in the range of fruit available: avocados, passion fruit, star fruit, kiwi fruit and mangoes, largely unknown in Britain in the 1960s, are now widely available in supermarkets. The increased consumption of convenience foods, generally reheated rapidly by microwave cookers, has provided a major market for new dishes. Foreign alcoholic drinks, and foreign types and brands of beer have become much more important, a process that also in part reflects technological and retail shifts, most obviously the growing sale of canned beers and the development of supermarket sales of alcohol. Supermarkets have also been responsible for the decline in independent retail activity. High streets have become more uniform and outlets are increasingly dependent on a relatively small number of suppliers.

Regional differences, nevertheless, remain substantial. The wealthiest regions are those that grew fastest: in England in 1977–89, Greater London and much of southern England. Conversely, there were low levels of both GDP (gross domestic product) per head and of economic growth in Cleveland, Merseyside and South Yorkshire. The impact in the 1980s and 1990s of the Conservative policies of monetarism, deregulation, privatisation and an abandonment of the goal of full employment exacerbated regional economic differences. So also did greater regional specialisation in which management, research and development jobs were increasingly separate from production tasks: the former were increasingly concentrated in south-east England. The recession of 1990–3 hit the south and East Anglia disproportionately hard, but economic growth in 1994–5 was of greatest advantage in these regions. In 1994, the average weekly earnings of a working man was £419.40 in the south-east, £327.80 in the north and £319.20 in Northern Ireland.

Until the 1970s there was a strong labour market for skilled and semi-skilled jobs and many jobs for the unskilled, but extensive de-industrialisation since has reduced opportunities for unskilled labour. The bottom tenth of manual workers earned only 64 per cent of average income in 1991. Thus, the differentiation within the workforce related to skills has widened greatly and this has strong regional consequences. Differential opportunity also affects migration, leading people to move from the north to the south of England, although this process is hindered by inflexible public housing policies and a limited low-cost private rental sector. Despite a growth in GDP of 4 per cent in 1994, the unemployment rate in March 1995 was 8.4 per cent, although that was a fall from 9.8 per cent in December 1993. De-industrialisation continues: the last British match factory closed in 1994 after it had been acquired by a Swedish company. Despite efforts to cut it during the 1980s, public spending as a proportion of GDP fell only slightly in the period 1975–95 and is far higher than earlier in the century and than in the USA.

Socio-economic change has created unease for the many who pursue an essentially defensive search for stability and comfort. Such defensiveness is difficult to manage given the impact of global economic and financial shifts. Social hierarchies have always been more fluid than might at first appear, tempered and complicated as they have been by mobility (both up and down), marriage and problems of classification. They have become far more fluid in recent decades, not least because a society that increasingly structured round liquid wealth has had to adapt to the volatility of the latter.

A stress on the importance of individual customers and consumers affected not only business but also administration in general with an emphasis on responsiveness to customers in both government and the public sector, for example in the NHS. This was expressed in the 1990s in terms of 'charters', setting out the rights of patients, pupils, etc. and the responsibility of management. This was linked to a so-called 'quality revolution' and to an improvement in the management of both the public and the private sector. A major problem of the 1960s and 1970s, this was partly resolved by better training and education.

The older landed society, which in fact benefited from links with the more commercial aspects of society for centuries, saw some traditional means of classification decline. In 1958 the ritual presentations of débutantes (young aristocratic women) at the royal palace was abolished. Presentations were the centrepiece of a London society that had already been sapped by the decline of landed wealth. Britain as a propertied society has long seen little need for the traditional possessors of most property, and the aristocracy is increasingly treated, like the monarch and established churches, as a form of heritage and tourism for the nation, not as a power in the nation. Yet this has left them with considerable privileges. For example, public access is still closed to most of the open moorland in England and Wales so that it can retain its value as grouse moorland for the favoured few. Nevertheless, the aristocracy, like the Crown and other traditional defenders and products of a hierarchical society, have been affected by a postwar decline in deference that began to gather force in the 1960s and became very prominent in the early 1990s with particular crises of confidence in the monarchy, the Church of England and the Conservative party. These have been matched by a sense of social change if not crisis. By 1994 less than 73 per cent of children under the age of 16 lived with both their natural, married parents.

By the mid-1990s relations with the EU played an increasing role in politics, and the domestic political world appeared less divisive, in large part because of the shift in Labour policies away from socialist objectives and the emergence of less combative party leaders. Labour had moved a long way from its call in the October 1974 manifesto for 'substantially extending public enterprise' by a programme of mass nationalisation. However, the more radical

constitutional proposals of the Labour party in 1994–5 suggested
the possibility of major changes in that sphere.

MODERN IRELAND

In the late 1980s and early 1990s it seemed apparent that the Anglo-
Irish agreement of 1985 was not going to serve as the framework
for a settlement in Northern Ireland. The political and security
situation continued to deteriorate. Violence became increasingly an
economic issue with, for example, the construction industry subject
to threats. In addition to nationalist terrorism – the explosions by
which the Provisional IRA emphasised its presence – 'loyalist'
terrorism, by the Ulster Defence Force, the Ulster Freedom Fighters and similar bodies, increased. Alongside specific acts of directed
terrorism, there were also 'tit for tat' killings: the random murder of
members of the other denomination designed to instil terror. Indeed in 1992 more Catholics were killed than Protestants, though
not all Catholics were killed by Protestants. This might have
emphasised the failure of nationalist politics and of terrorism to
protect the Catholic community. At the same time, the bloody
disintegration of Yugoslavia, and the development of 'ethnic
cleansing' there, led to new fears about the future of Northern
Ireland. Since the troubles began there has been a process of ethnic
concentration operating in Ulster, with Protestants moving to the
east and Catholics to the west. In the possible future absence of the
British army, it appeared possible that terrorists from the more
numerous and better-armed Protestant community, worried by the
greater demographic growth of the Catholic population, might
follow the tactics of ethnic cleansing.

As before, the impact of terrorism in the north was both all-
pervasive in its effect on the general political environment, and yet
also very specific. The violence of the sectarian housing estates of
working-class north Belfast was not matched in leafy middle-class
south Belfast; indeed, a significant number of the Catholic middle-
class who had benefited greatly from moves against discrimination
over the previous quarter-century moved from largely Catholic
areas to the hitherto mostly Protestant south Belfast. Sinn Fein
only enjoyed the electoral support of about 10 per cent of Northern
Ireland's population. Yet in 1993 IRA terrorism in small towns

that had hitherto been largely exempt from the troubles, and in particular the devastation of their commercial centres by bombs, underlined yet again the danger of assuming that violence could be restricted. These attacks, a counterpart to the use of car bombs to attack financial targets in the City of London in 1992–3, revealed the IRA's awareness of the economic weapon that terrorism offered; in London there was great concern about the insurance implications. Mainland terrorism increased the cost of the troubles, although, in hopes of winning nationalist support, the policy of the IRA Army Council was not to attack targets in Scotland or Wales. The cost to the United Kingdom of supporting social welfare in Ulster was also heavy. In the summer of 1994 unemployment was 40 per cent higher than in the rest of Britain and male earnings 11 per cent below the British average. In 1993 there was a net transfer to Ulster of £3.4 billion, excluding the cost of the security forces.

Attacks on the small towns in Ulster led Unionist politicians to declare that the terrorists were winning. Angry at what they saw as inadequate policing and suspicious of a dialogue between the government and the IRA, they pressed unsuccessfully for the reintroduction of internment and increased their criticism of the Anglo-Irish agreement. New talks, however, between the British and Irish governments that began in November 1993, in response to yet more carnage, produced that December the Downing Street Declaration in which John Major and Albert Reynolds, the Prime Ministers of the two countries, agreed to a shared sovereignty that would guarantee the rights of nationalists while unionists were assured that they would not be forced into a united Ireland. A cease-fire followed in 1994: the IRA declared a 'complete cessation' of violence on 31 August, followed shortly by the Loyalists. The cease-fire was slowly and hesitantly followed by preliminary talks. On 10 May 1995 leaders of Sinn Fein met a British government minister, the first such public meeting for seventy-five years. The cease-fire was followed by inward investment and a rise in house prices.

As elsewhere in the British Isles de-industrialisation has been a major problem. This has affected both traditional heavy industries, such as shipbuilding and heavy engineering, and newer light industries. Thus, synthetic fibre plants established in the 1960s closed in the early 1980s. In the south, the economy continued to be greatly influenced by the impact of Ireland's entry into the European Union in 1973. This led to a substantial infusion of development aid, a process of transfer of wealth from the richer European states, that has continued and was reaffirmed in 1993 with a new allocation of substantial funds for the poorer members of the EU. In addition, the stress on agricultural production in the EU has benefited Ireland, protecting her large farming sector from the impact of world competition and the more efficient agricultural economies of, for example, North America. Thus more people still live on or close to the land than would otherwise be the case.

Yet there are also important forces for change. Development aid has played a major role in a substantial measure of industrialisation since the 1960s, although much is in the form of multinational branch plants with restricted local linkages. Thanks to strong export expansion, the annual average growth rate in GDP in Ireland in 1990–4 was over 5 per cent, the highest in the EU: Britain's in contrast was only 0.7 per cent, the lowest bar Sweden. Ireland also benefited from low inflation, and government borrowing, which had risen substantially in the 1970s and 1980s, has been brought under control. There has been significant rebuilding in Dublin. The revival of the Irish language has made only limited progress. Secondary and university education has expanded considerably and the television has become important. Yet the south suffers the same problems as the north, and has much in common with it, not least a more rural and religious society than that of Britain. Compared to the rest of the EU, both suffer from low incomes, a relatively small population (3.6 million in the south in 1994) and high unemployment, which combine to produce limited demand and low economies of scale. Despite economic growth in the south, unemployment remains high, a consequence of a high birth rate, movement from the land and only a limited supply of new jobs. 26.2 per cent of under-25-year-olds were unemployed in April 1992. Fortunately for Irish society, emigration, especially to the USA, continues to provide an outlet. Emigration rose from the mid-1980s, and could not be blamed, as so much nineteenth-century emigration was, on British rule.

The republic has also experienced a substantial measure of secularisation. There have been legal and political battles over such issues as divorce, homosexuality, abortion and contraception, as the authority of the Church has been contested. Irish society is still more sectarian than that of England, but the lesser role of the

Church in Irish politics, society and culture is readily apparent. It has been linked to a measure of emancipation for women that culminated with the selection of Mary Robinson as President in 1990. In contrast, in Ulster neither the unionist nor the nationalist cause has had much time for feminism, although a number of active IRA members have been women, and there is a strong tradition of female involvement in Irish and Scottish nationalism.

New money has helped to change the character of Irish politics. Charles Haughey, Taoiseach in 1979–81, 1982 and 1987–92, was associated with new social forces and accused of corruption. A charismatic figure, Haughey's opportunistic policies and favouritism helped to divide Fianna Fáil, leading eventually, after charges of illegal telephone-tapping, to his replacement by Albert Reynolds in 1992, but Reynolds's apparent misuse of governmental patronage led to his fall in 1994. The instability of the republic's politics reflected the strength of sectional interests and the difficulty of moving beyond a politics of personality, but thanks to EU money the Irish were spared the worst consequences of their politicians. It is far from clear, however, that the republic would be able to escape the consequences of a total breakdown of civil order in the north. The republic's politicians have done little to lessen the fears of the Ulster Protestants and found it difficult to distance themselves from the nationalist cause. Despite common membership of the EU, and although most people loathe the IRA, there has been little economic co-operation between north and south. It is difficult to feel optimistic about the future. It is unclear whether the legacy of the catastrophic dimension of much Irish history – conquest, expropriation, colonisation, discrimination, poverty, myth-making and bitterness – can be lessened by economic growth, secularisation and social change.

MODERN SCOTLAND

Over the last decade Scotland has substantially shared the same economic and social trends as the rest of Britain, but its political trajectory has been different, as has more generally been the case since 1959 with the decline of Scottish Conservatism. As in England and Wales, there has been a decline in 'smoke-stack' industries, the traditional heavy manufacturing sector. The size and economic importance of the coal, heavy engineering, shipbuilding and steel industries have all declined and in Scotland there has been particular sensitivity about the fate of the Ravenscraig steel works. The textile industry has also been badly hit. What was once the biggest linen damask factory in the world, that of Erskine, Beveridge and Co. in Dunfermline, closed, and was converted to flats in 1983–4. Economic decline has hit Strathclyde particularly badly, and the urban fabric there has been under considerable challenge, despite urban regeneration.

New technology has led to new industry and employment, for example in offshore oil fields, but the pattern of the workforce is very different to that in the nineteenth-century townscapes of industrial decline. Instead, much of the new work places little stress on manual strength or traditional skills, and in areas such as Glenrothes there are higher rates of female than male employment. The bitter dispute over attempts to introduce new working practices at the US-owned Timex plant at Dundee in 1993 indicated that economic change was not welcomed by all, but it also revealed the consequences of growing foreign ownership of Scottish concerns: the management decided to shut the plant. The continued success of the long-established financial services industry in Edinburgh and of service-industry employment in Glasgow, the 'city of culture', have brought a measure of prosperity, but it is significant that Wales has been more attractive to foreign investors. It is unclear whether independence would not create fresh economic problems; Scotland would be part of the EU, but very peripheral to its markets. The most recent prominent Scottish literary declaration of cultural self-determination, James Kelman's novel *How Late It Was, How Late* (1994) was published in London by an English publisher and won the Booker prize, a national award. In the mid-1990s 50 per cent of the Scottish sales of tabloid newspapers were of London titles and 75 per cent of those of the 'quality' press. 72 per cent of total tourism expenditure in Scotland in 1994 was by English tourists.

Socially, Scotland has experienced shifts similar to England. The role of the Church continued to decline, there has been a broadening out of the middle class, and the nuclear family is under strain. Rates of heart disease remain very high. It and cancer were each responsible for more than ¼ of the deaths in 1994. Edinburgh has acquired a new reputation as a major centre of drug abuse and AIDS. The percentage of owner-occupiers has risen from 25 in 1979 to 40 now, but is still below the United Kingdom average. Emigration continues to be important: in the period 1900–90 there was only one year (1932–3) in which Scotland gained from migration. Combined with declining birth-rates, now lower than those of England and Wales, this had led to a fall in population: 152,000 people in 1976–86. In 1994 there were only 61,656 live births in Scotland, the lowest figure since records began in 1855. The population in 1994 was 5,132,400. Within Scotland there has been a substantial move from the urban areas of Strathclyde – 172,360 people in 1976–86 – and net gains in the Highlands and Islands, the Border region and south-western Scotland. In 1988–9 30 per cent of Scottish graduates from Scottish universities got their first job in England and Wales, whereas only 0.3 per cent of English and Welsh graduates from English and Welsh universities gained their first post in Scotland.

Politically, the late 1980s and early 1990s lent fresh impetus to the debate about the constitution. This had abated after the devolution referendum of 1979, but the unpopularity in Scotland of Mrs Thatcher's Conservative government (1979–90) and contrasting electoral results in Scotland and England led to a revival in agitation about what *The Times* called 'the Scottish question'. The extent to which administrative responsibility for Scottish affairs was transferred from Whitehall to the Scottish Office in Edinburgh helped to encourage a sense of governmental autonomy and responsibility in Scotland, but there was little real element of democratic control over the office. Scottish ministers effectively determined policy on the domestic front. In 1987 Labour won fifty of the seventy-two seats, the Conservatives only ten. The link between the Conservative party and working-class Protestant culture declined markedly: there were no Tory seats in Glasgow after 1982. In 1989 the introduction of the Poll Tax, a year ahead of England and Wales, was particularly unpopular, and the Conservatives won only 21 per cent of the vote in the European elections, compared to 25 per cent for the SNP. The previous year, Jim Sillars had won the Govan by-election from Labour for the SNP, suggesting that the party had broken through among the Strathclyde working class; although earlier hopes based upon victories in Hamilton (1969) and Govan (1973) had proved deceptive.

In March 1989 the first meeting was held of a Constitutional Convention designed to produce plans for a Scottish parliament. Supported by Labour and Liberal Democrats, but not Conservatives and SNP, it agreed plans in February 1992. The Conservatives, however, supported the union in its current form, while the SNP proposed 'independence in Europe', a more radical step than the devolution backed by the convention.

The 1992 election results were a surprise. Far from the anticipated decimation of the Conservatives, they benefited from an overall positive swing of 2.5 per cent, in contrast with the swing away from them in the south of England and the Midlands. The results reaffirmed what is too often disguised by the first-past-the-post system, namely that Scotland is a four-party system. Although Labour considers itself the natural party of government there, it enjoys the support of less than half the population and, in 1992, several of the ten seats where there was the greatest fall in the Labour share of the vote were in Scotland. In 1992 the Nationalists increased their share of the Scottish vote by 7 per cent to 21 per cent, although their highest poll – in Banff and Buchan – was only 47.5 per cent, and only in Moray, Angus East, Tayside North, Western Isles, Glasgow Govan and Galloway did they poll more than 36 per cent. It is noteworthy that SNP success in local government and European elections has a much broader base.

The better-than-anticipated Conservative vote in 1992 (although it was still far lower than in the 1960s and 1970s: 50 per cent in 1955, 31 per cent in 1979), and the failure of the SNP to break through, reflected continued support for the Union and the role of 'bread-and-butter' issues in the election. Despite the diatribes about the consequences of 'rule from London', Scotland continued to enjoy a disproportionately high share of government expenditure, especially in health and education, while the economy was in a less parlous state than elsewhere. Unemployment fell between the 1987 and 1992 elections, while house prices were less hit by the recession than were those in southern England. Anger with the government, however, ensured that in the 1994 local elections the Conservative vote fell to its lowest ever (11 per cent), while Labour rose to 44 per cent, and the SNP and Liberal Democrat percentages also rose.

Scotland remains over-represented in Westminster: Scottish MPs looked after fewer than 55,000 voters each in 1994 compared to 59,000 for the average Welsh MP and 69,000 for his English counterpart. While the Labour party remains so much stronger than the SNP, it is difficult to see it endorsing independence: that would end any chance of a Labour government at Westminster. Indeed Labour strategy is in many respects a cynical attempt to use the idea of a Scottish parliament to undercut the SNP and obtain more British funds for their Scottish power-base, while at the same time using Scotland for their own ends south of the border. There has been no proposal from Labour to match a Scottish parliament with a reduction in the number of Scottish MPs at Westminster.

It is unclear what the SNP's notion of independence means in the context of a federal Europe, although doubtless there would be more autonomy. An independent Scotland would have to search for a sense of identity: opposition both to England and the notion of Britain would not prevent divisions within Scotland from becoming more apparent, whatever the fate of a pseudo-irredentist movement centred on Berwick.

An 'independent' Scotland, however, constrained by federalism and multinationals, would represent a marked discontinuity, whether presented in terms of return to past identity (and glories) or not. This will pose serious problems for the understanding of Scotland after the Union. Patriotism and nationalism will be refocused, history serving as a powerful aspect of public myth. The most damaging consequence may be the failure to address the regional theme in Scotland, past, present and future. While aware of the extent and role of regional economic differences, many commentators fail to consider adequately the nature of the regional political and cultural experience. Yet, alongside the vitality of Scotland and the Scots, there are also tremendous differences between Strathclyde and Shetland, between Ayr and Aberdeen. Politicians and others will need to work with this diversity in mapping out the future for Scotland.

MODERN WALES

Alongside nationalist pyrotechnics, it is worth noting that the principal political shift in the late 1970s was the rise of the Conservatives, who won eleven seats in 1979 and fourteen in 1983. Although harmed by the unpopularity of aspects of Conservative rule from 1979, the Conservatives continued to have a political presence far larger than that of Plaid Cymru. They took eight seats in 1987 and six in 1992 on 29.6 and 28.6 per cent of the Welsh vote respectively. The rise in Conservative support was linked to social changes, not least the growth of a white-collar workforce for whom traditional loyalties had scant interest. This was a workforce living not in the valleys but on the north and south coasts and in the Cardiff urban region. Expansion in service industries and, in particular, in administrative agencies based in Cardiff (declared capital of Wales by Parliament in 1955) created much new employment, as did investment, especially from Japan, in new industrial plants. These were concentrated in South Wales, the economic importance of which was boosted by a new proximity to markets, thanks to the opening of the Severn Bridge (which had been called for since the 1930s) and the extension of the M4 motorway into South Wales. Under Peter Walker, Mrs Thatcher's effective and interventionist Secretary of State, Wales benefited from considerable public investment, in particular on road links: economic planning brought benefits. Tourism, now Wales's leading industry, fortifies the Welsh sense of history.

A new geography of wealth and employment greatly favoured Cardiff and to a lesser extent Bridgend, Newport, Swansea and Wrexham. Ford invested £180 million in its Bridgend engine plant. Conversely, coal and steel were badly hit in the late 1970s and 1980s. The expansion of the late 1940s, in particular in the Port Talbot steelworks opened in 1951, was succeeded by closures and massive layoffs. By 1957 economic decline had already left large areas of derelict land, 8,227 hectares of disused spoil heaps, 3,090 of disused mineral workings and 7,567 of disused buildings and installations. The Aberfan disaster, in which an unstable spoil-heap engulfed a school, indicated the price of early industrialisation that was to be paid in the mid-twentieth century. Restoration of the valleys and countryside was another consequence of the virtual disappearance of the coalmines. The industrial heritage has been used increasingly in the leisure industry. Despite the cushioning of social security, economic problems had a serious impact on the social framework. Average annual household income in Wales in 1991–2 was £22,015, lower than the north of England or Scotland, but the average difference concealed major regional and social variations and these were reflected in Wales's politics.

Wales, like Scotland, has a four-party system. With 49.5 per cent of the vote in 1992 (45.10 per cent 1987), Labour was by far the largest party, much more so than in Scotland (39 per cent), but the amount of support enjoyed by the other parties was also important. Conservatives and Liberal Democrats had 41 per cent (47.5 per cent 1987), and were thus greatly under-represented by the first-past-the-post electoral system. The problem that language creates for Plaid Cymru is indicated by the far greater degree of nationalist support in Scotland (21.5 per cent), where it is not an issue, than in Wales (8.8 per cent) where it is difficult to see the campaign for the Welsh language, and Plaid Cymru's association with it, as anything other than divisive. From the perspective of, for example, Swansea with its enterprise zone near the M4, its retail parks and its new waterside developments, it is hard to see the causes of Welsh independence and cultural nationalism as anything other than a potentially dangerous irritant. Wales, however, despite its relatively small size, is a very strongly regional country, and what goes on in Swansea has very little relevance – or at least is perceived as having little relevance – to developments in, for example, North Wales.

In part this is a cultural and political reassertion of the profound geographical differences that have always characterised Wales and that economic growth made even more central. The creation of Welsh agencies provided a new occasion for the voicing of regional anxieties. Thus, at the 1941 annual general meeting of the National Industrial Council of Wales and Monmouthshire, Councillor G. O. Williams of Flintshire county council emphasised that postwar reconstruction must be considered by two separate regional committees, 'stressed the difficulties of travelling from North Wales' and declared that 'very little consideration had been given to the convenience of North Wales . . . a fatal step to have so few representatives of North Wales on the Reconstruction Committee . . . to justify the title of "national" it must have behind it the full backing of the whole of the people of Wales'.

However much eroded by all Welsh preoccupations with Non-conformity and rugby football, such regional differences are particularly apparent in Wales because of the language issue and everything that that represents and can be made to symbolise. The *eisteddfod* movement and the *Urdd Gobaith Cymru* (League of Welsh Youth, founded in 1922) are both strong. Thanks to language, many of the Welsh are, at least in this respect, far more distinct from the English than are the vast majority of Scots; but, equally, the Welsh as a whole are, as the devolution vote and subsequent election results have revealed, far more likely to identify with a British future than are the Scots. A federal Europe offers a possible alternative, and Plaid Cymru make much of being good Europeans, arguing that they can campaign for EU investment far more effectively than will London-based parties. The regional dimension is currently on the European political agenda, as there is pressure for a movement back to smaller societies within a European framework. This comes particularly from political movements based on groups with a national consciousness, such as the Basques, Bretons, Catalans, Scots and Welsh, all of whom want to retain their separate identities while remaining part of Europe. Yet the strongly regional nature of support for Plaid Cymru within Wales, combined with the divisive nature of the language issue, suggests that an autonomous Wales might well face an uneasy future: the different interests of South Wales and Gwynedd would be very difficult to reconcile. Much would depend on the electoral system. An autonomous Wales might resemble an England dominated by the demographic and economic weight of the south, but the degree to which this would be acceptable elsewhere in the two countries is unclear. For the present, the Welsh have an ability to pursue their different views without an excess of bitterness, whilst Wales has an attractive diversity that rewards both inhabitants and visitors alike.

CONCLUSION

History is like travel. To go back in the past and then to return is to have seen different countries, other ways of doing things, various values. The traveller might not have the time or resources to appreciate fully what he or she is seeing, but is nevertheless made aware of variety and change. To travel today is to be made aware of some of the strengths and weaknesses of the British Isles and its inhabitants and it also serves to confirm a sense of identity with place and people. Reviewing the history of the British Isles it is possible to conclude by stressing continuity, to emphasise a constant expression of a deep sense of history, an organic, close-knit society, capable of self-renewal, and the rooted strength of institutions and culture. The British certainly have a genius for the appearance of continuity, but the manufacture of traditions often masks shifts in the centres of power. Writing in 1995, it is also possible to stress the role of chance. The relative stability of Britain in this century, it can be argued, was due not only to deep-lying forces and trends, but also to victory in both world wars. Most continental countries were defeated and occupied, with the accompanying strains. Many right-wing political groupings were contaminated, or at least stained, by collaboration; their left-wing counterparts compromised, or at least affected, by the rise of communism. In Britain, as in Ireland, in contrast, there was no foreign invasion, no seizure of power by undemocratic forces from left or right. Similarly, in the longer term, it was far from inevitable that Britain would survive French invasion attempts in the eighteenth century and the Napoleonic period. There have also been domestic crises whose peaceful resolution was far from inevitable, as well as civil conflicts whose outcome was far from certain to contemporaries. The result of the conflicts involving John and Henry III, the English Civil War and the '45 are obvious examples.

While, therefore, stressing chance, it is also necessary to draw attention to those in the past who were unsuccessful. British society can be presented as both organic and divided. The Glorious Revolution, for example, plays a role in the British public myth, but many, particularly in Ireland, were not comprehended within the Whig consensus, and both the Revolution Settlement and the Hanoverian regime were only established by force. For all their talk about being the natural party of government in Britain, only thrice this century (the Conservatives and their allies in 1900, 1931, and 1935) has either the Labour or the Conservative Party gained more than 50 per cent of the popular vote. Deterministic approaches to the past are suspect, and it is necessary to qualify any emphasis on patterns by stressing the role of chance and contingency.

Selected Further Reading

The following is necessarily a selective list, concentrating on recent books. Other works and articles can be traced through the bibliographies in these books.

GENERAL WORKS

C. Bayly (ed.), *Atlas of the British Empire* (1989).
M. Falkus and J. Gillingham (eds), *Historical Atlas of Britain* (1981).
B. J. Graham and L. J. Proudfoot, *Historical Geography of Ireland* (1993).
C. Haigh (ed.), *The Cambridge Historical Encyclopedia of Great Britain and Ireland* (1985).
P. Jenkins, *A History of Modern Wales 1536–1990* (1992).
H. Kearney, *The British Isles. A History of Four Nations* (1989).
R. Mitchison (ed.), *Why Scottish History Matters* (1991).
K. Morgan (ed.), *The Oxford Illustrated History of Britain* (1984).
N. J. G. Pounds, *The Culture of the English People* (1994).
B. Short (ed.), *The English Rural Community* (1992).
E. A. Wrigley and R. S. Schofield, *The Population History of England, 1541–1871* (1981).

BRITONS AND ROMANS

M. W. Barley and R. P. C. Hanson (eds), *Christianity in Britain 300–700* (1968).
A. R. Birley, *The People of Roman Britain* (1979).
B. W. Cunliffe, *Iron Age Communities in Britain* (1974).
B. Jones and D. Mattingly, *An Atlas of Roman Britain* (1990).
P. Ottaway, *Archaeology in British towns: From the Emperor Claudius to the Black Death* (1992).
M. Todd, *Roman Britain* (1981).

400–1066

J. Campbell (ed.), *The Anglo-Saxons* (1982).
D. Hill, *Atlas of Anglo-Saxon England* (1981).
D. Kirby, *The Earliest English Kings* (1990).
L. and J. Laing, *The Picts and the Scots* (1994).

J. Morris, *The Age of Arthur: A History of the British Isles from 350 to 650* (1973).
C. Thomas, *Britain and Ireland in Early Christian Times A.D. 400–800* (1972).

MEDIEVAL BRITAIN

R. H. Britnell, *The Commercialisation of English Society 1000–1500* (1992).
A. D. Carr, *Medieval Wales* (1995).
M. T. Clanchy, *England and its Rulers, 1066–1272* (1983).
A. Curry, *The Hundred Years War* (1993).
R. R. Davies (ed.), *The British Isles. 1100–1500: Comparisons, Contrasts and Connections* (1988).
D. C. Douglas, *William the Conqueror* (1964).
B. Golding, *Conquest and Colonisation. The Normans in Britain, 1066–1100* (1994).
R. A. Griffiths, *Conquerors and Conquered in Medieval Wales* (1994).
M. Keen, *England in the Later Middle Ages* (1973).
J. Le Patourel, *The Norman Empire* (1976).
H. R. Loyn, *The Norman Conquest* (1982).
W. M. Ormrod, *Political Life in Medieval England, 1300–1450* (1995).
A. J. Pollard, *The Wars of the Roses* (1988).
M. Prestwich, *The Three Edwards* (1980).
M. Prestwich, *English Politics in the Thirteenth Century* (1990).
W. L. Warren, *Henry II* (1973).

SIXTEENTH-CENTURY BRITAIN

P. Collinson, *The Religion of Protestants: The Church in English Society 1559–1625* (1982).
C. S. L. Davies, *Peace, Print and Protestantism: 1450–1558* (1977).
S. Gunn, *Early Tudor Government, 1485–1558* (1995).
J. Guy, *Tudor England* (1988).
C. Haigh (ed.), *The Reign of Elizabeth I* (1984).
C. Haigh, *Elizabeth I* (1988).
R. A. Houston and I. D. Whyte (eds), *Scottish Society 1500–1800* (1989).
R. Hutton, *The Rise and Fall of Merry England. The Ritual Year 1400–1700* (1994).
J. G. Jones, *Early Modern Wales, c.1525–1640* (1994).
D. Loades, *The Mid-Tudor Crisis 1545–1565* (1992).
D. MacCulloch, *The Later Reformation in England 1547–1603* (1990).
D. Palliser, *The Age of Elizabeth* (1983).
R. Rex, *Henry VIII and the English Reformation* (1992).
C. Russell, *The Crisis of Parliaments, 1509–1660* (1974).
J. J. Scarisbrick, *Henry VIII* (1983).
P. Williams, *The Tudor Regime* (1979).

STUART AND INTERREGNUM BRITAIN

K. M. Brown, *Kingdom or Province? Scotland and the Regal Union, 1603–1715* (1992).

B. A. Holderness, *Pre-Industrial England* (1977).

A. Hughes, *The Causes of the English Civil War* (1991).

R. Hutton, *Charles II* (1989).

R. Hutton, *The British Republic 1649–1660* (1990).

J. R. Jones, *Country and Court, 1660–1714* (1978).

P. Laslett, *The World We Have Lost* (1972).

P. Seaward, *The Restoration, 1660–1688* (1991).

M. Spufford, *Contrasting Communities: English Villagers in the Sixteenth and Seventeenth Centuries* (1974).

K. Wrightson, *English Society 1580–1680* (1982).

1689–1815

J. Black, *Robert Walpole and the Nature of Politics in Early Eighteenth-Century Britain* (1990).

J. Black, *Culloden and the '45* (1990).

J. Black, *War for America* (1991).

J. Black, *The Elder Pitt* (1993).

S. J. Connolly, *Religion, Law and Power. The Making of Protestant Ireland 1660–1760* (1992).

M. Daunton, *Progress and Poverty. An Economic and Social History of Britain 1700–1850* (1995).

J. Derry, *Politics in the Age of Fox, Pitt and Liverpool* (1990).

R. Harding, *The Evolution of the Sailing Navy 1509–1815* (1995).

R. A. Houston, *Social Change in the Age of Enlightenment. Edinburgh 1660–1760* (1994).

P. Langford, *A Polite and Commercial People: England, 1727–1783* (1989).

P. Mathias, *The First Industrial Nation: An Economic History of Britain, 1700–1914* (1969).

K. Perry, *British Politics and the American Revolution* (1990).

R. Porter, *English Society in the Eighteenth Century* (1982).

J. Rule, *Albion's People. English Society 1714–1815* (1992).

J. Rule, *The Vital Century. England's Developing Economy 1714–1815* (1992).

AGE OF REFORM AND EMPIRE, 1815–1914.

R. Barker, *Politics, Peoples and Government. Themes in British Political Thought since the Nineteenth Century* (1994).

G. Best, *Mid-Victorian Britain 1851–1870* (1970).

R. Blake, *Disraeli* (1966).

A. Bourke, 'The Visitation of God'? The Potato and the Great Irish Famine (1993).

A. Briggs, Victorian People (1954).

A. Briggs, The Age of Improvement 1783–1867 (1959).

A. Briggs, Victorian Cities (1963).

A. Briggs, Victorian Things (1988).

G. Crouzet, The Victorian Economy (1982).

T. M. Devine (ed.), Scottish Emigration and Scottish Society (1992).

E. J. Evans, The Forging of the Modern State 1783–1870 (1983).

R. F. Foster, Paddy and Mr Punch: Connections in Irish and English History (1994).

K. Jefferys, The Labour Party since 1945 (1993).

T. A. Jenkins, The Liberal Ascendancy, 1830–1886 (1994).

M. Mason, The Making of Victorian Sexuality (1994).

R. Pope (ed.), Atlas of British Social and Economic History since 1700 (1989).

K. G. Robbins, Nineteenth-Century Britain: Integration and Diversity (1988).

G. R. Searle, The Liberal Party. Triumph and Disintegration 1886–1929 (1992).

R. Stewart, Party and Politics 1830–1852 (1989).

F. M. L. Thompson, The Rise of Respectable Society. A Social History of Victorian Britain, 1830–1900 (1988).

THE TWENTIETH CENTURY

C. J. Bartlett, British Foreign Policy in the Twentieth Century (1989).

D. G. Boyce, The Irish Question and British Politics 1868–1986 (1988).

J. Campbell, Edward Heath (1993).

D. Cannadine, The Decline and Fall of the British Aristocracy (1990).

R. Floud and D. McCloskey (eds), The Economic History of Britain since 1700 (1981).

T. R. Gourvish and A. O'Day (eds), Britain since 1945 (1991).

J. Grigg, Lloyd George (1978, 1985).

D. Harkness, Ireland in the Twentieth Century (1995).

C. Harvie, Scotland and Nationalism. Scottish Society and Politics 1707–1994 (1994).

R. Hoggart, Townscape with Figures. Farnham – Portrait of an English Town (1994).

G. Hussey, Ireland Today (1994).

D. Kavanagh and A. Seldon (eds), The Thatcher Effect (1989).

D. Kavanagh and A. Seldon (eds), The Major Effect (1994).

A. Marwick, British Society since 1945 (1982).

H. Perkin, The Rise of Professional Society: England since 1880 (1989).

D. Powell, British Politics and the Labour Question, 1868–1990 (1992).

M. Pugh, The Making of Modern British Politics, 1867–1939 (1982).

M. Pugh, *State and Society. British Political and Social History 1870–1992* (1994).
D. Reynolds, *Britannia Overruled* (1991).
K. G. Robbins, *The Eclipse of a Great Power: Modern Britain 1870–1975* (1983).
Social Trends 1995 (1995).
J. Stevenson, *British Society 1914–1945* (1983).
M. Thatcher, *The Downing Street Years* (1993).
J. Young, *Britain and European Unity, 1945–1992* (1993).